Methods for Teaching Culturally and Linguistically Diverse Exceptional Learners

John J. Hoover
University of Colorado, Boulder

Janette K. Klingner
University of Colorado, Boulder

Leonard M. Baca
University of Colorado, Boulder

James M. Patton
The College of William and Mary

Upper Saddle River, New Jersey
Columbus, Ohio

Library of Congress Cataloging-in-Publication Data

Methods for teaching culturally and linguistically diverse exceptional learners /
John J. Hoover. . . [et al.].
  p.   cm.
Includes bibliographical references and index.
ISBN 0-13-172023-6
  1. Multicultural education—United States.   2. Education, Bilingual—United States.
3. Second language acquisition.   I. Hoover, John J.
LC1099. 3. M48 2008
370. 117—dc22   2007001264

Vice President and Executive Publisher:
Jeffery W. Johnston
Executive Editor: Ann Castel Davis
Editorial Assistant: Penny Burleson
Production Editor: Sheryl Glicker Langner
Production Coordination: GGS Book
Services

Design Coordinator: Diane C. Lorenzo
Cover Design: Thomas Borah
Cover Image: Super Stock
Production Manager: Laura Messerly
Director of Marketing: David Gesell
Marketing Manager: Autumn Purdy
Marketing Coordinator: Brian Mounts

This book was set in Minion by GGS Book Services. It was printed and bound by R. R.
Donnelley & Sons Company. The cover was printed by R. R. Donnelley & Sons Company

Pearson Education Ltd.
Pearson Education Singapore Pte. Ltd.
Pearson Education Canada, Ltd.
Pearson Education—Japan

Pearson Education Australia Pty. Limited
Pearson Education North Asia Ltd.
Pearson Education de Mexico, S.A. de C.V.
Pearson Education Malaysia Pte. Ltd.

10 9 8 7
ISBN-13: 978-0-13-172023-7
ISBN-10:   0-13-172023-6

Dedicated to our mentor, friend, and colleague Herbert Grossman
for his support and long-lasting contributions
to bilingual special education

Preface

Throughout our teaching and research careers in special education, we have found that effective education for students with disabilities can only be achieved when their needs are addressed in comprehensive ways. Today's educational assessment and instructional environments challenge even the most seasoned educators to continuously grow personally and professionally if all students' needs are to be appropriately met. One of the more pressing issues we currently face is increasing numbers of diverse learners in our schools, many of whom have disabilities. Our experiences, including many years of work with students who bring diversity to the classroom, have taught us that education for these learners must blend culture, language, and disability needs to be most effective. This text provides readers with a wealth of knowledge in instructional methods for culturally and linguistically diverse learners with and without disabilities; it is designed to help differentiate between learning *differences* and learning *disabilities* and appropriately meet associated needs. We hope that as readers progress through this text and apply their learning, their competence in educating diverse learners will increase and they will see a direct and positive impact on student learning in their classrooms and schools.

AUDIENCE

This book is written for any educator directly or indirectly involved in the K–12 education of culturally and linguistically diverse exceptional learners. It is appropriate for use with both practicing as well as pre-service educators in college or university courses that are designed to teach methods for assessing and educating culturally and linguistically diverse learners with disabilities. This book may also serve as a valuable resource for professional development staff, school administrators, school psychologists, and other related service providers as well as content teachers for identifying and selecting appropriate methods for meeting diverse needs in the classroom.

ORGANIZATION OF THE BOOK

The book is organized into four major sections with three chapters in each section.

Part I provides an overview and introduction to teaching culturally and linguistically diverse exceptional (CLDE) learners. Chapter 1 establishes the foundation for the topics covered in the book, including an overview of current legislation, instructional practices, and terminology. An instructional model is also presented along with suggested teaching qualities to best meet the needs of CLDE learners. Chapter 2 discusses, in detail, qualities and characteristics necessary to implement culturally responsive education with diverse learners. Chapter 3 addresses the topic of second language acquisition and its significance to meeting disability needs.

The chapters in *Part II* discuss instructional models, assessment, and behavior management for culturally and linguistically diverse learners. Chapter 4 offers examples of various education models typically used in today's schools to educate CLDE learners along with the application of technology to meet diverse needs. Chapter 5 discusses various assessment practices and procedures to effectively assess CLD learners, bearing in mind the need to consider culture, language, and disability needs simultaneously. Chapter 6 provides an in-depth discussion of classroom and schoolwide approaches for managing student behaviors.

In *Part III* the topic of culturally responsive instructional methods is addressed. Chapter 7 provides detailed discussions of methods for teaching reading to culturally and linguistically diverse learners. This chapter suggests examples of the application of selected methods for successfully teaching reading to diverse learners with or without disabilities. The content area of writing is addressed in Chapter 8, where a variety of methods for teaching CLDE learners written expression are presented. Chapter 9 concludes this section with a discussion of numerous methods to support learning in different content areas while also meeting diverse cultural and linguistic demands. This includes a presentation of several instructional adaptations and modifications to best facilitate student learning in the content areas.

Part IV covers several related yet highly significant topics associated with effective instructional methods for educating CLDE learners in today's schools. Chapter 10 provides important information about methods and strategies for collaboration in education, including a suggested model and associated practices to facilitate collaboration among general and special educators. Chapter 11 includes detailed discussions of study skills and study strategies that support academic content learning as well as behavior management in culturally competent ways. Chapter 12 concludes this section and book with discussion of a variety of transition issues confronting CLDE learners as they progress through school and move into postsecondary education.

Collectively, the methods discussed in these four sections and 12 chapters address many of the most timely and relevant instructional needs of CLDE learners. In addition, the contents of this book provide readers with information, knowledge, and skills to develop further their own cultural competence necessary to provide CLDE students with high-quality opportunities to learn.

CHAPTER FORMAT

Each chapter follows a consistent format designed to challenge the reader with content, methods, and classroom situations that reflect the education of CLDE learners in today's instructional environments. Each chapter contains the following:

1. *Chapter Objectives* provide specific targeted skills and abilities the reader should possess upon completion of the chapter.

2. A *Vignette* describes a typical educational situation for a learner with cultural and linguistic differences in today's schools. The vignettes challenge the reader to consider various topics to be covered in the chapter. Each vignette is followed by *Vignette Reflective Questions* that guide the reader to further evaluate possible solutions or practices to best meet the needs described in the situation. The specific chapter content follows the vignette, providing the reader with an in-depth discussion of the major issues illustrated in the vignette.

3. *Figures, Diagrams, and Guides* are used throughout the chapters to illustrate and further clarify the various principles and suggested methods and models presented to the reader.

4. *Discussion Questions* conclude each chapter to help the reader reflect on the knowledge and skills acquired through study of the chapter content.

ACKNOWLEDGMENTS

A variety of professionals were involved in the development of the first edition of this text. Appreciation is extended to both Allyson Sharp and Ann Davis of Pearson for their expertise and guidance throughout the initial development of the text, its two formal external reviews, and associated revisions based on the feedback. Their knowledge and expertise contributed significantly to this final product and we are grateful to them. We also wish to thank Penny Burleson and Kathy Burk for their excellent editorial assistance and support.

Our text was submitted to two separate field reviews, and we wish thank all of these individuals for their time and expertise in providing us succinct and valuable feedback. Their contributions helped to significantly improve our text, and we are grateful to have benefited from their expertise. Thanks go to Stephanie A. Dhonau, University of Arkansas at Little Rock; Barbara Fulk, Illinois State University; Willard S. Gilbert, Northern Arizona University; Rita van Loenen, Arizona State University; Gina Zanolini Morrison, Wilkes University; Lori Navarrete, University of Nevada, Las Vegas; Robert W. Ortiz, California State University, Fullerton; Philip P. Patterson, California State University, Bakersfield; Cathi Draper Rodriquez, University of Nevada, Las Vegas; and Laura M. Saenz, The University of Texas, Pan American. Chapter contributions to this text were also provided by several professionals with specific expertise in selected areas, with three of the chapters written by contributing authors. Chapter 6 was written by Dr. Alicia Moore (Southwestern University) and Drs. Julie Armentrout and LaVonne Neal (University of Colorado, Colorado Springs). Chapter 8 was written by Dr. Anne Graves (San Diego State University) and Chapter 12 by Drs. Audrey Trainor (University of Wisconsin, Madison) and James Patton (Austin, Texas). Their chapter contributions are an integral part of this text, and we are very appreciative of their willingness to contribute their knowledge and expertise to this book. Also, several other individuals provided selected contributions to various chapters throughout the book. We wish to thank Mr. Michael Orosco and Ms. Amy Saks (Doctoral Candidates at the University of Colorado, Boulder) for their contributions to the development of several of the vignettes. Michael assisted with the vignettes in Chapter 1, 5, and 11, and Amy assisted with the vignettes in Chapter 3, 4, and 10. In addition, Ms. Veronica Koussai, Ms. Michele Kissinger, Mr. Patrick Humphrey (Doctoral students at The College of William and Mary) and Dr. Arletha McSwain (Norfolk State University) are recognized for their contributions to the vignette in Chapter 2. Dr. Jennifer Urbach (University of Northern Colorado) contributed content to Chapter 7, and Dr. Shanan Fitts (California State University, Fullerton) provided content to Chapter 9. Each of these individuals enhanced the quality of this text, and we are grateful for these excellent contributions.

Lastly, we wish to acknowledge all the teachers and students we have had the privilege of knowing and working with over the years. Their tireless efforts in helping to meet the needs of culturally and linguistically diverse exceptional learners provide inspiration for the development of this text, along with the continued hope for improved education for all learners who have disabilities.

JJH
JKK
LMB
JMP

Discover the Merrill Resources for Special Education Website

Technology is a constantly growing and changing aspect of our field that is creating a need for new content and resources. To address this emerging need, Merrill Education has developed an online learning environment for students, teachers, and professors alike to complement our products—the *Merrill Resources for Special Education* Website. This content-rich website provides additional resources specific to this book's topic and will help you—professors, classroom teachers, and students—augment your teaching, learning, and professional development.

Our goal is to build on and enhance what our products already offer. For this reason, the content for our user-friendly website is organized by topic and provides teachers, professors, and students with a variety of meaningful resources all in one location. With this website, we bring together the best of what Merrill has to offer: text resources, video clips, web links, tutorials, and a wide variety of information on topics of interest to general and special educators alike. Rich content, applications, and competencies further enhance the learning process.

The *Merrill Resources for Special Education* Website includes:

- Video clips specific to each topic, with questions to help you evaluate the content and make crucial theory-to-practice connections.
- Thought-provoking critical analysis questions that students can answer and turn in for evaluation or that can serve as basis for class discussions and lectures.
- Access to a wide variety of resources related to classroom strategies and methods, including lesson planning and classroom management.
- Information on all the most current relevant topics related to special and general education, including CEC and Praxis™ standards, IEPs, portfolios, and professional development.
- Extensive web resources and overviews on each topic addressed on the website.
- A search feature to help access specific information quickly.

To take advantage of these and other resources, please visit the *Merrill Resources for Special Education* Website at

http://www.prenhall.com/hoover

About the Authors

John J. Hoover is a Senior Research Associate and Adjunct Faculty in the Graduate School of Education at the University of Colorado, Boulder. He holds a Ph.D. in Curriculum, Administration, and Supervision with an emphasis in Special Education from the University of Colorado, Boulder. He is a former special education teacher and supervisor, working with diverse learners in grades K–12 who had learning disabilities and emotional/behavioral disorders. In the field of special education, he has over 60 publications, ranging from university texts and textbook chapters to refereed journal articles in multicultural, special, and general education. His book (co-authored with James R. Patton) *Curriculum Adaptation for Students with Learning and Behavior Problems: Differentiating Instruction to Meet Diverse Needs* (2005) is in its third edition. In addition to curricular methods, his other research and writing interests include study skills, school district policies for meeting the needs of immigrant students with special needs, and the role of special educators in multilevel instruction and response to intervention.

Janette Klingner, Ph.D., is an Associate Professor in Bilingual Special Education at the University of Colorado, Boulder, in the Division for Educational Equity and Cultural Diversity. She was a bilingual special education teacher for 10 years before earning her doctorate in reading and learning disabilities from the University of Miami. Currently she is a co-Principal Investigator for The National Center for Culturally Responsive Educational Systems (NCCRESt). One research focus is the disproportionate representation of culturally and linguistically diverse students in special education. Another is reading comprehension strategy instruction. She and Beth Harry recently published the book, *Why Are so Many Minority Students in Special Education? Understanding Race and Disability in Schools.* In 2004 she won AERA's Early Career Award.

Leonard Baca has an Ed.D. from the University of Northern Colorado. He has been a professor of Education at the University of Colorado, Boulder, since 1973. He has taught courses in bilingual and bilingual special education and served as the program chair. Professor Baca is founder and director of the BUENO Center for Multicultural Education. He is the author of *The Bilingual Special Education Interface*, Merrill Prentice Hall (2004), and several other articles dealing with English language learners with disabilities.

James M. Patton is a Professor of Leadership and Special Education at the College of William and Mary in Virginia and spearheads a major effort to infuse cultural responsiveness into leadership and special education. He was formerly Associate Dean of Academic Programs and Director of Project Mandala, a federally funded research and development project aimed at developing culturally responsive systems for identifying and serving selected culturally, linguistically, and socioeconomically diverse students and their families who exhibit at-risk and at-promise characteristics. Dr. Patton has taught special education in the public schools of Louisville, Kentucky, where he also directed the Career Opportunities Program, a federally funded effort to increase the number of indigenous inner-city ethnically and culturally diverse teachers in the Louisville Public Schools. A former member of the Executive Committee, the Board of Governors, and Board of Directors of the Council for Exceptional Children (CEC), Dr. Patton has been a Senior Scholar in the Shaklee Institute, a special education think tank. Dr. Patton has authored or co-authored over 50 articles in refereed publications and two books, which have cultural, class, and linguistic responsiveness as their major themes. His major research interests include the educational and psychosocial development of African Americans, particularly those with gifts and talents; the holistic development of African American males; the social, political, and economic correlates of mild disabilities; curriculum and pedagogical issues around multicultural education; cultural competency development; and analyses of policies that affect people of color and those from low socioeconomic circumstances. His funded external grants approximate $4.8 million. His grant development mentoring of faculty approaches $12.0 million.

Brief Contents

Contents

Note: Every effort has been made to provide accurate and current Internet information in this book. However, the Internet and information posted on it are constantly changing, so it is inevitable that some of the Internet addresses listed in this textbook will change.

PART I

Overview of Teaching Culturally and Linguistically Diverse Exceptional Learners

Chapter 1

Introduction to Instructional Methods for Culturally and Linguistically Diverse Exceptional (CLDE) Learners

Chapter Objectives

Upon completion of this chapter the reader will be able to:

1. Articulate current general instructional needs of CLDE learners in today's schools.
2. Identify a variety of factors influencing the instructional climate in today's schools.
3. Discuss strategies for selecting appropriate language of instruction.
4. Briefly summarize culturally competent teaching characteristics.
5. Describe teaching qualities necessary for instructing CLDE learners.
6. Describe an instructional model for meeting the needs of CLDE learners in the classroom.

VIGNETTE

Danh is a third grader who has not developed the skills to be successful in the third-grade classroom. Danh is a child of a second-generation immigrant family from Vietnam and is a culturally and linguistically diverse (CLD) learner. Although Danh's parents' native language is Vietnamese, his primary language at home and at school is English. All of his teachers care about him and want him to learn so that he may live a fully productive life in America. Danh has been in U.S. schools for 3 years and is currently in a school that has recently implemented a three-tiered instructional model of learning along with response to intervention methods. While at school, Danh continues to listen to his teachers and fellow students read, and tries to do his homework. Having little success in the general education classroom, Danh is referred to his school's child-study team. A meeting is called to see what may be done to best help Danh succeed in school. The team brainstorms ideas and decides that more intensive supplemental instruction may help Danh to meet his reading needs. Danh is provided supplemental support in basic reading skills along with additional English language development.

Although Danh is being provided supplemental academic assistance, the child-study team neglected to consider several important factors in his life that contribute to better understanding his situation and associated needs. For example, Danh has had limited exposure to formal U.S. schooling and is experiencing difficulties acculturating to the new school environment. Also, he learns best in small group situations rather than independent seatwork. The strategy selected to help Danh with reading was implementation of a reading method completed independently, supported by paraprofessional assistance. For 5 weeks, Danh is provided extra learning assistance, but still continues to make inadequate progress. Embedded within this supplemental instruction is regular monitoring of his progress in reading and English language development, using approved assessment instruments within the school district. However, these testing instruments lack cultural relevancy to Danh's needs and in turn yield inaccurate or invalid results. Unaware that the instructional methods and associated assessment of Danh's response to the instruction are not culturally responsive to Danh's needs, the child-study team erroneously believes that Danh may have a learning disability in reading or language and is referred for formal special education testing. This in turn leads to other mistakes in providing inappropriate opportunities to learn for Danh and students like him in our schools.

The authors wish to acknowledge Michael Orosco for his assistance in developing this vignette.

Danh is a culturally and linguistically diverse learner that the system was unable to effectively educate because it did not possess adequate knowledge of linguistic and cultural competences that Danh brought to school. Because of this, the school was unable to develop effective instructional methods to educate him. The system lacked the comprehensive knowledge that should influence use of effective educational methods consistent with cultural and linguistic diverse needs. This process may have set Danh and others like him up for a series of failures because the system neglected to provide sufficient opportunities to learn.

Unfortunately, many diverse learners experience the type of educational structure provided to Danh, where lack of knowledge of cultural and linguistic diversity contributes significantly to misinterpreting a learning difference for a learning disability. Danh's situation also highlights the critical need for culturally competent educators who implement appropriate instruction and associated assessment with diverse learners, with or without a disability.

Reflective Questions

1. To what extent does your school or district accommodate instruction to meet cultural and linguistic needs?
2. What should Danh's child-study team have done prior to selecting and implementing supplemental instructional methods?

INTRODUCTION

Mandated curricula, recent legislation, and increased diversity are some of the educational issues currently impacting the education of students with disabilities from culturally and linguistically diverse backgrounds. Throughout this text, we will stress the importance of meeting the instructional needs of diverse learners with disabilities by simultaneously addressing three interrelated learner aspects as illustrated in Figure 1.1.

As shown, culturally and linguistically diverse exceptional (CLDE) learners bring to the classroom three areas of diversity:

1. *Culture.* Culture represents the communication, socialization, interactions, values, and behaviors of a particular group or subgroup of people (Baca & Cervantes, 2004).
2. *Language.* Language encompasses the systematic way in which verbal and/or nonverbal communication occurs among individuals, reflecting cultural values and linguistic symbols (de Valenzuela & Niccolai, 2004).
3. *Disability Needs.* Disability needs include the special education services needed to help students who have a disability (e.g., learning disability, developmental disability, visual impairment, significant emotional/behavior disorders) reach their full potential (Hallahan & Kauffman, 2006).

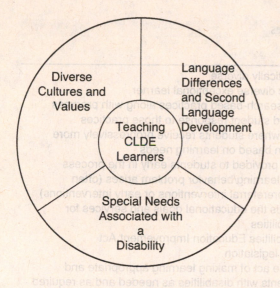

FIGURE 1.1 Diverse Elements for Teaching CLDE Learners

As a result, educators of students with disabilities who also reflect cultural and linguistic diversity are challenged with understanding the interrelated needs associated with two types of learners:

1. Culturally and linguistically diverse (CLD) students who are learners bringing cultural and language diversity to the learning environment. A CLD learner often brings different values, expectations, and experiences to the classroom, and frequently speaks a first language other than English. Currently, there are over 400 different languages spoken by students in our schools, with Spanish being the most prevalent (U.S. Department of Education, 2001). Other highly prevalent languages spoken by learners in our schools include Vietnamese, Hmong, Russian, Arabic, Chinese (Cantonese and Mandarin), Navajo, or Korean (U.S. Department of Education, 2001). (The methods discussed in this book apply to learners from various cultural backgrounds who speak the many different languages found in today's classrooms.)

2. Culturally and linguistically diverse exceptional (CLDE) learners who are CLD learners with an identified disability as defined by special education laws or regulations.

To best meet the needs of CLD and CLDE learners, teachers must become familiar with several interrelated elements of education, including linguistically diverse education, second language acquisition, special education needs and characteristics, and the role of culture in teaching and learning. Table 1.1 provides a glossary of terms and practices important for teachers to be familiar with to best meet the needs of CLD learners. These will be referred to throughout this text, and we recommend readers refer back to this glossary as necessary.

TABLE 1.1 Glossary of Terms and Educational Practices

Term	Explanation
CLD	Culturally and linguistically diverse
CLDE Learner	Cultural and linguistic diverse exceptional learner
Response to Intervention (RTI)	Implementation of research-based practices along with progress monitoring to record student response to those practices
Multi- or Three-Tiered Learning	System of education where students receive progressively more intensive instruction based on learning needs
Early Intervening Services	Educational services provided to students early in the process when a suspected learning/behavior problem arises (often synonymous with prereferral interventions or early interventions)
Individualized Education Plan (IEP)	Document that records the educational goals and services for students with disabilities
IDEA (2004)	Individuals with Disabilities Education Improvement Act
NCLB (2001)	No Child Left Behind legislation
Accommodations	*Accommodation* is the act of making learning appropriate and accessible to students with disabilities as needed and as required by law; applies to both instructional and assessment tasks
Standards-Based Learning/ Assessment	Instruction/assessment designed to emphasize student's proficiency on grade-level standards of learning
ESL Method	English as a second language method such as approaches intended to help students who are nonnative speakers of English
English Language Learner (ELL)	English language learner is a student in the process of acquiring English but who is not yet fully proficient; the term *limited English proficient* is sometimes used to describe an ELL, though it is not the preferred term
Cultural Competence	Valuing diversity as strengths incorporated into the educational curriculum and process

As we begin our discussion about the most appropriate strategies to use for teaching culturally and linguistically diverse students (with or without disabilities), an overview of the current educational situation is important to ensure that all readers are familiar with preferred educational practices and prevailing policies. Some general teaching implications that will be further explored in our text are also provided for each of the topical areas covered in this chapter. We begin with a discussion of the current instructional climate in schools.

INSTRUCTIONAL CLIMATE IN TODAY'S SCHOOLS

A variety of recent events and current practices directly affect instruction, curriculum, and assessment in today's learning environments. Several of these have a direct impact on teaching diverse learners, including (1) reauthorization of the Individuals with Disabilities Education Improvement Act (IDEA); (2) No Child Left Behind (NCLB);

(3) three-tiered instruction; (4) response to intervention; (5) standards-based learning and assessment; (6) immigrant students with special needs; and (7) misdiagnosis of disabilities. Each of these topical areas is discussed along with significant teaching implications for educators of CLD/CLDE learners.

Reauthorization of the Individuals with Disabilities Education Improvement Act (IDEA, 2004)

Effective July 1, 2005, the new provisions associated with the reauthorization of IDEA (2004) took effect (Beekman, 2005). A variety of new provisions are included in the reauthorization, and several of these pertain specifically to the education of CLD and CLDE learners. The following is a summary of relevant points within IDEA (2004) as found in the *Federal Register* (2006) and discussed by the Council for Exceptional Children (CEC, 2004) and Beekman (2005).

Overidentification and Disproportionality IDEA requires school districts that have an overrepresentation of minority students in special education to refocus their efforts at the prereferral stage to reduce inappropriate placements of these students in special education.

Teaching Implications: Educators must strive to provide more effective and relevant prereferral services to CLD students prior to any formal efforts to assess and place into special education.

Early Intervening Services IDEA (2004) authorizes school systems to use funds for at-risk learners not identified with a disability who require supplemental services to meet academic or socioemotional needs. These educational efforts may also be referred to by some as early intervention or prereferral services. However, whichever term is used, the intent of this provision in IDEA (2004) is to facilitate identifying and addressing potential learning and/or behavior problems early in the process before placement into special education.

Teaching Implications: Special educators may provide early intervening services in the general education setting. This practice attempts to prevent potential problems from escalating by providing more timely support and assistance to CLD learners who are at risk either academically or behaviorally.

Criteria for Determining a Learning Disability Specific criteria for identifying and placing a student into special education for a learning disability was also further clarified in IDEA (2004). Relevant specifics for identifying a learning disability include the provisions that states must (1) not *require* the use of significant discrepancy data (although significant discrepancy data may still be used if districts elect to do so), and (2) *permit* the use of response to intervention as criteria (Federal Register, 2006).

Teaching Implications: As more and more schools move to the use of student responses to evidence-based interventions as major criteria for determining a learning disability, teachers of CLD students need to become more proficient with response to intervention methodology and three-tiered learning and apply these appropriately to meet cultural and linguistic needs. (Each of these is discussed in greater detail in a subsequent section in this chapter.)

Individualized Education Plan (IEP) The IEP contains a few new or expanded provisions. Two of these include emphasizing *academic and functional performance* rather than the previous more broadly used term *educational performance*. In addition, short-term objectives are no longer required as annual goals are stated in measurable terms.

Teaching Implications: Educators must become more proficient in writing measurable annual goals and think in terms of functioning skills to be acquired. IEPs for CLDE learners must include functioning abilities relative to the interrelated needs associated with language, culture, and disability.

Transition Services IDEA requires schools to document goals for transitioning students beyond secondary education, including skills and outcomes related to employment, independent living, and adult training. (Chapter 12 addresses this topic in detail.)

Teaching Implications: Secondary teachers of CLDE learners must become familiar with transition services and supports available to students. In addition, educators must document the student's IEP transition goals to facilitate successful transition beyond secondary education.

Accommodations IDEA includes specific provisions to ensure that a CLDE learner is provided appropriate accommodations and/or alternative assessments, if necessary, to best assess student progress toward "academic achievement and functional performance." Accommodations and alternative assessments must be documented on the IEP along with the justification for the modifications.

Teaching Implications: Teachers of CLDE learners need to be aware of approved accommodations and alternative assessments within their districts. Educators must advocate to include these on the student's IEP to ensure the best opportunities for appropriate assessment of student progress toward the measurable annual goals.

No Child Left Behind (NCLB)

No Child Left Behind (NCLB, 2001) legislation was designed to ensure that all students meet rigorous education standards. Collectively, NCLB and IDEA require all students, including CLDE learners, to be educated within and assessed through district and statewide curriculum and assessments. As a result, several recent provisions relate specifically to the instruction of CLDE learners. These include:

1. Annual testing of student progress relative to state standards
2. Paraprofessionals who are highly qualified and well trained
3. Academic and behavioral supports provided to students failing to meet minimum proficiency level standards
4. Provision to implement accommodations for students with disabilities should these be determined necessary to adequately assess progress

Currently, most states have adopted some form of standards-based mandated education and assessment (Hoover & Patton, 2004). As stipulated in NCLB, all students are to be provided sufficient opportunities to succeed in the state-mandated curricula and associated assessment.

Teaching Implications: Teachers of CLDE learners must acquire needed skills to ensure that students are provided sufficient opportunities to learn within the parameters of mandated curriculum and testing. Additionally, differentiated instruction is often necessary to provide appropriate education to CLD/CLDE learners. Teachers must become proficient in balancing the needs of district curricula with cultural and linguistic needs of CLDE learners.

Three-Tiered Instruction

The use of three-tiered or multilevel instruction is another important recent educational practice (Vaughn, 2003; Klingner & Edwards, 2006). This type of educational model includes three levels of instruction, which collectively may facilitate effective education for CLD/CLDE learners (Hoover & Patton, 2005). The model is frequently depicted as a triangle (Winston, 2006; Hoover, 2006; Yell, 2004) similar to that illustrated in Figure 1.2.

The type of education received through each tier is characterized as follows:

Tier 1: High-Quality Core Instruction is systematic instruction in an evidence-based and challenging curriculum implemented in the general education classroom.

Tier 2: High-Quality Targeted Supplemental Instruction includes more focused interventions designed to supplement tier 1 core instruction to learners at risk academically or behaviorally.

Tier 3: High-Quality Intensive Intervention is specialized intervention to meet the needs of students who have more significant needs, including those with disabilities.

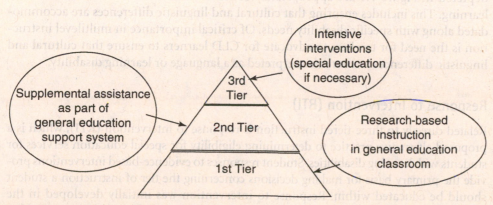

FIGURE 1.2 Three-Tiered Instruction

In three-tiered learning, as depicted in Figure 1.2, students are initially provided *high-quality core instruction* in the general education curriculum (tier 1). Within the total population of tier 1, some learners need additional support in the form of *high-quality targeted supplemental instruction* (tier 2). This supplemental instruction (1) directly supports the general education curriculum, (2) is often implemented in the general education setting, and (3) targets specific areas of need exhibited by the learner. An important element in multilevel instruction is the documentation of how well the student responds to the tier 2 supplemental intervention. This is referred to as *response to intervention* and is discussed further in the next section. Based on student response to the interventions, learners who continue to exhibit significant educational needs, and who fail to make adequate progress, may require *high-quality intensive intervention* (tier 3). Instruction at this level is provided to those students with more significant learning and behavior needs, including those associated with disabilities. Although three tiers are most frequently discussed in multilevel instruction, as a variation, Klingner and Edwards (2006) suggested a four-tier model approach, and the reader is referred to that source for additional information on their model. Also, Hoover and Patton (in press) illustrated the levels of instruction as a circular process to depict the interconnectedness between and among the tiers.

In reference to expected numbers of learners educated within each tier, particularly in the area of reading, approximately 80 to 90 percent of all students are expected to be successful in tier 1, 15 to 20 percent will require some supplemental tier 2 instruction, and approximately 1 to 5 percent will require tier 3 intensive special services (Winston, 2006; Yell, 2004; Hasbrouk, 2002). If implemented appropriately, most CLD learners who continue to experience difficulties with tier 1 instruction will receive tier 2 supplemental interventions, with few needing tier 3 instructional services.

Teaching Implications: In a three-tiered instructional system, special educators' roles and responsibilities are most defined for tier 3 where intensive intervention occurs to meet more significant educational needs. However, special educators also have important roles in the education of at-risk learners in tiers 1 and 2 (Hoover & Patton, in press). Educators of CLDE learners must ensure that all three elements depicted in Figure 1.1 are appropriately considered and addressed in three-tiered learning. This includes ensuring that cultural and linguistic differences are accommodated along with specific disability needs. Of critical importance in multilevel instruction is the need for teachers to advocate for CLD learners to ensure that cultural and linguistic differences are *not* misinterpreted as a language or learning disability.

Response to Intervention (RTI)

Related directly to three-tiered instruction is response to intervention (RTI), which is a proposed alternative practice to determining eligibility for special education services for students with learning disabilities. Student responses to evidence-based interventions provide the primary basis for making decisions concerning the tier of instruction a student should be educated within. Response to intervention was initially developed in the 1980s as a potential strategy for identifying learning and/or reading disabilities (Vaughn,

Linan-Thompson, & Hickman, 2003). Currently, use of some form of response to intervention as an alternative to determine special education eligibility is supported by several educational organizations (Fuchs, Mock, Morgan, & Young, 2003). Also, as previously discussed, IDEA (2004) includes provisions that allow states and school districts to use alternative methods for identifying a learning disability. RTI is the primary alternative currently being proposed by special educators. According to Vaughn and Fuchs (2003), this alternative method of RTI includes the implementation of research-based instructional practices along with the monitoring and documenting of student progress. If students fail to make sufficient progress, additional differentiated instruction is implemented with continued student progress monitoring. Students who continue to make unsatisfactory progress (as evidenced by documented responses to attempted interventions) would be considered for formal special education evaluation and/or placement (Fuchs et al., 2003).

Although there is limited research on using RTI with culturally and linguistically diverse students, recent investigations have produced promising results and initial support for the use of this model with at-risk English language learners (Linan-Thompson, Vaughn, Hickman-Davis, & Kouzekanani, 2003; Linan-Thompson, Vaughn, Prater, & Cirino, 2006; Vaughn et al., 2003; Vaughn, Mathes, Linan-Thompson, & Francis, 2005). For example, Vaughn et al. (2005) found that ELLs responded well to focused reading interventions combined with language development activities that incorporated ESL best practices (e.g., modeling, use of facial expressions and gestures in teaching vocabulary, explicit instruction in English language usage).

The success of the RTI model for culturally and linguistically diverse students will depend on several factors (Klingner & Bianco, 2006). The first is whether the learning environment nurtures academic success and views students' cultural and linguistic diversity as a rich resource (Ortiz, 1997, 2002). The second is whether teachers have received adequate preparation for teaching in culturally and linguistically diverse settings and have developed culturally responsive attributes (Gay, 2000; Ladson-Billings, 2001; Villegas & Lucas, 2002). The third is whether teachers have available to them a wide variety of research-based instructional approaches specifically designed for culturally and linguistically diverse students who show signs of struggling (McCardle, Mele-McCarthy, Cutting, Leos, & D'Emilio, 2005). Teachers need to know whether their interventions are effective and how to adjust instruction for students who do not respond to the first, second, or third tier of intervention (McCardle, Mele-McCarthy, & Leos, 2005). Each level of support in an RTI model must be culturally and linguistically responsive (Ortiz, 2002) and provide effective, research-based interventions with ongoing, culturally sensitive progress monitoring.

Teaching Implications: Currently, efforts are underway to further clarify and research the benefits of RTI relative to special education and cultural and linguistic diversity. However, several states have begun to formally use RTI in special education eligibility decision making, and therefore its practice has critical significance to special educators. Specifically, the implementation of instruction for CLD/CLDE learners requires ongoing differentiation, accommodation, and documentation to make informed and culturally and linguistically relevant decisions concerning opportunities to learn and progress toward goals. Further, to effectively implement RTI for CLD learners, diverse perspectives and cultural diversity must be examined and valued (Klingner & Edwards, 2006). Also, teachers must become proficient at progress monitoring and efficient in documenting results if RTI is implemented in their schools. See Klingner and Bianco (2006) and Klingner and Edwards (2006) for more detailed descriptions of possible RTI models for culturally and linguistically diverse students.

Standards–Based Learning and Assessment

Standards-based curriculum was initially developed in the 1970s as "minimum competencies" (Hoover & Patton, 2005), and over the past few decades, significant advancements have occurred in the curriculum for and assessment of students relative to meeting defined standards. Specifically, proficiency levels associated with assessment (e.g., not proficient, partially proficient, proficient, highly proficient) have evolved within our schools (Linn & Herman, 1997). This approach to documenting student progress is a major departure from the more traditional pass/fail or multiple-choice, norm-referenced tests. Also, a standards-based curriculum must contain educational standards written so expected achievement outcomes are clearly understood by all concerned (Education Commission of the States, 2003).

However, perhaps the most important aspect of standards-based education is the direct and more authentic connection between assessment and classroom instruction. As a result, standards-based curriculum and associated assessments are interconnected, with student progress documented in terms of proficiency levels. Overall, standards-based curriculum provides educators a clearer description of what should be taught and of what students should learn (Hoover & Patton, 2005), resulting in the opportunity for teachers to differentiate instruction for all students while meeting defined standards (Quenemoen, Lehr, Thurlow, & Massanaair, 2001).

Teaching Implications: A significant result of standards-based reforms is the opportunity for educators to reverse recent trends associated with the lowering of standards for CLDE students (Hoover & Patton, 2004). In effect, standards-based education requires more accountability and teacher competence to raise and meet expectations, rather than lowering the standards for culturally and linguistically diverse learners who also may have a disability. As teachers become more knowledgeable of the value of cultural and linguistic diversity in education the more effective standards-based learning will become for all students.

Immigrant Students with Special Needs

Immigrant students comprise a significant percentage of many educational classrooms nationwide, including both urban and rural school systems. The continuous and sometimes dramatic increases in the numbers of immigrant students places tremendous pressure on educators in our schools (Suarez-Orozco & Suarez-Orozco, 2001). Although different variations of definitions exist describing who qualifies as an immigrant student, most include the following (Emergency Immigrant Education Program, Office of English Language Acquisition—OELA):

1. Born outside of the United States
2. Enrolled in U.S. schools for less than 3 years
3. Are between the ages of 3 and 19

Suarez-Orozco and Suarez-Orozco (2001) described the new immigrant population as possessing wide diversity and socioeconomic characteristics ranging from high to minimum education, including various levels of economic status, and representing numerous languages. Although a recent government document (OBEMLA, 2000) concluded that nearly 75 percent of immigrants are of Spanish-speaking origin, several hundred different languages are represented by recent immigrants. Additionally, immigrants of this generation are more highly educated as compared to immigrants of the early 1990s (Suarez-Orozco & Suarez-Orozco, 2001). Of specific concern to educators and educational systems is that immigrant youth comprise the fastest growing segment of the overall population of children (Landale & Oropesa, 1995). Projections are that by 2040 one in three children will be children of immigrants (Rong & Prissle, 1998).

Issues such as the overrepresentation of immigrant students in special education, the lack of adequate support systems for new immigrant students, equal access barriers, inadequate teacher training to meet the unique needs of immigrant students, or the pervasive misperception that a language difference is a learning disability are but a few of the challenges confronting immigrant students, their families, and the educational system (Suarez-Orozco & Suarez-Orozco 2001; Smith-Davis, 2000; Chaifetz, 1999; Haynes, 2002). An example of potential issues associated with misinformed educators about cultural and linguistic diversity was illustrated in this chapter's vignette. As described, Danh, who is the son of Vietnamese parents, is improperly considered for special education due to misinterpretation of second language needs as a learning disorder. In addition, immigrant students with disabilities, who are properly placed into special education, often receive inadequate services and their teachers lack relevant training (Chaifetz, 1999; Smith-Davis, 2000). Grossman (1995) wrote that immigrant students experience three major problems in regards to special education: (1) misplacement, (2) culturally inappropriate services, and (3) linguistically inappropriate services.

To better understand the impact of increasing immigrant populations on today's schools continued research is needed to further explore the following concerns:

1. Immigrant students are overrepresented in special education.
2. Language difference is often misunderstood to be a learning disability.
3. Some immigrant students with disabilities go unreferred to special education.
4. Inadequate special education supports exist for immigrant students with disabilities.
5. Teacher shortages exist nationwide in the education of immigrant students, including special education teachers.

Teaching Implications: Teachers of CLDE learners need to acquire greater understanding of immigrant students' instructional, social, and emotional needs, including the following:

1. More effective assessment strategies must be developed to correctly refer and identify immigrant students who have special needs (Stefanakis, 2000).
2. Educators must create more learning environments for immigrant students where diversity is viewed as a resource rather than a barrier (Suarez-Orozco & Suarez-Orozco, 2001), as well as support their social and emotional needs.
3. Specific special education teacher training practices and programs for educating immigrant students with disabilities must be developed or improved upon along with the evaluation of those programs (Smith-Davis, 2000).

Misdiagnosis of Disabilities

Harry and Klingner (2005) discussed the complexities of overrepresentation of minority students in special education, indicating that many students are placed, for a variety of reasons, who do not actually have internal deficits (i.e., disabilities). The misinterpretation of cultural and linguistic diversity in our schools plays a significant role in the misdiagnosis and misplacement of CLD learners in special education. The overrepresentation of African American students in special education has and continues to be a significant issue in our schools (Harry & Klingner, 2005; Donovan & Cross, 2002). In addition, Artiles, Trent, and Palmer (2004) wrote that overrepresentation and misdiagnosis of diverse learners continues to exist, resulting, in part, from ineffective language assessment practices in schools. Also, recent data confirm that approximately 50 percent of students in special education are still placed with the eligibility of a learning disability (OSEP, 1998), many of whom also represent cultural and linguistic diversity. As educators continue to differ in opinions concerning ability to differentiate between low achievement and potential learning disabilities (Hallahan et al., 2005), the implications for accurate eligibility decisions must continue to be addressed. Most significant is the reality that language differences are often misunderstood for reading or language disabilities, resulting in misdiagnosis of a learning disability contributing to the overrepresentation of CLD learners in special education (Klingner, Artiles, & Barletta, 2004). As a result, students from culturally and linguistically diverse backgrounds continue to have a high risk for placement into special education (Donovan & Cross, 2002), particularly for needs associated with reading and language.

Teaching Implications: Eligibility decisions and culturally competent instruction begin with knowledge and skills necessary to differentiate between a learning difference and a suspected disability. Educators must acquire a greater understanding of the similarities among cultural, linguistic, and disability behaviors to make more informed and accurate decisions concerning special education eligibility of CLD learners (see Table 1.2). This critical issue is addressed throughout the text.

TABLE 1.2 Similarities Among Cultural/Linguistic Behaviors and Suspected Learning/Behavior Problems

Learning/Behavior Problems Often Associated with a Disability	Expected Behaviors in Stages When Learning a Second Language (English-L2)	Cultural Behaviors or Values
Verbal reticence (silence) Poor attention span for age Poor phonological processing skills Difficulty in verbal organization Poor verbal memory retrieval Difficulty in verbal expression Difficulty in graphic organization Stress, anxiety Low self-esteem Difficulty following directions Poor motivation and engagement Poor time management Difficulty in changing activities Poor interpersonal skills May prefer to be alone (social withdrawal) Problems in developing relationships Outspoken Acting out/aggressive behaviors	**Silent Period Stage** Focus on active listening skills Very little English spoken by learner Learner may not respond when spoken to Learner may experience confusion with locus of control May be withdrawn/show low self-esteem May seem to exhibit poor attention and concentration **Production Stage** May be withdrawn/show signs of frustration Learner begins to speak single words and short phrases in L2 Phrases may contain notable grammatical errors **Intermediate Stage** Learner is approaching age-appropriate levels in English (academic, behavioral, cultural, social); still makes errors in speech, reading, and writing **Advanced Stage** Language usage, meaning, and fluency are age appropriate; learner has very good comprehension Academic, behavioral, cultural, and social skills are L2 age appropriate	Learner may view time differently (e.g., starting times, deadlines) Anxiety, stress due to process of adapting to new cultural environment Acting out may reflect lack of experience with formal schooling Differences in preferred style of learning may reflect cultural norms External locus of control may be emphasized in some cultures Time management abilities reflect cultural values toward time Independent work may be discouraged in favor of group work/collaboration Coping strategies may vary by culture Confusion with time and space may be due to lack of familiarity with new cultural expectations Behavioral involving touch, movement, proximity to others may vary Kinesthetic strategies may receive greater emphasis over verbal interactions Ways of showing respect may vary (e.g., lowered eyes vs. eye contact) Discourse styles may vary (e.g., overlapping talk vs. waiting one's turn) Offering a different opinion may be considered a sign of disrespect Gender differences may influence the extent to which girls speak Learner may not be used to learning through question-answer exchanges (e.g., preferring observation)

Sources: Baca & Cervantes (2004); Collier & Hoover (1987); Cummins (2000); Hoover & Collier (1985); Jerrell (2000); Ortiz & Wilkinson (1991).

SELECTING APPROPRIATE LANGUAGE OF INSTRUCTION

As previously stated, students bring over 400 different languages to classrooms nation-wide. Many of these students are in the process of acquiring English, and this must be considered when selecting the most appropriate language of instruction. When providing instruction to an English language learner who has special needs, one of the first issues a teacher must address is whether to provide instruction in English, the child's native or first language, or both languages. In an ideal classroom situation where all necessary resources are available, education for a CLD learner with limited English proficiency should occur in the student's most proficient language, and if that language is other than English, then English language development must also occur to further advance that student's English language proficiency. However, since school districts have varying policies regarding language of instruction, educators must make informed decisions given those resources, policies, and potential restrictions (Baca & Cervantes, 2004). For example, states or school districts that have an English-only policy limit one's ability to instruct in the native language if that language is the primary language and other than English. For CLDE learners, the IEP should designate the language of instruction and this should be adhered to during classroom teaching. In the event that the IEP does not specify language of instruction for a CLDE learner, the building principal and/or program supervisor should be consulted to clarify language of instruction and/or the IEP team should reconvene to determine instructional language.

If native language is the most proficient language and native language instruction is permitted either by district policy and/or IEP specification, bilingual professionals or paraprofessional staff (should the teacher not be bilingual) should provide instruction in the native language (especially in reading), while also developing English language proficiency (Baca & Cervantes, 2004). The bilingual/English as a second language (ESL) special education delivery models presented in Chapter 4 provide more specific guidance on how to provide bilingual and ESL services to CLDE learners with limited English proficiency.

Teaching Implications: Teachers of CLDE learners must identify and use native language for instruction until English proficiency is sufficiently developed to allow the students to succeed academically in English. The following questions should be addressed to guide educators to determine and select the most appropriate language of instruction:

What is the student's native language?

What is the student's English language proficiency level?

What is the student's most proficient language—English or native language?

What native language instructional resources are available?

What English language development instructional resources are available?

Does the student's IEP specify language of instruction?

If not specified on IEP, what is district policy for selecting language of instruction?

Throughout this text, various models, strategies, and content-area methods are presented. We encourage readers to use the above questions as a guide to determine the most proficient language of instruction (whether it is English or the student's first language, such as Spanish, French, Chinese, etc.) to best meet the instructional and assessment needs addressed in this text.

STATUS OF BILINGUAL AND ESL EDUCATION IN TODAY'S SCHOOLS

Given the fact that this chapter and book are concerned with the education of culturally and linguistically diverse exceptional learners, it is important that the national context regarding bilingual and ESL education be addressed. Although bilingual education has a long and rich history in the United States dating back to the mid-1800s (Baca & Cervantes, 2004), it has a more current history that dates back to 1968 with the passage of the Bilingual Education Act (PL90-247) by the U.S. Congress. This law established bilingual education as one of the major programs administered by the U.S. Department of Education. The initial programs promoted a transition model of bilingual education. This meant that schools were encouraged to use the native language of the students to help them transition into English. As soon as this transition took place the rest of their education would be in English.

The bilingual education act was amended several times. The law eventually permitted what was known as developmental bilingual programs (Crawford, 2004). These programs did not require early transition into English but supported the goal of biliteracy. The law was also amended to allow English-only or ESL approaches to educating limited English proficient students (Crawford, 2004). Most recently with the passage of the No Child Left Behind Act, the term *bilingual education* itself has been replaced with *English language acquisition* (Ovando, Collier, & Combs, 2006). For example, the Bilingual Office in the Department of Education is now called the Office of English Language Acquisition, and the National Bilingual Clearinghouse is now called the National Clearinghouse for English Language Acquisition.

Ever since the U.S. Congress passed the Bilingual Education Act there have been those who have opposed the implementation of bilingual education. A national organization (U.S. English) was organized for this purpose. U.S. English has supported the passage of English-only laws or amendments in 24 states across the country (Ovando, Collier, & Combs, 2002). This opposition to bilingual education has reinforced the idea that bilingual education is a controversial issue. With this background in mind there seems to be two trends that have developed. The first is that some states and school districts have discontinued their bilingual programs and replaced them with ESL programs. On the other hand, some school districts have worked even harder to strengthen and maintain their bilingual programs. A second trend that seems to have developed is the growing support for dual language programs, which provides the opportunity for students to become bilingual. One thing is clear, the student population in our schools is becoming more and more linguistically diverse. Therefore, all schools need to implement either bilingual or ESL programs to help these students attain high levels of academic achievement.

In summary bilingual education is alive and well across the country. A growing body of research supports its effectiveness. At the same time public policy and discourse has gradually shifted toward an ESL approach in some states and school districts. The field of special education has been influenced by this national context. For example, a recent study of bilingual special education in California (Baca, Almanza De Schonewise, & Vanchu-Orosco, 2004) revealed that proposition 227, an English-only amendment, has caused some special education teachers to opt for an ESL rather than a bilingual approach, even though, IDEA, the national special education law takes precedence over a state mandate such as proposition 227. However, whichever approach is used, culturally competent teaching is necessary to meet CLD students' needs in the classroom.

OVERVIEW OF CULTURALLY COMPETENT TEACHING

Cultural competence occurs when educators grow beyond cultural awareness/sensitivity to become more competent in their abilities to implement culturally relevant curriculum and instruction (Mason, 1993). In this section we provide a brief overview of this important topic, and in Chapter 2 we present a more detailed description of cultural competence in teaching. Cultural competence is achieved when teachers value cultural and linguistic diversity as strengths incorporated into the overall educational process. Hoover (in press) wrote that culturally competent teaching in behavior management occurs by valuing diverse family expectations so as to not conflict with cultural values/norms. Cross, Bazron, Dennis, and Issacs (1989) and Mason (1993) identified five stages to develop cultural competence:

1. *Cultural Destructiveness.* Cultural differences are . . .
   - Not acknowledged in any way in the teaching/learning process
   - Viewed as problems to be punished or suppressed
2. *Cultural Incapacity.* Cultural differences are . . .
   - Ignored and not supported by the teacher
   - Provided little or no attention as cultural awareness and individual identity are viewed indifferently
3. *Cultural Blindness.* Cultural differences are . . .
   - Acknowledged by teachers, yet they also believe that cultural differences are of little importance or significance to education in the classroom
   - Recognized, but viewed only relative to the mainstream Western culture, resulting in the devaluing of other cultures in the overall learning experience
4. *Cultural Precompetence.* Cultural differences are . . .
   - Acknowledged and responded to by teachers in the classroom
   - Recognized as necessary for cultural competence in teaching to occur
   - Incorporated in teachers' personal/professional growth to better understand diversity

5. *Cultural Competence Proficiency.* Cultural differences are . . .
   - Genuinely valued and explored in the educational process
   - Integrated in meaningful ways throughout the learning process

Teaching Implications: Teachers of CLDE learners must become culturally competent educators in order to provide the most appropriate education to all learners. Readers are encouraged to identify in which stage of competence they currently perceive themselves and to make efforts to continue progressing toward stage 5.

INSTRUCTIONAL FRAMEWORK FOR TEACHING CLDE LEARNERS

The Instructional Framework for Educating CLDE Learners (Figure 1.3) provides educators a structure for ensuring that the main components necessary to successfully educate CLDE learners are considered, addressed, and implemented in culturally and linguistically competent ways. Our framework was developed from information found in Hammill and Bartel (2004), Baca and Cervantes (2004), and Hoover and Patton (2005).

This figure is not considered all inclusive; rather it reflects several critical aspects necessary to effectively educate CLDE learners in a variety of educational settings within which different educators may possess varying degrees of qualifications.

As shown, the framework contains four major components, each building on specific knowledge and skills:

1. Underlying Instructional Framework Elements
2. Instructional Considerations
3. Instructional Cycle
4. Ongoing Assessment

Initially, our framework addresses five critical elements that form the foundation for successful implementation of methods for teaching CLDE learners. It begins with a working knowledge of CLDE learners. Also important is the overarching need to acquire an in-depth understanding of the interrelationship among disability, cultural, and linguistic needs. Additionally, educators must identify and understand their own perceptions of the role of the teacher (e.g., facilitator of learning, one who imparts knowledge to students, cooperative versus individual teaching) as well as the role of the learner (e.g., passive recipient of knowledge, active learner, cooperative versus individual learner). The philosophical slant in which educators view the role of teachers and learners is reflected in the selection of teaching and student strategies, the establishment of classroom structures, and the procedures used to implement classroom management. The foundation for this framework also requires educators to know and understand the purposes for and processes within the use of selected bilingual/ESL instructional programming (e.g., English as a second language instruction).

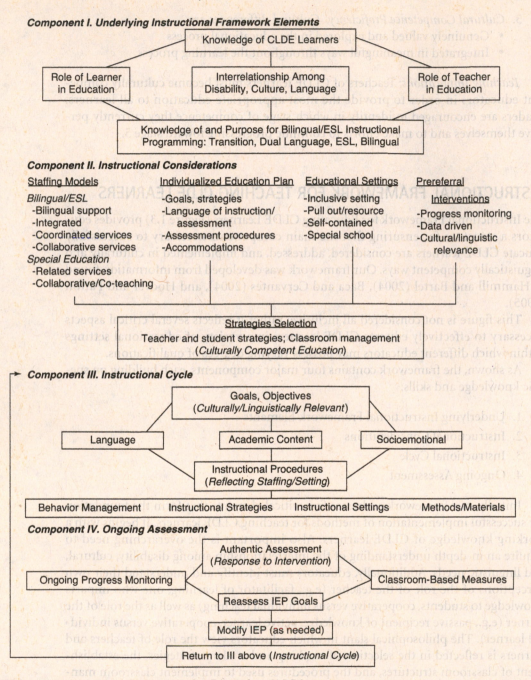

Component I. Underlying Instructional Framework Elements

Knowledge of CLDE Learners

Role of Learner in Education

Interrelationship Among Disability, Culture, Language

Role of Teacher in Education

Knowledge of and Purpose for Bilingual/ESL Instructional Programming: Transition, Dual Language, ESL, Bilingual

Component II. Instructional Considerations

Staffing Models

Bilingual/ESL
-Bilingual support
-Integrated
-Coordinated services
-Collaborative services

Special Education
-Related services
-Collaborative/Co-teaching

Individualized Education Plan
-Goals, strategies
-Language of instruction/ assessment
-Assessment procedures
-Accommodations

Educational Settings
-Inclusive setting
-Pull out/resource
-Self-contained
-Special school

Prereferral Interventions
-Progress monitoring
-Data driven
-Cultural/linguistic relevance

Strategies Selection
Teacher and student strategies; Classroom management
(*Culturally Competent Education*)

Component III. Instructional Cycle

Goals, Objectives
(*Culturally/Linguistically Relevant*)

Language

Academic Content

Socioemotional

Instructional Procedures
(*Reflecting Staffing/Setting*)

Behavior Management   Instructional Strategies   Instructional Settings   Methods/Materials

Component IV. Ongoing Assessment

Authentic Assessment
(*Response to Intervention*)

Ongoing Progress Monitoring

Classroom-Based Measures

Reassess IEP Goals

Modify IEP (as needed)

Return to III above (*Instructional Cycle*)

FIGURE 1.3 Instructional Framework for Educating CLDE Learners

The second component of our model reflects various aspects of the educational setting and process. This includes bilingual/ESL and special education staffing models based on available educational staff, educational placement settings (e.g., self-contained, pull out, inclusive classroom) within which CLDE learners receive instruction, prereferral interventions and the results of those interventions (e.g., response to intervention, progress monitoring, data-driven decisions), as well as the major aspects found on the students' Individualized Education Plan (IEP). Specifically, attention must be paid to the IEP elements of:

1. Educational goals and associated cultural and linguistic competent strategies, materials, and management techniques.

2. Accommodations for appropriate assessment and sufficient opportunities to learn within prescribed curricula.

3. Identification of the most appropriate language of assessment based on the purpose(s) for the assessment (e.g., English language skill abilities, higher order thinking abilities).

4. Selection of the most appropriate language of instruction with clearly defined purposes for its selection and use. For example, a teacher may instruct in a selected language for the purpose of drawing on student strengths in that language to best understand a concept in reading or social studies. In another situation, however, the teacher may use that same language for the sole purpose of helping the student acquire that language (e.g., learning English, French, Spanish, etc.). Teachers must be clear in identifying the purpose(s) for selecting a language of instruction in order to best assess the intended outcomes associated with those purposes. Once clear purposes for language of instruction are identified and articulated, appropriate methods, materials, and associated classroom management techniques are selected.

The third component within the framework is the instructional cycle used to teach the knowledge and skills based on factors discussed in component II. Within this cycle, language, academic, and socioemotional goals/objectives are identified and addressed relative to the specific staffing model(s) and educational setting(s) within which the student is educated. At this stage in the instructional cycle, educators must identify the most appropriate evidence-based instructional practices and strategies to best educate the CLDE learner, within the specific staffing model and educational setting(s) selected. Each staffing model and educational setting reflects unique ways to address the education of students (e.g., the bilingual/special education coordinated services model, discussed in Chapter 4, contains both a monolingual special educator and a bilingual educator, and the strategies to educate CLDE learners through this staff arrangement must reflect this reality). However, knowing the particular staffing model or educational setting is only the prerequisite first step in providing effective education. Use of instructional strategies, materials, and management procedures specific to the selected staffing model and educational setting is critical to providing the most appropriate education to CLDE learners. (Chapter 4 discusses various staffing models in detail.)

Component IV of our framework pertains to ongoing authentic assessment of the goals and objectives achieved by (1) using culturally/linguistically appropriate methods, materials, and management (component III); (2) reflecting the IEP, prereferral intervention, staffing models, and educational setting specifics (component II); and (3) basing instruction on knowledge and skills reflective of competent education and programming by blending disability, culture, and language needs into one integrated program, while simultaneously advancing the most appropriate teacher and learner roles in education (component I). As both classroom-based and more formal assessment procedures are implemented, students' IEP goals must be revisited and revised, if necessary, to best differentiate strategies and use selected materials to provide the best education possible to CLDE learners. (Chapter 5 covers assessment for CLD learners.)

Each of the aspects presented in this framework are discussed in greater detail throughout this text. We encourage readers to periodically refer to this framework to ensure that they are acquiring necessary skills and experiencing the necessary personal growth to successfully educate CLDE learners, no matter which staffing model or educational setting they must operate within.

EFFECTIVE INSTRUCTIONAL QUALITIES FOR TEACHING CLDE LEARNERS

Along with the implementation of an instructional framework, educators must possess a variety of instructional competencies or qualities to help all learners succeed in school. Within today's classrooms, a value-added component brought by CLDE learners is diversity in culture, experiential background, language, and values. Ovando, Collier, and Combs (2002) discussed several principles that are relevant to implementing effective instruction with culturally and linguistically diverse learners. These are not all inclusive; however, we have found that they provide a general foundation for effective teaching, which we will further explore and develop throughout this text. The following principles are applicable to CLDE learners:

1. Academic content must be related to the cultural environment and prior experiences of the learners.
2. Multiple content areas should be addressed in integrated ways so acquired knowledge and skills are reinforced over time.
3. Both cognitive and academic instructional goals should be addressed, including higher order thinking abilities.
4. Educators must challenge, through high expectations, all learners.
5. Teachers must value diversity within the classroom and view this as a positive learning opportunity for all students.
6. Students should be engaged in active learning and inquiry-based tasks.

In addition, cooperative learning to facilitate student responsibility for their own learning should be included in the implementation of classroom instruction. Also, Garcia (2001) stressed the importance of active and student-centered learning to address cultural and linguistic needs of diverse learners. The unique needs of CLDE learners must be addressed in comprehensive ways. As previously discussed, the academic and socioemotional needs of CLDE students exhibited in the classroom may be due to a variety of different factors, including diverse linguistic and cultural background, limited English proficiency, adjustment to a new cultural environment, and/or the presence of a disability.

Teaching Implications: Expanding on the discussions above, we included in Table 1.3 several qualities that will assist educators in their personal assessment of effective teaching for CLDE learners.

Although not all inclusive, these various qualities assist to effectively meet cultural, linguistic, and disability needs. Readers are encouraged to initially evaluate their current knowledge and skills in these areas to identify their specific strengths and areas requiring further development. Knowledge and skills presented in Table 1.3 will be strengthened through further exploration of effective teaching methods for CLDE learners discussed throughout the remainder of this text. Educators of CLD learners must keep in mind that some suspected academic and/or

TABLE 1.3 Instructional Qualities for Educating CLDE Learners

Effective education for CLDE learners includes these minimum instructional qualities:

Student learning is facilitated through cooperative activities.

Learner's prior knowledge is accessed during instruction.

Instructional activities are provided within the context of the student's prior experiences and acquired prerequisite skills.

Students are challenged to engage in higher level thinking/problem-solving tasks.

Ongoing verbal dialogue facilitates student learning.

Academic content is relevant to students' own cultural values and experiences.

Integration of knowledge/skills across content areas is emphasized.

Instructional goals for both cognitive and academic areas are addressed.

Instruction challenges students to aspire to and attain high expectations.

Student's present language functioning abilities (communicative/academic) are identified.

Acculturation effects on student learning are identified and accommodated.

Diverse cultural values are integrated into the learning environment.

Compatibility between teaching and student preferred learning styles are identified and accounted for in instructional methods.

Instruction reflects teacher's positive cultural competence.

Learner's special needs are accommodated in the classroom environment in culturally relevant ways.

socioemotional behaviors are expected behaviors due to differences in language and culture and *not* due to disabilities, even though similar behaviors often associated with a disability may be present. This complex situation requires educators to possess sufficient background in all three areas illustrated in Figure 1.1—cultural diversity, language differences, disability needs—to provide appropriate and effective instructional methods to all learners.

SUMMARY

Educators must possess a minimum level of linguistic and cultural competence in order to effectively implement instructional methods to educate CLDE learners. This includes a working knowledge of the influences of cultural and linguistic diversity on special education eligibility and placement decision making, along with skills necessary to blend interrelated needs associated with English as a second language development, disabilities, and cultural values. Our hope is that as you read, study, internalize, and implement the topics and ideas related to instructional methods and assessment for CLD/CLDE learners throughout this text, an increase in professional knowledge about and advocacy for these learners will emerge.

Discussion Questions

1. How might culture, language, and disability needs converge to define the education of a CLDE learner?

2. What are some of the recent educational practices found in today's schools and how might these be of benefit to teaching CLDE learners?

3. What is your current level of cultural competence and which areas must you further develop to advance your teaching abilities with CLDE learners?

4. What is your local school district's language of instruction policy and its implications for teaching CLD/CLDE learners?

5. What instructional qualities do you currently possess for implementing effective instructional methods for CLDE learners?

References

Artiles, A. J., Trent, S. C., & Palmer, J. (2004). Culturally diverse students in special education: Legacies and prospects. In J. A. Banks & C. M. Banks (Eds.), *Handbook of research on multicultural education* (2nd ed., pp. 716–735). San Francisco, CA: Jossey-Bass.

Baca, L., Almanza De Schonewise, E., & Vanchu-Orosco, M. (2004). Teaching English language learners with disabilities in an English-only environment: A pilot study. *NABE News, 27*, 5.

Baca, L., & Cervantes, H. T. (2004). *The bilingual special education interface* (3rd ed.). Upper Saddle River, NJ: Merrill/Prentice Hall.

Beekman, L. (2005, January). *IDEA 04: What's new and so what.* Presentation at the annual Colorado Special Education Directors meeting, Denver, CO.

Chaifetz, J. (1999, December). *Meeting the educational needs of English language learners.* Testimony before New York State Assembly Education Committee and Task Force on New Americans, NY.

Collier, C., & Hoover, J. J. (1987). Sociocultural considerations when referring minority children for learning disabilities. *LD Focus, 3*, 39–45.

Council for Exceptional Children. (2004). *The new IDEA: CEC's summary of significant issues.* Arlington, VA: Author.

Crawford, J. (2004). *Educating English learners: Language diversity in the classroom* (5th ed.). Los Angeles, CA: Bilingual Education Services.

Cross, T., Bazron, B., Dennis, K., & Issacs, M. (1989). *Towards a culturally competent system of care.* Washington, DC: CASSP Technical Assistance Center, Georgetown University Child Development Center.

Cummins, J. (2000). *Language, power, and pedagogy: Bilingual children in the crossfire.* Clevedon, England: Multilingual Matters Limited.

de Valenzuela, J. S., & Niccolai, S. L. (2004). Language development in culturally and linguistically diverse students with special educational needs. In L. M. Baca & H. T. Cervantes (Eds.), *The bilingual special education interface* (pp. 124–156). Columbus, OH: Merrill.

Donovan, M. S., & Cross, C. T. (Ed.). (2002). *Minority students in special and gifted education.* Washington, DC: National Academies Press.

Education Commission of the States. (2003). *No child left behind issue brief: A guide to standards-based assessment.* Denver, CO: Author.

Federal Register. (2006, August 14). *Assistance to states for the education of children with disabilities and preschool grants for children with disabilities: Final rule.* 34 CFR Parts 300 and 301. Washington, DC: Author.

Fuchs, D., Mock, D., Morgan, P. L., & Young, C. (2003). Responsiveness-to-instruction intervention: Definitions, evidence, and implications for the learning disabilities construct. *Learning Disabilities: Research & Practice, 18*(3), 157–171.

Garcia, E. E. (2001). *Hispanic education in the United States: Raíces y alas.* Lanham, MD: Rowman & Litchfield.

Gay, G. (2000). *Culturally responsive teaching.* New York: Teachers College Press.

Grossman, H. (1995). *Special education in a diverse society.* Boston, MA: Allyn & Bacon.

Hallahan, D. P., & Kauffman, J. M. (2006). *Exceptional learners* (7th ed.). Boston, MA: Allyn & Bacon.

Hallahan, D. P., Lloyd, J. W., Kauffman, J. M., Weiss, M. P., & Martinez, E. A. (2005). *Learning disabilities: Foundations, characteristics, and effective teaching.* Boston, MA: Pearson.

Hammill, D. D., & Bartel N. R. (2004). *Teaching students with learning and behavior problems.* Austin, TX: Pro-Ed.

Harry, B., & Klingner, J. K. (2005). *Why are so many minority students in special education?: Understanding race and disability in schools.* New York: Teachers College Press.

Hasbrouck, J. (2002). *Washington state reading initiative.* Washington Department of Education.

Haynes, J. (2002). *Myths of second language acquisition.* Everything ESL.net

Hoover, J. J. (2006, April 25). *Framework for implementing culturally competent response to intervention.* Invited presentation at the NYC Summit on Differentiated Instruction and Academic Intervention, New York.

Hoover, J. J. (2006). Managing behavior problems by differentiating curriculum and instruction. *Teaching English as a Second Language (E-Journal), 10*(2).

Hoover, J. J., & Collier, C. (1985). Referring culturally and linguistically different children: Sociocultural considerations. *Academic Therapy, 20*(4), 503–509.

Hoover, J. J, & Patton, J. R. (2004). Perspective: Differentiating standards-based education for students with diverse needs. *Remedial and Special Education, 25*(2), 74–78.

Hoover, J. J, & Patton, J. R. (2005). *Curriculum adaptations for students with learning and behavior problems: Differentiating instruction to meet to diverse needs* (3rd ed.). Austin, TX: Pro-Ed.

Hoover, J. J., & Patton, J. R. (in press). Role of special educators in a multi-tiered instructional system. *Intervention in School and Clinic.*

IDEA. (2004). *Individuals with Disabilities Education Improvement Act Amendments of 2004.* Washington, DC.

Jerrell, I. A. (2000). Natural approach to second language acquisition. *Modern Language Journal, 6,* p. 325, 337.

Klingner, J., & Bianco, M. (2006). What is special about special education for culturally and linguistically diverse students with disabilities? In B. Cook & B. Schirmer (Eds.), *What is special about special education?* Austin, TX: Pro-Ed.

Klingner, J. K., Artiles, A. J., & Barletta, L. M. (2004, November). *English language learners who struggle with reading: Language acquisition or learning disabilities?* Paper presented at the Research Conference English Language Learners Struggling to Learn: Emergent Research on Linguistic Differences and Learning Disabilities, Scottsdale, AZ.

Klingner, J. K., & Edwards, P. E. (2006). Cultural considerations with response to intervention models. *Reading Research Quarterly, 41*(1), 108–115.

Ladson-Billings, G. (2001). *Crossing over to Canaan: The journey of new teachers in diverse classrooms.* San Francisco: Jossey-Bass.

Landale, N. S., & Oropesa, R. S. (1995). *Immigrant children and the children of immigrants: Inter- and intra-ethnic group differences in the United States.* (Population Research Group Research Paper No. 95-2). East Lansing: Michigan State University.

Linan-Thompson, S., Vaughn, S., Hickman-Davis, P., & Kouzekanani, K. (2003). Effectiveness of supplemental reading instruction for second-grade English language learners with reading difficulties. *Elementary School Journal, 103,* 221–238.

Linan-Thompson, S., Vaughn, S., Prater, K., & Cirino, P. T. (2006). The response to intervention of English language learners at risk for reading problems. *Journal of Learning Disabilities, 39(5),* 390–398.

Linn, L. R., & Herman, J. L. (1997). *A policymaker's guide to standards-led assessment.* Denver, CO: Education Commission for the States.

Mason, J. L. (1993). *Cultural competence self-assessment questionnaire.* Portland, OR: Portland State University. Multicultural Initiative Project.

McCardle, P., Mele-McCarthy, J., Cutting, L., Leos, K., & D'Emilio, T. (2005). Learning disabilities in English language learners: Identifying the issues. *Learning Disabilities Research & Practice, 20*(1), 1–5.

McCardle, P., Mele-McCarthy, J., & Leos, K. (2005). English language learners and learning disabilities: Research agenda and implications for practice. *Learning Disabilities Research & Practice, 20,* 68–78.

No Child Left Behind Act. The Elementary and Secondary Education Act of 2001, P. L. 107–110, 115, *Stat.* 1425 (2001). Washington, DC.

OBEMLA. (2000). *Survey of states limited English proficient students and available educational programs and services: 1997–98.* Washington, DC: U.S. Department of Education.

Office of Special Education (OSEP). (1998). *Distribution of disabilities by category: 1998.* Washington, DC: U.S. Department of Education.

Ortiz, A. A. (1997). Learning disabilities occurring concomitantly with linguistic differences. *Journal of Learning Disabilities, 30,* 321–332.

Ortiz, A. A. (2002). Prevention of school failure and early intervention for English language learners. In A. J. Artiles & A. A. Ortiz (Eds.), *English language learners with special education needs: Identification, placement, and instruction* (pp. 31–48). Washington, DC: Center for Applied Linguistics.

Ortiz, A. A., & Wilkinson, C. Y. (1991). Assessment and intervention model for the bilingual exceptional student. (AIM for the BESt). *Teacher Education and Special Education, 14,* 35–42.

Ovando, C. J., Collier, V. P., & Combs, M. C. (2002). *Bilingual and ESL classrooms: Teaching in multicultural contexts* (3rd ed.). Boston: McGraw-Hill.

Quenemoen, R. F., Lehr, C. A., Thurlow, M. L., & Massanaair, C. B. (2001). *Students with disabilities in standards-based assessment and accountability systems: Emerging issues, strategies, and recommendations.* Minneapolis, MN: National Center on Educational Outcomes.

Rong, X. L., & Prissle, J. (1998). *Educating immigrant students: What we need to know to meet the challenge.* Thousand Oaks, CA: Corwin Press.

Smith-Davis, J. (2000). *Immigrant students with disabilities in the U.S. public schools: Preliminary findings of a pilot study.* Nashville, TN: Alliance Project, Peabody College/Vanderbilt University.

Stefanakis, E. (2000). Teachers' judgments do count: Assessing bilingual students. In Z. Beykont (Ed.), *Lifting every voice: Pedagogy and politics of bilingual education* (pp. 139–160). Cambridge, MA: Harvard Education Publishing Group.

Suarez-Orozco, C., & Suarez-Orozco, M. (2001). *Children of immigration*. Cambridge, MA: Harvard Education Publishing Group.

U.S. Department of Education. (2001). *Survey of the states' limited English proficient students & available educational programs and services, 2000–2001*. Washington, DC: Author.

Vaughn, S. (2003, December). *How many tiers are needed for response to intervention to achieve acceptable prevention outcomes?* Paper presented at the National Center on Learning Disabilities Responsiveness-to-Interventions Symposium, Kansas City, MO.

Vaughn, S., & Fuchs, D. (2003). Redefining learning disabilities as inadequate response to instruction: The promise and potential problems. *Learning Disabilities: Research & Practice, 18*(3), 137–146.

Vaughn, S., Linan-Thompson, S., & Hickman, P. (2003). Response to instruction as a means of identifying students with reading/learning disabilities. *Exceptional Children, 69*(4), 391–409.

Vaughn, S., Mathes, P. G., Linan-Thompson, S., & Francis, D. J. (2005). Teaching English language learners at risk for reading disabilities to read: Putting research to practice. *Learning Disabilities Research & Practice, 20*, 58–67.

Villegas, A. M., & Lucas, T. (2002). Preparing culturally responsive teachers: Rethinking the curriculum. *Journal of Teacher Education, 53*, 20–32.

Winston, M. L. (2006, July 31–August 2). *From unique to universal: An urban district's journey toward universally designed instruction*. Research presentation at the Annual OSEP Project Directors' Conference, Washington, DC.

Yell, M. (2004, February). *Understanding the three-tier model*. Presentation at the Colorado State Directors of Special Education Meeting, Denver, CO.

Chapter 2

Culturally Responsive Teaching and Learning:
Curriculum and Pedagogical Implications from Theory to Practice

Chapter Objectives

Upon completion of this chapter the reader will be able to:

1. Better understand concepts of race, culture, class, and language at deep structural levels and their implications for teaching CLDE learners.

2. Obtain the knowledge and dispositions needed to understand their own culture, class, and language "baggage" and that of their learners.

3. Understand and be able to apply theoretical, conceptual, and pedagogical elements needed to ground special education teacher preparation programs that are culturally responsive.

4. Know and apply key theoretical, conceptual, and pedagogical elements needed to "ground" special education teacher preparation programs to make them culturally responsive.

5. Understand and apply curricular and pedagogical programmatic components that result in preparing special education teacher candidates to become culturally *responsive* and *competent* in improving outcomes for diverse exceptional learners.

VIGNETTE

The Kern School District is one of the largest school districts in the state. Until rezoning, the district had a very homogenous, mainly White, middle-class student body. According to the rezoning, in each school at least 40 percent of the student population is to represent cultural, class, and linguistic diversity. To further complicate matters, the district is in the midst of a reform movement for high-stakes testing, which has resulted in the exclusion from the assessment process of many students who have been identified as needing special education.

To achieve the required state accreditation, some schools have increased the number of referrals to special education. Not surprisingly, this has included a disproportionate number of students who are culturally, linguistically, socially, and ethnically diverse.

The rezoning has also created a cultural, class, and language clash between suburban and urban mindsets and experiences of both students and teachers. Many of the White students had not attended school before with students from low socioeconomic environments or those from other racial and ethnic groups. In addition 90 percent of the teachers and 85 percent of the administrators in the school districts were White and middle class, and they lacked experience educating diverse learners. Believing that there was no need to provide special professional development programs for its administrators, teachers, and related personnel staff, the school district began the new school year with the revised zoning and new composition of students with business as usual. However, within the first week at Kern Elementary School, there were subtle and overt examples of separation of students by race, ethnicity, and class within the school. The students would exchange negative racial comments, and student conflicts would occur on a regular basis. Further, many teachers seemed to be challenged to make appropriate "connections" with many of the "new" students.

At lunchtime students typically sat at separate tables by race or other groupings. An assistant principal, Mr. Thomas, noticed this division while visiting with Ms. Torres, a ninth-grade teacher. Coincidentally, Ms. Torres was sitting with a group of teachers who were mostly Latinos. During the same conversation, Mr. Thomas wanted to know the details of a fight and the context of the racial slurs that had precipitated this fight. Several Latino students, who were involved in the conflict, happened to be in Ms. Torres' class. Ms. Torres stated that the Latino students were not the aggressors and had

The authors wish to acknowledge contributions to this vignette on the part of Ms. Veronica Koussai, Ms. Michele Kissinger, Mr. Patrick Humphrey, and Dr. Arletha McSwain.

attempted to avoid any conflict. She indicated that a group of White students began to berate the Latinos and eventually attacked several of them. They then attempted to make others believe that the Latinos initiated the conflict.

As time progressed, the parents became more and more concerned and eventually requested a meeting with the school board. It was determined that an advisory board would be established to address the cultural, class, and linguistic diversity issues. In addition, the school board hired Dr. Jesus Rodriquez, nationally known for his experiences and research in cultural responsiveness, to serve as a consultant. Dr. Rodriguez had strong roots in the community. Having assisted numerous local school districts in becoming more culturally responsive, Dr. Rodriquez understood the predicament of the students and teachers, and was determined to facilitate cultural responsiveness among the administrators, teachers, and students.

Reflective Questions

1. As a member of the advisory board, you would be working with Dr. Rodriguez to determine a professional development plan and direction for the Kern School District. Based on your understanding of the scenario and the conflicts presented, what recommendations would you make and what steps would you take to assist the school district in creating learning environments that were culturally responsive?

2. The advisory board also includes teacher educators who represent several colleges and universities. What recommendations should the board make to teacher educators so as to make their special education teacher education programs more culturally responsive?

INTRODUCTION

We live in a society in which culture, class, and language serve as significant educational markers more than at any other time in American history. At the same time, and as a consequence of this reality, those in power demonstrate a historical and natural inclination to support and perpetuate *their* dominance by reinforcing cultural, class, and language norms, conventions, and traditions in a way that best suits them and their class. As a result, those who have had the power to define have often associated the cultures, classes, and linguistic affiliations that deviate from the dominant ones as being different, at best, or deviant.

Consequently, the deep structural elements of culture, class, and language that have profound and pervasive power in the larger social, political, economic, and cultural sectors of society have not been generally and routinely embraced and responded to positively in special education teacher education programs. This reality has resulted in the absence of culturally responsive and competent teachers who possess the knowledge, skills, and dispositions required to respond to the strengths and needs of culturally, socioeconomically, and linguistically diverse exceptional learners. At the very moment when public K–12 classrooms have become the *most diverse* cultural, class, and linguistic institutions in all of our society, special educators and their teacher candidates have become increasingly culturally, class, and linguistically homogenous. All demographic indicators and census extrapolations consistently predict no end to this cultural, class, and linguistic mismatch and incongruity between students and their teachers (Hodgkinson, 1998).

As special educators and teacher trainers, we find ourselves challenged to move beyond our traditional ways of thinking and knowing to arrive at a destination that allows us to better understand how to authentically educate and prepare a new set of professionals who can respond to this ever-expanding cultural, class, and linguistic diversity that permeates our society and today's schools. To reach that goal requires that we create special education teacher education programs that educate individuals and communities to become competent, caring, committed, and culturally responsive to diverse exceptional learners. Special education teacher educators must design holistic teacher education cultures and climates that support the development of culturally responsive special education teacher candidates.

This chapter will first explore the conceptual elements of the *nexus* of culture, class, language, diversity, and disabilities and how diverse exceptional learners embody these forces more now than ever. Second, this chapter will identify and discuss some salient and common theoretical, conceptual, and pedagogical elements needed to ground culturally responsive special education teacher preparation programs. Last, a set of curricular and pedagogical components that result in preparing special education teacher candidates to become culturally responsive and competent will be offered.

THE CHALLENGE OF EDUCATING TEACHERS TO BE CULTURALLY RESPONSIVE AND COMPETENT

The terms *race* and *culture* are often used interchangeably; seldom are they recognized as *not* being synonymous. As discussed by Patton and Day-Vines (2002), the term *race* has historically been employed by dominant legal, social, political, and economic groups to sort individuals and groups of individuals on the basis of phenotypic or physical characteristics. Barkan (1992) reminds us that during the 18th century certain researchers and other powerful individuals and groups believed that they could hierarchically order "racial" groups to determine moral and racial *superiority* by developing a classification system of races similar to the one Carl Linnaeus developed to classify and sort plants. Linnaeus is further credited with developing a classification system that divided human beings into four "subspecies" called variously Native Americans, Europeans, Asians, and Africans. Later, in 1795, the German scientist Johan Friedrich Blumenbach proposed that humans could be divided into five races, which he called

Caucasian, Negro, American, Mongolian, and Malayan (Barkan, 1992). However erroneous these systems were, they were eventually promulgated under the guise of evidence-based scientific fact in order to legitimize the oppression and subordination of various cultural, ethnic, and lower socioeconomic groups. Originally, therefore, the term *race* connoted biological distinctions that were deemed to be permanent characteristics of *Homo sapiens*. Many distinctions among individuals, such as language, class, and disability, have been made and continue to be made based on physical differences. Too often these distinctions or differences have been used to marginalize, oppress, and deny equal protection and education to those individuals and groups so targeted by those in power. Certain critical theorists (Bourdieu, 1986; Rorty, 1998) refer to this notion of marginalizing as "othering," a tactic designed to set individuals and groups apart from the so-called norm in order to justify their disparate treatment. Once individuals are perceived as negative, then individuals and society are justified in treating them as such.

However, today's advances in cultural and linguistic anthropology, sociology, and genetics are undermining these previous notions about race and the distinct physical, class, and linguistic differences that this term implies. As a result it has been found that human beings are close to 99.9 percent the same genetically, with as much within-group variation as between-group differences (Roylance, 2004). Therefore, race generally functions as a social construction that frequently refers to social and political interactions and dynamics in addition to skin color, genetics, or biological features. However, there are ways to avoid this detour of race as we attempt to better understand CLDE learners.

Culture refers to the sum total of ways of living developed by a group of human beings to meet their biological, ethical, and psychosocial needs (Leighton, 1982). Leighton also refers to culture as the patterns of thought, behavior, language, customs, institutions, and material objects unique to a group. Culture, then, encompasses the unique metaphysical, axiological, and epistemological orientations of a group, as expressed through their native language. Accordingly, although all individuals of a given culture do not always subscribe to an identical value or belief system, individuals within a particular cultural group often share distinct ways of behaving and communicating that are grounded along certain similar axiological, metaphysical, and epistemological continua. As a consequence, cultural, linguistic, and class differences within, between, and among groups exist and often result in cultural conflicts or "clashes." When this occurs, dominant groups often tend to respond in ways that assume that their ways of knowing, thinking, speaking, behaving, or responding to the world are superior to those of individuals and groups who have previously been "othered," commonly referred to as ethnocentrism.

Further, these differences, when not properly understood and responded to, can become imagined and defined as *deviancies*, thus limiting their legitimate and authentic cultural, social, and linguistic transformational power. The more we as special educators and teacher educators understand the nature, extent, kind, meanings, values, and "capital" associated with these differences the better we can build on cultural, class, and linguistic knowledge and add culturally responsive skills and dispositions that better connect us to ourselves and our "others." Other "deeper" level cultural constructs have been created to assist us with this transformation.

Weaver (1986) used an iceberg metaphor to illustrate the many layers of culture and language associated with culture. Weaver conceptualized culture as containing three advancing and concentric levels referred to, in turn, as "surface," "folk," and "deep" culture (see Figure 2.1). As one views an iceberg, one will notice that the majority of the iceberg is out of view of the observer, not apparent and out of consciousness. However, this unseen aspect of the iceberg encompasses most of its power. This out-of-awareness portion of the iceberg or "culture" is referred to as "deep" culture. One's metaphysical, axiological, and epistemological orientations are often manifested at this "deep" structural level of culture that is usually not explored or challenged. As an example, concepts of beauty, sin, justice, ordering of time, and concepts of past and future are contained in the "deep" structural layer of culture. Contrariwise, elements of

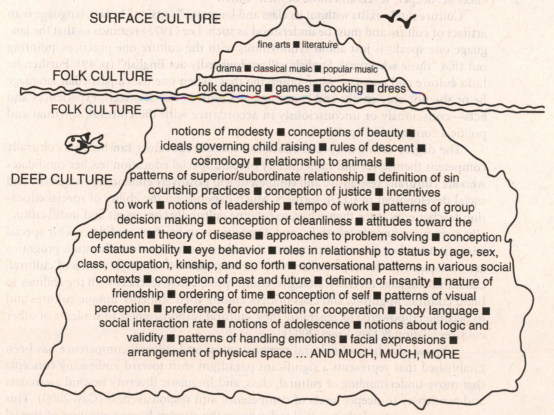

SURFACE CULTURE

fine arts ■ literature

FOLK CULTURE

drama ■ classical music ■ popular music

folk dancing ■ games ■ cooking ■ dress

FOLK CULTURE

DEEP CULTURE

notions of modesty ■ conceptions of beauty ■ ideals governing child raising ■ rules of descent ■ cosmology ■ relationship to animals ■ patterns of superior/subordinate relationship ■ definition of sin courtship practices ■ conception of justice ■ incentives to work ■ notions of leadership ■ tempo of work ■ patterns of group decision making ■ conception of cleanliness ■ attitudes toward the dependent ■ theory of disease ■ approaches to problem solving ■ conception of status mobility ■ eye behavior ■ roles in relationship to status by age, sex, class, occupation, kinship, and so forth ■ conversational patterns in various social contexts ■ conception of past and future ■ definition of insanity ■ nature of friendship ■ ordering of time ■ conception of self ■ patterns of visual perception ■ preference for competition or cooperation ■ body language ■ social interaction rate ■ notions of adolescence ■ notions about logic and validity ■ patterns of handling emotions ■ facial expressions ■ arrangement of physical space … AND MUCH, MUCH, MORE

FIGURE 2.1 Iceberg Model of Culture

Source: From "Understanding and Coping with Cross-Cultural Adjustment Stress," by G. Weaver, 1986. In R. Paige (Ed.), *Cross-Cultural Orientation: New Conceptualizations and Applications* (pp. 137–167). Copyright 1986 by University Press of America. Adapted with permission of the author.

"surface" and "folk" culture that are usually readily apparent in an iceberg or "culture" provide the foci of most cultural exchanges, even though these elements represent limited manifestations of deeper structures of cultural existence.

Only small portions of "deep" structured culture are consciously "visible" to most untrained individuals and groups, thereby residing in the unconscious or dysconscious. As a result, that which we know about culturally, class, and linguistically diverse exceptional learners and their families is frequently limited to those "surface" or "folk" aspects of culture that are normally in the direct view of the observer and often not considered contextually or with the knowledge of "deep" structured culture. For instance, we can easily identify the traditional dress of Native Americans but are often unable to discern their more deep-seated cultural and linguistic meanings that embody the dress. As special education teacher educators and their candidates develop a more astute and insightful knowledge of deep-structured culture, language, and class, they can better understand and respond to their own culture, class, and language preferences at "deeper" levels and those of their "other."

Culture rarely exists without its class and language "cousins." In fact, language is an artifact of culture and must be understood as such. Lee (1973) reminds us that the language one speaks is just about synonymous with the culture one practices, pointing out that "those who speak English will undoubtedly act English" (p. 49). Further, he links culture and language when observing that "when one uses a particular language he or she not only speaks and communicates with it, but also feels, experiences and acts—consciously or unconsciously in accordance with the cultural, spiritual and political context of it" (p. 50).

The degree to which special education teacher educators can become culturally competent themselves and subsequently prepare special education teacher candidates who are culturally responsive and competent will positively enhance the academic and social development of CLDE learners. Much depends on the ability of special education teacher educators, themselves, to become culturally competent and instill culturally responsive knowledge, skills, and dispositions in teacher candidates. Our special education teacher education programs as well as general teacher education programs are challenged to develop teachers who are responsive to multiple forms of cultural, class, and language diversity. Doing so equips prospective teachers with the abilities to build cultural, linguistic, and class bridges among their students' unique cultures and to become empowered to generalize their cultural responsiveness to students of other cultures (Patton & Day-Vines, 2002).

A knowledge base of cultural responsiveness and cultural competence has been established that represents a significant paradigm shift toward embracing concepts that move understanding of cultural, class, and linguistic diversity beyond awareness and sensitivity to deeper levels of competence and responsiveness (Gay, 2000). This movement is particularly essential today given the current homogenization of special education teacher education candidates.

A host of researchers (Banks, 1997; Brown, 2000; Nieto, 1998; Sleeter, 2001) have found that most prospective teachers enter teacher education programs with limited knowledge about their own cultural selves and with even more narrow and often stereotypical knowledge of the culture of their "other." Brown (2004) observed that the attitudes and behaviors that many of these students bring to teacher education programs is evidence of this reality. Unfortunately, these attitudes tend to be maintained and often reinforced in teacher education programs unless specific culturally responsive interventions are incorporated into these programs. Too often these teacher candidates bear "knapsacks" that are filled with *unwashed* perceptions, assumptions, predilections, mythologies, images, and stereotypical beliefs about themselves and their culturally, class, and linguistically diverse exceptional learners (see Figure 2.2).

Special education teacher education programs need to create environments that allow their teacher candidates to explore, examine, and critically analyze the oftentimes invisible cultural, class, and linguistic "knapsacks" that they bring to these programs and then move them along the path of becoming culturally responsive and competent educators of diverse exceptional learners. There is a need today and in the future to help special education teacher candidates to engage in what Singleton and Linton (2006) call "courageous conversations." These conversations can serve as a means of confronting cultural and racial disconnects by requiring individuals to confront their prejudices and the biases held by all in order to see the perspective of their "other," who is often culturally, class, and linguistically different. In addition to this attitudinal reexamination or cultural assessment that should become commonplace in all special education teacher education programs, culturally responsive principles, critical teaching behaviors, and essential culturally responsive best practices must also be infused into

Examining Our Cultural and Class Knapsack in Order to Be Culturally Competent—Cultural Assessment or Cultural Therapy

- Assumptions about the self and the "other"

- Perceptions and predilections of the "other"

- Images of the "other"

- Stereotyping and beliefs of the "other"

- Engaging in some "courageous conversations" a la Singleton and Linton

FIGURE 2.2 Cultural and Class Knapsacks

these programs as we attempt to respond to the needs of diverse exceptional learners (Sorrells, Webb-Johnson, & Townsend, 2004). So what can we do?

GUIDEPOSTS FOR CULTURALLY RESPONSIVE SPECIAL EDUCATION TEACHER EDUCATION

Pioneering research that has emanated from social scientists and teacher educators has provided special education teacher education with some refreshing and enlightened guideposts for better understanding the significance of culture, class, and language and the need for special education teacher trainees to foster authentic knowledge, skills, and dispositions that will result in more culturally responsive and competent special education teachers (Banks, 2001; Bennett, 1995; Gay, 2000; Hanley, 1999; Irvine, 1992; Ladson-Billings, 1995; Morey & Kitano, 1997; Sleeter, 1992; Villegas & Lucas, 2002). The theoretical, conceptual, and pedagogical conventions offered by these and other researchers and practitioners have provided some much needed clarity as special education teacher educators grapple with discerning the conceptual, curriculum, and pedagogical direction necessary to generate a new breed of special education teachers who can respond in authentic, culturally responsive ways to the needs of diverse exceptional learners. Specifically, the recent writings of Gay (2000), Villegas and Lucas (2002), and Hanley (1999) offer conceptual clarity in this regard. The following discusses salient elements from their works, identifies common concepts contained in these bodies of literature, and suggests missing elements that offer implications specific to the education of teachers of diverse exceptional learners.

Gay (2000) postulated that different terms have been used to represent the idea that curriculum and pedagogy employed by teachers in our schools should respond to the cultural, class, and linguistic capital that all students bring to the classroom. Terms such as *cultural relevance, cultural sensitivity,* and *culturally responsive practices* have been used throughout the literature to express this belief and have been used to inform teacher educators (Gay, 2000). Gay defines her preferred descriptor as *culturally responsive teaching,* which in her words means "teaching that uses the cultural knowledge, prior experiences, frames of reference, and performance styles of ethnically diverse students to make learning encounters more relevant to and effective for them" (p. 29).

Gay (2000) offers a thoughtful and sometimes provocative approach to culturally responsive teaching and teacher education by suggesting that this cultural responsiveness embeds notions of power, caring, and ethnic, cultural, and linguistic knowledge into pedagogy and curriculum. Her latest work provides descriptive characteristics and roles and responsibilities of culturally responsive teachers. For example, her discussion of "power pedagogy through cultural responsiveness," exposes the fallacy of noncontextualized teaching and calls into question the "culturally neutral" or "blind" pedagogical approaches that characterize many of today's special education teacher education programs. This power pedagogy outlines a highly connected knowledge and application approach to helping teachers to move students, especially CLD learners, from an internalized locus of "I can't" to one of "I can" (Gay, 2000).

Another important pillar of cultural responsiveness discussed by Gay (2000) is the multidimensional concept of "caring." Noddings (1984) has defined the concept of caring as taking on, as much as possible, the perspective and reality of another along with a commitment to act on behalf of the other. Similarly, Gay's concept of unconditional caring, like that of a mother for her child, connects individuals to each other, to their communities, and to a common good or goal. This approach also implies that culturally responsive teachers engage in the necessary and appropriate actions and effort to make manifest this concept.

Gay (1993) suggests that teachers in the future must become cultural brokers and be able to "translate students' expressive cultural behaviors into pedagogical implications and actions" (p. 48). These "bicultural actors" must be able to acquire the cultural knowledge of their learners, translate this knowledge into their curriculum and pedagogy, and become cultural change agents (Gay, 1993). Building on these ideals, Gay (2000) has argued that culturally responsive teachers need to acquire the ability to use curriculum and pedagogy that allows their learners to discern what one might call "mirrors" and "windows" in the curriculum and pedagogy employed by their teachers. By "mirrors," she means that diverse exceptional learners must see themselves actualized and played out in the curriculum, its content, and the pedagogy their teachers use. Additionally, special education teachers must be able to use curricula and pedagogical approaches that foster and accentuate their learners' current social, cultural, and linguistic capital and their present and future aspirations, hopes, powers, and capabilities. In other words, this transformation should allow diverse exceptional learners to view the curriculum, its content, and the pedagogy used by culturally responsive teachers as a "window" that allows them to imagine otherwise.

Villegas and Lucas (2002), like Gay (2000), have outlined a set of characteristics of culturally responsive teachers that they believe must be infused in special education teacher education programs. They have designed six teacher educator curriculum strands of humanistically and constructivist-grounded organizing constructs to guide the education of those who will teach a rapidly changing and diverse student population. They propose that each of these strands be infused into the coursework and field experiences of teacher education programs.

The first three of those strands, like those of Gay (2000), are focused on the need for these teachers to (a) obtain a foundational understanding of the sociocultural context of teaching and learning; (b) examine their understanding of diversity in all of its manifestations; and (c) reflect on the role of today's teacher (Villegas & Lucas, 2002). The second three strands address more directly conceptions of teaching and learning, the need to teach students only after one has a cultural knowledge base of them, and how to use the previous two strands in ways that transform the education of diverse exceptional learners. These strands appropriately represent an amalgam of the elements needed to educate students in the specific domains. These six orientations will allow prospective teachers to be responsive to the needs of culturally, socioeconomically, and linguistically diverse exceptional learners. The authors recommend that the strands be systematically infused throughout the courses, practica, and student teaching experiences of teacher candidates.

The first strand challenges teacher candidates to see the world from "moccasins of one's other." This social consciousness curriculum strand (Villegas & Lucas, 2002) pushes teacher candidates to understand that individuals view the world through their own cultural, class, and linguistic lenses and that those lenses are not the only ones relevant to a teaching/learning transaction and should be consciously and continuously examined. Thus, these authors, like those referenced earlier in this chapter, suggest that the base of a curriculum to educate culturally responsive teachers should contain a focused and reinforced component of cultural assessment or therapy (Spindler & Spindler, 1994).

The second strand of courses and experiences will require that teacher candidates develop the knowledge, skills, and dispositions that affirm the culture, class, and language of their students and that result in them having the internal and pedagogical power and confidence to move them and their students from a powerlessness perspective to one of self-efficacy. This translates to the need for teacher candidates to know, respect, affirm, and understand their own cultural, class, and linguistic identities and those of their diverse exceptional learners.

Within this context, the term *no arrangement is neutral* has been used to suggest that social, cultural, political, and economic "arrangements" usually result in serving one group well, while at the same time disadvantaging another group (Starrat, 1994). As an example, an arrangement existed throughout this country that resulted in local education agencies using a portion of their public funds to exclusively support boys' athletic programs. Although this arrangement served boys' athleticism as a group and individually, it did not serve the interest or welfare of girls' athleticism. At some point someone or a group of individuals challenged this arrangement and, as a result, eventually Title IX of the 1972 Higher Education Act was legislated to require equitable athletic programming for males and females. In this vein, Villegas and Lucas (2002), like Gay (2000), urge teacher educators to develop programs that include a strand of courses and field experiences that address the need to prepare teacher candidates to become ethical change agents, the same kind of individuals who had the liberating and empowering knowledge, skills, and dispositions to create the changes that resulted in the passage of Title IX.

Additionally, Villegas and Lucas (2002) propose in their third strand that there is a need to develop curricula and teacher pedagogy that enable teacher candidates to develop connections between the knowledge, experiences, and "capital" of their diverse exceptional learners and those of their own. This notion implies deliberate cultural reciprocity and a genuine responsiveness from each participant. Once established, culturally responsive curricular and pedagogical scaffolds can be developed that move students from what they have previously experienced and known to what they need to experience and know.

Both Gay (1993) and Villegas and Lucas (2002) strongly advocate that culturally responsive teacher education programs must require that teacher candidates have a foundational, historical, and contemporary deep-structured sociocultural knowledge base of their learners. This suggestion seems to reflect the generally understood reality that no prospective teacher can have a distinct and authentic knowledge base of all of the cultural groups in any given classroom or school. Nonetheless, teachers can gain a foundational understanding of the fact that there are disparate cultural, class, and linguistic groups who possess distinct worldviews and heritages, the knowledge of which must become a part of the curricula and pedagogy of special education teacher education programs.

The fourth strand proposed by Villegas and Lucas (2002) encourages teacher educators and their teacher candidates to use and model principles of constructivism in their curriculum and pedagogical approaches. It is their belief that cultural, class, and linguistically diverse learners bring valuable "capital" and lived experiences to college classrooms. Accordingly, it is the role of the culturally responsive teacher educator to make manifest these resources and to assist learners in "unearthing" the gifts, talents, and resources that they bring with them. The role, then, of all teacher educators has shifted to what Freire (1994) referred to as one of *co-intentionality*. In this sense teacher educators build scaffolds of learning and experiences that allow them and their teacher candidates to work in collaborative and co-intentional ways that enhance critical thinking, reflective problem solving, and decision making that allow for viewing, analyzing, and evaluating multiple perspectives.

Similar to the cultural competency curriculum designed by Patton and Day-Vines (2002), the fifth strand offered by Villegas and Lucas (2002) suggests strongly that knowledge and experiences of culturally distinct groups be infused into the coursework and field experiences of all teacher education programs. Teacher candidates must understand the history, nomenclature, and values, and social, educational, and political experiences of culturally distinct groups. This can be accomplished through total cultural immersion of teacher candidates into the culture of these distinct groups, through studying these groups, or through a combination of the two so that teacher candidates develop deep cultural, class, and linguistic knowledge of these groups. The totality of this form of cultural, class, and linguistic knowledge has profound implications for teacher education programs and serves as antecedents for implementing authentic culturally responsive interventions in teacher candidates' future classrooms.

Last, Villegas and Lucas (2002) call for another conceptual change in all teacher education programs that allows teacher candidates to model and practice culturally responsive pedagogy in their future classrooms. This knowledge, skill, and disposition development strand focuses teacher candidates on the development of specific strategies that they can employ to enhance their efficacy levels in future classrooms of diverse exceptional learners. Some of these strategies include:

- Creating classrooms organized as communities of learning in which dialogue and reflective learning are the hallmarks.
- Utilizing highly interactive classroom strategies such as inquiry projects, action plans, debates, simulations and games, and storytelling.

- Exploring personal and family histories and issues around power and privilege.
- Using case study approaches.

This next section discusses curriculum and pedagogical programmatic components that prepare special education teacher candidates to become culturally *responsive* and *competent* in their use of curriculum and pedagogy for diverse exceptional learners.

BECOMING A CULTURALLY COMPETENT TEACHER

Another term that is used sparingly in educational or special education literature, *cultural competence*, conveys a meaning similar to cultural responsiveness but contains several additional conceptual elements that allow special education teacher candidates to more easily move beyond cultural awareness and sensitivity to cultural competence in their pedagogy and use of curriculum.

Cultural competence refers to a set of congruent attitudes, practices, policies, and structures that come together in a system or organization that enables professionals to work more effectively with members of culturally, class, and linguistically diverse groups in a manner that values and respects the culture and worldviews of those groups (Hanley, 1999). The attainment of cultural competence by today's special education teachers is especially important given the (a) previously discussed rapid cultural, class, and linguistic diversity in our schools; (b) the history of oppression experienced by many CLD learners; and (c) the current disproportionate representation of culturally, class, and linguistically diverse learners in special education (Patton & Day-Vines, 2002). Both terms, *cultural competence* and *cultural responsiveness*, are comparable and convey a similar conceptual understanding of the need for today's teachers of diverse exceptional learners to know their own cultural identities, orientations, and knowledge and to connect those elements with similar realities of their students.

This concept validates *biculturalism*, a concept that has allowed ethnic minority groups to exist within the dominant group in a given society and, *at the same time*, value their own indigenous cultural, class, and linguistic values. To become bicultural, individuals and groups are challenged to learn to be *situationally intelligent*, which refers to the additive ability to know and understand the norms, conventions, language, and behavioral expectations of a given cultural, class, or linguistic group and respond in ways that enable individuals or groups to meet those demands, while maintaining their own deep-structured cultural, class, and linguistic orientations (Patton & Day-Vines, 2002).

The result should allow these individuals to switch their cultural, class, and linguistic "codes" in response to the demands of the dominant culture or the culture of their "other" without surrendering the core elements of their own culture, class, and language. This reality is seen when a speaker of Ebonics or Spanish is able to speak so-called Standard American English in situations that require that particular language pattern and switch back into his or her own indigenous language when Standard

American English is not required. The meaning of this biculturalism discussion is that culturally responsive special education teacher educators and teachers must know and understand these concepts and be able to build on this knowledge in their curriculum and pedagogy (Patton & Day-Vines, 2002).

Hanley's Components of Cultural Competence

Hanley (1999) suggests that three major components are involved in becoming culturally competent. All of these components can only be obtained through the interaction of knowledge and practical application. The first and most important component of cultural competence includes deep knowledge of one's own cultural, class, and linguistic self that serves as a form of "cultural therapy" (Spindler & Spindler, 1994). This process of cultural self-assessment roughly corresponds to the sociocultural strand suggested by Villegas and Lucas (2002) and Gay's (2000) power curriculum. The remaining two cultural competency components are built on this foundation. As previously discussed, this dynamic process of constantly assessing one's invisible cultural, class, and linguistic "knapsacks" provides a context and foundation for special education teacher candidates to know themselves at deep and introspective levels, thus situating them to better understand the culture, class, and language of their diverse exceptional learners.

Hanley's second component of cultural competence includes the development of knowledge of culturally distinct groups (1999). Hanley proposes that this can best be accomplished, not just through books, videos, or classroom experiences, but through unmediated experiences with the cultures of diverse exceptional learners. This knowledge and experience base then can serve as a mediator through which culturally responsive and competent teacher candidates can relate to, build on, and incorporate into the curriculum and pedagogy used with diverse exceptional learners. As such, this concept focuses on positive change at both *individual* and *organizational* levels.

Hanley's third component of cultural competence incorporates and extends the change agentry challenge discussed by Gay (2000) and Villegas and Lucas (2002). According to Hanley (1999), it is impossible to obtain cultural competence without positive change in one's behavior or that of the system or organization. It is his view that "cultural competence replaces the earlier ideas of cultural sensitivity and awareness that were often embraced with no corresponding change in behavior" (p. 11).

The Patton and Day-Vines Model of Cultural Competency

Patton and Day-Vines (2002) remind us that given the cultural, class, and language chasm between diverse exceptional learners and that of their teachers, American institutions (such as schools and special education teacher education programs) must adapt their structures, policies, and routines in ways that respond to different cultural, class, and linguistic practices and values. The education of special education teacher candidates, then, must inculcate them with authentic knowledge, skills, and dispositions that value culture and cultural and linguistic diversity and that embrace cultural competence. To be effective, cultural competency must move beyond awareness and sensitivity to take into account the different cultural histories of diverse exceptional learners, as well as legacies of inequality and exclusion that have characterized their past and present (Patton & Day-Vines, 2002).

Patton and Day-Vines (2002) have developed a cultural competency curriculum and pedagogical guide that incorporates many of the design features offered by Gay (2000) and Villegas and Lucas (2002). They suggest that their guide can be used in the construction of all teacher education programs that prepare special education teacher candidates in culturally competent and responsive ways. This curriculum and pedagogical model also incorporates the cultural competence framework and components of Cross, Bazron, Dennis, and Isaacs (1989) and Mason (1993) and is also grounded in the cultural and cross-cultural competency work of Mason, Benjamin, and Lewis (1996) and Pedersen (1994). Table 2.1 provides a summary of the major components of the Patton and Day-Vines guide.

The next section discusses these frameworks and their application to the cultural competence curriculum and pedagogical guide suggested by Patton and Day-Vines

TABLE 2.1 Summary of the Major Components of the Patton and Day-Vines Cultural Competency Curriculum and Pedagogy Guide

I. Cultural Assessment
II. Awareness Competencies

- Race as a construct related to cultural competency
- Ethnicity as a construct related to cultural competency
- Culture as a construct related to cultural competency
- Dimensions of personal identity as a construct related to cultural competency
- Worldview as a construct related to cultural competency
- Recognizing and responding to oppression
- Recognizing and responding to racism
- Recognizing and responding to power and privilege

III. Knowledge Competencies

- Racial and cultural identity
- Knowledge of major culturally distinct groups in U.S. schools

IV. Skills Competencies

- Strategies and skills for developing cultural competency
- Integrating knowledge and skills

Source: Patton and Day-Vines (2000).

(2002). Accordingly, constructs of cultural competence offered by Cross et al. (1989) and Mason (1993) will be outlined, followed by a discussion of Pedersen's (1994) concepts of cultural and cross-cultural competence.

THE FRAMEWORK OF THE CULTURAL COMPETENCE CURRICULUM

Although Pedersen's (1994) cultural competency model focus on developing awareness, knowledge, and skills of individuals relative to cultural competency, Mason et al. (1996) focus their work on creating culturally competent organizations and services through institutional and organizational responsiveness that emanate from changes in individuals and organizations. Both of these approaches are valid and important and, together, provide the theoretical and conceptual bases for the cultural competency curriculum and pedagogical model proposed by Patton and Day-Vines (2002).

Cultural Competence Continuum

Mason (1993) discussed a cultural competence continuum based on the previous work of Cross et al. (1989) that could be used as content to form the basis for individual and organizational cultural assessment. This continuum allows individuals and school systems to engage in honest cultural assessments to determine their present locus on the continuum and measure positive change as they move along the continuum (see Table 2.2). The exploration of this continuum forms the foundational content for programs that prepare culturally competent and responsive teachers. This dynamic cultural competence continuum consists of six progressive stages:

- Cultural destructiveness
- Cultural incapacity
- Cultural blindness
- Cultural precompetence
- Cultural competence
- Cultural proficiency

Cultural Destructiveness Stage According to Cross et al. (1989) and Mason (1993), this extreme stage of *cultural destructiveness* reflects a training model in which individuals and teacher educators refuse to acknowledge the presence or significance of cultural, class, and linguistic differences. In addition, any perceived or real differences from dominant mainstream culture are usually suppressed. Individuals and special education teacher education programs operating at this level tend to endorse a mythology in which all teacher candidates would conform to a standard, mainstream, middle-class imperative. At this stage, cultural, class, and linguistically diverse learners

TABLE 2.2 Cultural Competence Continuum

Cultural Destructiveness	• The individual or organization *refuses to acknowledge the presence or importance of cultural differences* in the teaching/learning process. • Differences are punished and suppressed. • Teachers and schools endorse the myth of universality.
Cultural Incapacity	• The individual or organization *chooses to ignore cultural differences*. • No attention is devoted to supporting cultural differences. • Emphasis may be on the cognitive growth and maturity of youngsters versus addressing the issues of cultural awareness.
Cultural Blindness	• The individual and organization *believes that cultural differences are of little importance*. • Others are viewed through a Western cultural mainstream lens. • Messages are communicated to students that their culture is of little consequence to the learning experience.
Cultural Precompetence	• The individual or organization *recognizes and responds to cultural differences*. • An open acknowledgement of the need for cultural competence exists. • Educators may seek out new information about diversity by attending training sessions or interacting with those individuals who have insider cultural information.
Cultural Competence	• The individual or organization *values and appreciates cultural differences*. • Issues related to equity, cultural history, knowledge, and social justice are explored. • Students' cultural experiences are valued and integrated into the learning process.
Cultural Proficiency	• The individual or organization *holds cultures in high esteem*. • The individual or organization seeks to add to its knowledge base. • The individual or organization advocates continuously for cultural competence throughout the system.

Source: T. Cross, B. Bazron, K. Dennis, & M. Isaacs (1989). *Towards a Culturally Competent System of Care*. Washington, DC: CASSP Technical Assistance Center, Georgetown University Child Development Center.

are generally expected to shed retentions of their culture, class, and language of origin in favor of those of the dominant culture and socioeconomic class. Ordinarily, learners who depart from this mainstream imperative are viewed as deviant, deficient, or inferior. It is not unusual for special education teacher education programs in this stage to endorse and perpetuate curricula and pedagogical polices and practices that penalize individuals and groups for their seeming differences (Patton & Day-Vines, 2002).

Cultural Incapacity Stage The *cultural incapacity* stage reflects the inability of special education teacher education programs to respond to cultural, class, and language differences while, at the same time, not intentionally purporting to be culturally destructive. This occurs when special education teacher educators lack the capacity to respond to these differences and, at the same time, choose to ignore them. Since individuals functioning at this level generally lack sociocultural knowledge, skills, and dispositions, little or no attention, time, or resources are devoted to developing teacher candidates who will leave with the skills to be culturally competent. Often special educators and their institutions at this stage appear to be ambivalent about the importance of cultural competence. More attention may be devoted to more generic curricular issues or to other priorities in the program that are responsive to the dominant, mainstream culture of teacher candidates, rather than to considerations specific to culture, class, or language (Patton & Day-Vines, 2002).

Cultural Blindness Stage *Cultural blindness* represents the stage in which special education teacher educators, under the guise of being unbiased, actively advance the notion that cultural, class, and language differences are inconsequential. At this stage special education teacher educators may have the individual and institutional capacity to act in more culturally responsive ways but consciously choose to ignore important cultural, class, and linguistic considerations. It is at this stage that the mythical "melting pot" analogy of culture prevails, rather than the current and more accurate "salad bowl" analogy of culture. The desired state of existence of special education teacher educators at this stage is color, class, cultural, and linguistic blindness. Special education teacher education programs at this stage also generally provide few resources and little attention, time, or teaching to understanding the cultural, class, and linguistic differences of their teacher candidates or the diverse exceptional learners they will educate, and rarely view these differences as strengths.

Although some progressive-minded teacher educators may perceive this approach as a superior one for appearing free of bias, such a strategy often denies deep structural cultural, class, and linguistic aspects of teacher candidates and the diverse exceptional learners they are being prepared to educate (Patton & Day-Vines, 2002). Special education teacher educators, who prepare candidates to *not see* the culture, class, or language of their diverse exceptional learners and to treat all of them the same, fail to realize that treating learners the *same* is not synonymous with treating them equally or fairly. When these significant sociocultural markers are not *seen* by their teacher candidates, both subtle and overt messages are communicated to their subsequent learners that:

- Their culture, class, and language are of little consequence to their learning experience.
- Members of their cultural/ethnic group have made few meaningful contributions to society.
- Cultural, class, and linguistic experiences are not legitimate in academic settings.

Whereas the first three stages of Cross's cultural continuum demonstrate hostility, incapacity, and a certain indifference to the significance of cultural competence, the next three stages illustrate a conscious transformational shift toward developing special education teacher candidates who can address their own cultural, class, and linguistic differences and those of their diverse exceptional learners (Cross et al., 1989; Mason, 1993).

Cultural Precompetence Stage At the *cultural precompetence* stage, special education teacher educators design coursework and experiences that allow for teacher candidates to recognize and respond to their own cultural, class, and linguistic differences and those of their diverse exceptional learners. The creation of transparent programs that openly acknowledge the need for cultural competency training represents an important first step toward addressing those curricular and pedagogical practices that enhance the educational and social progress of CLDE learners. Special education teacher educators functioning at this stage usually seek out sociocultural knowledge and information through study and experience and often elicit the guidance and support of cultural, class, and linguistic informants who possess insider deep-structured cultural, class, and linguistic knowledge and experience (Patton & Day-Vines, 2002).

Cultural Competence Stage The *cultural competence* stage represents a reality at the opposite extreme of the cultural destructiveness stage, wherein special education teacher educators and their teacher candidates aggressively learn deep-structured sociocultural knowledge of their own selves and of others and value cultural, class, and language differences (Cross et al., 1989; Mason, 1993). Further, rather than viewing differences as deviant, teacher candidates see strengths in these differences and attempt to creatively seek out ways to celebrate, encourage, and respond to these differences within and among themselves and their learners. Special education teacher candidates at this stage are taught to continue to build on their cultural assessment work; expand their cultural, class, and linguistic knowledge and experience; explore issues of equity, social justice, and privilege and power relations in schools and in society; and be committed to positive change and to do so in naturally occurring, routine, and often subconscious ways (Patton & Day-Vines, 2002). It is this conscious attempt to engage in positive change that differentiates cultural "competence" from the notions of cultural "sensitivity" or cultural "awareness," which often do not convey a corresponding change in behavior (Hanley, 1999).

When special education teacher educators and their teacher candidates are culturally competent, the culture, class, and language that their students bring to school are viewed as important capital for educators, the children themselves, and their families. Their learners' cultural, class, and linguistic funds of knowledge are valued and affirmed in contrast to the experiences of many previous generations of diverse exceptional learners.

Cultural Proficiency Stage The highest level of cultural competence, *cultural proficiency*, represents the epitome of the conscious transformational shift toward developing special education teacher candidates who *routinely* and *expertly* practice the art and science of cultural competence. In addition to addressing all of the elements in the previous cultural competence stage, individuals and organizations in this stage hold all cultures in high esteem and persistently act to incorporate cultural knowledge to their individual and organizational knowledge base. At this level diversity is valued and actualized in natural ways and systems are in place to attract cultural brokers and to institutionalize cultural competence.

In this stage, special education teacher educators and their candidates act in individual and corporate ways by continuously advocating for the infusion of cultural competence throughout all systems involved in the education of teacher candidates.

It is as if all the individuals and systems involved become "cultural fighters." These cultural competence and proficiency elements have been incorporated into the Patton and Day-Vines model of cultural competency training.

Pedersen's Tripartite Model

As mentioned, the culturally competency teacher education curriculum model developed by Patton and Day-Vines (2002) also incorporates ideas from the work of Pedersen (1994). Pedersen (1994) developed a tripartite model designed to promote cultural and multicultural understanding among teachers and other related service professionals. This model includes the following domains:

- Awareness
- Knowledge
- Skills

These three domains, then, serve as the basis for the three strands that form the core of the Patton and Day-Vines cultural competency curriculum and pedagogy guide.

Each of Pedersen's competency domains builds successively on the previous one (Pedersen, 1994). Accordingly, mastery of an earlier domain is a prerequisite for proceeding to subsequent ones. Similar to the cultural assessment domains of Mason (1993) and Villegas and Lucas (2002), Pedersen's awareness competency domain requires that teacher candidates recognize their own cultural, class, and linguistic biases as well as develop an awareness of the larger sociopolitical issues that confront their culturally, class, and linguistically diverse exceptional learners. Competencies in the knowledge domain, in turn, challenge teacher candidates to acquire deep-structured factual information about different groups relative to their cultural, class, and language differences. Last, teacher candidates acquire competencies in the skills domain by integrating their previously acquired competencies from the awareness and knowledge domains in an effort to positively impact culturally, class, and linguistically diverse exceptional learners. Given this developmental framework, special education teacher educators are challenged to include the provision of strands of coursework and experiences that allow special education teacher candidates to master the requirements in each of the three competency domains. The following contains a more detailed explication of those requirements that, if mastered, result in preparing culturally competent and responsive special education teachers.

THE REQUIREMENTS OF THE CULTURAL COMPETENCE CURRICULUM

Two essential elements encompass Pedersen's (1994) *awareness* competency domain. According to Pedersen, special education teacher candidates must first confront their own preconceived attitudes, values, and biases that may influence their teaching and the learning of their students. The elements of this competency domain represent the essentials in the previous discussion that deal with cultural self-assessment and the examination of one's cultural, class, and linguistic "knapsack." However, Pedersen (1994) adds a pointed, introspective orientation that requires teacher candidates to examine *critically*, *analytically*, and *experientially* the following:

- How they obtained their attitudes and biases
- How these biases impact the diverse exceptional learners served by them
- More importantly, how they can eliminate those biases

If special education teacher candidates fail to constantly confront and resolve the issues in the awareness domain, mastering the knowledge competency domain is usually difficult. Coursework and field experiences in special education teacher education programs that explore elements of this awareness domain are critical in providing a foundation for the first strand embedded in the Patton and Day-Vines guide designed to prepare culturally competent and responsive special education teachers.

Second, Pedersen's awareness model of cultural competence challenges students to develop an awareness of sociopolitical factors that confront culturally different groups. These constructs generally include race, ethnicity, culture, dimensions of personal identity, and worldview. All of these constructs are addressed by Villegas and Lucas (2002), except for dimensions of personal identity. Race, ethnicity, and culture serve as important sociopolitical forces that must be continuously addressed in all teacher education programs that are designed to educate culturally competent and responsive teacher candidates. The deep-structured elements of culture have been previously discussed in this chapter. Some distinctions between race and ethnicity may be instructive here.

Ethnicity, according to Robinson and Howard-Hamilton (2000), refers to groups of which members generally share a cultural heritage from one generation to another. Although similarities between *race* and *ethnicity* do exist, significant and important differences between the two abound. For example, Robinson and Howard-Hamilton (2000) remind us that *race* as a broad encompassing term generally reflects physical characteristics and social status, whereas *ethnicity* often refers to one's nationality and country of origin. Pedersen's third sociopolitical construct, culture, is very similar to notions of culture previously discussed.

The fourth sociopolitical construct suggested by Pedersen (1994) includes dimensions of personal identity. These dimensions, which are included in the cultural competence curriculum and pedagogy outlined by Patton and Day-Vines (2002), are not addressed by the other previously discussed culturally responsive models. Arredondo et al. (1996) have developed a paradigm for addressing the complexity of human differences by looking at individual differences and shared identity. These authors have identified three primary areas of an individual's identity, which they call "A," "B," and "C" dimensions of identity. The "A" dimension demands some discussion. Accordingly, "A" dimensions of personal identity include characteristics over which individuals have little or no control. Thus, characteristics of "A" dimensions include age, race, ethnicity, and language function. Since these characteristics are visible and apparent, another notable feature of "A" dimensions of personal identity is that they frequently create stereotypes about people. As such, it is important that special education teacher educators create experiences that allow for their teacher candidates to constantly explore this dimension of their own identities and those of their students (Patton & Day-Vines, 2002).

A discussion of worldview in the curriculum and pedagogy guide proposed by Patton and Day-Vines (2002) forms the last sociopolitical construct and provides a helpful framework for understanding how different cultural and linguistic groups make sense of and interpret their experiences and worlds, including schooling and the educational process. Both Villegas and Lucas (2002) and Gay (2000), like Patton and Day-Vines (2002), stress the importance of including this dimension in teacher education programs designed to produce culturally competent and responsive educators of diverse exceptional learners. As previously discussed, special education teacher educators need to accept the reality that various cultural, class, and linguistic groups have vastly different fundamental beliefs and philosophical orientations than their own. Worldviews consist of one's attitudes, values, opinions, concepts, thoughts and decision-making processes, as well as how one behaves and defines events (Sue & Sue, 1999).

Two distinctions must be made to understand various cultural worldviews. First, a Western cultural orientation refers more generally to people of various European ancestries and usually approximates a White, middle-class norm. A non-Western cultural orientation often refers to those culturally distinct groups that ordinarily include people of African, Asian, Latino, and Indian ancestry (Patton & Day-Vines, 2002). Although there are many differences within and between non-Western groups, in the main, at deep-structured cultural levels they often share some very broad characteristics. In addition to this general discussion of worldview, it is important to note that special education teacher education programs must include coursework and field experiences that allow a special education teacher candidate to know, understand, and respond to more specific issues of oppression, racism, power, and privilege. These concepts are explored in the Patton and Day-Vines guide and are discussed next.

Reynolds and Pope (1991) defined oppression as "a system that allows access to the services, rewards, benefits, and privileges of society based on membership in a particular group" (p. 174). In general, *oppression* operates as an umbrella term that protects all forms of domination and control, including racism, sexism, heterosexism, and classism. In its maximum levels of functioning, individuals, especially those marginalized by culture, class, and language, can experience single or even multiple forms of oppression. For instance, an African American female student receiving special education services may experience:

- Racism, as a representative of a culturally different group
- Sexism, as a result of her gender
- Linguicism, if she does not speak Standard English

- An internalized sense of shame and embarrassment because of the stigma associated with a diagnosed learning disability

Racism constitutes a particular form of oppression that refers to the systematic process of enlisting institutional resources not only to support and promote a belief in the inferiority of groups on the basis of skin color, but also to deny opportunities to one group and subsequently grant them to a preferred group (Nieto, 1996; Tatum, 1997). According to Pinderhughes (1989), the insidious nature of racism prevails because "policies and institutions interlock and reinforce one another in their capacity to deprive and cripple many people while offering preparation, support, and opportunity" to members of a dominant group (p. 89). Tatum (1997) noted that if racism victimizes one group of individuals, then, by default, another group profits. Culturally competent special educators equipped with this knowledge, perspective, and understanding of oppression and racism have a better framework and foundation for providing culturally competent and responsive education to diverse exceptional learners (Patton & Day-Vines, 2002).

Pinderhughes (1989) clarified the function of *power* and powerlessness when individuals from different racial and cultural groups interact. Educators from dominant cultural groups wield power, both individually and institutionally, and have influence both as members of an esteemed group and as authority figures in the classroom. In striking contrast, culturally, class, and linguistically diverse exceptional learners may feel powerless and vulnerable as members of marginalized and devalued groups. Culturally responsive teaching requires that teachers remain cognizant of power dynamics both in the classroom and in society and work to consciously eliminate power arrangements that jeopardize the learning of diverse exceptional students (Patton & Day-Vines, 2002).

Furthermore, power is a sociopolitical process that refers to the capacity to effect change and wield influence over others, especially in a manner that diminishes one's sense of personhood (Pinderhughes, 1989). Powerlessness, on the other hand, refers to the inability to effect and influence the outcomes in one's life (Sue & Sue, 1999). This juxtaposition of power and powerlessness occurs especially under circumstances in which status differentials exist between one with more power and one with less. Although power can be exercised in a manner that is just and equitable, too frequently power is abused in ways that result in individuals with less power being manipulated. As an example, the common practice of tracking has been described as an institutional practice that severely limits the educational opportunities for students whose cultures, language, and socioeconomic status differ from those in the dominant American culture (Robinson & Howard-Hamilton, 2000). Thus, the power and degrees of freedom of the targeted, marginalized groups are often reduced. Those who wish to be culturally competent in the ways they teach diverse exceptional learners must understand and effectively respond to the sociopolitical construct of power.

McIntosh (1989) provided an in-depth and frank discussion of "White privilege" as an obligatory dimension of oppression and racism. As such, *privilege* provides dominant groups with decided social, cultural, political, economic, and educational advantages relative to marginalized learners. Privilege grants a set of benefits and systemic rewards to one group while simultaneously depriving other groups' access to those very advantages. Additionally, McIntosh (1989) defined White privilege as "an invisible weightless knapsack of special provisions, assurances, tools, maps, guides, codebooks, passports, visas, clothes, emergency gear and blank checks" (p. 1). More notably, she acknowledged that systems of dominance remain firmly entrenched in our society because beneficiaries of White privilege remain perpetually in a state of denial and repression about their advantages. She catalogues a series of unearned privileges to which Whites have consistent and uninterrupted access. Some of these include the ability to:

- Reside in a community in which all the people look like them
- Purchase flesh-tone Band-Aids
- Walk around in a store without someone assuming you are there to steal

Within the context of special education teacher education, White privilege, or the protective mechanism of skin color, often predisposes middle-class Caucasian children to:

- Fewer discipline referrals
- The reduced likelihood of being falsely identified as having disabilities
- More recommendations for gifted and talented programs
- Advanced and college-bound classes
- More preferential treatment by teachers
- Greater recognition for accomplishments

These privileges and systems of dominance are seldom acknowledged but continuously place students who meet a White, middle-class imperative at an advantage while penalizing students from marginalized groups. McIntosh would argue that maintenance of such a system of privilege relies on an unwillingness to confront these social realities and the necessity of pretending in order to reinforce it. Special education teacher educators and their teacher candidates must work toward eliminating this system of privilege. The next step in developing cultural competence and proficiency embedded in the Patton and Day-Vines guide involves attaining knowledge competencies.

The knowledge competencies embedded in the second strand of the curriculum and pedagogical guide developed by Patton and Day-Vines (2002) provides a strand of information that can be used by teacher educators to enable teacher candidates to better understand the demographic, cultural, and educational experiences of major culturally distinct groups and individuals often served by our educational system. The knowledge competency component of the curriculum and pedagogical guide provides important knowledge and information relative to the formation of racial and cultural identity models as well as factual information and sociopolitical and educational experiences of African Americans, American Indians, Latinos, and Asian Americans. As a developmental aspect of cultural assessment, special education teacher candidates must continuously explore their racial or cultural identities in order to better know themselves racially so that they can better relate to diverse exceptional learners. An extensive discussion of the racial identity models of Cross (1995), Helms (1984), and Sue and Sue (1999) is provided in the guide developed by Patton and Day-Vines (2002). Further, deep cultural specific knowledge and information about the major culturally distinct learners represented in this nation's schools, which have important implications for implementing culturally responsive interventions in the classroom, are included in this guide.

Although information about each group is important, the authors caution against using it in stereotypical ways. Often there is a high level of heterogeneity within a particular cultural group and, as educators, we must avoid the temptation to regard culturally different groups as monolithic entities. As special education teacher education candidates acquire and apply new information about different cultural groups, they must continue to consider the varying viewpoints and values of various cultural group members.

The third strand of competencies needed by culturally competent special education teachers consists of the ability to integrate the previously discussed awareness and knowledge competencies in a manner that results in positive outcomes for diverse exceptional learners. Thus the *skills* competencies embedded in the curriculum and pedagogical guide proposed by Patton and Day-Vines (2002) focus on specific strategies needed by culturally competent teachers that allow them to build on the previously discussed awareness and knowledge competencies.

BEYOND CULTURALLY COMPETENT CURRICULUM AND PEDAGOGY

The curricula and pedagogical changes needed to create special education teacher education programs that prepare culturally responsive and competent teacher candidates have implications far beyond curriculum, pedagogy, and teacher education. Indeed, to create and sustain programs guided by the notions presented in this chapter requires changes that touch upon the school, the university, the public school systems, and the entire community. A sample of those implications is discussed next.

Morey and Kitano (1997) proposed a framework, in the form of a continuum from the cursory to the transformative, to analyze the level of infusing "diversity" into teacher education programs. This framework is outlined in Table 2.3. At the basic level, only minor aspects of diversity are begrudgingly discussed at surface levels, thus usually resulting in reinforcing stereotypical thinking about culture, class, and language. At the second level of infusion, which Morey and Kitano (1997) call the inclusive level, diversity issues are discussed usually in comparison with the dominant cultural norms as the denominator. Deep structural issues around culture, class, and language, along with elements of a culturally responsive and competent teacher education curricula

TABLE 2.3 Morey and Kitano Continuum of Diversity Infusion into Teacher Education Programs	
Level One—Basic Level	At the basic level, minor aspects of diversity are discussed at surface levels, usually resulting in reinforcing stereotypical thinking about culture, class, and language.
Level Two—Inclusive Level	At the inclusive level, diversity issues are discussed, usually in comparison with the dominant cultural norms that usually serve as the denominator.
Level Three—Transformative	At the transformative level, deep cultural issues around culture, class and language are discussed along with elements of culturally responsive teacher education curriculum and pedagogy. In addition, at this level challenges are made to replace the norms, traditions, conventions, and ways of training of traditional special teacher education programs with practices that form cultural responsiveness traditions.

Source: From *Multicultural Course Transformation in Higher Education* by A. Morey and M. Kitano, 1997, Needham Heights, MA: Allyn & Bacon. Copyright 1997 by Allyn & Bacon. Reprinted with permission.

and pedagogy, are usually not addressed and if so at perfunctory levels. The transformative level is the highest as it challenges the norms, traditions, conventions, and ways of training of traditional special teacher education programs. The very foundations of traditional enterprises are challenged and argued to be replaced by practices that flow from cultural traditions articulated by Gay (2000), Villegas and Lucas (2002), and Patton and Day-Vines, (2002). All of those elements of transformative, culturally responsive, and competent teacher education—from cultural, class, and linguistic awareness and self-assessment through cultural knowledge development to culturally responsive and competent skill development—are a part of the transformative curriculum level as articulated by Morey and Kitano (1997). At the very least, special education teacher educators must not and cannot be satisfied if they do not design programs that begin at the transformative level of curriculum and pedagogy. Furthermore, this same continuum of levels of change can be employed when analyzing changes needed in special education teacher education programs beyond curricular and pedagogical considerations.

This suggestion of additional implications of changes needed to create transformative special education teacher education programs is presented here as illustrative rather than exhaustive. A framework that may be helpful when analyzing the levels of changes needed to transform special education teacher education programs would allow us to view change in a concentric manner beginning at the levels of self, classroom or course, department, school, university, community, state, national, and international. The proposed changes in special education teacher education programs have implications at all levels. If these changes are to be accomplished, thoughtful and tactical strategies must be created and implemented at all of levels, concomitant with the suggestions for culturally responsive and competent transformative curricula and pedagogy. As an example, the total culture and climate of an institution of higher education and local school system—from the board of trustees and board of education to the teacher education and special education faculty member—must support and advocate for culturally responsive and competent policies, practices, curricula, and pedagogy. Accordingly, the institutional, organizational, fiscal, and instructional policies and practices of the university and local school systems must be changed and routinized in ways that advocate for culturally responsive and competent special education teacher education practices. Culturally competent leadership at the university and school system levels must prevail in order to reach the transformative level. And yet, most of this work is accomplished through the development of human resources.

Institutions of higher education and local school systems must recruit, retain, and constantly reinvigorate a corps of special education teachers who are culturally responsive and competent. Accordingly, it is incumbent upon those who select special education teacher educators and teacher candidates and those who hire special education teachers to insist that candidates be able to document and present evidence that they are culturally responsive or competent or that they have begun that developmental journey.

SUMMARY

The need to educate special education teachers to be culturally responsive and competent in the totality of their work has never been greater. Deep structural elements of culture, class, and language must be embedded into special education teacher education programs that initially focus teacher candidates on examining their invisible cultural, class, and linguistic "knapsacks." After this form of "cultural therapy," strands or domains of culturally responsive and competent practices must be embedded into their coursework and field experiences. The culturally responsive models of Gay (2000) and Villegas and Lucas (2002) delineated in this chapter should be considered, because of their conceptual clarity and comprehensiveness, in the creation of such special education teacher education programs. A model of cultural competence articulated by Patton and Day-Vines (2002) that contains coursework and experiences that include awareness, knowledge, and skill domains was also presented as a guide to developing transformative culturally competent theory and practice that can be used in special education teacher education programs.

All of the changes suggested in this chapter have implications far beyond curriculum and pedagogy. If culturally responsive and competent special education teacher education programs are developed at transformative levels, significant changes and support must be secured at institutional levels beyond the individual. These changes will take time and must be pursued with a clear vision in mind by all. When accomplished, our diverse exceptional learners and their families will be the ultimate beneficiaries.

Discussion Questions

1. Identify, discuss, analyze, and critique the major conceptual elements embodied in the discussion around the nexus of culture, class, language, diversity, and disabilities. What are the curriculum and pedagogical implications of these elements?

2. To what extent must these elements be embraced by special education teacher candidates?

3. To what extent are these elements embodied in today's CLD learners? How will their learning and behavior improve if they are taught by teachers who embody these elements?

4. What are some salient and common theoretical, conceptual, and pedagogical elements needed to ground special education teacher preparation programs that are culturally responsive? How can these elements be infused into special education teacher preparation programs? Describe the special education teacher candidate who does not embrace these elements. Describe the special education teacher candidate who does embrace these elements.

5. How can these elements be applied to curricular content and the teaching and learning of culturally and linguistically diverse learners and enhance their learning and behaving?

6. Identify and discuss four curriculum and pedagogical programmatic components that result in preparing special education teacher candidates to become culturally responsive and competent in their use of curriculum and pedagogy for diverse exceptional learners.

7. How can these elements be applied to curricular content and the teaching and learning of culturally and linguistically diverse learners and enhance their learning and behaving?

8. What are the implications for diverse exceptional learners when teachers are not culturally responsive?

References

Arredondo, P., Toporek, R., Brown, S., Jones, J., Locke, D., Sanchez, J., & Stadler, H. (1996). Operationalization of the multicultural counseling competencies. *Journal of Multicultural Counseling and Development, 24,* 42–78.

Banks, J. A. (1997). *Teaching strategies for ethnic studies* (6th ed.). F. Helland (Series Ed.). Needham Heights, MA: Allyn & Bacon.

Banks, J. A. (2001). *Cultural diversity and education: Foundations, curriculum, and teaching* (4th ed.). Boston: Allyn & Bacon.

Barkan, E. (1992). *The retreat of scientific racism: Changing concepts of race in Britain and the United States between the world wars.* Cambridge, England: Cambridge University Press.

Bennett, C. I. (1995). Preparing teachers for cultural diversity and national standards of academic excellence. *Journal of Teacher Education 46*(4), 259–265.

Bourdieu, P. (1986). The forms of capital. In J. G. Richardson (Ed.), *Handbook of theory and research for the sociology of education* (pp. 214–258). New York: Greenwood.

Brown, E. L. (2000). Developing the ethical multicultural classroom tenets of preservice teachers: A social cognitive instructional model. *Journal on Excellence in Teacher Education, 9*(3), 81–108.

Brown, E. L. (2004). What precipitates change in cultural diversity awareness during a multicultural course: The message or the method? *Journal of Teacher Education, 55*(4), 325–340.

Cross, T., Bazron, B., Dennis, K., & Isaacs, M. (1989). *Towards a culturally competent system of care.* Washington, DC: CASSP Technical Assistance Center, Georgetown University Child Development Center.

Cross, W. E., Jr. (1995). The psychology of Nigrescence: Revising the Cross model. In J. G. Ponterotto, J. M. Casas, L. A. Suzuki, & C. M. Alexander (Eds.), *Handbook of multicultural counseling* (pp. 93–122). Thousand Oaks, CA: Sage.

Freire, P. (1994). *Pedagogy of the oppressed.* New York: The Continuum Publishing Company.

Gay, G. (1993). Building cultural bridges: A bold proposal for teacher education. *Education and Urban Society, 25*(3), 285–299.

Gay, G. (2000). *Culturally responsive teaching.* New York: Teachers College Press.

Hanley, J. (1999). Beyond the tip of the iceberg: Five stages toward cultural competence. *Today's Youth: The Community Circle of Caring Journal, 3*(2), 9–12.

Helms, J. E. (1984). Towards a theoretical explanation of the effects of race on counseling: A Black and White model. *Counseling Psychologist, 12*(4), 153–165.

Hodgkinson, H. (1998, October). Demographics of diversity for the 21st century. *The Education Digest, 64*(2), 4–7.

Irvine, J. I. (1992). Making teacher education culturally responsive. In M. E. Dilworth (Ed.), *Diversity in teacher education* (pp. 79–92). San Francisco: Jossey-Bass.

Ladson-Billings, G. (1995). Multicultural teacher education: Research, practice, and policy. In J. A. Banks & C. A. M. Banks (Eds.), *Handbook of research on multicultural education* (pp. 747–759). New York: Macmillan.

Lee, D. L. (1973). *From plan to planet.* Chicago: Broadside Press.

Leighton, D. L. (1982). As I knew them: Navajo women in 1940. *American Indian Quarterly, 6*(1–2), 34–51.

Mason, J. L. (1993). *Cultural Competence Self Assessment Questionnaire.* Portland, OR: Portland State University. Multicultural Initiative Project.

Mason, J. L., Benjamin, M. P., & Lewis, S. A. (1996). The cultural competence model: Implications for child and family mental health services. In C. A. Heflinger & C. T. Nixon (Eds.), *Families and the mental health system for children and adolescents: Policy, services, and research. Children's mental health services* (pp. 165–190). Thousand Oaks, CA: Sage Publications.

McIntosh, P. (1989, July/August). White privilege: Unpacking the invisible knapsack. *Peace and Freedom,* 10–12.

Morey, A., & Kitano, M. (1997). *Multicultural course transformation in higher education: A broader truth.* Needham Heights, MA: Allyn & Bacon.

Nieto, S. (1996). *Affirming diversity: The sociopolitical context of multicultural education* (2nd ed.). White Plains, NY: Longman.

Nieto, S. (1998). From claiming hegemony to sharing space: Creating community in multicultural courses. In R. Chavez & J. O'Donnell (Eds.), *Speaking the unpleasant: The politics of (non) engagement in the multicultural education terrain* (pp. 16–31). Albany: State University of New York Press.

Noddings, N. (1984). *Caring: A feminine approach to ethics & moral education.* Berkeley: University of California Press.

Patton, J., & Day-Vines, N. (2002). *A curriculum and pedagogy for cultural competence: Knowledge, skills and dispositions needed to guide the training of special and general education teachers.* Unpublished manuscript.

Pedersen, P. (1994). *A handbook for developing multicultural awareness* (2nd ed.). Alexandria, VA: American Counseling Association.

Pinderhughes, E. (1989). *Understanding race, ethnicity, and power: The key to efficacy in clinical practice.* New York: Free Press.

Reynolds, A. L., & Pope, R. L. (1991). The complexities of diversity: Exploring multiple oppressions. *Journal of Counseling and Development, 70*(1), 174–180.

Robinson, T., & Howard-Hamilton, M. (2000). *The convergence of race, ethnicity, and gender: Multiple identities in counseling.* Upper Saddle River, NJ: Merrill.

Rorty, R. (1998). *Achieving our country*. Cambridge, MA: Harvard University Press.

Roylance, F. D. (2004). Genetics disputes notions about race: Humans are 99.9 percent identical, but our society still sets up constructs that divide. *Daily Press*, pp. A1, A9.

Singleton, G., & Linton, C. (2006). *Courageous conversations about race*. Thousand Oaks, CA: Corwin Press.

Sleeter, C. (1992). *Keepers of the American dream: A study of staff development and multicultural education*. London: Falmer.

Sleeter, C. (2001). Preparing teachers for culturally diverse schools: Research and the overwhelming presence of whiteness. *Journal of Teacher Education, 52*(2), 94–106.

Sorrells, A. M., Webb-Johnson, G., & Townsend, B. L. (2004). Multicultural perspectives in special education: A call for responsibility in research, practice, and teacher preparation. In S. M. Sorrells, J. H. Reith, & P. T. Sindelar (Eds.), *Critical issues in special education* (pp. 73–91). Boston: Pearson Education.

Spindler, G., & Spindler, L. (1994). *Pathways to cultural awareness: Cultural therapy with teachers and students*. Thousand Oaks, CA: Corwin Press.

Starrat, R. (1994). *Building an ethical school*. London: Falmer.

Sue, D., & Sue, D. (1999). *Counseling the culturally different: Theory and practice* (3rd ed.). New York: John Wiley & Sons.

Tatum, B. D. (1997). *"Why are all the Black kids sitting together in the cafeteria?" And other conversations about race. A psychologist explains the development of racial identity.* New York: Basic Books.

Villegas, A. M., & Lucas, T. (2002). *Educating culturally responsive teachers*. Albany: State University of New York Press.

Weaver, G. (1986). Understanding and coping with cross-cultural adjustment stress. In R. Paige (Ed.), *Cross-cultural orientation: New conceptualizations and applications* (pp. 137–167). Lanham, MD: University Press of America.

Chapter 3

Second Language Acquisition and Students with Disabilities

Chapter Objectives

Upon completion of this chapter the reader will be able to:

1. Present the major theories of second language acquisition.
2. Show the similarities and differences between L1 and L2 acquisition.
3. Present the common fallacies regarding second language acquisition.
4. Describe a sociocultural model for second language acquisition for use with CLDE learners.
5. Describe best practices for second language learners.
6. Discuss the implications for special education teachers.

VIGNETTE

When Han Vu began third grade at Hillside Elementary School in a suburb of Dallas, she spoke almost solely Vietnamese. This was the native language of her parents who had immigrated to Texas from Vietnam over the summer. Although Han's two older cousins, who had lived in the United States for 6 years and were bilingual, practiced English words with her over the summer as requested by Han's parents to help prepare her for school, Han was really only familiar with the English vocabulary words for some numbers, colors, and shapes.

Han's teacher, Ms. Taylor, paid close attention to Han's and the other English language learners' second language acquisition progress. After 5 years of working collaboratively with her bilingual aide, Mrs. Nguyen, Ms. Taylor had begun to feel confident in creating a classroom where the needs of her many ELLs could be met. She recognized the interrelatedness of social, cognitive, and linguistic processes, and she and Mrs. Nguyen designed learning activities that incorporated all three. She had also become comfortable with the quietness exhibited by her ELLs, recognizing that at times part of second language acquisition included comprehension without production. In observing Han, however, Ms. Taylor and Mrs. Nguyen noticed a refusal to verbalize in English or Vietnamese. Han tended to cry frequently, a behavior normal for many kindergartners at first, but for Han it continued several times a day throughout the first 2 months. Ms. Taylor and Mrs. Nguyen thought that these may have been side effects of acculturation, but because the behaviors continued and were quite dramatic, they consulted Han's parents and together decided to have an assessment conducted to try to better understand some of the difficulties Han was experiencing. Following an ongoing, broadly based, nonbiased assessment of Han, several potential teaching strategies were suggested to Ms. Taylor and Mrs. Nguyen.

Anxious to create a learning environment that met Han's needs more appropriately, Ms. Taylor and Mrs. Nguyen immediately implemented some of the suggestions. Recognizing the importance of Han receiving as much instruction as possible in her native language, Mrs. Nguyen worked individually with Han regularly throughout the day, and Han also spent part of each day in ESL with a special educator. Also, they frequently paired Han with her classmates who were also learning English, using peer tutoring to help Han with cognitive, linguistic, and cross-culturally appropriate emotional development. This also afforded Han the opportunity to see similarities and

The authors wish to acknowledge Amy Saks for her assistance in developing this vignette.

differences from other children in the class and to experience success. As a way of proactively helping all the children in this multicultural, multilingual classroom setting develop appropriate linguistic skills and emotional responses to conflict, Ms. Taylor and Mrs. Nguyen often used role-playing to have students act out and discuss potential responses.

As Han began to feel more comfortable in the learning environment, the emotional difficulties she had been experiencing began to diminish and her acquisition of English began to progress. She was more willing to speak in class in both English and Vietnamese, and although the teachers encouraged Han's parents to continue speaking to her in Vietnamese at home because that was their dominant language, Han expressed a desire to practice speaking English with her cousins who were proficient in English and Vietnamese. She felt comfortable code switching with her cousins and was more willing to take linguistic risks with them as she acquired more and more English-speaking skills. Now, in the second half of the year, Han still demonstrates a tendency to withdraw when she feels overwhelmed by the learning task at hand, but this occurs only rarely. Instead, Han actively participates in classroom activities in both English and Vietnamese on a daily basis and enjoys working collaboratively with all her classmates.

Reflective Questions

1. What would you have done as the teacher with Han if you had not had the help of a Vietnamese-speaking paraprofessional to assist you?
2. If you as Han's teacher were going to use peer tutoring to help Han, how would you go about preparing for this intervention?

INTRODUCTION

This chapter explores the field of second language acquisition in general as well as how students with disabilities develop a second language. It starts out by defining language and discusses the difference between language acquisition and language learning. The various stages of language acquisition are presented along with suggestions for teachers who support students with disabilities with their learning of English as a second language.

WHAT IS LANGUAGE?

On the surface defining language may appear to be an easy task. We might say that language is a system of sounds and symbols used for communication. However, delving into this question a little deeper, we will find that this is a difficult task. Language scholars or linguists are themselves not in agreement about how to define language. These scholars have written many volumes proposing definitions and debating with one another about how to best define language. Brown (1980) reviews multiple definitions of language and produces a comprehensive list of the characteristics of language. He maintains that:

1. Language is systematic—possibly a generative—system.
2. Language is a set of arbitrary symbols.
3. Those symbols are primarily vocal but many also be visual.
4. The symbols have conventionalized meanings to which they refer.
5. Language is used for communication.
6. Language operates in a speech community or culture.
7. Language is essentially human, although possibly not limited to humans.
8. Language is acquired by all people in much the same way—language and language learning both have universal characteristics.

Having provided this succinct summary of the definition of language, Brown (1980) goes on to caution that this is not a simple matter and that the study of language is a complex area of scientific inquiry.

Teaching Implications: Every special education teacher is a language teacher. In this book, attention is focused on the special education teacher who is working with English language learners who also have a documented disability as defined by special education law. The challenge for the special education teacher working with culturally and linguistically diverse exceptional learners is enormous. Nonetheless, some basic theories and ideas about both first and second language learning will be helpful in facing this challenge. As we review this material the special education teacher should continue to ask: How can I use this information with my work with CLD learners with special needs?

LANGUAGE ACQUISITION VS. LANGUAGE LEARNING

Do we learn a language or do we acquire a language? This question suggests that we can take a formal and conscious approach to learning a language by studying the language and taking language classes. On the other hand, we can simply be exposed to the language and acquire it without formal study (Krashen, 1981). Young children acquire the language of their parents without formal instruction. When they enter school, they formally study and further learn that same language. Krashen (1981) popularized this distinction between acquisition and learning and based it on Chomsky's (1957) notion of a genetic predisposition to language learning known as the language acquisition device (LAD). This supports the idea that some of language learning occurs naturally at the subconscious level and without formal schooling. So it can thus be said that we both acquire and learn a language. Regardless of whether language is acquired or learned, there are certain conditions that optimally support language acquisition and learning.

Language acquisition is most successful when there is a safe and stress-free environment. Also important is that exposure to the language occurs in a natural setting and that language is being used for authentic communication. Perhaps most important is that there is comprehensible input. This is supported by a highly contextualized environment that includes body language, the use of concrete referents, pictures, and visual support. Also important are the availability of good language models or individuals who speak the language well, such as the teacher and other students. Finally, there should be ample opportunity to practice and use the language both as a listener and as a speaker.

Language Learning and the Exceptional Child

The next logical question thus becomes, what do we know about language learning and the exceptional child? Is a child with a disability able to learn a second language? Some have argued that the disability will prevent or interfere with language learning. As far as we have been able to determine, there is no reliable research to support this position. On the other hand, we know from direct observation that many children with disabilities do know and speak two languages. If we look at the research literature on this topic, we see evidence that children with disabilities can and do learn second languages and benefit from bilingual instruction. Others have argued that special education students with lower levels of intelligence cannot learn a second language and that they need all their intelligence to learn English. This, however, is a fallacy. McLaughlin (1985) indicates that intelligence does not seem to be related to aptitude for second language learning. Again we know from direct observation that students with severe retardation are capable of learning a second language. In terms of research, Malherbe (1969) conducted a study on the impact of bilingual instruction on students with low levels of intelligence. He found:

> Not only the bright children but also the children with below normal intelligence do better school work all round in the bilingual school than in the unilingual school. What is most significant is that the greatest gain for the bilingual school was registered in the second language by the lower intelligence groups. Not only do they more than hold their own in the first language (in comparison to equivalent children in monolingual schools), but in their second language their gain was nearly twice as big as that registered by the higher intelligence groups. (p. 78)

Teaching Implications: Given that children with disabilities, including children with low levels of intelligence, benefit from bilingual and native language instruction, we argue that staffing committees should include native language support in the IEPs of these students. Although this recommendation may seem reasonable and warranted, the large majority of bilingual students with disabilities receive all of their instruction in English. This is true in all states across the country and especially true in states that have adopted English-only amendments (Baca, Almanza De Schonewise, & Vanchu-Orosco, 2004). Federal law, such as the Individuals with Disabilities Education Act (IDEA), takes precedence over state law, such as proposition 227 in California, so it is appropriate to use native language instruction for students with disabilities in states with English-only policies.

HISTORICAL PERSPECTIVE REGARDING LANGUAGE THEORY

Language scholars have conducted many studies in an attempt to explain how language is acquired. Linguists have advanced multiple perspectives but have not come to a consensus on how language is acquired. In 1916 Saussure (1916/1959) made an important distinction between language performance and language competence. This led to the development of two competing theories. Since the mid-1900s two corresponding major schools of thought have dominated the field. In the 1940s and 1950s the structural-descriptive (language performance) school of thought prevailed (Brown, 1980). A good example of this perspective is seen in the work of B. F. Skinner (1957) in his book *Verbal Behavior*. According to this perspective, language could be broken down into smaller parts that could then be studied scientifically and then reassembled to form a whole. In the 1960s the generative school of thought (language competence) became popular. Noam Chomsky argued against the behavioral perspective and argued that humans are "hard wired" for language. He proposed the existence of what he called a language acquisition device (LAD) that humans are born with which makes it possible for them to develop a complex language system.

Teaching Implications: As a special education teacher working with second language learners, your challenge is to help your students develop their language or languages to the fullest extent possible. Thus you will have to build your own personal theory of how language is developed and learned. Because you will want your students to develop both language competence and performance, you may want to draw from both of these major schools of thought and formulate your own eclectic personal theory of language acquisition. You will also need to be familiar with the research on second language acquisition. The age of the student will be an important factor to consider. The younger the student the more likely second language acquisition will be similar to first language acquisition.

SECOND LANGUAGE ACQUISITION

The study of second language acquisition clearly fits within the above theoretical debate. Understanding how second language learners best acquire a new language may shed more information about the relative influence of cognition, language-specific brain functions, and environmental influences. Unlike the process of first language acquisition in young children, the process of second language acquisition can be observed under a variety of circumstances. The relative influences of age, personality, social context, type of language input, and other factors can be better isolated and explored. This information can, in turn, inform our understanding of how language acquisition as a generic process unfolds (De Valenzuela & Niccolai, 2004).

Although there is not complete consensus as to how second languages are acquired, there are a few tentative conclusions we can suggest at this time. For example, we can conclude that the process of grammatical development, the relationship of comprehension to production, and the role of hypothesis testing and formulaic speech are somewhat similar in first and second language development. In other words, grammatical development will be orderly and systematic. Second language learners will learn a grammatical rule and then through hypothesis testing they will overextend its use; for example, they may say "goed" instead of "went." They may imitate phrases they hear (formulaic speech) such as "liar, liar panzon fire." Second language learners will comprehend more than they produce; in fact, they will go through a silent period where they focus more on comprehension and on gaining familiarity with the grammar of the language.

Noting the differences between first and second language acquisition is also important. One major difference is the social setting of the language. More than likely the greatest social exposure to the language will be at school and not at home. Another difference will be the rate of acquisition. Because of increased age and maturity second language learners will acquire the language faster by drawing on what they already know from their first language, which may even include reading and writing. Language status is also an important difference. Because English has a higher status in this country, this will contribute to native language loss and possible difficulty acquiring English.

The following individuals have made significant contributions to the theory of second language acquisition:

- Stephen Krashen (1981) is one of the foremost theorists in second language acquisition. He has developed a number of interrelated hypotheses based on the idea that individuals learn language best in authentic settings, when they are made to feel relaxed and comfortable, and when the second language input that they are receiving is only slightly more advanced than their current level of proficiency.

- Lilly Wong Filmore (1991a) focuses on the importance of social, linguistic, and cognitive settings that encourage native speakers and language learners to interact in meaningful ways. She claims that the social environment and the status of language influence language acquisition and development, including language loss.

- Jim Cummins has postulated three basic principles related to second language acquisition (Cummins, 1979, 1989). These have come to be known as the conversational/academic language proficiency principle, the linguistic interdependence principle, and the additive bilingual enrichment principle. It is the first of these three principles that has given rise to the now famous distinction between basic interpersonal communication skills (BICS) and cognitive academic language proficiency (CALP).

- Saville-Troike has focused on the social settings and academic skills necessary for maximum academic achievement of CLD students (Saville-Troike, 1984, 1988). Among other things, she found that a well-developed vocabulary is the most important aspect of oral English proficiency for academic achievement. However, an academic focus on structural patterns, such as basic grammar rules, appears to contribute little toward meeting students' immediate academic needs. At the root of her theory is the belief that students need opportunities to discuss academic concepts in their native language if they are to master content area knowledge. Thus, social interaction among students is not sufficient for development of academic English language skills.

- Roland Tharp's work on sociocultural theory (D'Amato & Tharp, 1997; Tharp, 1997; Tharp & Dalton, 1994) and his development of five principles for cross-culturally compatible education, while not explicitly a theory of second language acquisition, can be readily applied to creating environments that encourage language development and bilingualism. Tharp's theory and its application are discussed in more detail in the final section of this chapter.

STAGES OF LANGUAGE DEVELOPMENT

Most theorists argue that there is a continuum of language learning that can be broken down into specific stages (see Table 3.1).

Stage I: The Silent/Receptive or Preproduction Stage

This first stage of language development usually lasts from 1 to 6 months and is often referred to as the silent stage because it is focused solely on comprehension. Students in this stage have up to 500 receptive words they understand but are not able to use. These students rely on body language or simple yes-no responses. Teachers should not force these students to speak until they are ready. Teachers should speak clearly and slowly and write key words on the board for students to see and copy but not pronounce.

Stage II: The Early Production Stage

This stage generally lasts about 6 months. These students have up to 1,000 words they can understand and use, and comprehension has now expanded into production. Speech is very limited and usually in one- or two-word phrases and utilizes yes-no answers to simple questions. At this stage the teacher should use visual aids and

TABLE 3.1 Language Development Stages	
Stage I	Silent/Receptive or Preproduction Stage
Stage II	Early Production Stage
Stage III	Speech Emergence Stage
Stage IV	Intermediate Language Proficiency Stage
Stage V	Advanced Language Proficiency Stage

gestures along with manipulative materials. The teacher should also use charts and graphs as well as environmental print and local newspaper ads to help focus on authentic language use. In addition the teacher should use role-playing activities and encourage open dialogue.

Stage III: The Speech Emergence Stage

This stage can last up to 1 year. These students usually understand and use up to 3,000 words. They can use longer utterances including short phrases and simple sentences to communicate but often make grammatical errors. The teacher at this stage should use class discussions and the use of skits and performances. Also helpful at this stage is multimedia technology. The teacher should also introduce written compositions at this stage. Error correction should be kept to a minimum.

Stage IV: The Intermediate Language Proficiency Stage

This stage may last up to 1 year. Now these students can understand and use up to 6,000 words. They can now make complex statements, give opinions, and ask for clarification. Teachers should encourage these students to write essays on current events and be part of panel discussions.

Stage V: The Advanced Language Proficiency Stage

This stage may take from 5 to 7 years. Students now have content area vocabulary and can participate in grade-level discussions. Student grammar and vocabulary is comparable to that of a same-age native speaker. These students are ready for critiquing stories and legends as well as newspaper editorials. Writing should be at an advanced level with emphasis on drafting, redrafting, and editing one's writing. Error correction is now an important strategy.

Teaching Implications: Teachers who understand this continuum and these stages of language development can use stage-appropriate strategies and materials that will maximize language learning. Based on the above-mentioned theory, Jameson (1998) maintains that teachers should follow four principles with ELL students:

1. *Increase comprehensibility.* This involves the use of nonverbal clues, pictures, real objects, and gestures. This is especially useful when students are in stages I and II.
2. *Increase interaction.* Students are now ready to interact with one another and negotiate meaning with one another in real-life situations. This is known as authentic language use. This is important when students are in stages II and III.
3. *Increase thinking/study skills.* Here the teacher challenges the students to develop higher level thinking skills and the use of abstract language. This is an advanced strategy that can be best used when students are at stage IV in their language development.

4. *Use a student's native language to increase comprehensibility.* This is an easy way of building on existing knowledge. Students are able to transfer knowledge and skills from their native language into English and improve their ability to understand and communicate. This strategy can be used at all stages but is especially powerful at stage V.

FALLACIES ABOUT SECOND LANGUAGE ACQUISITION

Fallacy #1: Parents of CLD students should speak with their children at home in English.

This advice, although popular, is incorrect for several reasons. As discussed above, students will best acquire a second language if their first language is well established. Second, asking parents who may not be able to provide an adequate language model in English to restrict the use of their more proficient language is absurd. Parents will neither be able to stimulate their child's language development nor will they be able to communicate easily for social purposes with their child. Wong Fillmore (1991b) makes the following poignant observation:

> When parents are unable to talk to their children, they cannot easily convey to them their values, beliefs, understandings, or wisdom about how to cope with their experiences. They cannot teach them about the meaning of work, or about personal responsibility, or what it means to be a moral or ethical person in a world with too many choices and too few guideposts to follow. What is lost are the bits of advice, the *consejos* parents should be able to offer children in their everyday interactions with them. Talk is a crucial link between parents and children: It is how parents impart their cultures to their children and enable them to become the kind of men and women they want them to be. When parents lose the means for socializing and influencing their children, rifts develop and families lose the intimacy that comes from shared beliefs and understandings. (p. 343)

Teaching Implications: The main implication here is that teachers should always advise parents to continue using the native language at home as much as possible. This is really important because sometimes parents think that using the native language at home will confuse the child or interfere with his or her learning of English. Actually the very opposite is the case. If the parents continue interacting actively in the native language, the new learning and language stimulation will improve their English language development.

Fallacy #2: Acquiring more than one language is "difficult" and can lead to academic problems.

Cummins' (1979) additive bilingualism enrichment principle and the research on the cognitive benefits of bilingualism clearly suggest that it is not a burden for students. In fact, in many parts of the world, it is a common part of daily life. When fluently bilingual parents are encouraged to raise their children monolingually, as in the case of a 1995 child custody case in which Texas State District Judge Samuel C. Kaiser equated raising the child of a bilingual mother in a Spanish-speaking home as tantamount to child abuse, beliefs about bilingualism as a cognitive deficit are reinforced. Regardless of the cognitive benefits, bilingualism is of social benefit in our global village and can have only positive outcomes when students leave school and seek employment.

Teaching Implications: Teachers should look at language as a way to increase understanding and the ability to communicate. Reducing children to English only restricts their ability to learn, understand, and communicate.

Fallacy #3: Some bilingual students don't speak any language to a real extent and are "semilingual."

This idea of "semilingualism" can be compelling when we do not understand language acquisition. Educators may confuse students undergoing a "silent period" as demonstrating a lack of ability to communicate. Remember all that children have to know to be able to say even one word is their first language. Even those children who demonstrate little expressive language in the school environment (in their first or second language) bring with them a wealth of information about the phonology, morphology, syntax, lexicon, and language use patterns of their native language. Additionally, standardized tests based on standard dialects in English and the student's native language may fail to identify their communicative competence. There are three important concepts that relate to language competence in bilingual children: language attrition, semilingualism, and code switching.

Language attrition is a recognized and completely normal phenomenon in which individuals lose all or part of their native language competence. It can happen naturally as a result of immigration and the lack of opportunities to communicate in a particular language. For adults who have immigrated without their families to a new country and rarely return for visits, this may occur over time. It can also happen to young children who are exposed to a new language at school before their first language has been well established or where there is a significant discrepancy between the social prestige of the two languages. Language attrition is a common phenomenon in the United States among children from discriminated and dominated ethnic groups, such as Hispanics. The preliminary results of the National Association for Bilingual Education (NABE) No-Cost Study on Families indicate that the early exposure to English, by enrollment of non-English background children in preschool programs that are not conducted exclusively in the children's home language, results in a shift in use of the native language at home and leads to language attrition (Wong Fillmore, 1991b). Merino (1982) found that among the native-Spanish-speaking children in her research project, language attrition occurred by the fourth grade, and sometimes even earlier. She also found that language attrition initially affects later developing skills and abilities. The dynamic relationship between increasing second language proficiency and first language loss can result in a temporary stage in which the child appears limited in both languages.

The problem with applying the label of "semilingualism" to these children is twofold:

1. This term suggests a difficulty in acquiring language and does not recognize that children may have lost language skills they once possessed.
2. This term implies a resultant *cognitive deficit*.

Although bilingual children from nondominant culture backgrounds do have a higher percentage of below-average academic performance, there is no evidence that this stems from a cognitive deficit caused by their bilingualism. Inappropriate academic programs and home–school incongruities have been suggested as reasons for these academic problems. Some students may not have had the opportunity to acquire the academic concepts or vocabulary. In fact, one of the major problems facing our school system today is the lowered academic achievement of all culturally different youth, regardless of whether they speak a home language other than English or not. However, poor academic achievement should not be confused with a cognitive deficit—do we really mean to say that our students are cognitively impaired because of their exposure to more than one language? If not, then we need to be careful about the implications of this term.

Sometimes the term *semilingual* is applied because educators observe students speaking what they consider to be a mixture of two languages. However, research has indicated that what may appear to a monolingual speaker to be a random hodgepodge of two different languages is in fact a systematic and socially governed interplay between two separate and well-developed linguistic systems (Genishi, 1981). In fact, that students are able to switch back and forth between two distinct codes is a sign of linguistic maturity. Code switching refers to "the use of two or more linguistic varieties in the same conversation or interaction" (Scotton & Ury, 1977, p. 5). This can involve switching between social styles or registers or between different languages. Most people code switch as a regular part of social interactions, but we don't even recognize what we are doing because it is such a normal part of communication. When we are talking with a friend and using informal speech and then start speaking more formally when the boss walks by, we are engaging in code switching. Research suggests that bilingual children are able to differentiate between their two languages at a very early age, even as young as age 2 (Lindholm & Padilla, 1978; Meisel, 1987). Therefore, we can conclude that the use of two different languages, as well as a range of social styles, merely makes a bilingual individual able to communicate in a wider range of social contexts. Depending on the social situation and the community norms, bilingual code switching may be more or less prevalent. However, regardless of the frequency of code switching, it should not be taken as evidence that a child is "semilingual."

Teaching Implications: Teachers should realize that labeling a child as semilingual is a serious mistake with devastating consequences. First, it is not accurate because the child's languages are still emerging and have not yet been mastered. Second, this label has very serious negative consequences, such as the lowering of expectations and the imposition of a negative and stigmatizing label.

A SOCIOCULTURAL MODEL FOR SECOND LANGUAGE ACQUISITION

The sociocultural model that is presented here is meant to address the complexities of second language acquisition, including the challenges faced by CLD students and the importance of creating a classroom environment that does as much as possible to help these students cope, survive, and thrive within the challenges of school in an alien culture and a foreign language. As mentioned earlier, the model we present is based largely on the work of Roland Tharp (D'Amato & Tharp, 1997; Tharp, 1997; Tharp & Dalton, 1994) and his colleagues. Tharp's model is composed of five standards for culturally congruent education. These standards are meant to provide a framework for creating a classroom environment (both social and academic) that serves as a starting point for addressing the challenges we have discussed.

Although Tharp does not consider himself a cultural anthropologist, his model can be categorized within the anthropological framework known as cultural difference theory. The five principles can be expanded and strengthened by looking to a newly emerging framework from cultural anthropology known as practice theory. Therefore, our sociocultural model for second language acquisition starts with Tharp's five standards, and adds a sixth, awareness of cultural productions. Together, these six principles are meant to push students to succeed academically, while helping to create a safe and comfortable social environment where they will not be intimidated and will not have their prior knowledge devalued.

We begin here by briefly outlining the framework of cultural difference. Cultural difference theory is grounded in the idea that cultural differences arise when groups face different historical, social, and economic conditions (Holland & Eisenhart, 1990; Levinson & Holland, 1996). Children learn the culture of the group through child-rearing practices in the home and the local community. Different child-rearing practices across groups lead to consistent patterns of behavior, language use, thinking, and feeling for individuals within groups. However, these patterns differ from the behavior, language use, thinking, and feeling of members of other groups coming from different historical, social, and economic conditions. Further, the relationship between groups is rarely symmetrical. Some groups enjoy greater power, prestige, and status than other groups. One of the strengths of cultural difference theory is that this view lends itself to developing interventions based on cultural differences that can be successful in certain settings. For example, strategies that address uses of time, space, motivation, and language that are more compatible with and build on community-specific features can help engage students who are otherwise prone to disengagement and failure in school (Heath, 1983; Moll et al., 1992).

Tharp's five principles (see Table 3.2) have been derived from working with such diverse populations as native Hawaiian elementary school students (Tharp & Gallimore, 1988), adult Hawaiian vocational education students (D'Amato & Tharp, 1997), and Native Americans on the Navajo and Zuni reservations (Tharp & Dalton, 1994). The effectiveness of these principles comes from studying and making use of broad cultural patterns of behavior. The principles that have emerged as seemingly cross-culturally compatible are as follows:

1. *Learning joint productive activity* is the process of both teacher and students working together to produce something that is of value to everyone involved. The main idea is that a tangible product should be produced by the learner such as a drawing or a book report.

2. *Developing the language and literacy of instruction* in all activities means that there is an overt focus on learning the discourse of the content area concurrent with learning the concepts. The emphasis here is on developing language across the entire curriculum and not just in language arts.

3. *Contextualizing schooling* in students' lived experiences refers to making connections (in an overt manner) between the content being learned and the students' personal prior experiences, both within and beyond school. The emphasis is on making the curriculum relevant in terms of the students' everyday life.

4. *Teaching for cognitive complexity* means making sure that every student is cognitively challenged, which implies individualization of tasks so that everyone is working on a task that is appropriate for his or her knowledge and ability. The emphasis is on high academic standards for every student.

5. *Engaging in instructional conversation* refers to the teacher engaging in conversation with an individual or group of students where the topic of conversation is of importance to all involved, the teacher does not already know the answer to the question he or she is asking, and the teacher has an authentic reason for wanting to know the answer. These informal conversations should be related to the curriculum.

Teaching Implications: Special education teachers should memorize these five principles and make every effort to apply them daily in lesson planning and in carrying out their daily instruction. The special education teacher should review each student's IEP and build in strategies and activities that incorporate these five principles. For example,

TABLE 3.2 Tharp's Five Principles for Effective Teaching and Learning

Principle 1	Learning through joint productive activity
Principle 2	Developing the language and literacy of instruction
Principle 3	Contextualizing schooling
Principle 4	Teaching for cognitive complexity
Principle 5	Engaging in instructional conversation

teachers in the Zuni Pueblo Public Schools decided that principle 3, *contextualizing schooling*, meant that they had to relate reading and writing to the culture and experience of their Zuni students. They thus designed a language experience unit based on the cultural tradition of *piñon harvesting*. The students recounted their weekend outing to the hillside to pick or harvest piñon nuts. The teachers recorded these stories and created their own books, complete with student-made illustrations, retelling this experience. In this very direct way the teachers made literacy an extension of their sociocultural world and experience.

Critiques of Sociocultural Theory

Despite the various successes of educational approaches grounded in cultural difference theory, in recent years cultural anthropologists have begun to critique the underlying framework on several counts. These critiques can provide insight into how Tharp's principles can be enhanced. The first criticism is that cultural difference theory pays insufficient attention to power relations (Mehan, 1993). For example, how can the gap between poor, urban Latino culture and the culture of a discipline of power, such as math or science, be successfully negotiated when there is such a great power differential between the two?

The second critique is that cultural difference theory focuses almost exclusively on the structural (macro) level when defining culture, by focusing on class, race, and/or gender issues. This overlooks the more micro-level influences such as peer groups, or the culture of the individual institution (Geertz, 1973).

The third critique deals with cultural difference theory's inattention to issues of identity and individual agency (Minick, 1993). From this perspective, there is no room for an individual to develop a cultural identity that is at odds with his or her structurally defined culture of origin, whereas in reality, such individuals clearly do exist.

The final argument is that cultural difference theory paints a monolithic perspective of culture. For example, all students from the same cultural group are thought to have developed the same patterns of thinking, talking, and acting during childhood and can likewise be aided by the same classroom interventions (Eisenhart & Graue, 1993).

Simply by examining one's own cultural background and the variety of factors that affect it, it becomes clear that cultural difference theory is an oversimplification of how culture helps shape an individual's identity in practice. For this reason, we turn to a second anthropological tradition, practice theory, which addresses some of the more intricate dynamics in the interactions between structural features and individual agency.

Practice theory is concerned with a number of different aspects of culture, including (1) the sociohistorical development of cultural groups and their members over time (Levinson & Holland, 1996); (2) the interplay of cultural productions (resistance) and cultural reproductions (conforming voluntarily or involuntarily to the cultural and structural norms) (Levinson, 1996); (3) power relations within and across cultural groups (Luykx, 1996); and (4) the dialectic between structural (macro-level) features and individual agency (Holland & Eisenhart, 1990). Practice theory explores how historical persons are formed in practice, within and against larger societal forces and structures. These structures provide the (tacitly understood) framework that governs the functioning of schools, as well as other social institutions.

By focusing on the dialectic between structure and agency, practice theory gives equal weight to macro-level structures (e.g., gender, class, race) and micro-level factors (e.g., an individual's agency and capacity to resist). From this perspective, culture is seen not as a set of characteristics as it is in cultural difference theory, but rather as a process, continually being constructed in practice. Individuals are not seen as passively accepting the conditions in which they live and function. Instead, they are given agency to counter the determining structures, though they must still do so while functioning within those structures. Through agency, individuals may have the opportunity to create a different vision for the culture in which they function, and ultimately, act on that vision in ways that challenge the status quo. However, at the same time, there are pressures on the individual to conform to the culture as currently practiced.

A consideration of practice theory gives rise to the need for a sixth principle in our sociocultural model: awareness of cultural productions. As stated above, cultural productions are the actions that individuals take both within and against the cultural confines in which they find themselves. This perspective implies that each CLDE student will react in different ways to his or her particular academic and social settings. Students from nearly identical cultural backgrounds may react to their school environment in different ways based on a range of factors, including their interpretation of the power structure in place in the classroom or school, their interactions and place in the social hierarchy of their peer group, or the opinion of the value of education held by individual family members.

Given these individual idiosyncrasies, each student will determine the arenas in which he or she will attempt to conform to the culture of the classroom and school and those arenas in which he or she will resist the system. The importance of these avenues of resistance cannot be overstated, because it is through this resistance that transformation of the cultural norms that govern the education setting can occur.

Thus, awareness of cultural productions is an important principle in considering culturally compatible academic settings for CLDE students, because it calls into question the entire notion of cultural compatibility. Although there are, without question, certain cultural norms that will be found in the majority of the members of a given cultural group, the very nature of being a CLDE student means that one will be thrust into a dynamic cultural milieu that will challenge and alter the beliefs inherited from one's heritage culture. An awareness of cultural productions means that a teacher will not make assumptions about a student's academic needs, desires, or preferences based on cultural overgeneralizations. Rather, the teacher will attempt to get to know each student as an individual, to understand why the student accepts and rejects the aspects of the school's culture that he or she does, and perhaps even work with the student to transform those aspects of the social and academic setting that he or she opposes.

Teaching Implications: Teachers of CLDE students should recognize that optimal language learning occurs in a warm and welcoming environment. This means that the teacher should do everything possible to create a sociocultural environment in the classroom that is an extension of the history and culture of the student. A White, middle-class, English-only environment will be an obstacle to maximizing learning. This being the case, the teacher should select learning activities, language, and materials that are culturally and linguistically familiar to the student. The teacher should not expect all students to react the same way. Some students may find a particular culture-based lesson very meaningful and other students from the same culture may approach the same lesson or exercise with resistance, using their personal agency to express their own uniqueness or individuality.

BEST PRACTICES FOR SECOND LANGUAGE LEARNERS

Next we want to focus on some of the specific practices that are beneficial to a wide range of students and that are consistent with the theories of second language acquisition described above, as well as with the sociocultural model of teaching. From the perspective of this model, every student brings to the classroom a wide range of prior skills and knowledge. To take advantage of this rich background, as well as to provide students with the skills and knowledge that they need to be successful in our schools, teachers must focus on authentic and meaningful language use. Authentic language use takes place when students are active participants in language use focusing on topics that are meaningful to them and are related to their own family and cultural background.

One important factor in fostering authentic language usage is to focus on the social organization of the classroom. Research with CLD students (Garcia, 1991; Miramontes, Nadeau, & Commins, 1998) demonstrates the importance of teachers making the shift from the traditional classroom model where the desks are in straight rows and the teacher is in front to a model of classroom organization emphasizing student centers and a mixture of guided, group, and independent work. Not surprisingly, the same organizational models have been shown to be successful with dominant culture students as well (Resnick, 1987a, 1987b). When such a shift in social organization occurs, it is almost impossible for teachers not to change their pedagogy to one that is more closely aligned with the sociocultural model of teaching and learning.

Assessment of the following conditions can be used to provide a rough estimate of whether a school is providing an adequate learning environment for CLD students that is aligned with what we know about best practices:

1. Classrooms should be student-centered and offer a nonthreatening environment that is informal and literature-rich.
2. Classroom climate should be comfortable in terms of space, temperature, and freedom from distractions, and offer access to technology, curriculum, and supplies that allow for plentiful and appropriate learning choices.

TABLE 3.3 Checklist of Recommended Practices for Teachers of CLDE Students	
Practice Questions	**Yes/No**
Do I focus on authentic and meaningful language use in my classroom?	
Do I introduce topics in my classroom discussion that are related to my students' home life and culture?	
Is my classroom organized in such a way that it promotes cooperative learning and authentic language use among my students?	
Is my classroom environment nonthreatening, informal, and literature-rich?	
Do I support native language use both at home and in the classroom to the fullest extent possible?	
Do I use comprehensible English throughout the curriculum?	
Do I use ESL strategies, including sheltered English, in my classroom?	

3. To be equitable, CLD students should be participating in all activities the school offers including honors classes, programs for the gifted and talented, and all manner of extracurricular activities.

Teaching Implications: The information covered above has important implications for special education teachers working with second language learners. Most important is the understanding that native language support, development, and instruction are practices that are helpful to the second language learner and are supported by research. This means that the special education teacher should use the child's native language for instruction whenever possible. Because this is not always the case, the special education teacher should encourage the parents to continue using the native language at home and use a bilingual paraprofessional to work with the student in his or her native language to the extent possible. Finally, the special education teacher should focus on using comprehensible input in English throughout the curriculum (see Table 3.3). This means that the special education teacher should learn more about English as a second language (ESL) techniques and strategies, including the use of sheltered English, which will be discussed in the next chapter.

SUMMARY

In this chapter we have briefly defined language and discussed language learning and the exceptional child. We have outlined the most important aspects of first and second language acquisition along with some of the prevalent fallacies regarding second language acquisition. A sociocultural model of second language acquisition was presented, and an overview of the best practices for second language learners was introduced. The implications for teachers of CLDE students were addressed throughout the various sections of the chapter.

Discussion Questions

1. Why is language such a difficult concept to define and explain?
2. Why is the distinction between language acquisition and language learning important?
3. Why do some people mistakenly think that a student with a disability is not capable of learning a second language?
4. Why is it important for a special education teacher to develop a personal theory relative to first and second language acquisition?
5. What are some of the similarities and differences regarding first and second language acquisition and what are the implications for special education teachers?
6. What are some of the common fallacies regarding second language acquisition and how can you as a teacher use this information?
7. Discuss Tharp's principles for effective teaching and learning and why they are important in every special education classroom.

References

Baca, L., Almanza De Schonewise, E., & Vanchu-Orosco, M. (2004). Teaching English language learners with disabilities in an English-only environment: A pilot study. *NABE News, 27*(5).

Chomsky, N. (1957). *Syntactic structures.* The Hague: Mouton.

Collier, V. P. (1995). *Acquiring a second language for school.* Directions in Language & Education. National Clearinghouse for Bilingual Education, Vol. 1, No. 4.

Cummins, J. (1979). Cognitive/academic language proficiency, linguistic interdependence, the optimal age question and some other matters. *Working Papers on Bilingualism, 19*, 197–205.

Cummins, J. (1989). A theoretical framework for bilingual special education. *Exceptional Children, 56*(2), 111–119.

D'Amato, J. D., & Tharp, R. G. (1997). *Culturally compatible educational strategies: Implications for native Hawaiian vocational education programs.* Honolulu, HI: Center for Studies of Multicultural Higher Education.

De Valenzuela, J., & Niccolai, S. L. (2004). Language development in culturally and linguistically diverse students with special education needs. In L. Baca & H. Cervantes (Eds.), *The bilingual special education interface.* Upper Saddle River, NJ: Merrill/Prentice Hall.

Eisenhart, M., & Graue, M. (1993). Constructing cultural difference and educational achievement in schools. In E. Jacob & C. Jordan (Eds.), *Minority education: Anthropological perspective* (pp. 165–179). Norwood, NJ: Ablex Publishing.

Garcia, E. E. (1991). *Education of linguistically and culturally diverse students: Effective instructional practices.* Santa Cruz, CA: National Center for Research on Cultural Diversity and Second Language Learning.

Geertz, C. (1973). Thick description: Toward an interpretive theory of culture. In C. Geertz (Ed.), *The interpretation of culture* (pp. 3–30). New York: Basic Books.

Genishi, C. (1981). Language across the contexts of early childhood. *Theory into Practice, 20*, no. 2, 109–115.

Heath, S. B. (1983). *Ways with words: Language, life and work in communities and classrooms.* Cambridge, England: Cambridge University Press.

Holland, D., & Eisenhart, M. (1990). *Educated in romance: Women, achievement and college culture.* Chicago, IL: University of Chicago Press.

Jameson, J. (1998). Three principles for success with English language learners in mainstream content classes. *From Theory to Practice,* no. 6. Tampa, FL: Center for Applied Statistics, Region XIV Comprehensive Center.

Krashen, S. D. (1981). *Second language acquisition and second language learning.* Oxford: Pergamon.

Levinson, B. A. (1996). Social difference and schooled identity at a Mexican secundaria. In B. A. Levinson, D. E. Foley, & D. Holland (Eds.), *The cultural production of the educated person: Critical ethnographies of schooling and local practice* (pp. 211–238). Albany: State University of New York Press.

Levinson, B. A., & Holland, D. (1996). The cultural production of the educated person: An introduction. In B. A. Levinson, D. E. Foley, & D. Holland (Eds.), *The cultural production of the educated person: Critical ethnographies of schooling and local practice* (pp. 1–54). Albany: State University of New York Press.

Lindholm, K. J., & Padilla, A. M. (1978). Language mixing in bilingual children. *Journal of Child Language, 5,* 327–335.

Luykx, A. (1996). From indios to profesionales: Stereotypes and student resistance in Bolivian teacher training. In B. A. Levinson, D. E. Foley, & D. Holland (Eds.), *The cultural production of the educated person: Critical ethnographies of schooling and local practice* (pp. 239–272). Albany: State University of New York Press.

Malherbe, E. (1969). Commentary to N. M. Jones: How and when do persons become bilingual. In L. Kelley (Ed.), *Description and measurement of bilingualism* (p. 78). Toronto: University of Toronto Press.

McLaughlin, B. (1985). *Second language acquisition in childhood: Vol. 2 School-age children* (2nd ed.). Hillsdale, NJ: Lawrence Erlbaum.

Mehan, H. (1993). Beneath the skin and between the ears: A case study in the politics of representation. In S. Chaiklin & J. Lave (Eds.), *Understanding practice: Perspectives on activity and context* (pp. 241–268). Cambridge, England: Cambridge University Press.

Meisel, J. M. (1987). Early differentiation of languages in bilingual children. In K. Hyltenstam & L. K. Obler (Eds.), *Bilingualism across the lifespan: Aspects of development, maturity and loss* (pp. 13–40). New York: Cambridge University Press.

Merino, B. J. (1982). Order and pace of syntactic development of bilingual children. In J. A. Fishman & G. D. Keller (Eds.), *Bilingual education for Hispanic students in the United States* (pp. 446–464). New York: Teachers College Press.

Minick, N. (1993). Teacher's directives: The social construction of "literal meanings" and "real worlds" in classroom discourse. In S. Chaiklin & J. Lave (Eds.), *Understanding practice: Perspectives on activity and context* (pp. 343–374). Cambridge, England: Cambridge University Press.

Miramontes, O., Nadeau, A., & Commins, N. (1998). *Restructuring schools for linguistic diversity: Linking decision making to effective planning.* New York: Teachers College Press.

Moll, L., Amanti, C., Neff, D., & Gonzalez, N. (1992). Funds of knowledge for teaching: Using a qualitative approach to connect homes and classrooms. *Theory into Practice, 2,* 132–141.

Resnick, L. (1987a). *Education and learning to think.* Washington, DC: National Academy Press.

Resnick, L. (1987b). Learning in school and out. *Educational Researcher,* 13–20.

Saussure, F. (1959). *Course in general linguistics* (Wade Baskin, Trans.). New York: McGraw-Hill. (Original work published 1916)

Saville-Troike, M. (1984). What *really* matters in second language learning for academic achievement? *TESOL Quarterly, 18*(2), 199–219.

Saville-Troike, M. (1988). Private speech: Evidence for second language learning strategies during the "silent" period. *Journal of Child Language, 15,* 567–590.

Scotton, C. M., & Ury, W. (1977). Bilingual strategies: The social functions of code switching. *Linguistics, 193,* 5–20.

Skinner, B. F. (1957). *Verbal behavior.* New York: Appleton-Century-Crofts.

Tharp, R. G. (1997). *From at-risk to excellence: Research, theory, and principles for practice* (Research Report 1). Santa Cruz, CA: Center for Research on Education, Diversity and Excellence.

Tharp, R. G., & Dalton, S. (1994). Principles for culturally compatible Native American education. *Journal of Navajo Education, XL* (Spring), 21–27.

Tharp, R. G., & Gallimore, R. (1988). *Rousing minds to life: Teaching, learning, and schooling in social context.* Cambridge, England: Cambridge University Press.

Wong Fillmore, L. (1991a). Second language learning in children: A model of language learning in social context. In E. Bialystok (Ed.), *Language processing in bilingual children.* Cambridge: Cambridge University Press.

Wong Fillmore, L. (1991b). When learning a second language means losing the first. *Early Childhood Research Quarterly, 6,* 323–346.

PART II

Culturally Competent Instruction and Classroom Management

Chapter 4

Instructional Models and Technology for Teaching CLDE Students

Chapter Objectives

Upon completion of this chapter the reader will be able to:

1. Provide a historical context for bilingual/ESL special education.
2. Discuss bilingual education goals and models.
3. Present bilingual education methods.
4. Introduce English as a second language (ESL).
5. Present English as a second language (ESL) models.
6. Discuss a range of ESL methods.
7. Provide bilingual/ESL special education strategies.
8. Review bilingual/ESL special education models.
9. Discuss available technology for working with CLDE students.

VIGNETTE

When Jose Garcia, a recent immigrant from Mexico, was placed in Mrs. Peterson's fourth-grade class in Utah halfway into the school year, Mrs. Peterson wanted to be sure she provided Jose with an effective educational environment. From her experiences working with other children whose families had recently emigrated from Mexico, Mrs. Peterson recognized the importance of creating a learning environment that was biculturally and bilingually inclusive for her students. However, since Mrs. Peterson's class was not bilingual, but rather all instruction was conducted in English, Jose was placed in an ESL pullout program where he received English language instruction and a minimal amount of supplementary assistance in the content areas. Mrs. Peterson, a bilingual English and Spanish speaker, often worked one-on-one with Jose while he was in her classroom, repeating parts of lessons in Spanish and informally assessing Jose's understanding of the content material. Mrs. Peterson noticed that Jose was struggling with the material, even with the additional assistance he received from her and from his ESL instructor, Mr. Stefano. Although Jose seemed quite comfortable with the material when it was presented orally by Mrs. Peterson and Mr. Stefano, he demonstrated quite a bit of difficulty when asked to read the material, whether in Spanish or English. Following several conferences between Mrs. Peterson and Mr. Stefano regarding Jose's progress, the two decided to have Jose evaluated by the school's prereferral team.

In their district, the Teacher Assistance Child Intervention Team (TACIT) process is used to best meet the needs of CLDE learners. The first step involved building the team. Mrs. Peterson, as the classroom teacher, and Mr. Stefano, as the ESL instructor, were the first team members. A bilingual special education consultant and a child psychologist were also included. Jose's parents were also invited to the team meetings to provide their insight into Jose's learning and progress at home. Once the team was formed, they began to gather information about Jose's learning experiences, identifying those areas and contexts in which he appeared most successful and those areas and contexts in which he seemed to struggle the most. With the help of Jose's parents, the team was also able to contact Jose's school in Mexico and speak with one of Jose's former teachers who explained that although Jose demonstrated strengths in oral expression and listening comprehension, there was a large discrepancy between his ability in those areas and basic reading skills and reading comprehension. This discrepancy, as observed by Mrs. Peterson and Mr. Stefano, and confirmed by his teacher in Mexico and the other members of the intervention team, led the team to suspect that

The authors wish to acknowledge Amy Saks for her assistance in developing this vignette.

Jose might have a learning disability. Jose was then referred for special education assessment. In the meantime the team recognized both his needs as a second language learner and his needs as a student with a possible learning disability. They decided to keep Jose in the regular classroom and his ESL pullout program, but also made modifications to both to better meet his needs. In identifying interventions that Mrs. Petersen and Mr. Stefano should implement when working with Jose, the team selected modeling processes and strategies and presenting information in multiple ways. Once the implementations were identified, Mrs. Peterson and Mr. Stefano began to use them in their work with Jose. For example, when teaching addition using counting blocks, Mrs. Peterson used instructional conversations where she talked through her thinking process so that process became visible to Jose and the other students. She then worked one-on-one with Jose and presented the concept using role-playing. After 2 weeks of implementing the interventions, and again after 1 month, the team met to evaluate how successful the implementations were. Mrs. Peterson, Mr. Stefano, Jose's parents, and the rest of the team agreed that modeling processes and strategies and presenting information in multiple ways were working well in meeting Jose's needs as an English language learner. Together, the team documented the consultation, agreed to continue implementing the interventions, and exited TACIT.

Reflective Questions

1. As a teacher of an ELL student with special needs, how would you use the strategy of instructional conversation mentioned above?
2. How does the prereferral system work in your school? How effective is it in meeting the needs of ELLs with special needs?

INTRODUCTION

This chapter reviews the historical context out of which instructional methods and strategies for second language learners developed. Instructional models and approaches including bilingual education, English as a second language and bilingual special education are explained. Technology resources for working with second language learners are also presented.

HISTORICAL CONTEXT FOR SPECIAL EDUCATION AND ENGLISH LANGUAGE LEARNERS

About 50 years ago the field of special education was in a rapid growth stage. The All Handicapped Children's Act of 1974 was challenging educators to find every child with a disability and bring them into the public school system. Full services for all children with disabilities was an ambitious goal at that time. As special education expanded rapidly to meet the needs of all these students, some noted that many of the students going into special education were minority students from culturally and linguistically different (CLD) backgrounds (Dunn, 1968; Mercer, 1973; Presidents Committee on Mental Retardation, 1969). In effect, a problem of overrepresentation of minority students in special education was rapidly developing. This development prompted leaders in the field as well as national organizations to respond with various initiatives.

The American Association on Mental Deficiency reexamined the definition of mental retardation in 1974 and revised it so that the cutoff score on the IQ test criteria would be changed from one to two standard deviations. This meant that an IQ cutoff score of 85 was changed to 70 as one of the criteria for the classification of educable mentally retarded. The association also stated that impairment in adaptive behavior would also be required for classifying a student as mentally retarded. In 1973 the Council for Exceptional Children sponsored its first national conference on Cultural Diversity and Special Education. These initiatives were all aimed at examining the problem of overrepresentation and proposing solutions to the problem.

While these reforms were underway, professionals in the special education community also began to point out that some of these CLD students did have bona fide disabilities, but that their special education teachers did not have the language background and expertise to serve them appropriately. This being the case, they argued, the new federal law requiring a free and appropriate education for all handicapped students was not being complied with, because the curriculum and teaching methods were all in English and were based on a White, middle-class perspective.

In 1973, the field of bilingual special education emerged (Baca & Cervantes, 2004). Bilingual special education includes a bilingual multicultural approach along with advocacy for the integration of ESL. The primary purpose of an ESL special education program is to help each individual student achieve his or her maximum potential.

BILINGUAL EDUCATION: GOALS AND MODELS

Before moving into a discussion of bilingual/ESL special education, it is important to first have some basic understanding of bilingual education and the various bilingual programs and models that have been developed over the last 35 years. Although bilingual education is a long-standing and worldwide phenomenon, it wasn't until 1968 and the passage of the Bilingual Education Act that bilingual education became an integral part of our federal education policy. There is general agreement regarding the definition of bilingual education: "the use of two languages as media of instruction." The academic literature refers to the two languages as L1, which refers to the native language, and L2, which refers to English. Nonetheless, bilingual education is controversial and has become a hotly debated political issue. Strong opposition to bilingual education has come from the English-only movement. This movement has been successful in passing English-only legislation in 24 states, including California and Arizona. The English-only advocates argue that this is America and everyone should speak English and that the schools should not allow or promote bilingualism.

When one steps outside of the political arena and looks at bilingual education strictly as an education issue, a very different picture emerges. A strong majority of the research done on monolingual education versus bilingual education has shown that bilingual education is the most effective vehicle for improving the academic achievement of English language learners (ELLs). It has also shown that bilingual education is the most efficient way of helping children learn English. Ramirez (1991) traced the progress of more than 2,000 Spanish-speaking ELLs in nine school districts in five states over a 4-year period. They found that students in developmental bilingual programs—which feature a gradual transition to English—significantly outperformed their counterparts in quick-exit, transitional bilingual programs and in all-English immersion programs when all three groups were tested in English. Oller and Eilers (2002) compared 952 students in Dade County, Florida, enrolled in bilingual and English immersion programs. They reported that bilingual children scored higher in English literacy by second grade. Thomas and Collier (2002) confirmed the patterns reported by Ramirez and colleagues; ELLs in Houston did better academically in programs that stressed native-language development. They fared best in two-way dual immersion programs in which English-speaking children learned Spanish alongside ELLs learning English.

Bilingual education is not one unique and specific program; it is a general term that describes a wide variety of programs with different goals, models, and methods. For example, some bilingual programs promote biliteracy whereas others do not. Some programs separate the two languages and others mix them and use them side-by-side. Some programs may be remedial and others may be developmental. Cazden and Snow (1990) have summed this up well when they said that "bilingual education is a simple label for a complex phenomenon" (p. 126). The field of bilingual education uses many acronyms that may be somewhat confusing. The federal law refers to the bilingual student as limited English proficient (LEP), whereas most scholars refer to these same students as English language learners (ELLs), which is different from English as a second language (ESL).

What exactly are, or should be, the goals of bilingual education? This is an extremely important question because the answer one gives to this question establishes the philosophy of the program and gives direction to the program. Leaders in bilingual education maintain that the primary goal of bilingual education is the cognitive and affective development of the student (Blanco, 1977; Baca & Baca, 2006). However, when the language and cultural goals are made primary, the argument becomes more political. Legislators, for example, might argue that the primary purpose of bilingual education is to teach English as soon as possible and transition bilingual students into the mainstream of education. On the other hand, parents might say that the main purpose of bilingual education should be to maintain the native language and culture. This confusion regarding the primary goals of the bilingual program is what leads to the political controversy and such opposition as the English-only movement.

A variety of program models and methodologies have been proposed. A *transitional* or early exit bilingual program is one that uses the native language and culture of the student only to the extent necessary for the child to learn English and be able to function in the regular school curriculum. A *maintenance* or late exit bilingual program promotes biliteracy and the maintenance of the native language and culture. A bilingual *restoration* program is one that attempts to restore a native language that is gradually being lost such as one of the many Native American languages. Finally, a bilingual *enrichment* program is one that seeks to add a new language to a group of monolingual students as an enrichment to their overall education. An example of this would be a bilingual program for gifted, English-speaking students.

Teaching Implications: As a special education teacher of CLDE students, you must know as much as possible about your students' former and current educational environment. Some of your students' current regular classroom placements may be in bilingual programs. You should be aware of the type of program that they are receiving and the goals of that program. Likewise if your CLDE students have been exposed to bilingual education in the past, you need to know the type of program they participated in. For example, you should know if literacy instruction was in English or in the native language. Was the goal of the program rapid transition to English or was it full literacy in both languages?

BILINGUAL METHODS FOR TEACHERS OF ENGLISH LANGUAGE LEARNERS

Bilingual teaching methods also vary from program to program depending on the philosophy of the program and the model being implemented. The most common dual language instruction methods are listed in Table 4.1.

Two main factors influence the type of method selected for instruction. The first factor is the philosophy of the program. For example, if the program has adopted a language maintenance philosophy, the method would be total immersion. If the philosophy of the program was rapid transition, the method could be language separation. The second factor is language resources. If the teacher is only fluent in English, the method used could be the translation method using the help of a bilingual paraprofessional. On the other hand, if the teacher is bilingual, one of the other methods could be used.

TABLE 4.1 Bilingual Methods

Method	Key Features
Translation method	The monolingual teacher relies on a paraprofessional fluent in the native language. The paraprofessional translates what the teacher is saying to a small group of students.
Preview-review method	The teacher introduces the lesson in the native language, teaches it in English, and then reviews or summarizes it in the native language.
Alternate day method	The main objective is to separate the two languages by day or by subject matter.
Concurrent method	The teacher switches between the two languages on an ongoing and informal basis depending on student comprehension.
Eclectic method	The teacher uses a combination of two or more of the other methods listed here.
Total immersion	The teacher relies exclusively on the native language or English at first and then gradually introduces the second language.

ESL METHODS FOR TEACHERS OF ENGLISH LANGUAGE LEARNERS

ESL is not a bilingual method but it is an integral component of a good bilingual program. English as a second language is defined by Ovando, Collier, and Combs (2006), as follows:

> A system of instruction that enables students who are not proficient in English (English language learners) to acquire academic proficiency in spoken and written English, ESL is an essential component of all bilingual education programs in the United States for students who are English language learners. In addition, ESL classes taught through academic content are crucial for English language learners when first-language academic instruction is not feasible, as is the case in contexts where low-incidence language groups (too few speakers of one language for bilingual education to be provided) are present. ESL content (or sheltered) classes may be self-contained, or students may attend ESL content classes for part of the school day and participate in monolingual English instruction in grade-level classes (in the "mainstream") the remainder of the day. (p. 37)

There are a variety of approaches for teaching ESL. Usually these diverse approaches stem from the trends in language teaching, as it is approached by foreign language teaching. Before entering this discussion it is important to point out that ESL instruction in elementary and secondary schools must be presented in the context of child and adolescent development generally. In other words, English cannot be taught to ELLs in a vacuum but must be taught in the context of social, academic, and cognitive development since they all occur simultaneously. Thomas and Collier (1997) describe this broader context well through the use of their Prism Model of language acquisition. They maintain that there is a constant and simultaneous interaction among the four components of social, academic, cognitive, and language development. The student in a school setting is going through a complex sociocultural process that involves family, community, and school environments as he or she learns a second language. The student's anxiety level and self-concept are being affected by many variables, including prejudice, discrimination, family, and peer support. The language development that the student experiences includes both first and second language development and involves the many facets of language, including reading and writing as well as listening and speaking. While this is going on the student is also experiencing academic development as he or she learns in the various content areas. Academic development should never be delayed or sacrificed by focusing exclusively on language development.

The final component of the model involves cognitive development. The curriculum should always include and focus on cognitive development at the same time as language and academic development are being addressed. Some ESL models have neglected either academic or cognitive development in the past and thus the students have fallen behind the development of their peers. In the Prism Model, however, these four components are interdependent. If one is developed at the expense of the other, the student's overall growth will be hindered. Thus the teacher must structure the classroom and teaching environment to address all four areas simultaneously.

The most common ESL teaching models are listed in Table 4.2 and discussed in the following sections.

TABLE 4.2 ESL Methods

Method	Key Features
Traditional ESL	This is an adult model that is focused on teaching English and is not concerned with academic content.
Silent Way	Requires the teacher to be silent 90 percent of the time, thus encouraging students to generate language on their own.
Total Physical Response	The teacher gives oral commands and the students respond with body language.
Current ESL methods	These methods include an emphasis on cognitive and academic development.
Sheltered instruction	This method simplifies the language and uses realia to make it more comprehensible.
ESL in the content areas	Here the focus is on teaching English and academic content at the same time.

Traditional ESL Methods

English as a second language as a distinct discipline has traditionally focused on adult learners. For this reason, it has not always seen the need to incorporate academic and cognitive development. Thus when ESL was brought into the public schools to assist with the education of ELLs, it followed many aspects of the adult ESL approach as well as the foreign language teaching approach. The main characteristic of traditional ESL is that it was taught in isolation from the rest of the curriculum. It was highly structured, based on grammar structures, and did not focus on meaningful communicative competence. Some examples of this approach included the grammar-translation method, the audiolingual method, and the direct method. Fortunately, most schools have moved away from these traditional approaches and now integrate ESL with the rest of the curriculum.

As the field of ESL moved toward integration with the content areas of the curriculum, some traditional language teaching methods were used in this transitional period. Included here were methods such as the Silent Way, which required the teacher to be silent up to 90 percent of the time, thus encouraging students to generate language on their own (Gattengno, 1976). Other methods included Suggestopedia, an approach aimed at using the subconscious level of the learner (Lozanof, 1978), and the Total Physical Response (TPR) (Asher, 1982). With this approach the teacher gives commands and the students use physical movement in response.

The Natural Approach (Krashen & Terrell, 1983) comes closest to the current ESL approaches. This method puts an emphasis on the teacher simplifying the language to create "comprehensible input" that the student easily understands. It also emphasizes the creation of a low-anxiety environment and the use of natural and meaningful communication. Error correction is kept to a minimum.

Current ESL Methods

During the last decade, the influx of significant numbers of ELLs combined with current research on language learning has moved the profession forward to adopt ESL methods that incorporate some of the practices from the traditional ESL era with a better integrated use of ESL within the content areas and with emphasis on cognitive and academic development. Rather than ESL being taught as a separate disconnected subject, it is now integrated with the various academic areas, such as math and science. At the elementary level, schools hire teachers with ESL endorsement and training to teach in the regular classroom. At the high school level, ESL-trained teachers are also hired to teach ESL sections of history, science, math, and so forth. Current ESL approaches use what has been called *sheltered instruction*. This approach is based on the importance of comprehensible input. To achieve this, teachers use gestures, body language, visual aids, and demonstrations along with slower speech, simple sentences, controlled vocabulary, and frequent comprehension checks (Lessow-Hurley, 1996).

BILINGUAL/ESL SPECIAL EDUCATION

Not very many special education teachers have Spanish or other native language proficiency. However, when a teacher is fluent in the native language of the student and the student's ability in English is limited, a bilingual special education model should be implemented. If, on the other hand, the student is more proficient in English, an ESL approach should be used. Using the child's native language if it is more proficient than English is always the preferred strategy if at all possible. This would mean that in addition to using sheltered English as outlined above, the teacher would present the actual lessons in two languages. The languages would have to be separated according to a systematic plan based usually on subject matter or on days of the week or certain periods of the day. For example, reading could be taught in the native language and math could be taught in English, or English could be used on Mondays, Wednesdays, and Fridays and Spanish on Tuesdays and Thursdays. A concurrent method (alternating languages within a lesson as needed) could also be used but is not as highly recommended as a language separation model. Teachers interested in this approach should refer to a book entitled *The Bilingual Special Education Interface* (Baca & Cervantes, 2004).

STUDENT NEEDS

Much has been written about the needs of bilingual students with disabilities (Artilles & Ortiz, 2004). Rueda and Chan (1979) described them as the "triple threat students," having three major obstacles to contend with: the disability, the lack of English proficiency, and oftentimes the condition of living in poverty. Baca and Baca (2006) took a strengths-based approach and referred to them as students with three strengths to build on, namely, learning ability, native language, and native culture. Regardless of how they are described in the literature, the fact remains that a bilingual child with a disability has a range of cognitive, academic, and language learning needs that require careful planning and intervention on the part of special educators. Using a strengths-based model rather than a deficit model is important because it emphasizes high expectations for these students. The deficit model not only lowers expectations but also promotes learned helplessness and poor outcomes.

The challenge of meeting the needs of these students continues to increase as the number of bilingual students in the public schools expands dramatically each year. The latest estimate by Baca and Cervantes (2004) is that there are approximately 1,198,200 of these students in our schools today. Unfortunately, the number of teachers trained specifically to work with them is extremely limited.

TRAINING OPPORTUNITIES

There is not only a severe shortage of highly qualified teachers for this group of students, but also a serious shortage of training opportunities in U.S. colleges and universities. Although most of the major special education textbooks now include some information or a chapter on bilingual special education, as few as 12 institutions of higher education in the country today offer a specialized program, degree, or certification/endorsement in bilingual special education. In a recent meeting (January 2005) of the National Association of Bilingual Education, the Special Interest Group (SIG) discussed the possibility of sponsoring an online certificate in bilingual special education.

BILINGUAL/ESL SPECIAL EDUCATION MODELS

With the severe shortage of bilingual special education teachers nationwide, most schools have had to be creative in designing programs for ELLs in special education. The most obvious strategy has been to use collaboration and teamwork with the teachers and paraprofessional staff that are readily available. Ambert and Dew (1982) were the first to describe the following models.

Bilingual Support Model

The bilingual support model (see Figure 4.1) is the most basic and easiest to implement. It offers a minimal level of service and requires a monolingual special education teacher and a bilingual paraprofessional. Training and staff development are necessary as is planning time.

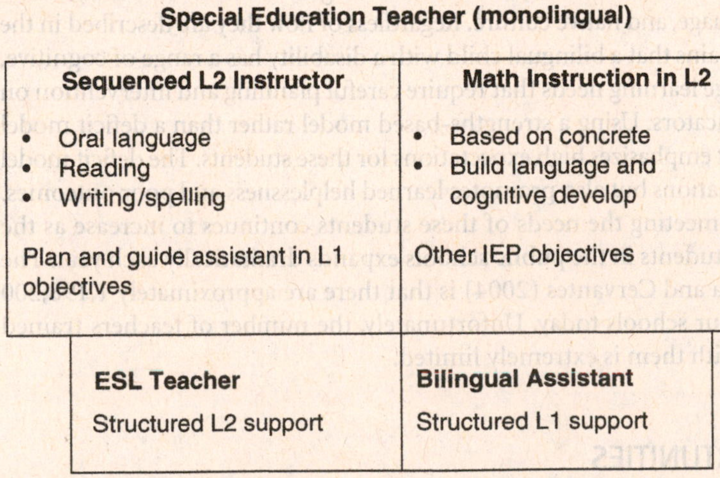

Special Education Teacher (monolingual)

Sequenced L2 Instructor	Math Instruction in L2
• Oral language • Reading • Writing/spelling Plan and guide assistant in L1 objectives	• Based on concrete • Build language and cognitive develop Other IEP objectives

ESL Teacher	Bilingual Assistant
Structured L2 support	Structured L1 support

FIGURE 4.1 Bilingual Support Model

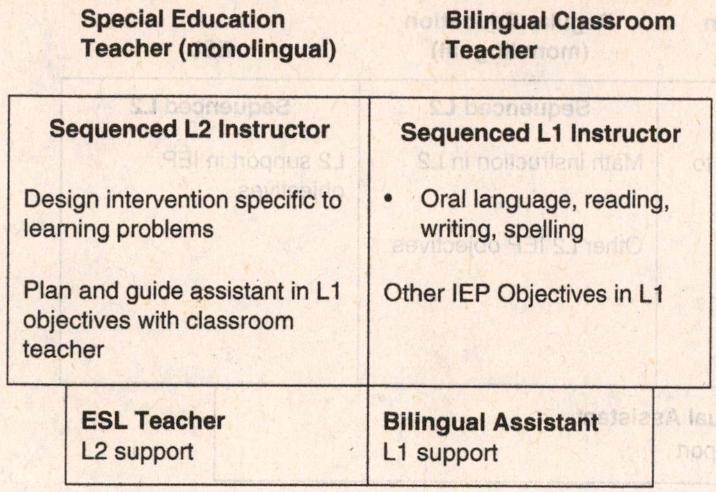

Special Education Teacher (monolingual)	Bilingual Classroom Teacher
Sequenced L2 Instructor Design intervention specific to learning problems Plan and guide assistant in L1 objectives with classroom teacher	**Sequenced L1 Instructor** • Oral language, reading, writing, spelling Other IEP Objectives in L1
ESL Teacher L2 support	**Bilingual Assistant** L1 support

FIGURE 4.2 Coordinated Services Model

Coordinated Services Model

The coordinated services model (see Figure 4.2) is considered more effective than the support model because it uses the services of two fully certified teachers. It also requires training and staff development so that both teachers understand the language and disability needs of the students and have ample time to plan and coordinate their services.

Collaborative Services Model

The collaborative services model (see Figure 4.3) is similar to the coordinated services model but involves more people, including the regular classroom teacher as well as the ESL teacher. Planning and coordination are more difficult because of the difficulty of finding a convenient time for planning.

Integrated Bilingual Special Education Model

The integrated bilingual special education model (see Figure 4.4) is considered the best and most comprehensive model because it uses a bilingual special education teacher who is trained in both fields and able to deliver the services independently.

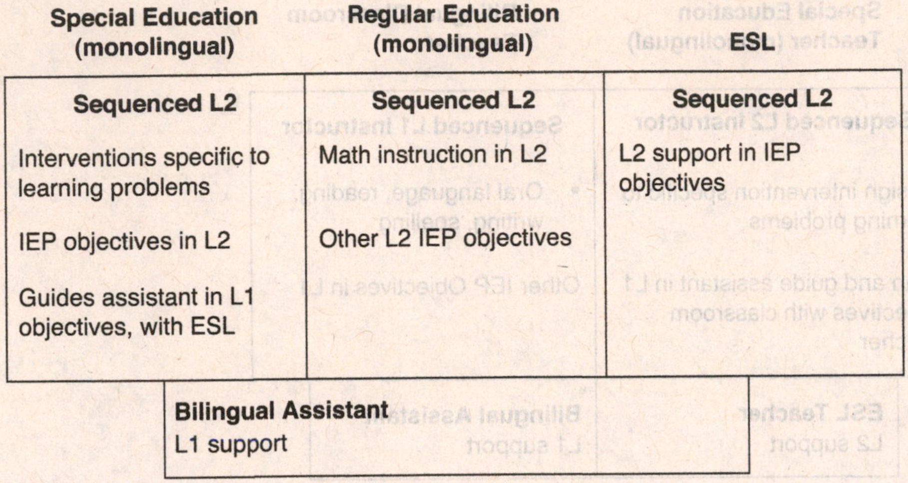

Special Education (monolingual)   **Regular Education (monolingual)**   **ESL**

Sequenced L2	Sequenced L2	Sequenced L2
Interventions specific to learning problems	Math instruction in L2	L2 support in IEP objectives
IEP objectives in L2	Other L2 IEP objectives	
Guides assistant in L1 objectives, with ESL		

Bilingual Assistant
L1 support

FIGURE 4.3 Collaborative Services Model

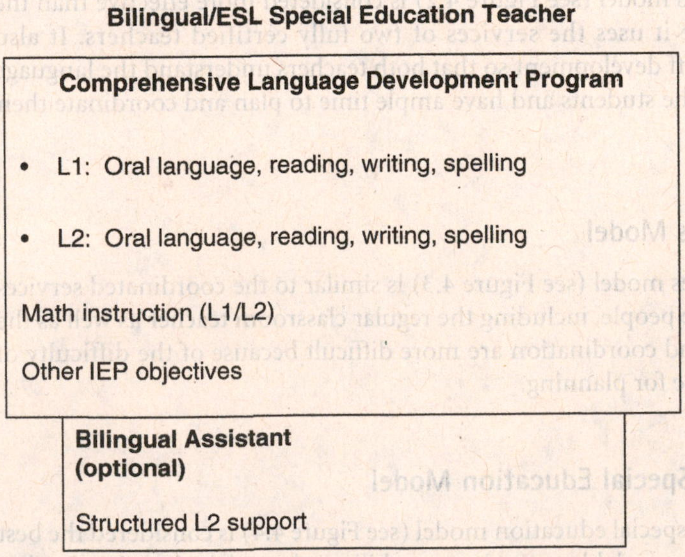

Bilingual/ESL Special Education Teacher

Comprehensive Language Development Program

- L1: Oral language, reading, writing, spelling

- L2: Oral language, reading, writing, spelling

Math instruction (L1/L2)

Other IEP objectives

Bilingual Assistant (optional)

Structured L2 support

FIGURE 4.4 Integrated Bilingual/ESL Special Education Model

TABLE 4.3 Characteristics of Bilingual/ESL Special Education Models

Models	Characteristics
Bilingual support model	This is a minimal and weak model and should be used only when a bilingual teacher is not available.
Coordinated services model	This is a good team-teaching model with both teachers working in the same classroom.
Collaborative services model	This model provides pull-out services and requires mutual planning.
Integrated bilingual special education model	This is a self-contained model and requires a highly trained, masters-level bilingual special education teacher.

Any of these models can be adopted and adjusted as necessary to be implemented in a school. The special education teachers in the building should meet with the principal and choose a model that best fits the needs of their special education students and the personnel available in the building. The adoption of a model should be a well thought-out and conscious choice rather than a passive acceptance of the status quo or default decision. Table 4.3 provides a summary of these models.

TEACHING STRATEGIES FOR ELLs WITH DISABILITIES

As a special education teacher working with ELLs with disabilities, one of your first options is to work collaboratively with your building's bilingual or ESL specialist. Through team teaching and/or consultation, you will be able to better meet the needs of your ELLs. This collaboration can also help you build your own expertise in using ESL and sheltered English techniques on your own. If you have no access to ESL professional collaboration in your building, you will have to seek out additional ESL training and use the information and suggestions presented here or in other appropriate texts. As a special education teacher, you already know about individualizing instruction and adapting the curriculum to accommodate the specific disability of the student. This same technique of adaptation and individualization is required relative to the English language learning needs of your students. Using sheltered English techniques is similar to what you already do in terms of adaptation. One could say that you are already sheltering for the disability and now you have to shelter for the English language learning needs of your student. In effect you will be "sheltering" for both the language and the disability.

Sheltered English requires the use of as much visual support as possible, including real-life objects, pictures, photographs, and illustrations. Hands-on manipulatives and various types of learning kits with materials are highly recommended. Various types of demonstrations should be used, from concrete examples such as constructing a terrarium to more abstract demonstrations such as modeling step-by-step the writing of a book report. When content is too difficult or too abstract, it should be adapted and made more comprehensible. Graphic organizers such as story maps, Venn diagrams, word maps, or timelines should be prepared ahead of time to serve as scaffolds for the English language learner. Other important adaptations include identifying and teaching key vocabulary words, highlighting essential text, and tape recording parts of the lesson for the student to listen to as he or she follows along in the textbook.

Another helpful resource is the use of the Sheltered Instruction Observation Protocol (SIOP). This protocol was developed by researchers at the Center for Research on Education, Diversity and Excellence (CREDE) at the University of California at Santa Cruz (Echevarria, Vogt, & Short, 2004). This protocol allows you, as the teacher, to review your lesson plan to ensure that you are indeed using optimal sheltered English techniques. The protocol is made up of the 30 items that are ranked on a Likert scale from 0, Not Evident, to 4, Highly Evident, such as:

- Content objectives clearly defined
- Language objectives clearly defined
- Student background and concepts being taught are clearly linked
- Various teaching techniques should be used to help students acquire concepts
- Adapt content as necessary to meet various student proficiency levels
- Implement instructions using hands-on materials/manipulatives when teaching new concepts

For additional information see Echevarria, Vogt, and Short (2004).

The special education teacher can rate his or her own lesson plans using the SIOP questions or a peer teacher can be invited in to observe a lesson and fill out the instrument. When the overall average scores are between 3 and 4, one can be assured that high-quality sheltered English instruction is being used. When the scores are at the low end of the scale, the teacher can go back to the planning stage and build in more effective language learning supports.

TECHNOLOGY AND STUDENTS WITH DISABILITIES

The advances that have been made in technology in recent years present educators with many additional resources for teaching and learning. This explosion of growth in technology has made technology more affordable and accessible to most schools and families. CLDE students stand to benefit from the incorporation of these new advances in technology in their classrooms. Some educators have gone so far as to say that technology can be viewed as a "cognitive prosthesis" for students with disabilities (Lewis, 1998). Regardless of how we view technology, it is clear that technology can be useful to both the teacher and the student.

TABLE 4.4 Technology Options for Students with Learning Disabilities

Barriers	Difficulties	Technology Solution
Print	Reading	Talking computers; Semantic mapping software
	Writing	Web-based texts
		Word-processing programs
		Desktop-publishing
		Computer-based thesauruses
	Spelling	Word prediction software
		Spell-checkers
Communication	Organization	Voice input devices manipulating graphics
		PowerPoint
		E-mail
	Speech	Voice output systems
		Synthesized speech
Solving problems	Calculating	Computer calculators
Being organized	Daily life	Spreadsheet software
		Personal organizers
		Electronic calendars
		Computer stickies
		Electronic address books
	Study skills	Organizing software
		Timing devices
Learning	Researching topics	CD-ROM reference books
		Internet databases
	Remembering	Outlining systems

Source: Adapted from Smith (2001).

Many types of technology could be discussed here, but the single most important one is the use of the computer and computer-related technology. Table 4.4 outlines how many student barriers can be overcome in different academic areas through the use of technology.

The use of the computer can be especially helpful when working with CLD students. They can now access a wide variety of programs and software aimed at helping them with their English language development. Many of the earlier computer-assisted language learning (CALL) programs were heavily focused on drill and practice exercises. These programs were not helpful and were inconsistent with current language learning theory and its emphasis on meaningful and natural communication. The advances made in the more current language learning software are much more interactive in nature and allow opportunities for the student to practice both the speaking and writing of English. What is still lacking in many of these programs is the integration of language teaching with the content areas of the curriculum.

SPECIFIC TECHNOLOGIES FOR CLDE STUDENTS

Many new technologies are being developed for special education students. These same technologies could easily be adapted to work with CLDE students. The following list from the Information Access Library (1998) are examples of the technologies currently being developed and utilized.

Haptic Visualization – intended to make multidimensional mathematical concepts accessible to visually impaired individuals through haptic and multimodal scientific visualization. Current development focuses on utilizing the Phantom haptic interface in conjunction with sonification methodologies to develop a multiresolution multimodal visualization interface.

Tactile Image Processing – intended to provide visually impaired individuals access to image based information through tactile rendering of images. Such rendering transforms color and gray scale images into a binary format that can be displayed on a tactile device, such as microcapsule paper, and manually explored. Current work focuses on the development of multiresolution edge extraction algorithms and texture analysis.

Virtual Instruments – intended to provide improved access to computer controlled laboratory instruments. Current work focuses on developing speech and audio interfaces for LabVIEW controlled instruments. Additionally, remote access methods are being developed to allow Web based control of laboratory experiments and the creation of a virtual laboratory.

Classroom Speechreading Aid – intended to provide hearing impaired individuals continuous visual access to an educator's lips in an everyday classroom setting where lighting, positioning, background noise, and other conditions may hinder perception. In this system, live video of the educator's lips is provided through a heads up display or a small desktop monitor. Research includes speechreading and multimodal studies, pilot testing, and further development of the system.

Sign Language Video Communications – intended to provide the deaf and hard of hearing individuals the ability to communicate through gestures and sign language over telephone line and Internet connections. MPEG-4 content-based coding techniques are being developed to allow perceptually improved transmission of high motion sign language sequences over low bandwidth channels. Further development is focusing on real-time, two-way sign language video conferencing over low bandwidth channels with effective picture quality.

Animated Sign Language for Literacy – intended to investigate and understand the relationship of animated sign language and language acquisition and literacy with an emphasis on multimedia applications in an educational environment. One application of particular interest under development is that of a signed closed caption system for broadcast television.

Speech to Braille Computer Interpreter – intended to equip deaf-blind individuals with a means for communicating without the assistance of an interpreter. While interpreters are often available for formal events, such as classes, they are not always available for less structured learning situations like group study and informal discussion, or tutoring and mentoring. Current work focuses on combining speech recognition technologies with Braille displays to allow interpreter free communications.

Today's classrooms include learners with a variety of needs and abilities; thus, CLDE teachers need to be sure that all students have access to not just the same content, but also the technology needed to facilitate, supplement, and enhance learning. With just a few free computer-based tools and online resources, almost any student can use technology successfully.

Many of the tools and technology devices that are available for students with special needs are available on the Internet. Jackson (2005) provides the following information in this regard.

Accessibility on a PC

Click Programs > Accessories > Accessibility in START > or go to Accessibility Options in the Control Panel to find these Windows tools:

Narrator: This tool for the visually impaired reads aloud (in English only) all windows and text.

On-Screen Keyboard: Users with physical limitations can open a window, Education World® Save Time with Macros, containing a keyboard layout and then use the mouse to type on that keyboard.

Magnifier: This tool for the visually impaired increases font and graphic size, and inverts text colors (changing white to black, for example).

Sticky Keys: With this tool, for users with limited hand or finger movement, keys such as SHIFT or ALT can be pressed once rather than held down for commands or typing.

Filter Keys: Students whose disabilities may cause them to type extra keystrokes will benefit from this tool, which eliminates extra characters or symbols.

For more tools and resources, go to Microsoft's Accessibility Technology for Everyone.

Accessibility on a MAC

The following tools can be found in the Apple System Preferences folder:

Speech Recognition: Users can speak commands—such as "Quit Microsoft Word"—instead of clicking a mouse or entering keyboard commands.

Text-to-Speech: This tool reads aloud alerts (and documents in some applications). A Spanish version also is available.

Close View: Magnify text and graphics with this tool.

Mouse Keys: With this tool, users with fine motor disabilities can operate the mouse using keys on the numeric keypad.

Sticky Keys: Users with limited hand or finger movement can press keys—such as SHIFT or ALT—once, rather than holding them down

Slow Keys: Students whose disabilities might cause them to type extra keystrokes will benefit from this tool, which eliminates extra characters or symbols.

Visual Alerts: Users with hearing disabilities can use this tool to display alerts on the computer screen rather than through beeps or other sounds. (Go to Sound in the Control Panel to access the feature.)

Go to Apple's Accessibility page for more information about these and other tools.

Websites

There are also many helpful Websites that teachers and students can go to for additional help and resources with technology. Siegel Robertson (2005) lists the following Websites:

General Information

MarcoPolo is the best single site for teachers who are researching lesson plans and ideas. You can find material for different level students so the lessons can often be adapted to various student needs.

Education World provides information and inspiration to all K–12 educators in its articles, resources, templates, and more. Type Special Education or Gifted into the search engine and get a ton of information.

Internet4Classrooms With links for content area resources, an excellent mini-Web Quest template called a Web Guide, and wonderfully helpful webmasters (who are local master teacher trainers as well). I find their list of links of K–12 subjects easy to use and have the best online activities.

Teacher Tools

4Teachers Great teacher tools such as: Organize learning on the Web (Trickster), test students online (Quiz Star), have students narrow down a research topic (Think-Tank), post your own Web site (Web Worksheet Wizard), and send (Castanets).

Discovery Channel's School page is a wealth of info and free tools for the teacher. Quiz center tests your kids, Puzzle maker will create printable puzzles and games, Clip Art Gallery, BJ Pinchbeck's Homework Help, and Kathy Schrock's Guide for Educators. She has a *Special Education* page too.

Family Education Network has a little bit of everything from teacher tools to information but it is well known for fun online activities at Fun Brain.

Learning Disabilities
LDOnline is the leading Website on learning disabilities for parents, students, and educators.
LD Resources has a fairly comprehensive list of online sites for LD.
Online Books Search for the text or html version of over 10,000 books. Great for text to speech devices.
Internet Public Library has many resources for online materials including literature and reference materials.

Education Internet Examples:
Teacher Tools
Vivisimo
Puzzlemaker
TrackStar

Student Sites
Search Engines for Kids
Mightybook.com
Merriam-Webster Dictionary
Education 4 Kids
Power Proofreading
A+Math
FunBrain
Scholastic Online
Ancient Empires
Man's Best Friend: A Dog's Tale

SUMMARY

This chapter has presented some of the background regarding the historical evolution of bilingual/ESL special education. A number of possible instructional models for bilingual/ESL special education were presented and discussed. A number of ESL models and teaching strategies were also discussed. In addition, the use of technology when working with ELLs with special needs were presented.

Discussion Questions

1. How did the issue of overrepresentation of minority students in special education develop historically?
2. Why did the American Association for Mental Deficiency redefine the definition and criteria for classifying students as educable mentally retarded?
3. When did the field of bilingual special education get started?

4. What have been some of the major changes that have occurred in the ESL teaching methods?

5. What are some of the strategies used when implementing sheltered English methodology?

6. Discuss some of the strengths and weaknesses of the bilingual/ESL special education models.

7. How can you as a teacher best use technology to work with CLDE students?

References

Ambert, A., & Dew, N. (1982). *Special education for exceptional bilingual students: A handbook for educators*. Milwaukee, WI: Midwest National Origin Desegregation Assistance Center.

Artilles, A., & Ortiz A. (2004). *English language learners with special needs*. Washington, DC: Center for Applied Linguistics.

Asher, J. (1982). *Learning another language through actions: The complete teachers guide book* (2nd ed.). Los Gatos, CA: Sky Oaks Productions.

Baca, L., & Baca, E. (2006). Bilingualism and bilingual education. In L. Baca and H. Cervantes (Eds.), *The Bilingual Special Education Interface*. Upper Saddle River, NJ: Merrill/Prentice Hall.

Baca, L., & Cervantes, H. (2004). *The bilingual special education interface*. Upper Saddle River, NJ: Merrill/Prentice Hall.

Bernal, E. (1974). A dialogue on cultural implications for learning. *Exceptional Children, 40,* 552.

Blanco, C. (1977). *Bilingual education: Current perspectives*. Arlington, VA: Center for Applied Linguistics.

Cazden, C. B., & Snow, C. E. (1990). Preface to C. B. Cazden & C. E. Snow (Eds.), *English plus: Issues in bilingual education*. (*The Annals of the American Academy of Political and Social Science*, Vol. 508). London: Sage.

Dunn, L. M. (1968). Special education for the mildly retarded—Is much of it justifiable? *Exceptional Children, 35,* 5–22.

Echevarria, J., Vogt, M., & Short, D. (2004). *Making content comprehensible for English learners: The SIOP model*. Boston: Pearson.

Gattengno, C. (1976). *The common sense of teaching foreign languages*. New York: Educational Solutions.

Information Access Library. (1998). *Technology*. Retrieved January 14, 2006 from http://www.ece.udel.edu/InfoAccess/Technology/index.html

Jackson, L. (2005). *Save time with macros*. Retrieved January 16, 2006 from http://www.educationworld.com/a_tech/techtorial/techtorial057.shtml

Krashen, S., & Terrell, T. (1983). *The natural approach: Language acquisition in the classroom*. Oxford: Pergamon.

Lessow-Hurley, J. (1996). *The foundations of dual language instruction*. New York: Longman.

Lewis, R. B. (1998). Assistive technology and learning disabilities: Today's realities and tomorrow's promises. *Journal of Learning Disabilities, 31,* 16–54.

Lozanof, G. (1978). *Suggestolgy and outlines of Suggestopedy*. New York: Gordon and Breach.

Mercer, J. R. (1973). *Labeling the mentally retarded*. Berkeley: University of California Press.

Oller, D. K., & Eilers, R. E. (2002). *Language and literacy in bilingual children*. Clevedon, UK: Multilingual Matters.

Ovando, C., Collier, V., & Combs, M. (2006). *Bilingual and ESL classrooms*. Boston, MA: McGraw-Hill.

President's Committee on Mental Retardation. (1969). *The six-hour retarded child*. Washington, DC: U.S. Department of Health, Education and Welfare.

Ramirez, J. D. (1991). *Final report: Longitudinal study of transitional bilingual education programs for language minority children*. San Mateo, CA: Aguirre International.

Rueda, R., & Chan, K. (1979). Poverty and culture in special education: Separate but equal. *Exceptional Children, 45*(7), 422–431.

Siegel Robertson, J. (2005). *Instructional technology for students with exceptionalities.* http://www.people.memphis.edu/~jsiegel/act/EX.HTML

Smith, D. (2001). *Introduction to special education: Teaching in an age of opportunity.* Boston: Allyn and Bacon.

Thomas, W., & Collier, V. (1997). *School effectiveness for language minority students.* Washington, DC: National Clearinghouse for Bilingual Education.

Chapter 5

Assessing Culturally and Linguistically Diverse Learners

Chapter Objectives

Upon completion of this chapter the reader will be able to:

1. Articulate the major cultural and linguistic factors that must be addressed in the effective assessment of diverse learners at risk academically and behaviorally.

2. Differentiate between learning difference and disability.

3. Apply various assessment procedures and methods within a culturally relevant context.

4. Integrate prereferral assessment activities and results with formal special education assessment eligibility.

5. Apply formal, informal, and alternative assessment in determining eligibility and instructional needs of diverse learners, including those with disabilities.

6. Reduce inappropriate and biased assessment practices for diverse learners.

VIGNETTE

Ms. Lomas, an elementary school principal, wants to develop a comprehensive special education assessment process for her culturally and linguistically diverse (CLD) student population. She is worried that her school is contributing to the ongoing national concern of disproportionality. She sees her school's CLD population underrepresented or overrepresented in several special education categories because she feels that her teachers are inadequately prepared in assessing this learner population. Ms. Lomas realizes that there is a great deal of trepidation and confusion in the field of education about how to distinguish between a learning disability and learning difference. She also realizes that this is a complex situation that has been created due to a variety of factors, such as:

1. Increased numbers in the CLD population.
2. Use of general assessment procedures, methods, and instruments that are more appropriate for an English-only population.
3. Teachers and other assessment staff who are not equipped to assess and instruct a CLD learner population.

Her long-term goal is to develop a comprehensive special education process that begins in the general education classroom by instructing teachers and other assessment personnel about cultural and linguistic factors significant to the assessment process, including:

1. Communicative and language differences used by CLD learners.
2. Interrelationships among cultural, language, and academic achievement in the education process.
3. Significance of knowing language proficiency in both native and English languages.

Specifically, students in her school bring a variety of cultural and linguistic backgrounds to the learning situation, which must be addressed to best differentiate between a learning difference and a learning disorder. These factors include second language acquisition behaviors and qualities, limited experiential background with formal U.S. schooling, and cultural values and norms that are misinterpreted as learning or behavior problems as well as misperceived as "problems" that must be "fixed" rather than diversity that should be valued.

The authors wish to acknowledge Michael Orosco for his assistance in developing this vignette.

Another aspect necessary to include when developing an effective assessment process for CLD learners is the use of a variety of authentic and diagnostic tests, valid for use with CLD learners. This includes development of a process that includes cross-cultural observations, family/home interviews, work sample analysis, ongoing authentic classroom-based progress monitoring (e.g., curriculum-based measurement), as well as valid and reliable achievement and socioemotional testing instruments. Additionally, once data have been gathered the school assessment team must engage in effective problem solving and decision making. This aspect must address potential biases relative to the instruments, process, and/or interpretation of assessment results.

Finally, professional development and training must be implemented to train multidisciplinary assessment team members (e.g., school psychologist, speech and language specialist, general class teacher, ESL teacher, special educator, school principal) in culturally competent assessment practices and procedures. Specific assessment training needs include:

1. Making unbiased decisions.
2. Implementing culturally competent instruction.
3. Use of culturally relevant assessment practices and testing instruments.
4. Implementing an ecological approach to assessment in which home, school, and student factors are considered in interrelated ways.

Ms. Lomas knows that effective assessment for diverse learners at risk academically and/or behaviorally will best occur through the implementation of a comprehensive process that accommodates language and cultural diversity as well as home, school, and student factors relative to the suspected learning or behavior needs.

Reflective Questions

1. How might Ms. Lomas best prepare her staff to differentiate between a learning disability and cultural and linguistic diversity? What are your current knowledge and skills related to the assessment of students from different cultural and linguistic backgrounds?
2. What process for assessing CLD learners is currently used in your school or district and how and to what extent are cultural and linguistic factors incorporated into the process?

INTRODUCTION

Over the past several decades, many issues pertaining to assessment of diverse learners have surfaced in our schools. These include the use of biased testing instruments and procedures, failure to assess students in their primary language, inappropriate uses of testing instruments for purposes outside of their intended uses, special education assessment and staffing teams lacking knowledge and expertise in diverse cultural and linguistic influences on academic learning and social behaviors, as well as a pervasive practice of misinterpreting that which is different as a disability. These and related issues must be addressed to ensure that effective assessment is conducted with students from diverse backgrounds. These also represent some of the more frequent, yet ineffective, practices educators should strive to avoid in their overall assessment programs.

The information we discuss in this chapter will assist educators to more effectively implement a culturally and linguistically competent assessment program to best identify the needs of CLD students at risk academically and/or behaviorally. We take a proactive view toward assessment in that, when implemented effectively, responsibly, and appropriately, assessment provides invaluable information about students' learning needs, strengths, and associated responses to evidence-based instructional practices. We begin with a discussion about some of the major issues confronting the assessment process of CLD learners followed by coverage of numerous assessment strategies to facilitate culturally competent assessment for all learners.

OVERVIEW OF ASSESSMENT ISSUES FOR CLD LEARNERS

The improvement of assessment practices to identify students' instructional needs is ongoing for CLD populations. One continuing controversial issue in the assessment of CLD students pertains to standardization and norming procedures of assessment devices. According to Stefanakis (1998), formal assessment in English of CLD learners (i.e., standards-based, norm-referenced) must address or accommodate several realities:

1. CLD students often take more time to complete tasks in their second language, yielding the results of timed tests less reliable and valid.

2. Reasoning strategies may vary according to native language so processes such as systematic, sequential testing may be unfamiliar to and of questionable validity to CLD learners.

3. Primary language proficiency assessment must precede assessment of learning potential.

4. Assessment for second language learners should be conducted in both native language (L1) and English (L2) prior to making formal educational decisions or judgments.

Only through the use of culturally relevant administrative procedures, testing, and other assessment techniques can reliable and valid results be obtained when assessing CLD learners (Figueroa & Newsome, 2004; Wilkinson, Ortiz, & Robertson-Courtney, 2004). However, most general aptitude and ability tests rely on a student's previous experience and exposure to mainstream cultural concepts and are often of limited educational value in assessing students from different cultural and linguistic backgrounds. Effective assessment must, above all, reduce bias, and this begins with a process that is culturally relevant for all students.

Although school district special education diagnostic assessment procedures vary, most contain four main elements within which decision making for CLD students are made:

Element	Description
Process	Identifying and following an established process
Administration	Appropriate selection, administration, and scoring of assessment instruments
Interpretation	Meaningful program and contextual application and interpretation of assessment results
Monitor	Continuous monitoring of assessment decisions

Within these four elements, educators of CLD learners must determine and reduce potential bias in the assessment process, instruments, and/or interpretation of results. A variety of factors can contribute to biased or misinterpreted assessment results by educators. These include lack of understanding of aspects such as diverse experiential background, socioeconomic status, family history, cultural background, or varying teaching styles (Chamberlain & Medeiros-Landurand, 1991).

However, whatever the particular process is for assessing students in the schools, several rights are provided to students and their parents when assessment for special education is involved. These are identified in Table 5.1.

In addition, Baca and Clark (1992) wrote that bias in assessment is found primarily in two areas: (1) 25 percent in the assessment instruments, and (2) 75 percent in the assessment process and/or interpretations. Issues of content and/or language bias necessitate a thorough evaluation of cultural and linguistic appropriateness in the most recent edition of tests, current assessment procedures, and cultural and linguistic competence of those administering and interpreting test results.

Emphasized throughout this chapter and text is the premise that to effectively refer, assess, and place a CLD learner into special education, distinctions between cultural and linguistic difference and a learning or behavior disorder must be made. Table 5.2 provides an overview of possible alternative explanations, reflecting cultural and linguistic differences, for exhibited behaviors often used as a basis for referrals to special education. Knowledge of these will help to reduce bias in the referral and assessment process.

To reduce bias and inappropriate referrals, educators must consider a variety of factors when considering CLD learners for possible special education. These and related issues are addressed and explored further throughout this text. Also, these types of alternatives should be considered at all times as the complex task of referring and assessing CLD learners is undertaken.

TABLE 5.1 Assessment Rights of CLD/CLDE Learners

Based on recent legislation, CLD/CLDE learners and their families have various rights to protect them in the overall education process:

1. Schools must provide a free and appropriate public education for children who have disabilities.
2. School districts must conduct a language screening at the beginning of each school year for all new students to determine if a language, other than English, is present and influences the development and education of the child. If a second language is found, then a language assessment must be completed to determine language dominance and proficiency.
3. If a child has limited English proficiency and a disability, then the student's Individualized Education Program (IEP) shall reflect the child's language-related needs as well as other identified needs.
4. When a child is evaluated, nondiscriminatory assessment instruments must be used and assessment is to be conducted in the child's most proficient language to yield the most accurate and valid results.
5. Assessment devices and materials must be validated for the specific purpose(s) for which they are used. They must also be administered by personnel trained in administration of the instruments consistent with procedures identified by the instrument developers.
6. Assessment must be tailored to identify specific areas of academic and behavior needs, and provide more than a general IQ score.
7. Assessment tests and procedures must accurately reflect the student's aptitude, achievement level, or other factors the tests purport to measure, rather than reflecting the student's language differences, cultural diversity, or impairments.
8. Overall, when interpreting evaluation data and in making special education placement decisions, information shall be drawn from a variety of sources, including aptitude and achievement tests, teacher observations, classroom assessments, or work samples.

Sources: IDEA (2004), Hoover (2001); Baca and Cervantes (2004).

In regards to districtwide assessment for CLD/CLDE learners, all students must be included in the state-mandated assessments (NCLB, 2001). Although some special education students with more severe disabilities may be exempt from the statewide testing, most learners with mild to moderate disabilities are included in the state-mandated testing programs. For most states this includes mandated, standards-based assessments in which proficiency levels are determined rather than a simple pass or fail score (Hoover & Patton, 2005a). Inherent within successful completion of mandated testing, whether individual or group, are:

1. Adequate test-taking abilities (see Chapter 11).
2. Sufficient opportunities to learn.
3. English language proficiency necessary to read and comprehend tests taken in English.

Throughout this text we emphasize the importance of each of these factors to ensure reliable and valid assessment results for diverse learners, which begins with

TABLE 5.2 Reducing Biased Decision Making When Referring Culturally and Linguistically Diverse Learners

Exhibited Behaviors	Decision-Making Considerations to Avoid Inappropriate Referral
Extended periods of silence	May be associated with limited English proficiency level and/or level of acculturation (i.e., process of adapting to new environment such as a new school or classroom); some cultures encourage children to be quiet as a sign of respect
Confusion with locus of control	Some cultures teach that things are out of the control of individuals (i.e., external locus of control) and this should not be misinterpreted as not caring or requiring intervention
Indifference to time	The concept of time is often perceived differently in various cultures and may be significantly different than time emphasized in U.S. schools
Social withdrawal	Shy behavior may be associated with the process of adjusting or acculturating to a new environment (e.g., U.S. schools/classrooms) and/or with learning English as a second language
Acting out/ aggressive behavior	Some cultures may teach that assertive behavior (e.g., standing up for oneself) is desirable social behavior; inexperience with U.S. classroom rules may also account for acting-out behaviors
Difficulty with independent work	Some cultures may value group performance over individual achievement and thus students may be unfamiliar with independent, competitive learning preferring cooperative group learning
Perceived lack of significance of school achievement	Value or significance of school may vary by culture as other priorities in that culture may take priority (e.g., family needs, spring harvest)
Poor performance on tests taken in English	Tests in English become an English test for limited English proficient students; test results in English must be interpreted relative to the learner's English proficiency level
Low self-esteem	Students from different cultures or linguistic backgrounds may initially experience difficulty while adjusting to new cultural expectations and learning a new language, temporarily negatively impacting a child's self-concept
Differences in perception of everyday items	Different cultures may view everyday concepts differently than the mainstream culture (e.g., personal space, sharing of belongings, gender, meaning of color, directions) and knowledge of how cultures view these and related items is necessary to make informed decisions
Increased anxiety	Stress associated with adjusting to a new culture and/or learning a new language often results in increased anxiety in learners until they feel more comfortable in the new environment and develop higher levels of English language proficiency
Difficulty observing school/class expectations	Unfamiliarity with formal schooling and classroom expectations is often experienced by children new to U.S. schools; they require additional time and support to become more accustomed to U.S. school's behavioral and learning expectations
Preferences in style(s) of learning	Preferred styles of learning are reflective of cultural values and styles of CLDs may be different than typically emphasized in school
Inability to learn through teaching/ classroom strategies	Teaching strategies typically used in today's classrooms may conflict with cultural views and/or be inappropriate for student's limited English language proficiency levels

Source: From "Reducing Bias Decision-Making when Referring Learners with Cultural and Linguistic Needs," by J. J. Hoover, in press. In J. Klingner, A. Artiles, L. Baca, and J. Hoover (Eds.), *English Language Learners Who Struggle with Reading: Language Acquisition or Learning Disabilities?* Copyright by Corwin Press.

possessing a minimum level of competence in assessment. Effective assessment of CLD learners requires educators to possess cultural competence necessary to identify biases, differentiate between a disability and cultural or linguistic diversity, and ascertain relevant uses of assessment results.

Assessment Competence

The definition and characteristics of culturally competent teaching and learning were presented in Chapter 2, and those principles apply to assessment procedures. Specifically, cultural competence in assessment requires, at minimum, knowledge and understanding of the following assessment topics:

Reliability/validity. The validity, reliability, and standardization data must be reviewed to determine the diversity represented in the population sample. Appropriate reliability and validity reduces bias in the assessment of CLD learners.

Uses of standardized instruments. Many standardized tests are constructed and normed so items become increasingly more difficult. The scoring and interpretation of such tests are based on the progression of item difficulty. These tests may not be appropriate for use with CLD students, yielding biased or inaccurate results. Detailed discussion of special considerations when using standardized instruments with CLD students is presented in a subsequent section of this chapter.

Classroom-based authentic assessments. Effective classroom assessments for CLD learners ensure that the assessment information is instructionally meaningful and culturally relevant. Detailed discussion of authentic assessment is presented in a subsequent section of this chapter.

Opportunities to learn. Fundamental to all effective assessment is the opportunity to learn the material and skills tested. Opportunities to learn must be documented and addressed as assessment of CLD learners is undertaken.

Response to intervention (RTI). Response to intervention includes the implementation of effective instructional practices along with the monitoring of results associated with that intervention. As prereferral activities are undertaken with CLD learners, the effects of these interventions must be documented and used in the overall assessment process. (See Chapter 1 for a more detailed description of RTI.)

Cultural/language factors. A variety of cultural and linguistic factors must be addressed to ensure that an appropriate and comprehensive assessment is completed. Detailed discussions of six of these factors are presented in a subsequent section of this chapter.

Familiarity with these items relative to assessment practices for CLD learners in school districts begins the process of ensuring assessment competence as CLD learners

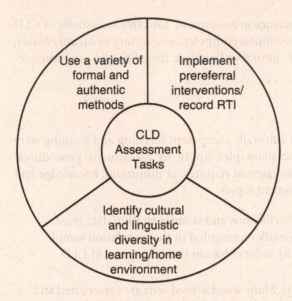

FIGURE 5.1 Essential Tasks for Assessing CLD/CLDE Learners

are considered for possible special education services. To further guide assessment personnel, Figure 5.1 illustrates three specific assessment tasks that are of specific relevance to CLD learners and should receive high priority within the overall comprehensive assessment process.

As shown, determining the positive impact of cultural and linguistic diversity in learning, implementing extensive prereferral interventions along with documented response to those interventions, and use of a variety of assessment methods are essential to the overall goal of identifying and addressing learning differences while not erroneously misidentifying a disability. An in-depth discussion of each of these three task areas is presented in subsequent sections of this chapter. It is beyond the scope of this chapter to address all aspects associated with comprehensive assessment, and the reader is referred to books on special education assessment, eligibility, and placement for additional information (Salvia & Ysseldyke, 2003; Cohen & Spenciner, 2003). Rather, the intent of this chapter is to focus on unique assessment needs or considerations necessary to determine disability from difference and uses of culturally appropriate assessment methods, strategies, and instruments.

Determining Difference versus Disability

The basic assessment issue challenging educators of CLD learners is that of determining whether a suspected problem or area of need reflects a learning disability or a learning difference resulting from cultural and linguistic diverse factors. A *learning difference* represents unique ways that individuals successfully acquire information, process learning, integrate knowledge, and generalize skills, which may deviate from what is typically accepted or preferred in schools or individual classrooms. A *learning disability* or *disorder* represents a condition within the learner that interferes with the acquisition, processing, integration, and/or generalization of knowledge and skills. A clear differentiation between difference and disability is that, although accommodations may be made, a disability is represented by characteristics that often limit or otherwise interfere with one's progress or learning (e.g., processing disorder, developmental disability), whereas cultural and linguistic diversity or differences are represented by characteristics that advance and support one's learning, relative to cultural/linguistic background. To make this distinction throughout the assessment process for a CLD learner, educators must continually determine and review the relationship between six major cultural/linguistic factors and a suspected disability. These factors are illustrated in Figure 5.2.

As shown, several cultural and linguistic factors that directly impact learning must be considered in the assessment of a CLD learner to best understand learning differences from disabilities (Banks, 1994; Rueda & Kim, 2001; Tharp, 1997; Hoover, 2005; Baca, 2005). Also, Lachat (2004) emphasized the importance of being knowledgeable of the interaction among culture, language, and diversity in education. Hodgkinson (2000) also wrote of the significance of understanding diverse values and historical traditions.

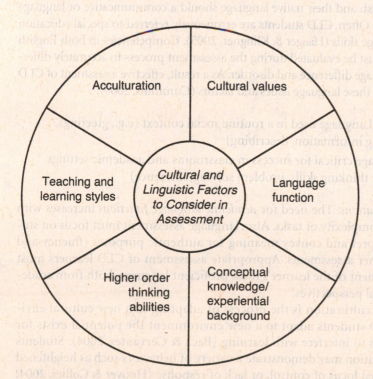

FIGURE 5.2 Factors to Consider When Determining Learning Difference from Disability

Addressing these six cultural factors within the overall assessment process will help ascertain whether potential learning and behavior needs exhibited by CLD students are reflective of cultural diversity, a learning problem or disability, or a combination of these factors. "Knowledge about each of these areas relative to English language learners (ELLs) with special needs is essential to providing effective education" (Hoover, 2005, p. 4). Consideration of these six factors early in the assessment process may alert educators to the fact that various cultural factors may be misinterpreted as learning and behavior problems, highlighting the need to further determine the positive impact of cultural and linguistic diversity in the education of the learner. Conversely, if diversity is considered early in the assessment process and appropriate interpretations made, issues underlying the learning problems may be more effectively and efficiently assessed. The following sections discuss these six factors and their relationship to effective assessment of CLD learners.

Language Function Language is the primary medium through which culture and experiences are shared and transmitted from generation to generation (Cummins, 1996). As suggested, when referring or assessing a CLD student's language competencies, the primary issue should be to discern the difference between linguistically different and linguistically disabled (Haager & Klingner, 2005). Only if students demonstrate speech or language problems both in English and their native language should a communicative or language disorder be considered. Often, CLD students are erroneously referred to special education due to deficient language skills (Haager & Klingner, 2005). Competencies in both English and native language must be evaluated during the assessment process to accurately differentiate between a language difference and disorder. As a result, effective assessment of CLD students must consider these language issues and factors (Cummins, 2000):

Communicative. Language used in a routine social context (e.g., greetings, requests, providing information, describing)

Academic. Language critical for success in classrooms and academic settings (e.g., higher order thinking skills, problem solving, inference)

Assessment Implications: The need for *academic language functions* increases with the grade levels and complexity of tasks. Also, language assessment must focus on student's ability to interpret and convey meaning for authentic purposes (fluency and accuracy) prior to other assessments. Appropriate assessment of CLD learners must begin with the assessment of the learner's most proficient language, both from academic and conversational perspectives.

Acculturation Acculturation is the process of adapting to a new cultural environment, and as CLD students adapt to a new environment the potential exists for behavioral side effects to interfere with learning (Baca & Cervantes, 2004). Students experiencing acculturation may demonstrate a variety of behaviors such as heightened anxiety, stress, confused locus of control, or lack of response (Hoover & Collier, 2004; Collier, 1988). If related to acculturation, these behaviors should be viewed as expected behaviors and not indicative of learning or behavior disorders.

The process of acculturation can be seen as either subtractive or additive and as a one-way or two-way process. *Subtractive* leads to the loss of one's native culture through assimilation to the dominant culture. *Additive* allows the learner to function in both the native community and the broader society. Acculturation as a one-way process occurs when the minority community adapts to the dominant culture, whereas a two-way process also sees change in the dominant culture (Baca & Cervantes, 2004).

Assessment Implications: Varied responses to acculturation (anxiety, withdrawal, stress) may be exhibited by the student and must be considered within the learning context. These behaviors should be viewed as expected behaviors, which will diminish over time, and not as disordered behaviors. Overall, the less time and opportunity the student has living in this country, speaking and using the English language, and being educated in U.S. schools the more impact acculturation will have on the learner. This may lead to acculturative stress, where the learner exhibits some or all of the behaviors described earlier. However, as suggested, these should not be viewed as behavior disorders.

Conceptual Knowledge/Experiential Background Differences in experience may account for much of the discrepancy between achievement and ability seen in CLD students. Since new information is built on existing knowledge (Gagne, Yekovich, & Yekovich, 1993), assessment must determine the student's prior and current conceptual background. CLD students with little previous school experiences may be unfamiliar with specific instructional strategies and behavioral expectations in U.S. schools and classrooms. In addition, many CLD students may lack early academic experiences, which are considered important to the learning foundation within the curriculum. Also, differences in experiential background affect students' responses to curricular expectations and must be known prior to a formal referral or placement to special education (Wilkinson et. al., 2004).

Assessment Implications: Determination of prior and current conceptual knowledge and experiential background related to the content area needs provides insight into a student's understanding of hierarchies and connections between concepts and the depth of knowledge in that content area. The assessment of CLD learners must initially determine conceptual and experiential background to accurately address issues related to learning differences versus disabilities.

Higher Order Thinking Abilities Various state curricula provide a framework for teaching and emphasizing thinking skills. To accurately determine learning ability, CLD students should be assessed in both native and English languages for these five higher order thinking abilities (O'Malley & Pierce, 1996):

- Comprehension—Organize or paraphrase information
- Analysis—Divide the whole into component elements, use sequencing
- Comparison—Articulate similarities/differences
- Synthesis—Combine elements to create a whole, form generalizations, use deductive/inductive reasoning

• Evaluation—Judge information/completed tasks (i.e., quality, worth, credibility) (Bloom et al., 1956)

CLD students in the process of learning English may lack appropriate responses to commonly used thinking strategies, and this may be mistakenly interpreted as a disability. However, Lachat (2004) wrote that CLD learners must be taught "in ways that will enable them to respond to the more complex and cognitively demanding tasks" (p. 104). As student use of higher order thinking skills is determined, a more complete and accurate assessment occurs.

Assessment Implications: Determination of student skills in applying these thinking abilities provides valuable insight into how the learner is interacting with and learning a curriculum. Inability to demonstrate one or more of these abilities may result from the acculturation process or lack of experiential background and not necessarily a learning problem. Higher order thinking abilities in both native language and English should be evaluated to avoid misdiagnosis of a disability.

Cultural Values and Norms Students represent a variety of backgrounds possessing different customs, lifestyles, values, and beliefs who often speak different languages (Lachat, 2004). Unfortunately, cultural and community needs are either inadequately identified or superficially integrated into the educational process (Baca & Cervantes, 2004). Respect for and sensitivity to local cultural values and norms are necessary to complete a culturally relevant assessment process. Culture has a comprehensive effect on one's thinking, perceptions, and behaviors, and educators who assess CLD learners must become familiar with the cultural background of their students to best understand CLD students (Garcia & Pearson, 1994). Differences in school behavior may be due to varying cultural values and norms and should not be viewed as disorders. (See Chapter 2 for additional information about culture and cultural competence.)

Assessment Implications: Assessment procedures for CLD learners must respect cultural and language differences and avoid oversimplified categorizations. Cultural values and norms that students bring to the classroom and assessment process must be viewed in positive and relevant ways to ensure appropriate assessment of CLD students.

Teaching/Learning Styles Effective assessment of CLD students must also include an understanding of the interactions and compatibility between teacher and learner in the instructional setting. Cultural and linguistic diversity shape characteristic ways in which an individual responds to learning tasks and the instructional environment reflecting preferred styles of learning (Farr & Turnbull, 1997). For example, some cultures may teach their children that cooperative work is more important than individual performance or that it is acceptable to take longer periods of time before responding to a question (Hoover & Collier, 2003). In these and similar situations, differences in styles of learning may be in conflict with teacher style preferences (e.g., desiring a quick response to a question) and should not be misinterpreted as a disability. As a result, identifying learning styles is an instructionally meaningful component of the assessment of CLD students (Hoover & Collier, 2003; Collier & Hoover, 1987). Preferred learning styles of the student and teaching styles of the educator must be documented to ensure effective assessment of learning needs. Therefore, an essential element within assessment is determining how the child is taught (teaching style), under what conditions (classroom variables), and whether these match with how the child best learns (learning style).

Assessment Implications: Consideration of the interactions between teaching and learning styles within the classroom is essential, since oftentimes CLD students may use different reasoning strategies according to their native language. These differences should not be viewed as a disability; rather, they should be viewed as productive strategies to facilitate learning most compatible with student learning styles.

An understanding of these important factors forms the foundation for implementing cultural and linguistic competent assessment for all learners. (The reader is referred to Chapters 2 and 3 for more detailed discussions of these topical areas.)

ASSESSMENT COMPONENTS FOR CLD LEARNERS

Although various school district models for assessing CLDs exist, each typically contains five major components: prereferral, referral, formal assessment, staffing, and placement. Within this process three aspects of assessment are of particular concern when assessing CLD learners for suspected disabilities: prereferral intervention, language proficiency assessment, and use of translators and interpreters.

One primary emphasis in the prereferral process is to clarify distinctions between a potential *disability* and a *difference.* Ultimately, the prereferral process should provide sufficient information to make informed decisions about the need for a formal referral to special education assessment and potential placement. In addition, the information obtained from all assessment procedures, including prereferral intervention, should be used to develop the Individualized Education Plan (IEP) documenting appropriate content, strategies, and classroom settings necessary to provide appropriate education. IEP development for CLDE learners is discussed in a subsequent section of this chapter. Table 5.3 identifies several key aspects that educators should consider prior to making a formal referral to special education. A variety of issues need to be addressed, ranging from determining language proficiency to meeting the parents to observing the student in the learning environment. Adhering to these will help ensure more appropriate referrals based on prereferral interventions results.

Prereferral Intervention and Early Intervening Services

The term *prereferral* refers to the time period following an indication by a teacher or a concerned person that the student is exhibiting a learning, communication, and/or behavior problem (i.e., the student has been referred to a child-study team or other

TABLE 5.3 Referral to Special Education of an English Language Learner

Before a formal referral to special education is justified for an ELL, the following should be completed and addressed:

_____ Student's most proficient language for instruction is identified

_____ Student's level of acculturation and adjustment to school environment is determined

_____ Discrepancies between teaching and learning style differences are identified

_____ Home visit and/or meeting with parent(s) is conducted

_____ A variety of culturally and linguistically relevant instructional interventions are attempted and results documented

_____ ESL and/or bilingual education instruction is implemented

_____ Sufficient time and opportunity for student to make satisfactory progress are provided relative to acculturation and English proficiency levels

_____ Recent vision and hearing exams are conducted

_____ Authentic or other criterion-referenced tests are used to assess student academic progress and socioemotional development

_____ One or more classroom observations are made to observe student interactions in the academic environment

Source: From "Reducing Bias Decision-Making when Referring Learners with Cultural and Linguistic Needs," by J. J. Hoover, in press. In J. Klingner, A. Artiles, L. Baca, and J. Hoover (Eds.), *English Language Learners Who Struggle with Reading: Language Acquisition or Learning Disabilities?* Copyright by Corwin Press.

person at the building level) and prior to a formal referral for special education assessment. Historically, prereferral interventions serve as an important safeguard against inappropriate formal referrals to special education by preventing potential problems from becoming more significant. Buck, Polloway, Smith-Thomas, and Cook (2003) wrote that "when prereferral intervention procedures are most effective, the number of inappropriate referrals to special education is reduced" (p. 358).

A key element of prereferral intervention is the implementation of curricular interventions prior to formal referral, should that be determined necessary, which includes differentiated instruction to meet specific needs (Klingner & Harry, 2004). The significance of prereferral interventions was further emphasized in the reauthorization of IDEA (2004), which referred to this practice as *early intervening services.* These services allow school districts to allocate up to 15 percent of funds to use special education expertise to provide early intervening services to students at risk academically or behaviorally (Beekman, 2005). Data from these evidence-based intervening or prereferral efforts is also important information to further clarify possible eligibility for formal special education assessment.

The process for prereferral varies by school district, but in most districts, teachers initially request assistance from a child-study or teacher-assistance team. This team outlines a process for gathering information relative to cultural and linguistic factors, such as those discussed earlier. Specific suggestions for academic assistance provided by teachers or by other specialists is also documented and results recorded (e.g., RTI). If the student is limited English proficient, prereferral interventions should include modifications to intervention techniques to accommodate the student's language and cultural background. Klingner and Harry (2004) stressed the importance of holding two referral meetings to allow educators to attempt and document interventions prior to making a formal referral to special education. The student's response to these prereferral interventions (RTI) should be documented and used as information to make informed decisions on the need for a formal special education assessment. As a result, prereferral helps educators to:

1. Resolve a suspected problem early and quickly before it becomes more serious.
2. Determine to what extent cultural and linguistic factors and not a disability influence the suspected learning or behavior problem.
3. Reduce the number of students inappropriately placed into special education (Hoover, in press a).

Prereferral interventions for CLD learners are significant for several additional reasons, as discussed by Baca and Cervantes (2004):

1. Special education placement, when the existence of a true disability is in doubt, does not benefit students.
2. The information gathered during prereferral interventions can help to clarify distinctions between a disability and cultural and linguistic differences.
3. Over 75 percent of ELL students formally referred for special education assessment and placement are placed in special education (Stefanakis, 1998).
4. Once placed in special education it takes an average of 6 years to be staffed out.
5. Often, placement and programming outcomes of special education assessments are determined by the teacher's initial referral rather than by the results of formal assessment.

As a result, prereferral intervention for CLD learners increases the possibility that relevant criteria are used to make informed decisions concerning a disability or difference. Many educational strategies appropriate for educating CLD learners also serve as a vital source of relevant information in the overall assessment process. These include use of experiential-based educational methods, hands-on enrichment activities, native language development and enrichment, instruction in literacy skills in the native language and in English, use of specialized ESL methods across curriculum areas, self-identity self-concept, and interpersonal skill development and strategies designed to develop behaviors appropriate to the academic setting (Baca & Cervantes, 2004).

As prereferral activities are implemented and results documented, educators become more informed about the specific needs of diverse learners. After attempting

TABLE 5.4 Factors to Consider in the Referral Process for an English Language Learner

Item	Consideration
Difference versus disability	Educators must ensure that limited English proficiency is not mistaken for a learning or language disability
Proper time for formal referral	Formal referral for special education evaluation should only occur after prereferral interventions have been implemented and results documented
Proper language of instruction/assessment	Referral teams must instruct/assess ELLs in their most proficient language to determine difference from disability
Limited English proficiency and IQ	Referral teams must be cognizant of the fact that limited proficiency in the use of English does not indicate low IQ or inability to use higher order thinking abilities
Opportunities to learn	Referral teams must ensure that students with limited English proficiency are provided sufficient opportunities to learn by providing necessary accommodations to facilitate language differences
Cross-cultural observations/interviews	Teams must ensure that observations and interviews conducted with ELLs are culturally and linguistically appropriate to the level of English proficiency of the learner
Proper interpretation and use of test scores	Referral teams must corroborate test score data with authentic, classroom-based information, observations, and interviews

Source: From "Reducing Bias Decision-Making when Referring Learners with Cultural and Linguistic Needs," by J. J. Hoover, in press. In J. Klingner, A. Artiles, L. Baca, and J. Hoover (Eds.), *English Language Learners Who Struggle with Reading: Language Acquisition or Learning Disabilities?* Copyright by Corwin Press.

various prereferral interventions and documenting their results, the teacher-assistance team may decide that a formal referral to special education is necessary. Once a formal referral for special education assessment is made, the legal constraints of P.L. 94–142/IDEA (2004) regarding assessment, timelines, staffing, placement, and IEP development must be adhered to. Should formal referral be determined, educators must keep in mind several factors throughout the referral and assessment process. As shown in Table 5.4, several overarching areas of consideration must encompass effective and appropriate assessment of CLD learners. These considerations, along with the items previously presented in Table 5.2, collectively help to ensure that a valid and meaningful referral and assessment process is implemented for CLD learners.

Language Proficiency Assessment

One step within prereferral for CLD students that must be undertaken prior to implementing other forms of intervention and assessment is determining English language proficiency. Determining written and oral language skills of CLD learners is critical to any effective assessment process. The language diversity that exists in society also exists in our schools and language proficiency assessment should be authentic (Richard-Amato, 1996). To be most effective, language proficiency assessment must include determining what students know about a language system and what they can do with that language, without mistaking these abilities for a language disability (Figueroa & Newsome, 2004). Conversational and academic language skills fall along a continuum denoting language functions acquired over time (Collier, 1995). Evaluators need to remember that the regular use of conversational language at school is not a guarantee of mastered academic language. As a result, the distinction between conversational and academic language is critical because misunderstandings about surface or conversational fluency often result in erroneously labeling CLD students as being poorly motivated or having a disability. When assessing language proficiency of CLD learners, the following should be addressed:

- Assessment of language should focus on abilities to interpret and convey meaning for authentic purposes in interactive contexts (O'Malley & Pierce, 1996).
- Language assessment should include determination of abilities in both native language and English (Ortiz & Yates, 2002).
- Language assessment for CLD learners should determine integrative uses of language skills while completing a task, rather than evaluation of individual language skills completed in a discrete or isolated manner (Richard-Amato, 1996).
- Language assessment for CLD students should be routine and ongoing.
- Baseline assessment of student strengths and needs in oral and written language should be conducted to determine instructional standards and objectives.
- When using standardized assessment instruments for the language assessment, the validity and reliability of the instruments must be clearly understood.
- Informal and authentic assessment procedures in language assessment should be used because they often more accurately reflect actual instructional activities.
- Classroom-based assessment tasks should be structured to facilitate student use of both communicative and academic language functions (Cummins, 1996).

Appropriate Use of Interpreters

The use of outside interpreters in the assessment of a CLD learner is necessary when:

1. A bilingual professional is not available.
2. It is inappropriate to have a peer or sibling translate.
3. The student is not literate in his/her dominant language.

4. No tests are available in the student's dominant language (Chamberlain & Medeiros-Landurand, 1991).

When using an interpreter, it is important to remember that speaking a language well and translating a language are two distinct skills. When used appropriately, an interpreter can:

1. Translate the test or other assessment materials.
2. Prepare the student and parents for the assessment process.
3. Interpret the student's responses.
4. Facilitate communication with the parents during the staffing and IEP meeting (Baca & Cervantes, 2004).

Also, interpreters must be able to translate both the language and the concepts being assessed (Chamberlain & Medeiros-Landurand, 1991). Qualifications of effective interpreters include (1) an understanding of student development, language variation (dialects, language domains, registers), and cross-cultural variables; (2) knowledge of special education terminology; and (3) training in the administration of tests, including how to transmit information about role-playing, how to cue a student during assessment, how to prompt for responses, and how to probe for pertinent information or responses (Yates & Ortiz, 2004; de Valenzuela & Baca, 2004).

ECOLOGICAL ASSESSMENT

An ecological perspective in education emphasizes the significance of the role of the environment in teaching and learning. When used effectively, an ecological model influences the environment to meet the needs of individual learners (Bronfenbrenner, 1979, 1995). To complete the most relevant and comprehensive assessment of CLD/CLDE learners, information relevant to the total environment (i.e., student, classroom, home/community) must be gathered and used in the special education decisions. Table 5.5 provides an overview of the three targeted areas (student, classroom, home/community) within an ecological assessment process along with suggested assessment measures and/or assessment outcomes. The overall assessment process should include information gathered at the student, classroom, and home/community levels using a variety of assessment techniques. The student factors are based on resources previously discussed; the classroom factors were derived from the research of Tharp (1997), who identified five practices necessary to ensure effective classroom opportunities to learn for students with cultural and linguistic diversity; and the home/community items reflect information found in Baca and Cervantes (2004). Many of the suggested assessment measures are discussed in the following section.

TABLE 5.5 Ecological Assessment Template for CLD Learners (Cultural and Linguistic Factors)

Component 1: Student Factors

Factor	Primary Outcome	Information to Gather	Suggested Measures
Language competence	Identify most proficient language for providing assessment/ instruction	Native language proficiency—oral English language proficiency—oral Native language proficiency—rdg/wrtg English language proficiency— rdg/wrtg	LAS[a] Links IPT[b] Woodcock Munoz Running records Language samples
Acculturation	Determine if exhibited behaviors reflect stress due to acculturation	Behavioral and emotional adjustment to school/community environment	Acculturation quick screen Cross-cultural interview Class observation/CBA
Experiential background	Determine if prior experiences are sufficient to meet academic/behavior classroom demands	Previous experiences with formal schooling Prerequisite academic skills (Native language) Prerequisite academic skills (English language)	Review of records Cross-cultural interview with parents and students
Cultural values/ norms	Ensure that values/ norms are understood relative to areas of need	Compatibility of native culture values/ norms with school/ classroom behavioral expectations Compatibility of native culture values/norms with academic expectations	Cross-cultural interview Curricular review Interview
Higher order thinking	Document critical thinking skills used by student	Student use of Bloom's taxonomy higher order thinking abilities in native language Student use of Bloom's taxonomy higher order thinking abilities in English language	Analytic teaching CBA/M[c] Performance-based assessment Work sample analysis
Teaching/ learning styles	Ensure that differences between teaching style and preferred learning style are not mistaken for learning problem	Most used teaching styles in classroom (e.g., lecture, drill/ practice, coop learning) Student styles of learning resulting in most effective educational progress	Classroom observations CBA/M Task analysis

(*continued*)

TABLE 5.5 (continued)

Component 2: Classroom Factors (Opportunities to Learn)

Topic	Specifics to Gather Through Observations/Interviews
Linguistic competence	Appropriate instruction; functional language usage; purposeful conversations; connect current and prior experiences
Contextualized learning	Home/community culture and student experiences are reflected in instruction
Joint productivity	Activities shared by teachers/students; interactive conversations
Instructional conversation	Ongoing teacher-student dialogue; form, exchange, express ideas interactively
Challenging curriculum	Curriculum must be appropriate and effective in challenging students cognitively

Component 3: Home/Community Factors

Topic	Suggested Assessment
Primary home language	Home language survey
Adjustment to new environment	Interview/checklist of important considerations
Education history (family/child)	Parent/caregiver interview/checklist/review of records

[a] LAS—Language Assessment Scales
[b] IPT—IDEA Proficiency Tests
[c] CBA/M—Curriculum-based assessment/measurement

Source: From "Reducing Bias Decision-Making when Referring Learners with Cultural and Linguistic Needs," by J. J. Hoover, in press. In J. Klingner, A. Artiles, L. Baca, and J. Hoover (Eds.), *English Language Learners Who Struggle with Reading: Language Acquisition or Learning Disabilities?* Copyright by Corwin Press.

ASSESSMENT TECHNIQUES

A variety of assessment techniques exist and may be effectively used in the assessment of CLD students. The manner in which these techniques are applied and results interpreted will determine their effectiveness with students. Several relevant techniques are discussed in this section and are summarized in Table 5.6. When used in the overall assessment process, including prereferral interventions, these alternative and authentic assessment techniques will provide valuable and meaningful information about the student.

Analytic Teaching

Analytic teaching, also referred to as diagnostic or prescriptive teaching, involves the observation of student behavior engaged in particular tasks subdivided into their constituent components (Moran & Malott, 2004). Analytic teaching provides insight into what students are doing, what they may be thinking, and what they are learning as they complete tasks. When used as an assessment method, it

TABLE 5.6 Assessment Techniques

Technique	Description	Uses with CLD/CLDE Learners
Analytic teaching	Analyzing a student's behavior while he/she is engaged in ongoing instructional situations	Cultural and linguistic differences should be noted and addressed by varying the sequence or nature of the analytic tasks
Cross-cultural interview	Discussing the cultural and linguistic background of the student in order to determine whether a student's behaviors are culturally or linguistically appropriate	The cross-cultural interview can provide meaningful information such as parents' perceptions about the student's behavior and developmental history, and family upbringing
Language samples/ journaling	Using journal writing or language samples to have students document what they have learned and teachers assess thinking processes as well as other literacy skills	Language samples are sensitive to cultural/language differences if administered and used appropriately and interpreted accurately
Observations	Firsthand observing and recording of classroom and learning behaviors	Cultural/linguistic values and behaviors are put into context through classroom observations
Review of existing records	Reviewing various student school records to determine instructional history	Examination of the existing records for evidence of the student's cultural and language background and prior school successes is essential in the assessment process
Work sample analysis	Analyzing student work samples to identify patterns, inconsistencies, strengths, and weaknesses in learning	Cultural/linguistic differences may become more apparent through student work samples along with strengths reflective of those differences
Task analysis	Breaking down learning into discrete parts in order to analyze student learning and thinking abilities	Task analysis ensures the incorporation of CLD students' culture and language in authentic assessment tasks within the learning environment
Running records	Using written narrative to record an observation completed over specified time period (e.g., 15 to 20 minutes)	Running records documents the effectiveness and cultural appropriateness of classroom interventions and teaching strategies

Sources: Moran and Malott (2004); Figueroa & Newsome (2004); Hoover, Patton, Hresko, and Hammill (in press); Hammill (1987); Peregoy and Boye (1997).

documents what tasks the student is able and unable to do. Analytic teaching provides meaningful information to (1) form hypotheses about student's needs, (2) determine subsequent steps in assessment or instruction, and (3) monitor student responses to intervention (Hammill, 1987). When implementing analytic teaching, teachers should change only one element at a time so the instructional element producing a change is more clearly identified. As a result, analytic teaching is an instructionally meaningful technique, especially in prereferral intervention activity. Intervention strategies in analytic teaching assessment should also focus on teaching enabling skills to perform more complex behaviors within culturally relevant contexts. This provides additional evidence-based documentation to assist in differentiating between learning difference and disability.

Interviews

Interviews are another useful assessment technique for examining the educational and social needs of CLD students (Stefanakis, 1998). The interviewer must be sensitive to cross-cultural communication and should at a minimum address or include the following (Figueroa & Newsome, 2004; Damico, Cheng, Deleon, Ferrer, & Westernoff, 1992):

1. Factors that affect test performance (e.g., family, community, classroom setting)
2. Significant people in the child's life interviewed in the native language
3. Evaluation, through interviews, of both native (L1) and English (L2) oral language/literacy proficiency
4. Determination of the teacher's primary instructional language
5. Identification of the home language of parents and siblings

Table 5.7 provides an example of a cross-cultural interview that may be used as a guide to gathering relevant information.

Language Samples/Journaling

Use of language and writing samples or journaling is another highly effective assessment method to support formal standardized language assessment (Hammill, 1987). When collecting and analyzing language samples, the following points are important to consider:

1. Collect samples in several different language contexts.
2. Use samples that involve a familiar and culturally appropriate conversational partner.
3. Provide a relaxing environment to best obtain meaningful language samples.

TABLE 5.7 Sample Questions for Parent/Family Cross-Cultural Interview

Interview Purpose: Discuss child's home life, school, and peer interactions.

Question	Response
When did you first arrive in this community?	
Why did you come to this community?	
What was your home community like?	
What work do you do?	
How is your family adjusting to this community?	
What problems are you experiencing adjusting to this new community?	
What do you miss the most/least about your previous community?	
What do you like most/least about this new community?	
Are you receiving needed medical/school services?	
What language(s) do you prefer to speak at home?	
What language(s) does your child speak at home?	
How has your child adjusted to the new school?	
How does this new school compare with other school(s) child has attended?	
What does your child like the most/least about school?	
What are your child's most/least favorite subjects?	
Who helps your child with homework?	
Has your child made friends in this new community?	
Does your child spend more time alone than in your previous community?	
What does your child like to do most with friends?	
What language(s) does (do) your child and friends use while interacting together?	

Sources: Garcia (2002); Figueroa and Newsome (2004); Winzer and Mazurek (1994).

4. Audio- and/or videotape language samples for later review (need parent permission).
5. Emphasize language function (communicative, academic) as well as form.
6. Exercise caution when comparing CLD student's language sample results to commercially published testing norms (Hammill, 1987; Baca & Cervantes, 2004).

Journaling is also an effective tool for CLD students as they write in their native language (L1) and/or English (L2). Journal responses may reflect or describe a variety of topics, such as story elements, personal events, relation of prior knowledge to new knowledge, personal ideas or thoughts, explanations about specific events, or illustration of various levels of thinking such as comprehension, evaluation, or synthesis (O'Malley & Pierce, 1996).

Collectively, language sampling and journaling complement an overall comprehensive assessment for CLD learners and should be an integral component in the process.

Observations

Observation is essential to a comprehensive assessment process for CLDE learners (Wilkinson et al., 2004; Stefanakis, 1998). To facilitate effective observations and accurate recording of information, checklists, surveys, or running records may be used. When used appropriately, checklists remind the evaluator what to observe, what to ask during interviews, and what response to record to share with others. The following are key elements of the observation:

1. Ensure that adequate length of time for the observation exists.
2. Observe an activity or period of time that provides comprehensive information about the student's performance.
3. Clearly document the content, strategies, and setting of the observed time period or activity.
4. Provide a comprehensive description of the observed behaviors and learning characteristics.

The information gained from observations, along with other information gathered from the various assessment methods, enables the evaluator to draw more authentic conclusions about the student's cultural background experiences, sociolinguistic development, and cognitive learning styles (Hoover & Collier, 2003). The observer must be someone who is sensitive to and knowledgeable about the student's culture and speaks the primary language of instruction.

Review of Existing Records

If current and complete, existing student records can be a major source of information about the student, particularly with regard to instructional history. Unfortunately, these records are often not comprehensive, inconsistent, incomplete, or disorganized and caution must be used when interpreting information from these types of student records. Anecdotal records vary in subjectivity depending on the experience, background, knowledge, and training of the person who wrote the report (i.e., factors important to providing meaning to the records). To assist with completing an accurate review of records, several items are presented in Table 5.8.

Accurate responses to these questions will provide additional background information necessary for a comprehensive assessment to occur. However, if existing records do not contain student's background information, it is critical to obtain this information from other sources (e.g., siblings, parents, or other community members).

TABLE 5.8 Items to Obtain from Review of Existing Records

Record Item	Recorded Documentation

Home/Language/Culture

Home language(s)
Student's English language proficiency
Student's native language proficiency
Student's cultural background
Evidence of trauma in homeland
Student's physical health history
Students socioemotional health history

School Experiences

Number of years residing in the United States
Number of years in U.S. schools
Types of instruction received (e.g., ESL)
Student progress in previous schools
Student's preferred instructional methods
Basic interpersonal communication skills (BICS)
Cognitive academic language proficiency (CALP)
Quality educational experiences provided

Socialization/Acculturation

Time spent interacting with peers
Quality of interactions with peers
Student's level of acculturation in the United States
Student's adjustment to U.S. classroom environments
Student's ability to work in cooperative groups
Comparison of social interactions at school and home

Sources: Wilkinson et al., (2004); Lachat (2004); Hammill (1987); Hoover (in press a).

Work Sample Analysis

Analysis of students' work samples is a meaningful assessment technique for instructional purposes for CLD learners (de Valenzuela & Cervantes, 2004) and may include both highly structured and informal methods depending on student needs. Samples of student work may be gathered and analyzed in any subject or content area, as well as speech, language, and fine or gross motor performance (Hammill, 1987). The accurate analysis of student work is best accomplished by an educator familiar with and sensitive to the student's cultural and linguistic background. Linguistic differences between English and other languages may pose considerable problems for CLD students in written and spoken classroom work, and work sample analysis may provide additional insight into student needs and current levels of development.

Task Analysis

Task analysis is an assessment technique designed to provide information on specific skills a student has acquired or must still master. Once targeted objectives have been identified, a variety of steps for successful use of task analysis in classroom assessment and instruction should be followed. These are adapted to address cultural and linguistic needs (Hammill & Bartel, 2004; Polloway, Patton, & Serna, in press; Baca & Cervantes, 2004):

1. *Identification.* Determine specific skills/subskills needed to facilitate achievement of the objective; list individual steps to follow to achieve the objective.
2. *Introduction.* Determine prior knowledge/skills possessed by learner in both native language (L1) and English (L2).
3. *Model.* Model desired skill/content using problem solving and direct instruction.
4. *Guided Practice.* Provide the learner meaningful opportunities to practice the skill or use the content in a variety of ways with direct teacher support (e.g., scaffolding).
5. *Student Feedback.* Provide the learner opportunities to describe either in writing (journaling) or orally what they are thinking, doing, and learning as they engage in a specific task.
6. *Independent Practice.* Provide reduced teacher direction to students so they more independently demonstrate the skill or use the content in varied ways.
7. *Assessment Review.* Record student performance during each step, documenting what is observed, discussed, and learned as the student engages in the learning task.

Overall, task analysis is an effective assessment method when clearly defined objectives are identified for the assessment following the steps identified above.

Running Records

A running record provides opportunity to collect and record data on student performance based on a specified time period rather than on the observation of a specific behavior (Alper, Ryndak, & Schloss, 2001). To implement the running records procedure, Peregoy and Boyle (1997) wrote that the teacher "stands behind the reader and marks words the student gets right with checks and takes notes (on the miscues) to code the reader's deviations from the text" (p. 300). Running records used in assessment assists the evaluator to provide detailed information documenting the effectiveness of classroom instruction, including text difficulty, student groupings, reading and other content area academic progress, learning difficulties, and individual student progress (Peregoy & Boyle, 1997). Running records provide another method for documenting and assessing student progress and classroom behaviors over time and should be integral to the comprehensive assessment process for CLD learners.

ASSESSMENT TYPES

A variety of types of assessments exist and are used to evaluate the academic progress and socioemotional development of CLD learners. Three of these assessment types include:

1. Authentic assessment
2. Standardized testing
3. Standards-based assessment

Each of these types is discussed with specific relevance to CLD/CLDE learners. Over the past couple of decades, two themes have emerged that highlight many issues in the area of assessment: accountability for and underachievement in the education of CLD learners (Cummins & Sayers, 1995). Data gathered from authentic assessment methods add support and relevance to standardized and standards-based assessment data and testing results. Specific issues associated with the use of formal, standardized testing and standards-based assessment with CLD learners are addressed in subsequent sections of this chapter. However, whichever assessment type is used it must reflect a nondiscriminatory assessment for CLD learners. Table 5.9 outlines several practices to insure a nondiscriminatory assessment. As shown, assessment practices must reflect cultural and linguistic diverse needs, primary language, cross-validation of results, and a variety of assessment techniques.

To minimize problems often resulting from the use of standardized testing with CLD learners, authentic assessment methods should be employed.

Authentic Assessment

When used in conjunction with prereferral interventions, authentic assessment provides more relevant and meaningful information concerning the educational needs of CLD learners. Two types of authentic assessment appropriate for use with CLD learners are curriculum-based assessment/measurement and performance-based assessment. The process for use of each of these is briefly described below. The reader is referred to Hammill and Bartel (2004); Polloway, Patton, and Serna (in press);

TABLE 5.9 Guide to Nondiscriminatory Assessment Practices

Tasks reflecting nondiscriminatory assessment practices . . .

1. Cross-cultural interviews are conducted and classroom observations are made.
2. Cross-validation of information from the home and family settings are made to corroborate formal assessment data or reasons for referral.
3. Assessment is conducted in student's primary language.
4. Effects of environmental and cultural influences on suspected problem are documented.
5. Assessment practices are completed by culturally and/or linguistically competent persons.
6. Linguistically appropriate goals and services are included in assessment practices.
7. Previous instructional programs and student progress in those programs are considered.
8. Adaptive behavior interventions are attempted and documented.
9. Home and family information is documented and accurate.
10. Student's language dominance and English proficiency are determined.
11. Translators/interpreters are properly used in assessment practices.
12. Basic interpersonal communication skills (BICS) and cognitive academic language proficiency (CALP) are determined in both dominant and second languages.
13. Alternative and authentic forms of assessment are included.

Source: From "Reducing Bias Decision-Making when Referring Learners with Cultural and Linguistic Needs," by J. J. Hoover, in press. In J. Klingner, A. Artiles, L. Baca, and J. Hoover (Eds.), *English Language Learners Who Struggle with Reading: Language Acquisition or Learning Disabilities?* Copyright by Corwin Press.

Choate et al. (1994); and Fuchs and Deno (1994) for more detailed discussions and descriptions on these assessment approaches.

Curriculum-Based Assessment Curriculum-based assessment (CBA) is an evidence-based alternative assessment method for determining specific instructional needs of students (Fuchs & Fuchs, 1997; Jones, 2001). Curriculum-based assessment is an alternative to formal, standardized tests and is typically conducted on an ongoing basis. Three elements must be included to effectively implement CBA (Fuchs & Deno, 1994):

1. Authentic class curriculum is used to determine student proficiency.
2. Assessment of learners occurs over extended period of time.
3. Results from CBA are linked directly to classroom instructional decisions.

Curriculum-based assessment provides a more direct correspondence between classroom curricular objectives and actual student performance (Hallahan & Kauffman, 2003). CBA is meaningful when assessing CLD/CLDE learners because it uses material directly related to the curriculum being taught in the classroom. In addition, Hoover and Patton (2005a) discussed several advantages that CBA has over formal standardized testing. These include the ability to more effectively:

1. Link scope and sequence with student needs directly in the assessment process.
2. Include more direct assessment of student needs based on actual curricular tasks, skills, and outcomes.
3. Implement effective decision making about classroom-level curricular issues.
4. Modify most, if not all, curricular content areas based directly on classroom performance.
5. Determine progress toward mastery of specific skills while also identifying those that require additional instructional support or intervention (RTI).

Curriculum-Based Measurement A more rigorous form of classroom-based curriculum assessment is curriculum-based measurement (CBM), which uses standardized procedures for assessing student performance (Hammill & Bartel, 2004; Paulsen, 1997). Research on CBM shows positive effects on student learning, particularly with students who have disabilities (Allinder, Fuchs, & Fuchs, 2004). Although CBM is similar to CBA by connecting interrelated aspects of teaching, learning, and testing, it also emphasizes these characteristics:

1. Focuses on long-term instructional goals rather than short-term objectives.
2. Blends alternative assessment with traditional testing.
3. Employs standardized methodology, whereas CBA relies primarily on teacher-made testing procedures (Fuchs & Deno, 1994).

When used appropriately, CBM is as reliable and valid as most standardized, norm-referenced tests (Hammill & Bartel, 2004). Additionally, CBM is evidence-based by including measurement over time, graphing of data or scores, and progress monitoring using objective, reliable, and valid instruments (Fuchs & Fuchs, 1997). When applied to CLD/CLDE learners, CBM is an alternative to standardized, norm-referenced instruments by including these special features:

1. Annual curriculum goals can easily be identified and measured.
2. Samples of the curriculum are systematically assessed through short, culturally appropriate tests.
3. Brief tests are administered following the same procedures (i.e., standardized) at regular intervals throughout the school year.
4. Results facilitate direct differentiation of curriculum to meet cultural and linguistic needs.

Both CBA and CBM complement other assessment methods by focusing on actual classroom behaviors, curriculum, and instructional strategies. For additional information about CBA and CBM, the reader is referred to Allinder, Fuchs, and Fuchs (2004) and Hammill and Bartel (2004).

Performance-Based Assessment Performance-based assessment consists of any form of assessment where students construct a response orally or in writing. Performance-based assessment for CLD/CLDE learners includes the following characteristics (O' Malley & Pierce, 1996; Herman, Aschbacher, & Winters, 1992):

1. *Constructed Response.* Students construct or expand on a response; generate product.
2. *Higher Order Thinking.* Student is challenged to use higher order thinking skills in the response constructed.
3. *Authenticity.* Assessment tasks must be meaningful, challenging, and engaging activities that model high-quality instruction.
4. *Integration.* Assessment tasks should integrate language and other skills across content areas.
5. *Process and Product.* Strategies for obtaining a response are assessed as well as the final product or response.
6. *Depth versus Breadth.* Assessment should measure a student's depth of mastery of skills and breadth of knowledge.

Performance assessments allow students to demonstrate proficiency with tasks involving higher order thinking abilities and problem solving (Lachat, 2004). They also provide opportunities for students to demonstrate skill proficiency associated with content knowledge. Use of scoring rubrics with performance-based assessment facilitates grading the performance tasks and more clearly helps to determine if and to what extent the student has mastered skills and employs higher order thinking.

The use of CBA/CBM and performance-based assessment with CLD/CLDE students allows teachers to:

1. Accommodate cultural and linguistic differences in assessment.
2. Determine specific skills/content that should be taught.
3. Identify appropriate teaching strategies.
4. Provide for frequent monitoring of progress.
5. Determine specific learning styles and strategies.

Formal Standardized Assessments

Any test administered in English to a nonnative English speaker becomes, to a great extent, a language test (Lachat, 2004). This leads to the possibility that, for CLD learners, a test may not measure what it is intended to measure. One of the most significant

TABLE 5.10 Guidelines for Using Unbiased Testing Devices

Formal standardized assessment devices are appropriate for CLD/CLDE learners if they contain or reflect the following:

Test examples and content are culturally appropriate.

Test has been validated for use with culturally and linguistically diverse populations.

Cultural and linguistic backgrounds are taken into account in test development.

Translated test has been validated and normed following proper procedures.

Concepts and vocabulary relevant to assessment tasks are familiar to student.

Topics assessed are familiar and culturally relevant to the student.

Test does NOT misdiagnosis second language needs for language disorders.

Time limitations do NOT penalize student because of limited English proficiency.

Limited English proficient students have the same opportunities to demonstrate knowledge as English proficient students.

Test format is familiar to the student.

Assessment manual discusses appropriate uses of the test with culturally and linguistically diverse learners.

Language of the test is in student's primary language.

Content of test does not mislead the student due to cultural or linguistic diversity.

Sources: Figueroa and Newsome (2004); Wilkinson et al. (2004); Lachat (2004); O'Malley and Pierce (1996).

concerns when using standardized testing with CLD learners is the possibility that differing cultural values may influence student responses to a point where results are rendered inaccurate. In addition to language issues, educators who assess CLD learners using standardized instruments must determine whether and to what extent cultural and linguistic diversity impacts the learner's test-taking abilities and subsequent test results (O'Malley & Pierce, 1996). This is best accomplished by addressing the six cultural factors previously discussed and through the use of a variety of assessment methods such as those previously presented. Also, although educators are aware of potential cultural and linguistic biases inherent in tests, many professionals often view formal standardized test scores as accurate measures of students' achievement and abilities (Baca & Cervantes, 2004).

Assessments Implications: When using formal standardized instruments to assess CLD learners for possible special education eligibility, educators should adhere to the suggestions described in Table 5.10. This guide contains several items to assist educators to be more confident that the assessment device and subsequent results are appropriate for CLD learners. Only through the use of a variety of culturally relevant assessment methods and testing devices can the detrimental trend of inappropriate assessment of CLDE learners be reversed.

Standards–Based Assessment

Standards-based education includes the establishment and assessment of standards for academic progress, emphasizing higher learner expectations (Hallahan & Kauffman, 2003; Thurlow, 2000). Currently, most states use some form of standards-based curriculum and assessment with all of their students, including CLD/CLDE learners. For standards-based assessment to be valid and reliable, learners must be properly instructed within standards-based curriculum, which is composed of three interrelated areas (Hoover & Patton, 2004; Glatthorn, 1998; McLaughlin & Shepard, 1995):

1. *Content Standards.* Includes subject area skills/knowledge to be learned
2. *Performance Standards.* Proficiency levels required to demonstrate mastery of content
3. *Opportunity to Learn Standards.* Materials, strategies, structure necessary for successful learning to occur in the classroom

All three of these types of standards must be addressed to successfully assess progress in standards-based curriculum for CLD/CLDE students (Hoover & Patton, 2005b). These authors also discussed other items that educators who use standards-based assessment with diverse learners should attend to:

1. Focus on what is important to learn in the curriculum.
2. Compare students' academic performance to a standard of proficiency, NOT other students.
3. Ensure that assessment is reflective of the existing curriculum and instruction.
4. Realize that standards-based assessment is intended to establish accountability and stimulate improvement.

Several underlying assumptions concerning standards-based assessment have been discussed in the literature (Hallahan & Kauffman, 2003; Lachat, 2004; Quenemoen, Lehr, Thurlow, & Massanaair, 2001; Hoover & Patton, 2005a). These assumptions include:

1. Emphasizing improved learning rather than ranking students based on test norms.
2. Viewing assessment as a tool to clarify proficiency levels relative to identified standards.
3. Determining the extent to which ALL students are learning at high levels.
4. Viewing intelligence as a dynamic not a fixed trait.
5. Seeing learning potential as developmental and related to experiential background.
6. Recognizing the need for more diverse means of assessment due to roles of multiple intelligences.

Assessment Implications: Standards-based curriculum and assessment has the potential to more accurately identify current levels of proficiency in CLD learners provided extensive opportunities exist to ensure that culturally and linguistically relevant teaching and learning occur in the classroom. As a result, of most concern for CLD/CLDE learners educated and assessed within a standards-based curriculum is their opportunity to learn. Without adequate access and participation in the curriculum, standards-based assessments will yield inaccurate and invalid assessment results, similar to norm-referenced standardized testing results. As educators acquire a greater understanding of appropriate uses of standards-based curriculum and assessment, CLD/CLDE learners will be provided better opportunities to learn as well as to demonstrate their learning in more valid and reliable ways.

ASSESSMENT ACCOMMODATIONS AND INDIVIDUALIZED EDUCATION PLANS FOR CLDE LEARNERS

As suggested throughout this chapter, a variety of cultural and linguistic needs interconnect with educational needs. Within the overall assessment and placement process, two additional areas that must be considered to ensure appropriate, valid, and reliable assessment and instruction for CLDE learners are (1) use of assessment accommodations and (2) IEP development.

Assessment Accommodations

Demands associated with the assessment of CLD learners for both general education annual performance and possible special education eligibility have highlighted the possible need for making appropriate accommodations to ensure that accurate results are obtained. Accommodations are modifications to the assessment environment so that students are provided an appropriate opportunity to successfully complete the assessment. Thompson (2004) suggested that accommodations allow students with disabilities to succeed. Most recently, IDEA (2004) provides provisions for making appropriate accommodations for students with disabilities, including CLDE learners. Accommodations are designed to alter conditions for assessment due to disability or language needs, which do not change the standards or benchmarks being assessed. While generally understood, the issue of equity in school assessment is a major concern to many special educators (Orosco, 2005). Educators of CLD/CLDE learners should be aware of accepted assessment accommodations and implement them if appropriate to ensuring valid assessment results. Specifically, five types of assessment accommodations are available for students with disabilities (Orosco, 2005; Thompson, 2004; Elliot, Braden, & White, 2001):

1. *Presentation.* Adjusting how material is presented; assessment may require more or less visual or auditory emphasis.
2. *Response.* Modifying method of response; assessment may require alternate response modes to accommodate a disability.

3. *Time.* Adjusting time allotments; more time to complete the assessment may be required due to needs associated with a disability or language difference.
4. *Scheduling.* Restructuring test-taking schedule; disability or language needs may require adjustments to assessment schedules.
5. *Setting.* Altering the location where student completes testing; assessment location in the school or classroom may need to be changed due to disability or language needs.

The need for appropriate accommodations for CLDE learners is reported on the student's IEP. Teachers of CLDE students should be aware of these accommodations, apply them as necessary to ensure appropriate assessment, and advocate for their inclusion in the student's IEP.

IEP Development

One of the final steps educators must complete if a CLD student's needs are determined to be due primarily to a disability is the completion of an Individualized Education Plan (IEP). The IEP is developed after a placement decision into special education is made. Placement decisions should be based on prereferral intervention and response to that intervention, along with a comprehensive assessment process and use of a variety of methods as discussed throughout this chapter. It should be based on a student's strengths and weaknesses in the areas of achievement, aptitude/ability, and emotional/behavioral competence within a culturally and linguistically relevant context.

In addition to identifying the child's general competence in these areas, IDEA (2004) specifies elements necessary to be addressed in an IEP, including emphasis on annual goals rather than short-term instructional objectives, measurable educational outcomes and progress, and provisions for academic and assessment accommodations (Sorrells, Reith, & Sindelar, 2004). Specific elements important for an IEP for CLDE learners include strategies and provisions for:

1. Native language development and English language acquisition.
2. The facilitation of acculturation and language of instruction.
3. Special education services and placements.
4. Integration of culture/linguistic interventions while simultaneously meeting special education needs.
5. Identification of all service providers responsible for implementing and monitoring the integration of these services, including ESL or bilingual educators.
6. Expected time limits and scheduled-for annual reevaluation.

The inclusion of these items in an IEP ensures that the most appropriate and culturally relevant special services available are provided to all CLDE learners. Overall, the IEP is developed in consultation with all concerned parties and must be a comprehensive presentation of the student's total learning needs. This includes documenting how culturally and linguistically appropriate instructional interventions will be used in meeting the student's special needs.

SUMMARY

The comprehensive assessment of CLD learners for possible special education services is a complex process that requires in-depth knowledge of general assessment procedures, methods, and instruments, as well as specific knowledge of cultural and linguistic factors that influence learning. This chapter has addressed many critical issues challenging educators involved in the assessment of CLD learners as they attempt to differentiate between learning differences and disabilities. This includes using a variety of standardized and classroom-based assessment procedures, various assessment methods and tests, along with specific consideration of six cultural factors that directly influence assessment results of CLD learners. The primary outcome when assessing CLD students is the ability to make informed decisions concerning whether a student's instructional needs are based primarily on learning differences or a disability that interferes with academic and/or socioemotional development. Various guides and checklists to assist educators in assessment were presented to facilitate an objective means to ensuring that the most culturally relevant, appropriate, and meaningful assessment process for CLD learners occurs. The current emphasis on standards-based curriculum and assessment, the need for English language assessment to precede all other assessment, and the development of effective IEPs for CLDE learners were also discussed.

Discussion Questions

1. Identify three examples of communicative and academic language use in the classroom for both oral and written language and discuss how to assess each in authentic ways.

2. Discuss how the six cultural/linguistic factors can affect assessment results and influence the assessment interpretation. How would these six areas affect an assessment team's "hypothesis" concerning a potential difference versus a disability?

3. Illustrate the relationship among culture, language, and academic achievement and show how this relationship must be considered in assessment.

4. Why is it important to know a student's non-English language abilities?
5. Select four assessment techniques and show how useful information in a non-biased assessment may be gathered.
6. Discuss how you have used various forms of authentic assessment with CLD/CLDE learners.

References

Allinder, R. M., Fuchs, L. S., & Fuchs, D. (2004). Issued in curriculum-based assessment. In A. M. Sorrels, H. Reith, & P. Sindelar (Eds), *Critical Issues in Special Education: Access, Diversity and Accountability* (pp. 106–124). Boston: Allyn & Bacon.

Alper, S., Ryndak, D. L., & Schloss, C. N. (2001). *Alternate assessment of students with disabilities in inclusive settings.* Boston, MA: Allyn & Bacon.

Baca, L. M. (2005). The education of English language learners with special needs. In J. J. Hoover (Ed.), *Current issues in special education* (pp. 25–33). Boulder, CO: University of Colorado, BUENO Center.

Baca, L. M., & Cervantes, H. T. (2004). *The bilingual special education interface* (3rd ed.). Upper Saddle River, NJ: Merrill/Prentice Hall.

Baca, L. M., & Clark, C. (1992). *EXITO: A dynamic team assessment approach for culturally diverse students.* Minneapolis, MN: CEC.

Banks, J. A. (1994). *Multiethnic education: Theory and practice.* Boston: Allyn & Bacon.

Beekman, L. (2005, January). *IDEA 04: What's new and so what.* Presentation at the annual Colorado Special Education Directors meeting, Denver, CO.

Bloom, B. S., Englehart, M. D., Furst, G. J., Hill, W. H., & Krathwohl, D. R. (1956). *Taxonomy of educational objectives: Handbook I. The cognitive domain.* New York: David McKay.

Bronfenbrenner, U. (1979). *The ecology of human development.* Cambridge, MA: Harvard University Press.

Bronfenbrenner, U. (1995). Developmental ecology through space and time: A future perspective. In P. Moen, G. Elder, & K. Luescher (Eds.), *Examining lives in context: Perspectives on the ecology of human development* (pp. 619–647). Washington, DC: American Psychological Association.

Buck, G. L., Polloway, E. A., Smith-Thomas, A., & Cook, K. W. (2003). Prereferral intervention processes: A survey of state practices. *Exceptional Children, 69*(3), 349–360.

Chamberlain, P., & Medeiros-Landurand, P. (1991). Practical considerations for the assessment of LEP students with special needs. In E. V. Hamayan & J. S. Damico (Eds.), *Limiting bias in the assessment of bilingual students* (pp. 111–156). Austin, TX: Pro-Ed.

Choate, J. S., Miller, L. J., Bebbett, T. Z., Poteet, J. A., Enright, B. E., & Rakes, T. A. (1994). *Assessing and programming basic curriculum skills.* Boston, MA: Allyn & Bacon.

Cohen, L. G., & Spenciner, L. J. (2003). *Assessment of children and youth with special needs.* Boston: Pearson.

Collier, C. (1988). *Assessing minority students with learning and behavior* problems. Boulder, CO: Hamilton Publications.

Collier, C., & Hoover, J. J. (1987). Sociocultural considerations when referring minority children for learning disabilities. *Learning Disabilities Focus, 3*(1), 39–45.

Collier, V. P. (1995). Acquiring a second language for school. *Directions in language and Education, 1*(4), 1–12. Washington, DC: National Clearinghouse for English Language Acquisition and Language Instruction Educational Programs.

Cummins, J. (1996). Primary language instruction and the education of language minority students. In *Schooling and language minority students: A theoretical framework* (pp. 3–46). Los Angeles: Evaluation, Dissemination, and Assessment Center, UCLA, School of Education.

Cummins, J. (2000). *Language, power, and pedagogy: Bilingual children in the crossfire.* New York: Multilingual Matters.

Cummins, J., & Sayers, D. (1995). *Brave new schools: Challenging cultural illiteracy through global networks.* New York: St. Martin's Press.

Damico, J. S., Cheng, J., Deleon, J., Ferrer, J., & Westernoff, F. (1992). *Descriptive assessment in the schools: Meeting new challenges with new solutions.* Minneapolis, MN: CEC.

de Valenzuela, J. S., & Baca, L. M. (2004). Procedures and techniques for assessing the bilingual exceptional child. In L. M. Baca & H. Cervantes, (Eds.), *The bilingual special education interface* (pp. 187–201). Upper Saddle River, NJ: Merrill/Prentice Hall.

de Valenzuela, J. S., & Cervantes, H. (2004). Procedures and techniques for assessing the bilingual exceptional child. In L. M. Baca & H. Cervantes (Eds.), *The bilingual special education interface* (pp. 168–187). Upper Saddle River, NJ: Merrill/Prentice Hall.

Elliot, S. N., Braden, J. P., & White, J. L. (2001). *Assessing one and all: Educational accountability for students with disabilities.* Arlington, VA: Council for Exceptional Children.

Farr, B., & Turnbull, E. (1997). *Assessment alternatives for diverse classrooms.* Norwood, MA: Christopher-Gordon.

Figueroa, R. A., & Newsome, P. (2004). *The diagnosis of learning disabilities in English language learners—Is it nondiscriminatory?* Paper presented at the 2004 NCCRESt Conference, English Language Learners Struggling to Learn: Emergent Research on Linguistic Differences and Learning Disabilities, Tempe, AZ.

Fuchs, L. S., & Deno, S. L. (1994). Must instructional-useful performance assessment be based in the curriculum? *Exceptional Children, 61*(1), 15–24.

Fuchs, L. S., & Fuchs, D. (1997). Use of curriculum-based measurement in identifying students with disabilities. *Focus on Exceptional Children, 30*(3), 1–16.

Gagne, E. D., Yekovich, C. W., & Yekovich, F. R. (1993). *The cognitive psychology of school learning* (2nd ed). Boston: Little Brown.

Garcia, S. B. (2002). Parent-professional collaboration in culturally sensitive assessment. In A. J. Artiles & A. A. Ortiz (Eds.), *English language learners with special education needs: Identification, assessment and instruction* (pp. 85–103). McHenry, IL: Center for Applied Linguistics and Delta Systems Co.

Garcia, G., & Pearson, P. (1994). Assessment and diversity. In L. Darling-Hammond (Ed.), *A review of research in education* (Vol. 20, pp. 337–391). Washington, DC: American Educational Research Association.

Glatthorn, A. A. (1998). *Performance assessment and standards-based curricula: The achievement cycle.* Larchmont, NY: Eye on Education.

Haager, D., & Klingner, J. K. (2005). *Differentiating instruction in inclusive classrooms: The special educator's guide.* Boston, MA: Pearson.

Hallahan, D. P., & Kauffman, J. M. (2003). *Exceptional learners: Introduction to special education.* Boston: Allyn & Bacon.

Hammill, D. D. (1987). An overview of assessment practices. In D. D. Hammill (Ed.), *Assessing the abilities and instructional needs of students.* Austin, TX: Pro-Ed.

Hammill, D. D., & Bartel, N. R. (2004). *Teaching students with learning and behavior problems.* Austin, TX: Pro-Ed.

Herman, J. L., Aschbacher, P. R., & Winters, L. (1992). *A practical guide to alternative assessment.* Alexandria, VA: Association for Supervision and Curriculum Development.

Hodgkinson, H. (2000). *Educational demographics: What teachers should know.* Alexandria, VA: Association for Supervision and Curriculum Development.

Hoover, J. J. (2001). *Assessment of English language learners* (CD-ROM). Boulder, CO: University of Colorado at Boulder, BUENO Center.

Hoover, J. J. (2005). Special challenges, special needs. In J. J. Hoover (Ed.), *Current issues in special education: Meeting diverse needs in the twenty-first century.* Boulder, CO: University of Colorado, School of Education, BUENO Center.

Hoover, J. J. (in press a). Special education referral and eligibility decision-making practices. In J. K. Klingner, A. J. Artiles, L. Baca, & J. J. Hoover (Eds.), *English language learners who struggle with reading: Language acquisition or learning disabilities?* Thousand Oaks, CA: Corwin Press.

Hoover, J. J. (in press b). Assessment issues and test validity for english language learners: Implications for practitioners. In J. K. Klingner, A. J. Artiles, L. Baca, & J. J. Hoover (Eds.), *English language learners who struggle with reading: Language acquisition or learning disabilities?* Thousand Oaks, CA: Corwin Press.

Hoover, J. J., & Collier, C. (2003). *Learning styles* (CD-ROM). Boulder, CO: University of Colorado at Boulder, BUENO Center.

Hoover, J. J., & Collier, C. (2004). Methods and materials for bilingual special education. In L. M. Baca & H. Cervantes (Eds.), *The bilingual special education interface* (pp. 276–197). Upper Saddle River, NJ: Merrill/Prentice Hall.

Hoover, J. J., & Patton, J. R. (2004). Perspective: Differentiating standards-based education for students with diverse needs. *Remedial and Special Education, 25*(2), 74–78.

Hoover, J. J., & Patton, J. R. (2005a). *Curriculum adaptations for students with learning and behavior problems: Differentiating instruction to meet to diverse needs* (3rd ed.). Austin, TX: Pro-Ed.

Hoover, J. J., & Patton, J. R. (2005b). Differentiating curriculum and instruction for English language learners with special needs. *Intervention School and Clinic, 40,* 231–235.

Hoover J. J., Patton, J. R., Hresko, W., & Hammill, D. (in press). *Prereferral assessment inventory.* Austin, TX: Pro-Ed.

IDEA. (2004). *Individuals with Disabilities Education Act Amendments of 2004,* Washington, DC.

Jones, C. J. (2001). CBAs that work: Assessing student's math content-reading levels. *Teaching Exceptional Children, 34*(1), 24–28.

Klingner, J. K., & Harry, B. (2004). *The special education referral and decision-making process for English language learners—Child study team meetings and staffings.* Paper presented at the 2004 NCCRESt Conference, English Language Learners Struggling to Learn: Emergent Research on Linguistic Differences and Learning Disabilities, Tempe, AZ.

Lachat, M. A. (2004). *Standards-based instruction and assessment for English language learners.* Thousand Oaks, CA: Corwin Press.

McLaughlin, W. W., & Shepard, L. A. (1995). *Improving education through standards-based reform.* Stanford, CA: The National Academy of Education.

Moran, D. J., & Malott, R. W. (2004). *Evidence-based educational methods.* Boston: Elsevier Academic Press.

No Child Left Behind Act (2001). The Elementary and Secondary Education Act of 2001, P.L. 107–110, 115, *Stat.1425* (2001). Washington, DC.

O'Malley, J. M., & Pierce, L. V. (1996). *Authentic assessment for English language learners: Practical approaches for teachers.* New York: Addison-Wesley Publishing.

Orosco, M. J. (2005). Accommodations in assessment and instruction to meet special needs. In J. J. Hoover (Ed.), *Current issues in special education: Meeting diverse needs in the twenty-first century* (pp. 87–94). Boulder, CO: University of Colorado, BUENO Center.

Ortiz, A. A., & Yates, J. R. (2002). Considerations in the assessment of English language learners referred to special education. In A. J. Artiles & A. A. Ortiz (Eds.), *English language learners with special education needs: Identification, assessment and instruction* (pp. 65–85). McHenry, IL: Center for Applied Linguistics and Delta Systems Co.

Paulsen, K. J. (1997). Curriculum-based measurement: Translating research into school-based practice. *Intervention in School and Clinic, 32,* 162–167.

Peregoy, S. F., & Boyle, O. F. (1997). *Reading, writing, & learning in ESL: A resource book for K-12 teachers.* New York: Addison Wesley Longman.

Polloway, E. A., Patton, J. R., & Serna, L. (in press). *Strategies for teaching learners with special needs* (9th ed.). Upper Saddle River, NJ: Merrill/Prentice Hall.

Quenemoen, R. F., Lehr, C. A., Thurlow, M. L., & Massanaair, C. B. (2001). *Students with disabilities in standards-based assessment and accountability systems: Emerging issues, strategies, and recommendations.* Minneapolis, MN: National Center on Educational Outcomes.

Richard-Amato, P. A. (1996). *Making it happen: Interaction in the second language classroom.* New York: Longman.

Rueda, R., & Kim, S. (2001). Cultural and linguistic diversity as a theoretical framework for understanding multicultural learners with mild disabilities. In C. A. Utley & F. E. Obiakor (Eds.), *Special education, multicultural education, and school reform: Components of quality education for learners with mild disabilities* (pp. 74–89). Springfield, IL: Charles C. Thomas.

Salvia, J., & Ysseldyke, J. (2003). *Assessment in special education and remedial education.* Boston: Houghton Mifflin.

Sorrells, A. M., Reith, H. J., & Sindelar, P. T. (2004). *Critical issues in special education: Access, diversity and accountability.* Boston, MA: Pearson.

Stefanakis, E. H. (1998). *Whose judgment counts?: Assessing bilingual children K–3.* Portsmouth, NH: Heinemann.

Tharp, R. G. (1997). *From at-risk to excellence: Research, theory, and principles for practice.* Santa Cruz, CA: Center for Research on Education, Diversity and Excellence.

Thompson, S. J. (2004). Choosing and using accommodations on assessments. *CEC Today, 10(6)*, 12.

Thurlow, M. L. (2000). Standards-based reform and students with disabilities: Reflections on a decade of change. *Focus on Exceptional Children, 33*(3), 1–16.

Wilkinson, C. Y., Ortiz, A., & Robertson-Courtney, P. (2004). *Appropriate eligibility determination for English language learners suspected of having reading-related learning disabilities—Linking school history, prereferral, referral and assessment data.* Paper presented at the 2004 NCCRESt Conference, English Language Learners Struggling to Learn: Emergent Research on Linguistic Differences and Learning Disabilities, Tempe, AZ.

Winzer, M. A., & Mazurek, K. (1994). *Special education in multicultural contexts.* Upper Saddle River, NJ: Merrill/Prentice Hall.

Yates, J. R., & Ortiz, A. A. (2004). Developing individualized educational programs for exceptional language minority students. In L. Baca & H. Cervantes, *The Bilingual Special Educational Interface* (pp. 204–229). Upper Saddle River, NJ: Merrill/Prentice Hall.

Chapter 6

Methods for Behavior, Classroom, and Schoolwide Management

Alicia L. Moore, Ph.D.

Julie A. Armentrout, Ph.D.

La Vonne I. Neal, Ph.D.

Chapter Objectives

Upon completion of this chapter the reader will be able to:

1. Understand the importance of multicultural competence and culturally responsive management strategies in managing today's classrooms and schools.
2. Describe classroom management strategies for working with students who exhibit difficult behaviors.
3. Understand the role of the school in supporting behavior management programs.
4. Describe methods for teaching social competence and self-management strategies to students.
5. Understand violence prevention strategies and their impact on student behavior.

VIGNETTE

"Sit down, Jarrod!" "Be quiet, DeMarcus!" Ms. Prichard was upset at both boys because she believed that they were being disrespectful to her and to each other. She had warned the boys several times to settle down after an altercation on the way from the cafeteria to the classroom. During the altercation, Jarrod and DeMarcus, both sixth-grade, African American males, made snide comments to each other that were related to topics that ranged from their clothing and sport shoes to their siblings and athletic prowess. With each remark, the other students would laugh and make noises that seemed to urge on this behavior. Though she had explained to them that their comments were not "very nice," and were inappropriate, the dialogue continued:

Jarrod: "Your pants look like they belong to your sister!"

Rest of the class (laughing): "Ohhh!"

DeMarcus: "Boy, you can't talk about me; your shirt looks like your grandmother picked it out for you!"

Rest of the class: "Ohhh, he got you good!!"

Jarrod: "What are you talking about? At least my grandmother doesn't buy me tight pants. You can't run in those pants. I can beat you running today!"

Rachael: "You two should race on the playground!"

DeMarcus: "I can still beat you running; you are slower than a turtle!"

Rest of the class: "Ohhh!"

When the class entered the classroom, the two boys continued to whisper insults to each other and did not immediately sit down as directed. This banter made Ms. Prichard nervous and she was afraid that their verbal barbs would lead to more aggressive behavior. She picked up the classroom intercom and called for an administrator before things got out of control. She felt that she had made a prudent decision. Though an administrator responded to the call, the boys soon returned to the classroom in a jovial mood. Ms. Prichard was perplexed. What had happened? Had the boys not been scolded for their disrespectful behavior? Ms. Prichard was a young, European American teacher who had been teaching for half a year. She was raised in a conservative, upper middle-class, predominantly White, suburban community, and her family owned the local hardware store and the "Big Burger" restaurant in the commercially zoned area of town. She had attended a very small private school and never had a Black or Hispanic person in any of her classes. The only contact she had ever had with culturally diverse populations was through service industry-related positions or through cable Music Television (MTV©).

When she graduated from high school and went to college, she attended a predomi-nantly White, private university that was nestled in a small rural community whose demo-graphics mirrored her hometown. The university's education program infused the tenets of culturally responsive teaching (Gay, 2002) into every one of her education-related courses. However, Ms. Prichard still had little or no substantive contact with culturally diverse populations. Unlike her own academic experiences, Ms. Prichard's first teaching assignment was in an inner-city elementary school in a large urban area. The school's demographics were 60 percent African American, 35 percent Hispanic American, and 5 percent European American and Native American. As well, the principal was African American, the assistant principal was Hispanic American, and at every grade level, there was at least one African American and one Hispanic American teacher. After school, in the grade-level team meeting, Ms. Prichard proudly relayed the story about Jarrod and DeMarcus, her proactive discipline decision, and the fact that the boys were soon returned to her classroom. The other teachers on her team chuckled. They told her that they did not know what she was so worried about—the boys were just "high-capping" on each other. Ms. Prichard had witnessed a cultural ritual called "verbal sparring" or "capping" (Irvine, 1990; McIntyre 1991). This type of sparring, she was told by her colleagues, was harmless joking that did not usually lead to aggression, but to more robust friendships. They further explained that when the students use this type of "humor" to poke fun at each other, the ritual is only in fun. Although teacher intervention may be needed if the verbal taunts are cruel insults, this episode was an innocent act of oral jousting.

Ms. Prichard was neither unqualified nor uncaring. On the contrary, she was well-prepared and truly wanted her students to be successful in her classroom. The decisions she made were sensible and proactive classroom management practices. However, she quickly realized that there was something implicitly cultural that she did not clearly understand. Weinstein, Tomlinson-Clarke, and Curran (2004) define this lack of under-standing as a lack of multicultural competence and assert that given the increasing diver-sity of our classrooms, a lack of multicultural competence can exacerbate the difficulties that novice teachers have with classroom management. Definitions and expectations of appropriate behavior are culturally influenced, and conflicts are likely to occur when teachers and students come from different cultural backgrounds. To reduce gaps in multicultural competence, Ms. Pritchard should make every effort to (a) learn about the history and experiences of diverse groups, (b) visit students' families and communities, (c) visit or read about successful teachers in diverse settings, and (d) develop an appreci-ation of diversity (Gay, 2002; Villegas & Lucas, 2002; Addressing Diversity in Schools, 2004).

Reflective Questions

1. What steps can Ms. Prichard take to gain multicultural competence?
2. Given the implicit cultural underpinnings of this situation, what would you do to make sure that students who are culturally different than yourself are given an opportunity to be successful both academically and behaviorally?

INTRODUCTION

Given the complexity of our country's changing demographics, and the resultant increase in diversity in today's classrooms, the incongruity between the cultural backgrounds of teachers and their culturally and linguistically diverse students may likely be a source of conflict. The differences in the cultural backgrounds of teachers and students may be associated with the cultural knowledge, experiences, beliefs, attitudes and values that both students and teachers possess. These cultural differences play an important role in teachers' interactions with students, expectations of students, inferences about student behaviors, and thus, their utilization of classroom management techniques and strategies. Conflicts arise when teachers misunderstand or misinterpret the behaviors of culturally and linguistically different students and use these misinterpretations to make management decisions. To decrease the likelihood of management problems related to cultural differences, teachers have to make an effort to explore them and consider them as assets that can be used to build strong student-teacher relationships.

OVERVIEW OF MANAGEMENT NEEDS OF CLDE LEARNERS

Nieto (2002) reported that U.S. demographic profiles of students and teachers illustrate an increasing number of culturally diverse students being taught primarily by White, middle-class, female teachers. As well, she found that U.S. teacher candidates, both current and projected, are White females and will be hired to teach in school districts that are becoming increasingly diverse. More specifically, recent statistics presented by the National Center for Education Statistics (NCES, 2003) found that in the United States the number of teachers of color is not representative of the number of students of color. Data from 2001–2002 show that 60 percent of public school students were White, 17 percent Black, 17 percent Hispanic, 4 percent Asian/Pacific Islander, and 1 percent American Indian/Alaska Native, whereas, 2001 data show that 90 percent of public school teachers were White, 6 percent Black, and fewer than 5 percent of other races (National Collaborative on Diversity in the Teaching Force, 2004). One solution related to the disparity in the demographic profiles of students and teachers is the recruitment and retention of more teachers from diverse backgrounds. The National Collaborative on Diversity in Teaching Report (2004) asserts that more teachers of color would (1) increase the number of role models for students of color; (2) provide opportunities for all students to learn about ethnic, racial, and cultural diversity; and (3) be able to enrich diverse students' learning because of shared racial, ethnic, and cultural identities and calls for those involved in education and education policy to examine its recruitment and retention strategies. In the meantime, Cartledge, Kea, and Simmons-Reed (2002) report that, by the year 2050, half of the U.S. population is projected to be of Hispanic, African American, Native American, or Asian/Pacific descent. Translating this projected composition of the larger population onto the school population has been the focus of a growing body of research over the past several years. For example, Anderson et al. (1998) state that the traditional "minority" groups will become the "majority" in public education settings throughout several states. One of the more pressing implications of this trend centers on developing proven methods for successfully meeting the academic and social needs of culturally and linguistically diverse exceptional (CLDE) children.

Culturally and linguistically diverse learners with cognitive, physical, and/or emotional needs have consistently been the target of misidentification, misrepresentation, and miseducation within the classroom (Anderson et al., 1998; Cartledge, Kea, & Simmons-Reed, 2002; Lo, Loe, & Cartledge, 2002; McCray & Neal, 2003). McCray and Neal (2003) assert that the miseducation of students of color continues to threaten the academic achievement, and subsequent economic and cultural vitality, of culturally diverse children, their families, and the broader community. Although federal regulations (Lopez, 1995) have mandated the provision of nondiscriminatory and culturally sensitive instruction and assessment services to all students, the current reality illuminates the seemingly perpetual trend of CLD students being disproportionately placed in special education (Neal, Webb-Johnson, & McCray, 2003).

In a report to the President's Commission on Excellence in Special Education (Cartledge, n.d.), data reveal that Black students, who make up 14.8 percent of the student population, account for 20.2 percent of the students in special education programs. These data further reveal that African American students are 2.9 times as likely to be identified as having mental retardation, 1.9 times as likely to be labeled with serious emotional disturbances, and 1.3 times as likely to be labeled learning disabled. Regarding disciplinary actions, Cartledge (n.d.) noted that Black males, as compared to White males, are much more likely to be suspended at a younger age; receive suspensions of longer durations; be tracked into classes for low-ability learners; be retained in their grade levels; be programmed into reactive, punishment-oriented juvenile detention centers; and given more pathological, deficit-oriented labels. Instead of focusing on creative intervention strategies that could enable these learners to experience success and self-determination, the emphasis throughout much of today's teaching practice and education literature has focused on a reductionism model that conceptualizes problem areas within these learners (Obiakor, Utley, Smith, & Harris-Obiakor, 2002).

McCray and Neal (2003) state that African American students are being placed in programs for students with disabilities, even as the special education discipline has admittedly faced challenges in locating the most culturally relevant tests to assess their cognitive, intellectual, behavioral, and social skill development. There is also an increased awareness that this discipline is falling short in preparing their general and special educators to appropriately modify curriculum and programs to accommodate for learning and cultural differences (Lo et al., 2002). Because of these glaring challenges, various researchers (Artiles, 1998; Artiles & Trent, 1994; Obiakor, 2001) have concluded that special education may not be so "special" for many culturally diverse students, particularly African Americans. The likelihood is high that placement in special education is a permanent status with few opportunities for students of color with disabilities to receive individualized, structured, and explicit learning that is culturally responsive

(McCray & Neal, 2003). Cultural and linguistic factors and their impact on behavior management strategies, then, need to be a part of the training of well-qualified teachers.

Cultural and Linguistic Factors and Behavior Management

Punishment and other coercive practices are often ineffective for culturally diverse learners, leading to negative modeling and causing students to devalue school, the schooling process, and school personnel (Cartledge, n.d.). For example, research (Artiles & Trent, 1994; Bacon & Kea, 1998; Chinn & Hughes, 1987) has shown that the emotional consequences of academic and social failure impact African American males more severely than any other group. Furthermore, families are faced with the added challenge of socializing these males in ways that lessen the prospect of school failure and other negative, self-destructive behaviors (Cartledge et al., 2002). The reality that males are taught to be aggressive, competitive, and assertive often serves as a source of conflict within the general classroom where a teacher, by virtue of being female (typically) and of a different cultural background, may view these males' behaviors as threatening and pathological (Cartledge, n.d.; Neal et al., 2003; McIntyre, 1991).

Teachers whose culture or class differs from that of their students are often likely to misinterpret the students' behaviors. If teachers are to create caring and culturally affirming classroom environments for CLDE students, culturally responsive instructional and management strategies must be developed. To enhance teacher effectiveness, Anderson et al. (1998) make the following recommendations: (a) know the cultural values and orientations of all students; (b) accept students as individuals and their cultural differences; (c) respect, relate, and build relationships with all students; (d) require high expectations of all students; (e) examine teacher behaviors and antecedent conditions in the classroom that may promote cultural misunderstandings; (f) realize that a mismatch between home and school culture may exist and create a system of familial responsibilities that approximate home communities in the classroom; (g) be aware of "culture-specific" behaviors regarding communication styles, social taboos, and motivational systems; and (h) redesign classrooms to accommodate cultural differences and styles via a relevant curriculum and cooperative learning.

Culturally Responsive Classroom Management

Weinstein, Tomlinson-Clarke, and Curran (2004) contend that classroom management is a powerful influence on student success, and its "ultimate goal is not to achieve compliance or control but to provide all students with equitable opportunities for learning" (p. 27). They propose that this type of equitable management can be accomplished through culturally responsive classroom management (CRCM). They further assert that culturally responsive classroom management includes (a) an examination and awareness of one's own biases; (b) knowledge of the backgrounds of students who are culturally diverse; (c) the creation of a caring classroom community; and (d) the "ability and willingness to use culturally appropriate management strategies" (p. 25). For teachers to embrace CRCM, they must examine their own personal challenges in multicultural competence. Teachers can then use their self-examination findings as a guide in developing a CRCM system that will be effective in their classrooms. CRCM systems should be developed as a purposeful and informed intersection of culture and behavior. One way to examine personal barriers to CRCM is for teachers of all races and ethnicities to facilitate their own personal self-assessment through a reflective process. This process is personal and is to be used to inform classroom management practices. It requires teachers to be starkly honest and to look "in the mirror." Through this honest and exploratory process, a teacher can assess personal preparedness to be culturally responsive and reflect upon action approach strategies for a successful classroom (see Chapter 2).

The CRCM Teacher Self-Assessment and Reflection Guide shown in Table 6.1 can be used by teachers to begin their self-assessment process. It provides *action approach strategies* that affirm culturally responsive practices (Gay, 2002) because it is important for teachers to understand that their personal attitudes can impact student learning and behavior. As well, teachers need to understand the communities in which their students live and its cultural customs. For example, teachers must understand that many students who come from urban communities have learned the conventions of the neighborhood streets and playgrounds, as well as other culturally connected behaviors. One of these behaviors includes being able to hold ones' own by being quick-witted and using snappy quips to show a complex tough prowess. These behaviors may be misinterpreted by teachers who are unfamiliar with these conventions and may incorrectly view the behaviors as being difficult or deviant within the context of the school culture. McIntyre (1991) wrote about these behaviors and their impact on teachers' decisions to refer students for special education services:

> What occurs oftentimes, is that educators, unfamiliar with other cultures, mistake their students' culturally determined behavior as being an indication of an emotional problem in need of special education services or at least disciplinary action (Grossman, 1990). Behavioral patterns often vary by culture (Light and Martin, 1985; Toth, 1990) and are commonly misinterpreted by teachers not from those cultures (Garcia, 1978; Grossman, 1990; Pusch, 1979). In fact, according to Garcia (1978), much of the minority group overrepresentation in special education may be due to this educator ethnocentricity. Much of the overrepresentation of black students in programs for the behavior disordered may also be due to a cultural misunderstanding (McIntyre, 1990).

Similarly, Cartledge and Loe (2001) describe all behavior as having a culturally constructed base. They contend that children who come from and identify with groups that are culturally diverse are likely to engage in behaviors that are atypical in the context of the school's culture. This difference in context can be described as cultural dissonance. Cultural dissonance (also known as the lack of multicultural competence) refers to the variance between a teachers' ability to acknowledge, comprehend, and/or knowledgeably interpret the beliefs, mores, and behaviors of those students who are culturally different based on their own personal cultural knowledge. Cultural dissonance, then, has serious implications for classroom management and student behavior.

TABLE 6.1 CRCM Teacher Self-Assessment and Reflection Guide

Personal Focus	Self-Reflection Questions	Action Approach Strategies
1. Personal biases	What are my personal biases about people who are _____ (insert race/ethnicity)? Do this for each race/ethnicity represented in your classroom. Are those beliefs stereotypical? Do I treat children who look like me differently than I treat those who do not?	I will be aware of my biases when I teach and manage my students. I am accountable for being culturally responsive. I will participate in professional development that informs my efforts to be culturally responsive.
2. Value analysis	How are my values different from those of the students in my classroom? If there are value differences, do I understand their perspectives? How are they the same?	If I don't agree with or understand my students' values, I will seek to understand their perspectives. I don't have to agree, but I will not let these differences interfere in my teaching.
3. Societal perceptions	Do I see the same behavior as appropriate for some students and inappropriate for others? Do I discipline one child who calls out and not others? Could this be based on race/ethnicity, disability, or language, for example?	I will make a concerted effort to examine my perceptions about appropriate and inappropriate behaviors. I will be aware of inconsistencies in my management style.
4. School climate	What is the overall attitude of my co-workers about students of color or who have disabilities? Is this attitude stereotypical? How does it affect my interactions with students?	I will have high expectations for all students. I know that my attitude impacts my teaching and management behaviors and affects student learning and behavior. I will look for positive ways to impact the schoolwide management program.
5. Economic disparity	What is the socioeconomic status of my students (upper, middle, lower, below poverty level)? Examine this focus for each student. Is it different than my socioeconomic status? What are my beliefs about groups of people whose socioeconomic status is different than mine? Are those beliefs stereotypical?	I will examine my beliefs about socioeconomic status. I will acknowledge that these differences are out of the control of my students and my attitudes and behaviors are important in student success.
6. Classroom materials and environment	Do my classroom materials and environment provide or add to a multicultural perspective? Do my bulletin boards, etc. positively	I understand that students need to see themselves in the materials and curriculum and that people of color should not only be presented during

(continued)

149

TABLE 6.1 (continued)

Personal Focus	Self-Reflection Questions	Action Approach Strategies
	present images of various cultures? Do the reading and curriculum materials present multicultural images? Do I make a concerted effort to present images that are reflective of society?	specific units or holidays (e.g., Black History Month, Cinco de Mayo, Thanksgiving). I understand that it does not matter whether all of the students are of one race, there should still be images of other races. Omission is not acceptable.
7. Teacher expectation	Do I have high expectations for all students? Do I truly have high expectations for those who are culturally, linguistically, economically, or ability different? Do I have lowered expectations due to outside influences (incarcerated parents, divorce, unstable home lives, other teachers' comments)?	I know that low teacher expectations equal low student performance. I will do my best to find ways to help the students to be successful while they are at school. I will not let outside influences negatively affect my student expectations. While the students are at school, I will do my best to provide a safe, inclusive and positive environment that values all students.

Cultural dissonance accounts for many of the cultural conflicts that teachers have when imposing disciplinary measures on students who do not behave in a manner that the teacher values as appropriate. Teachers may not realize that their image of the well-behaved student is culturally constructed and may not encompass those behaviors exhibited by CLD students. As an example, Gay (2000) described its impact as follows:

> While most teachers are not blatant racists, many probably are cultural hegemonists. They expect all students to behave according to the school's cultural standards of normality. When students of color fail to comply, the teachers find them unlovable, problematic, and difficult to honor or embrace without equivocation. (p. 46)

The impact of cultural dissonance on student success is significant, and prospective teachers should be cognizant of their own cultural beliefs and biases when making decisions about students and their behavior, as well as classroom management systems that value differences.

DETERMINING A BEHAVIOR DISORDER WITHIN A CULTURAL CONTEXT

As evidenced in the vignette at the beginning of this chapter, teachers are often likely to misinterpret differences in culture as cognitive or behavioral disabilities. When teachers are not aware of or do not understand the educational needs of students of color, or when they fail to infuse teaching strategies that are more compatible with students' cultures, the resulting outcomes center on inaccurate and inappropriate referrals to special education (Neal et al., 2003). What teachers consider to be discipline problems are often determined by their own culture, personal values, attitudes, and teaching style. Failure to understand the cultural context of a particular situation may only serve to increase negatively perceived behaviors (Goodwin, 1997).

Cultural misunderstandings can have a negative impact on students as well as on teachers. Cartledge, Kea, and Simmons-Reed (2002) state that when teachers do not share the same background as their learners, they are in jeopardy of viewing their students' behavior in stereotypical ways. The authors further state that these misunderstandings among teachers are based on the teachers' (a) lack of cultural knowledge and understanding of the impact of family beliefs, customs, and transitions on students' behavior; (b) failure to recognize methods of child-rearing and discipline choices in various cultures; (c) lowered expectations; (d) failure to understand the cultural context in which a behavior is exhibited; (e) limited or no interaction with cultures outside of their own; (f) little use of cultural relevance in the school curriculum; and (g) lack of appreciation and respect for the student's uniqueness.

Culturally different behaviors are not equivalent to deficits in social skills or behavioral disabilities (Bowman, 2000). Evans (1998) states that teachers must anticipate cultural differences, value these differences, and try to understand and recognize the perspectives of the students and their families. Teachers can connect with culturally diverse parents and their children with disabilities if they respect, acknowledge, and become grounded in their family patterns and values (Cartledge, Kea, & Simmons-Reed, 2002). When working with families, educators must move more toward a model that emphasizes family empowerment and strength and that provides a positive framework for conceptualizing and implementing services to culturally diverse families and their children with disabilities (Cartledge, Kea, & Simmons-Reed, 2002).

Teaching Implication: Teachers should make an effort to understand all facets of their culturally and linguistically diverse learners. Accordingly, teachers should take time to learn about their students' interests, hobbies, culturally and socially constructed behaviors (e.g., capping), favorite television shows, the music they listen to and the informal "languages" they speak. This calls for teachers to gain insight into students' worlds beyond their academic lives and to use the cultural knowledge, prior experiences, and performance styles of diverse students to make the learning environment more appropriate and effective for them (Gay, 2000).

Learning about the students in the class is an on-going process that requires teachers to take the initiative to create opportunities that support this learning. Opportunities to learn about the students may be found through student observation, interest inventories, and conversations that are not academically driven. Other ways to accomplish this goal include: (a) forming *Lunch Bunches* in which the teacher randomly chooses 3–5 students to eat lunch with periodically throughout the year (preferably each month), (b) using alternative assessment for selected academic assignments (e.g., writing a rap, a poem, or a song to show their mastery of content), and

(c) using two-way journaling in which the teacher and the students share their thoughts about a class, school or community issue, a class lesson, or a television program. Through this learning process, teachers are able to more effectively and efficiently meet the needs of all students.

Classroom and Schoolwide Management

> We have no evidence that suspension and expulsion make a positive contribution to school safety or improved student behavior; they may in fact have significant unintended negative consequences for students and school climate.
>
> —*Russ Skiba*
> *Testimony before U.S. House of Representatives*

Schools have become increasingly tough when meting out punishment and enforcing classroom and schoolwide discipline policies. This tougher stance is in direct response to the changing landscape of seemingly unorthodox school misbehavior and violence in which students no longer use their fists to settle disputes or concerns, but may yield weapons. As well, school violence was once thought to be a problem that solely affected the inner city. In the past several years, highly publicized incidents of school violence in suburban areas have shattered those beliefs and highlighted violence as one of the nation's highest priorities (U.S. Department of Health and Human Services, 1999). These violent events have now made inappropriate behavior more than just an act of defiance; inappropriate behavior is now scrutinized as a possible preliminary indicator of more extreme, underlying problems that may plague a student and lead to the commission of violent acts.

Consequently, schools have taken a more proactive position on discipline by increasing their focus on the development of schoolwide management plans that include zero tolerance for any semblance of aggressive behavior or weapon possession. However, this position has reduced neither the number of behavior or violence-related problems nor the amount of instructional time lost in schools each year. In fact, research suggests that behavioral consequences alone (without teaching or reinforcing prosocial behavior) are ineffective and have been associated with increases in aggression, vandalism, truancy, and dropping out (Mayer, 1995; Mayer & Sulzer-Azaroff, 1990; Skiba & Peterson, 1999).

School stakeholders should take a proactive stance and begin to reevaluate their schoolwide management programs in an effort to examine variables that influence the school environment (culture and climate). In addition, they should reexamine management components that are integral in fostering a sound framework for success—social skills and behavioral interventions. These aspects have lead to positive behavioral outcomes (Bandura, 1977; Gresham, 1998) for schools. Schools should develop culturally and linguistically diverse discipline and prevention teams consisting of faculty, staff, parents/guardians, and community stakeholders who will work together to ensure that the school fosters an environment that is safe, inclusive, and fair and values all students. The discipline prevention team should develop a schoolwide management program for implementing social skills instruction, behavioral intervention systems, and an inclusive and shared vision for behavioral expectations through organized student and staff development campaigns that focus on proactive (Lewis & Sugai, 1999), prosocial behavioral expectations (see "Understanding and Preventing School Violence" section).

Schoolwide Management Programs

A well-developed and effective schoolwide management program is at the core of an academically and behaviorally effective school. The management program sets the school climate or tone for success throughout all school and school-related activities. For the management program to be successful, schools must establish proactive (Lewis & Sugai, 1999) intervention practices that (a) establish a systematic approach to discipline; (b) establish student assistance teams (SATs) to identify and respond to students who are having behavioral difficulties; (c) plan for individualized preliminary academic and environmental adaptations and modifications as interventions; (d) use information about student behavior to guide lesson planning, instructional strategies, and behavior management decision making; and (e) set clear behavioral expectations, rules, and subsequent consequences for misbehavior. To implement these practices, schools must have supportive systems in place, such as:

- Administrative collaboration
- A team-based systematic implementation process
- A willing and committed faculty and staff
- Involved family and community members
- Time for training, planning, and implementation for both students and staff
- Budgeted support for all activities, materials, and training resources
- A system for ongoing data collection and analysis of student behavior and teacher strategies
- Procedures for regularly monitoring and assessing overall programmatic effectiveness
- Evaluation instruments to assess the school climate and culture
- Schoolwide policies and expectations that focus on prosocial behavioral expectations that support and encourage the schoolwide program in individual classrooms

Effective schoolwide management systems must be supported and must receive endorsements and commitments, especially from a majority of campus teachers. However, schools must not rely on individual teachers or groups of teachers to change the behavioral culture of a school; this requires a systematic approach that is supported by all stakeholders. Schoolwide positive behavior expectations and support systems provide a set of systemic and individualized strategies for preventing problem behavior and creating a school environment that supports student behavioral growth and development. These behavioral supports set forth responsibilities for students, teachers and staff, parents/guardians, administration, and community partners and should be reviewed, revised, and adopted collaboratively.

Students:

- Students are expected to practice and internalize social skills and behavioral expectations.
- Students are expected to continually expand their skill sets and expectations each school year.
- Students are responsible for learning strategies that support learning and self-regulation and for determining (with the input of teachers and parents/guardians) an individualized plan that provides a framework for behavioral success.

Teachers and Staff:

- Teachers and staff members should teach students the appropriate social skills and expected behaviors.
- Teachers and staff members are expected to demonstrate appropriate levels of culturally responsive, interpersonal, problem-solving, and conflict resolution skills.
- Teachers and staff members are expected to develop and implement opportunities for social skills practice and reinforcement that take place daily throughout the school year.
- Teachers and staff members must be willing to take part in ongoing culturally responsive classroom management (CRCM) staff development that focuses on implementing positive culturally and linguistically relevant supports for student behavior.
- Teachers and staff members should plan and host training sessions for parents and/or guardians that focus on home- and community-based behavioral support systems. These sessions should allow for parent/guardian input and sharing.
- Teachers and staff members should include family members in the planning of schoolwide activities that will improve educational and behavioral outcomes. They should also offer incentives for families who may be unable to attend by offering childcare, a light meal, or transportation. Faculty, administration, and support staff should be open, helpful, culturally competent, and accessible to families.

Parents/Guardians:

- Parents should be invited to all school-related functions to continually assess the schoolwide campus climate related to management.
- Parents should participate in the development of schoolwide behavioral expectations.

- Parents and guardians should be required to attend at least one behavioral support meeting during the school year. These meetings should be in conjunction with short Parent Teachers Association (PTA) meetings, class presentations, and/or back-to-school or family nights.

Administration:

- Administrators should set the tone for a shared, culturally responsive vision for a positive school climate that truly values, celebrates, and respects all school stakeholders.
- Administrators should develop initiatives that will strengthen collaboration between the school and the community by inviting community representatives to be a part of programs, violence prevention committees, and other activities that will positively affect student success.
- Administrators should take an active part in professional development opportunities that offer an ongoing examination of school practices, programmatic schoolwide management assessment, and strategies that support school stakeholders.
- Administrators should provide and facilitate opportunities for teachers to talk with parents, behavioral specialists, and culturally aware individuals to discuss what works and what does not while continuing to respect student worth and dignity.
- Administrators should provide staff development opportunities for the whole school that focus on culturally competent and linguistically appropriate exchanges and collaborations among families, professionals, students, and community members. Staff development should focus on equitable outcomes for all students and interactions that are responsive to issues of race, culture, gender, sexual orientation, disability, and social and economic status.

Community Partners:

- Community partners should be invited to all training sessions and other meetings that provide an insight into the school's vision for positive behavioral and academic supports that affect student success.

CHARACTERISTICS OF EFFECTIVE CLASSROOM MANAGEMENT

Schools with effective classroom management systems teach and support expected student behavior, provide support for at-risk students, provide proactive interventions for problem behavior, provide intensive support for challenging behavior problems (Horner, Sugai, & Horner, 2000), and provide training for school stakeholders. Schools that provide communal training have a shared vision about behavioral expectations among students, families, school staff, and communities. When all school stakeholders have an understanding of the rules, they become more relevant and meaningful to the students.

This mutual awareness of the rules helps to create an environment that is conducive to teaching and learning as a priority. On the other hand, when there is a lack of clarity about rules and behavioral expectations or these rules and expectations are inconsistently stated or reinforced, students may not value them, and thus may more easily break them. This creates an environment in which teaching and learning become challenging ancillary activities rather than a primary focus. Though programs that change the behavioral climate in a school and focus on behavioral expectations will create a learning environment that is conducive to learning, teaching and reinforcing these behavioral expectations cannot, alone, improve academic skills such as reading, math, and science. To improve academic skills, schools must employ well-trained, effective teachers who use quality culturally responsive core curricula and instructional practices that are research-based best practice. Improvement in student behavior in schools allows effective, well-trained teachers to attend to students' academic and behavioral needs. Accordingly, research studies suggest that when the behavior in a school improves, ultimately, improvements in achievement follow. An example of a strategy to accomplish improvements in behavioral and academic success is culturally responsive teaching (CRT).

Educational systems are designed to intellectually and socially develop all students into tomorrow's leaders (Davis & Jordan, 1995). For CLD students, the level at which these students are engaged academically must be increased (Anderson et al., 1998). Measures by which increased engagement and success are achieved must consider the learning, behavioral, cultural, and linguistic history of the individual students.

Neal, Webb-Johnson, and McCray (2003) defined culturally responsive teaching as using the cultural knowledge, prior experience, frames of references, and performance styles of ethnically diverse students to make learning encounters more relevant to, and effective for, them. CRT teaches to the strengths within students. Teachers provide their instruction within a context of caring for and appreciating differences. Student involvement and active learning are highly emphasized as well as using the students' community language and dialect throughout all modes of instruction.

Culturally responsive teachers know that pedagogical methods matter (Neal et al., 2003). These teachers also know how to engage learners in meaningful and productive ways. While recognizing various aspects of culture, they teach their students to access cultural strengths within the context of the classroom setting. Examples of CRCM strategies, which center on the active engagement of students in meaningful and productive ways, include the following:

- There are clear student expectations for behavior and academic success.
- Teachers are aware of culturally related behaviors.
- There are high student expectations for behavior and academic success.
- Class routines and transitions are practiced and systematic.
- Instruction is provided in a context of caring and worth.
- Content is presented in meaningful ways that infuse culturally and linguistically relevant information, prior knowledge, and experiences (Gay, 2002).

ASSESSING THE SCHOOLWIDE AND CLASSROOM MANAGEMENT ENVIRONMENT

Schoolwide management systems must be continually monitored and assessed to determine their effectiveness. Regular monitoring and assessment allows management teams to analyze discipline referrals in order to (a) determine which strategies, consequences, or policies are effective and which are not; (b) collect data to isolate specific behaviors or patterns of behavior that occur, when the behavior occurs, and the location of most problems; (c) identify strategies used by teachers before implementing a discipline referral; and (d) identify students who repeatedly break rules. Assessing schoolwide and classroom management environments is a task that should include faculty, staff, administration, students, and parents. Collaboratively, they must work to develop a system for collecting and analyzing behavioral data. Positive trends in the following areas denote successful schoolwide and classroom management environments:

- Increases in positive school climate and academic achievement
- Increases in positive student attitudes and behaviors
- Increases in student attendance
- Increases in parental support for the school's discipline processes and procedures
- Decreases in school suspensions and student discipline referrals
- Decreases in the total number of office discipline referrals
- Decreases in special education referrals and placements for behavioral reasons
- Decreases in student grade retention

Functional Behavior Assessment and Intervention Plans

One of the more popular assessment and intervention strategies for measuring the behavioral dimensions of culturally diverse students is functional behavior assessment (FBA). FBA is based on the premise that every behavior, regardless of the level of destructiveness, has a purpose. For example, an educator might ask the question, "is the purpose of the problem behavior to get something (e.g., attention) or is it aimed at avoiding something (e.g., a difficult assignment; social situations). The intent of FBA is to understand the *conditions* surrounding the particular negative behavior in order to successfully prevent the repetition of that behavior (Kirk, Gallagher, & Anastasiow, 2006).

Effectively conducting a functional behavior assessment includes seven steps:

1. *Conducting an Interview.* The person conducting the FBA interviews the student's parents and/or guardians to develop a clear definition of the problem behavior. A series of questions (Kirk et al., 2006) that guide the interview process serve to gather information about setting events, antecedents, behaviors, and consequences. Additional questions during the interview focus on the student's general health, discipline record, academic standing, general strengths, and the specific times when the student behaved well.

2. *Making Observations.* Observations of the student are conducted in the setting(s) in which the problem behavior occurs. These observations are conducted over the course of 3 to 5 days (Kirk et al., 2006) to identify the events, times, and situations that predict the occurrence of the problem behavior as well as to identify the consequences that maintain the problem behavior.

3. *Developing a Hypothesis.* A hypothesis, or summary statement, is developed to describe the problem behavior and provide a rationale as to the reason behind the occurrence of the problem behavior. The hypothesis is then "tested" during subsequent observations and interviews.

4. *Brainstorming.* Individuals significant to the student (e.g., teacher, parents) gather to generate ideas for changing the problem behavior. Issues pertaining to specific events are discussed and identified as needing to be changed in order to support more appropriate expressions of behavior by the student. These issues can include the behavior of the teacher, the proximity of the student to his/her peers in the classroom, the lighting and seating arrangement in the class, the events that occur in the home before and after school, and the type of academic work the student is being asked to complete. During a brainstorming session, all participants agree not to criticize the ideas that are generated.

5. *Developing a Behavior Support Plan.* After the brainstorming session, the participants prioritize the ideas that were generated and one or two ideas are selected for implementation. A behavior contract is then developed that provides the following information: (a) a definition of the appropriate target behavior, (b) a description of conditions under which the target behavior can occur, (c) a list of possible reinforcers the student may earn for exhibiting the target behavior, and (d) a list of possible consequences for failing to exhibit the target behavior.

6. *Monitoring the Intervention.* A simple system is implemented for collecting data on the student's response to the behavior support plan.

7. *Evaluating the Outcome.* After the behavioral observation data is collected, the student's significant others review the data and determine the areas of strengths and weaknesses of the behavior support plan. Modifications to the plan are made accordingly and the student is reintroduced to the new intervention.

SOCIAL COMPETENCE DEVELOPMENT

In order to address school violence and related discipline issues, schools are currently under tremendous pressure to create safe and effective instructional environments to best facilitate learners' acquisition of social and academic skills (Lewis & Sugai, 1999; Sugai et al., 2000; Walker et al, 2001). Schools face the challenge of developing students who are socially skillful, self-managing, and adaptable to a variety of situations. One way to ensure that students acquire these skills is to teach social skills concepts in the school setting. These social skills concepts should be taught using culturally responsive strategies.

School populations have become more diverse over the past two decades, resulting in the same instructional environments being charged with meeting more diverse needs. This includes various cultures, languages, and socioeconomic backgrounds. As a result more than academics must be taught in today's classrooms; learners must now be more skilled at understanding diverse values and norms (Vincent, Horner & Sugai, 2002).

Although different cultures and contexts value different social behaviors, there is nevertheless some broad consensus in most societies about what is desirable: establishing and maintaining a range of positive social relationships; refraining from harming others; contributing collaboratively and constructively to the peer group, family, school, workplace, and community; engaging in behaviors that enhance and protect health; avoiding behaviors with serious negative consequences for the individual or others or both. Maag (1999) noted that very "few behaviors are universally inappropriate or appropriate without first considering the context in which they occur" (p. 19). This helps frame student behaviors in a way more apt for objectivity. Looking for the purpose and context in which the target behavior occurs frames the motivation behind the student's actions. Maag reminded educators that most behaviors are appropriate in some situations.

For students to learn about behavioral contexts and how to identify and use appropriate social behaviors within these contexts, they should be taught social skills that focus on social competence. Social competence is the ability to identify and use strategies that give students the "ability to integrate cognitive (thinking), emotional (feeling), and behavioral realms to achieve constructive social tasks, relationships, and outcomes valued in the host context and culture. In a school setting, these tasks, relationships, and outcomes would include accessing the school curriculum successfully; meeting associated personal, social, and emotional needs; and developing transferable skills and attitudes of value beyond school" (Mahar & Lyndall, 2002, p. 3). Students best acquire social competencies when their learning environment models, teaches, and "lives out" social competence. This learning occurs mainly in the context of social relationships within the school environment (Mahar & Lyndall, 2002) in which:

- Peer relations contribute significantly to social and cognitive development.
- The curriculum incorporates students' personal and social issues.
- Learning is enhanced through positive social and emotional dynamics between students.
- A culture of inclusiveness strengthens students' sense of connection.
- Cultural diversity is appreciated, valued, and celebrated.
- The primary language is used to promote the understanding of social expectations (p. 15).

Specific components of social competence are called social competencies. Social competencies are learned through a developmental progression that includes providing "fairness and inclusiveness into the school's values, norms and skills" that will create socially competent learning environments (Mahar & Lyndall, 2002, p. 8). Social competencies differ depending on the context. Inappropriate behaviors in one context might be appropriate in another. Through the ability to think and feel, students who are socially competent are able to select and control which behaviors are appropriate in any given context. Social competencies include "(a) perception and interpretation of relevant social cues, (b) recognition and appropriate expressions of emotion, (c) communication in a range of social relationships, (d) constructive conflict resolution, (e) self-management, (f) responsible decision-making skills, (g) flexible coping skills, and (h) social problem solving" (Mahar & Lyndall, 2002 p. 8). These social competencies are important for students who do not exhibit behaviors that are contextually appropriate for school. Students must be given the opportunity to learn appropriate behaviors before labeling them as emotionally or behaviorally disturbed. Social competencies skills may give students the skills they need to be successful in social and academic environments.

A student's social competence should be assessed by the teacher(s), peers, parents, relevant related personnel, and the student. Input that is collected can provide valuable insight into the student's social behavior. First, teachers and related personnel can assess the student's progress in social competence through formal and informal observations. Second, the teacher may also gather information by viewing the child's interactions with peers to assess classroom relationships (e.g., Is the child aggressive toward peers? Does the child find it difficult to play cooperatively?). Third, parents can also provide insights by sharing information about outside activities such as sports, family relationships, or memberships in community organizations. Finally, since social competence involves a student's thoughts, feelings, and perceptions of social situations, depending on the child's age, information can be obtained from the child by asking questions related to his or her own self-monitoring data.

BEHAVIOR MANAGEMENT IN THE DIFFERENTIATED CLASSROOM

Management of student behavior is a major concern of teachers because of its importance in establishing a positive classroom learning environment. Creating the opportunity to learn and develop both academic and behavioral skills is essential to an effective classroom. The classroom management system should reinforce the schoolwide behavior program and should have explicit goals for classroom management, especially for students who exhibit challenging behaviors; promote positive behavioral supports; empower students through self-management and self-control plans; provide opportunities for students to learn and practice social competencies; and include CRCM strategies.

Managing Surface Behaviors

Antisocial, or externalizing, behaviors are among the most frequently occurring behavior patterns among students with emotional and behavioral disabilities. According to Heward (2006), externalizing (a.k.a. "surface") behaviors are often expressed in the following ways in the classroom:

- "Getting out of seat
- Yelling, talking out, cursing
- Disturbing peers
- Hitting or fighting
- Ignoring the teacher
- Complaining
- Arguing excessively
- Stealing
- Lying
- Destroying property
- Not complying with directions
- Having temper tantrums
- Not responding to teacher corrections
- Not completing assignments" (p. 224)

One commonly held belief is that most children who exhibit inappropriate external behavior will develop out of them and will become "normally functioning" adults (Gartin & Murdick, 2001). This belief is based primarily on cultural differences between the teacher and student. Based on these cultural differences, externalizing behaviors are perceived as disturbing to other members of the classroom and generally result in considerable disruption in the classroom.

Students who display emotional and behavioral disorders often have difficulties with academic achievements. Issues with aggression, blatant opposition, and peer relationships often hinder productive performance in an educational environment. Students identified with emotional or behavioral disorders (EBD) constitute the lowest grade point averages of all students receiving special services (Sutherland & Wehby, 2001). Fifty percent of the population of students with EBD often fail at least one class in an academic year, and one-third of all students with EBD fail to complete a high school education (Sutherland & Wehby, 2001). Wood and Cronin (1999) established that students with EBD often represent the highest dropout rate of any group of students with a disability status. Often, these failures with school and life outcomes are the result of academic difficulties (Meadows, Neel, Scott, & Parker, 1994; Ruhl & Berlinghoff, 1992) and misinterpretation of cultural norms (Cartledge, Kea, & Simmons-Reed, 2002). Various interventions have been sited in the literature as empirically validated approaches to substituting inappropriate external behaviors with more appropriate social- and academic-related behaviors among these students. These interventions include active student responding and positive behavior supports.

Active Student Responding. People learn by doing. Under current practices, the ability to actively participate in the educational setting is limited. Shin, Deno, Robinson, and Marston (2000) estimated that 75 percent of a single school day consists of immediate instruction, but only 20 percent of that same school day was spent in active academic responding. Narayan, Heward, Gardner, Courson, and Omness (1990) have determined that only 45 percent of students passively attend to a teacher's instruction in the classroom environment. Thurlow, Graden, Greener, and Ysseldyke (1983) further supported the finding that only 25 percent of a student's academic time is spent actively responding, but also concluded that special education students receive even fewer opportunities in the classroom.

Teachers must recognize the need to involve all students in classroom instruction. The most common strategy used by educators in the classroom is to pose a question to the entire class and call on a student to answer. This method of teaching only offers an active learning opportunity to a single student (Heward, Gardner, Cavanuagh, Courson, Grossi, & Barbetta, 1996). The individual chosen to answer the question will receive one-on-one positive or corrective feedback depending on the answer. One student learns while the other students watch passively or disengage from the conversation. The results of this methodology favor the academically advanced student over the low-achieving student. A student who rarely responds or offers no response to a question posed by the teacher is generally a low-achieving student (Heward et al., 1996; Maheady, Mallette, Harper, & Sacca, 1991; Gardner, Heward, & Grossi, 1994). Therefore, lower achieving students do not benefit as much as high-achieving students do from traditional classroom instruction. Students with EBD fall into this low-achieving category.

Studies show that there is a negative relationship between students with EBD and traditional teacher instruction (Gunter & Coutinho, 1997). Teachers often have the means to teach students with EBD but often do not use effective practices with enough consistency to be effective with this population of students (Shores, Gunter, & Jack, 1993; Wehby, Symons, & Canale, 1998). In addition, a student's problem behavior in the classroom environment often creates a bias with the teacher, and the teacher will not provide the student with the same opportunities for academic achievement (Wehby et al., 1998). Carr, Taylor, and Robinson (1991) established that when a teacher gives students an opportunity to actively participate in instruction, the teacher often chooses a student that displays acceptable classroom behavior over the student that displays disruptive classroom behavior. Furthermore, as a student displays increased levels of aggression, the more a teacher will avoid instructional opportunities with a child (Wehby et al., 1998). If teachers tend to avoid students with EBD, then how can students achieve academic success from the traditional method of classroom instruction? Students need to be actively involved in classroom instruction and have an opportunity to respond to the teacher's questions. The instruction needs to change to include the students with EBD so that they may achieve academic success.

An ongoing theme in educational research is that active student responding is closely related to academic achievement (Courson & Heward, 1988; Gardner et al., 1994; Narayan et al., 1990). Students who respond actively and frequently to ongoing instruction learn more than students who passively attend. Active responding is a teaching strategy that promotes an interaction between the teacher and multiple students in a simple, straightforward manner as well as provides some type of feedback to the student's response (Thornton & Gerlach, 1989). By providing multiple opportunities for all students, including those with EBD, to actively respond to a question, the teacher may assess whether each student is obtaining the desired information from the lesson through active participation and correct answers. If the student does not give a correct response, then the teacher has a chance to provide immediate error correction. Regardless, the teacher can continually evaluate the student's progress. In turn, the teacher can make instructional decisions based on a student's feedback (Davey, 1989). Methods of active responding should be enjoyable to both teacher and student and easy to implement (Narayan et al., 1990). Students will not accept a teaching method if the method is difficult to understand or too complicated to perform. Opportunities to respond should be stress-free to students, allowing all students to actively participate without risk of embarrassment for answering questions incorrectly (Tam & Scott, 1996).

Positive Behavior Supports. With the recognition that the environment can have either a positive or a negative effect on an individual's behavior comes the responsibility to create educational environments that enhance positive behavior outcomes (Kirk et al., 2006). Three forms of positive behavior support (PBS) have been documented as effective in promoting successful social and academic behaviors among a diverse array of students who have been identified as having emotional and behavioral disabilities (Gartin & Murdick, 2001). The first form of support includes Universal Group Behavior Support. The purpose of this approach is to establish schoolwide management strategies by establishing rules and standards for expected student behavior. The second form of support involves Specialized Group Behavior Support. This approach is most applicable for students with at-risk problem behavior (Gartin & Murdick, 2001). School staff develop a plan that identifies appropriate behavior in various school venues (e.g., classroom, school bus, cafeteria) as well as the contingencies associated with obtaining reinforcers for exhibiting the appropriate behavior. The third form of positive behavior support is Specialized Individual Behavior Support. This form is most effective for students with chronic problem behaviors. For these students, a functional behavior assessment is needed, which is discussed further in this chapter. Positive behavior support is an approach that involves a set of supportive strategies to the needs of the individual student, his or her family, and others across home and community settings. PBS is based on the belief that problem behavior results from unmet needs (Gartin & Murdick, 2001).

According to Stein and Davis (2000):

> positive behavior support is a term that includes effective teaching strategies in all areas (e.g., academic, social, and mental health). The components of positive behavior support are based on empirically validated strategies. Positive behavior support includes comprehensive multi-component interventions that are preventive, proactive, as well as educative. The intent of an educative intervention is to teach students to perform the skills necessary to achieve the same outcome (i.e., function) as that generated by the problem behavior. (p. 7)

The primary foundation behind the PBS intervention is that problem behaviors are context related; that is, behaviors must be observed and understood within the characteristics of the student's setting (Asmus, Vollmer, & Borrero, 2002). Additionally, the PBS intervention perceives problem behaviors as purposeful, and interventions should be designed with an understanding of the needs of the students and the function that the behavior serves; interventions should also enhance the dignity of the student (Heckaman, Conroy, Fox, & Chair, 2000). Examples of positive behavior supports to use with problem behaviors include the following (Gartin & Murdick, 2001): (a) setting/situation change, including level of demand/task change, change in noise level, voice change, sequence of task change, activity omission, and environmental enrichment; (b) direct instruction; (c) errorless learning; (d) communication training; and (e) assertion training with modeling and role playing.

PBSs are specifically mentioned in IDEA 1997 as a method to be used by both general and special education teachers in the education of children who need special education services (Gartin & Murdick, 2001). If a child's behavior impedes his or her learning or the learning of others, the IEP team must conduct a meeting to assess the child's needs and prepare an appropriate plan that considers the implementation of positive behavior interventions and the necessary supports that should be in place to help remediate the behavior. As a result, the plan can successfully identify academic and behavior targets that are endorsed and emphasized by students, families, and educators. Furthermore, the plan specifically implements interventions and strategies that are evidence based. Behavior observation data is also gathered on an ongoing basis toward identifying any necessary changes that must be made to the plan and the overall effects of the intervention. Finally, the plan targets the coordination of various systems within the school and home to enable the successful implementation of the practices of positive behavior supports.

DIFFICULT BEHAVIORS: MANAGING AGGRESSIVE BEHAVIOR, HYPERACTIVITY, AND DISTRACTIBILITY

Difficult behaviors vary in frequency and intensity. These behaviors vary from students having trouble paying attention to becoming physically and/or verbally aggressive. Teachers have to pick their battles. Is the behavior just annoying or does it prevent learning, including the student's learning? Does the behavior cause the student to be socially isolated? Can the behavior be avoided with proactive strategies? These are some questions that teachers need to ask themselves before determining whether a student's behavior can be considered difficult.

Strategies for working with students who exhibit challenging, aggressive, and difficult behaviors include:

- Identify individualized strategies for working with students who exhibit challenging, aggressive, and difficult behaviors.
- Become familiar with strategies to use when a student becomes aggressive:

Onset—Student begins to become upset.

1. Maintain composure—do not raise your voice.
2. Speak in a calm and reassuring voice.
3. Show concern for anguish the student is feeling.
4. Ask the student about the origin of stress: What or who is it/did it?

Ignition—Student begins to lose control.

1. Maintain composure.
2. Continue to speak in a calm and reassuring voice.
3. Tell the student that you are there to help.
4. Give student a nonthreatening command.
5. Remove origin of stress.
6. If necessary, remove other students from the classroom.

Departure—Student loses control (not aggressive).

1. Maintain composure.
2. Continue to speak in a calm and reassuring voice.
3. Repeat your command.
4. Be prepared for detonation.
5. If necessary, call for assistance. If you are unsure, call anyway.
6. If necessary, remove other students from the classroom.

Detonation—Student has become verbally and/or physically aggressive.

1. Maintain composure.
2. Continue to speak in a calm and reassuring voice.
3. Remove other students from the classroom.
4. If necessary, call for assistance. If you are unsure, call anyway.
5. If the student has become aggressive, remain at a safe distance.
6. Physically restrain student if necessary (provided you are trained in restraint techniques).

Reentry—Student begins to noticeably calm down.

1. Maintain composure.
2. Continue to speak in a calm and reassuring voice.
3. Provide positive reinforcement for calming down.
4. When appropriate, review self-control strategies that may be appropriate for future outbursts.
5. Write up anecdotal record of incident (provide copies to appropriate personnel).
6. Contact the parents to begin or continue dialogue about a collaborative strategy for assisting the student.

- Clearly state directions for classroom activities and expectations for behavior; give warnings when students are about to transition from one activity to another or from one setting to another.
- Teach students appropriate strategies for controlling their behavior and dealing with stress or anxiety (counting to 10, taking a self-determined time-out).
- Provide positive reinforcement for appropriate behaviors (catch them being good).

Strategies for working with students who exhibit hyperactivity or distractibility behaviors include:

- Identify individualized strategies for working with students who exhibit hyperactive or distractible behaviors.
- Become familiar with strategies to use with students who have attention or distractibility difficulties.
- Clearly state directions for classroom activities and expectations for behavior; give warnings when students are about to transition from one activity to another or from one setting to another.
- Assist the student with organizational strategies.
- Provide written objectives for assignments to keep the student from being frustrated.
- Allow hyperactive students to stretch when needed, work on the floor (carpeted areas), or walk to a designated location and back.
- Give preferential seating near the front of the class and away from distractions (doors, windows, bathrooms, etc.).
- Teach students appropriate strategies for controlling their behavior and staying focused and on task (moving to an area that is more conducive to staying on task, using a study carrel or a teacher- or student-crafted divider).
- Provide positive reinforcement for appropriate behaviors (catch them being good).
- Use proximity to refocus student or a signal that has been collaboratively determined by the teacher and student in private.
- Use reminders that are "specific student neutral" (e.g., *Remember to use a different map pencil to color each state*). This will refocus the students and remind the student of the task at hand.
- Work with the student one-on-one to help him or her recognize social skills; involve the parent in working on these strategies at home.

Applying systematic instruction in appropriate behavior in ways similar to teaching academic skills is an important strategy for increasing positive learning opportunities and classroom environments for culturally diverse students with behavior problems (Lo et al., 2002). This method of instruction is based on a proactive approach to successfully redirecting students who are at risk for developing serious emotional disturbance (SED) to becoming socially responsible individuals.

The education literature illuminates the fact that several components of effective social skills instruction have occurred outside of the general education classroom (Lo et al., 2002; Lewis, Sugai, & Colvin, 1998; Sasso, Melloy, & Kavale, 1990), whereas little attention has been given to using more natural and normalized environments. Van Acker and Talbott (1999) assert that social skills intervention programs are more effective in both the short- and long-term when teachers are actively involved in delivering the instruction. These researchers state that classroom teachers are in the best position to tailor a social skills program to meet the specific needs of their students. Furthermore, a powerful outcome of teacher involvement is the increased success in students maintaining and generalizing the skills they have been taught.

Lo, Loe, and Cartledge (2002) identify several components that characterize effective social skills instruction. First, students must be provided with direct teaching strategies that incorporate the use of exemplars and nonexemplars. The instruction should model for students what is, and what is not, appropriate social behaviors. Second, peers should be included in social skills groups to facilitate the learning of students with behavior problems. All social skills activities and groups should include peers. Finally, teachers and student-trainers should be aware of all opportunities during the school day to teach and reinforce appropriate social skills. Students who receive meaningful reinforcement for the acquisition of appropriate behaviors are more likely to maintain and generalize those behaviors.

Many activities can be added to the classroom routine that will increase opportunities for students to practice social skills (Maag & Webber, 1995). Peer tutoring can increase academic skills as well as confidence and social adjustment. Cooperative learning activities, such as team projects, provide many of the same benefits, requiring students to interact while focusing on academic assignments.

Kravetz, Faust, Lipshitz, and Shalhav (1999) suggest that students with learning disabilities also have a more difficult time with understanding interpersonal interactions and social adaptation to the classroom. Although the results of their study only provided limited support for this statement, it again supports the need for social instruction in the general education classroom (Kravetz et al., 1999).

Despite the goal of social development in the classroom, students with special needs may not be readily accepted by their peers into friendship groups and activities (Salend, 1999). Therefore, classroom discussions should incorporate information about individual differences and diversity across cultures and abilities. There should also be facilitation from both educators and counselors exploring the meaning of friendships. Salend (1999) also revisits the peer system of tutoring or support to students with special needs. All of these activities can facilitate the development of peer relations.

Kamps, Kravits, Stolze, and Swaggert (1999) also conducted a study regarding students at risk of being identified as having an emotional or behavior disorder. They noted that adding a component addressing social competency into the curriculum helped these students improve their behaviors that were previously of concern. During the implementation of the prevention programs, Kamps et al. (1999) also used a peer tutoring program and behavior management programs.

Goodwin (1999) noted that educators cannot expect students to know how to work cooperatively together in such programs as peer tutoring if they do not possess the necessary social skills. This provides yet another opportunity for general educators to infuse social skills instruction into the classroom curriculum. Accordingly, Maag (1994) researched the ways school counselors can help general educators add social skill instruction to their curriculum through consultation and collaboration. Reitz (1994) also supports frequent and structured opportunities for students to interact, even in classrooms consisting of students with emotional and behavioral disorders. A challenge counselors face in this situation is persuading some teachers to alter their current classroom structure to include more student participation and interaction.

Strategies for Improving Social Skills

Observing and monitoring student behavior should be the first step in implementing social skills instruction (Goodwin, 1999). Subsequently, instruction should convene as it would for any academic skill, allowing the child to observe proactively and receive feedback on the use of each skill.

Maag and Webber (1995) concede that providing social skills instruction to the diverse population that is now present in the general education classroom is a big challenge. To be successful with a direct instruction social skills curriculum, the educator must (a) identify the exact skills necessary to learn, (b) schedule regular times for students to receive instruction in these skills, (c) document the progress of the student, and (d) program for generalization (Maag & Webber, 1995). Due to the intensity of this training for both the student and the teacher, the researchers stated that a special educator or school counselor would be a more appropriate educator than the general teacher. Also, students with disabilities should receive some type of social skills training before being mainstreamed to the general education classroom. Once initial instruction and acquisition of social skills have been attained, the student may be successful in the general education classroom with collaboration from the special educator to help move the students toward cooperative learning (Maag & Webber, 1995). Korinek and Popp (1997) have noted that students struggle to generalize skills taught out of the general classroom back to this environment. This conclusion emphasizes the need for collaboration between general educators and special educators. Furthermore, environments and time planned for generalization training and fading completes this cycle.

Blake, Wang, Cartledge, and Gardner (2000) conducted a study in which middle school students with SED served as social skills trainers for either their middle school or elementary-level peers. Student trainers used a formal social skills curriculum, *Working Together: Building Children's Social Skills through Folk Literature* (Cartledge & Kleefeld, 1994), to teach their peers with SED more appropriate social interaction skills pertaining to participating in games and social communication. The study included 12 middle school boys, ranging in age from 10 to 13 years, who received their instruction in a self-contained classroom for students with SED. These students were selected based on teaching ratings and direct observations. The focus of this study was to measure three positive social skills: (1) positive initiation of a game, (2) positive communication, and (3) positive termination of a game. Instruction was provided under three conditions of teacher-directed instruction, peer-directed instruction, and follow-up. Results indicated that the peer-directed instruction approach was most successful in increasing the social skills among the elementary and middle school students with SED. In addition, the peer-directed approach also led to increases in positive social behaviors among the student trainers with SED. The authors concluded that using peer trainers with SED was an effective means for increasing positive peer interactions for students with significant emotional and/or behavioral disabilities.

A critical aspect of social skills instruction is instilling the ability to self-monitor behavior. DuPaul and Hoff (1998) researched the benefits of using self-management strategies to decrease inappropriate classroom behaviors. The results from this study indicate that self-management is an effective strategy to reduce disruptive behaviors in the general education classroom (DuPaul & Hoff, 1998). Mitchem (2001) defined self-management as having "at least two or more of the following strategies: self-monitoring, self-evaluation, and positive reinforcement" (p. 76). Mitchem, Young, West, and Benyo (2001) studied an additional self-management strategy that implements peer assistance.

Teaching Self–Management and Self–Control

Self-management is a planned, systematic approach that empowers students by teaching them strategies for use in managing their own behavior. Students can be taught to self-manage or use self-control strategies to manage their behavior by using a curriculum that gives them the opportunity to practice these skills. Skills that should be included are self-monitoring, self-regulation, self-assessment, and self-control.

A variety of studies that have addressed self-management for students with mild to severe disabilities have shown that this strategy is effective in changing behavior and producing higher quality academics (Daniels, 1998; McCarl, Svobodny, & Beare, 1991; Nelson, Smith, Young, & Dodd, 1991; Prater, Joy, Chilman, Temple, & Miller, 1991). Teachers have found that self-monitoring procedures improve target behavior, stress the student's personal role in behavior change, allow generalization to environments outside of the school, give teachers the freedom to focus on other tasks, and teach students responsibility and self-determination (Firth & Armstrong, 1986). Self-management abilities are easy to implement in a classroom and should be integrated into everyday instruction to ensure implementation of high quality instruction (Dunlap, Dunlap, Koegel, & Koegel, 1991). These authors provided several steps that should be followed to successfully implement self-management. These are summarized below:

1. Target behavior is clearly defined relative to that which is observed in the instructional environment
2. Date-collection or progress monitoring system is developed

3. Instruct the learner in the use of self-management; provided guided practice

4. Implement the self-management procedures

5. Gather data to monitor progress in student use of self-management

6. Evaluate student progress; revise self-management program as necessary

Students who exhibit challenging behaviors often need individual intense instruction in self-management. Additional steps for teaching students these skills may require the following procedures:

Self-Management Procedures

1. Identify the behavior that needs to be modified. Take into account cultural behaviors that may be misidentified as problem behaviors.

2. Identify what event(s) precede the behavior. Does the behavior happen in a specific location? At a specific time? During a specific subject? When interacting with a specific student or adult?

3. Identify the intended consequence(s). Is the student seeking attention? Avoidance? To release anger, frustration, or angst?

4. Teach the student how to identify factors that influence the onset of the inappropriate behavior(s) and the impact of this behavior on the intended consequence.

5. Teach the student the appropriate behavior that will take the place of the inappropriate behavior and the appropriate consequence.

6. Teach the student to self-manage the inappropriate behavior(s) by using self-control strategies. Self-control strategies include, but are not limited to, employing self-talk, physical movement, physical proximity, and visualization; using a self-monitoring form to monitor behavior (see Figure 6.1); removing themselves from the situation; and looking at photographs or pictures that remind them of the appropriate behavior or self-control strategy.

7. Plan a positive reinforcement schedule that is individualized and gives the student a sense of success and accomplishment.

Another recommended self-management strategy is called FAST (Bos & Vaughn, 1994):

1. **Freeze and think!** What is the problem?

2. **Alternatives?** What are my possible solutions?

3. **Solution evaluation.** Choose the best solution: safe? fair?

4. **Try it!** Slowly and carefully. Does it work? (p. 371)

Self-monitoring systems should be co-planned by teachers, parents, students, and other relevant service personnel. The systems do not have to be elaborate, though they do have to encompass self-management procedures that provide effective support for the system. The main goals of a self-monitoring system are that (a) the student has easy access to any materials used, (b) the student understands that the system presents opportunity to self-monitor behavior, (c) the student and parents or guardians

FIGURE 6.1 Sample Self-Monitoring Form for Young Children to Use

understand that the system is a useful tool for providing a framework for academic and behavioral success, and (d) the student will be given an opportunity to independently control inappropriate behaviors.

UNDERSTANDING AND PREVENTING SCHOOL VIOLENCE

Millions of parents and guardians send their children to school with the expectation that they will be safe, learn appropriate curriculum, and have the opportunities to interact with peers in positive social situations. In contradiction with this expectation, school shootings have produced a sense of uneasiness in our nation that has proliferated within the past several years. Though school violence has declined (Children's Defense Fund, 2001), these highly publicized, and seemingly random, shootings have left parents, guardians, and educators fearful for their children's safety. An April 2000 Gallup poll found that 43 percent of parents are concerned about their children's safety while they are at school (Gallup, 2000). Similarly, according to a March 2001 Gallup poll, more than 50 percent of parents who have school-age children believe that a school shooting is a possibility in their academic region. With the thought of school violence in mind, school personnel are charged with the task of creating safer, yet welcoming and inclusive schools.

Under pressure and scrutiny from the media and school communities, school district and campus administrators have taken numerous actions designed to improve school climate and safety. These include the presence of campus safety officers; the use of metal detectors; training in school social skills; character education and anti-bullying instructional curriculum for faculty, staff, and students; violence prevention programs (e.g., Positive Adolescent Choices Training, PACT; Bullying Prevention Program (BPP), Peace Builders, Responding in Peaceful and Positive Ways, RIPP); positive behavioral supports; clearly defined expectations for faculty, staff, and student behavior; and conflict resolution/peer mediation programs. Additionally, several Web sites provide guides for and lists of violence prevention action items for educators (e.g., www.safeyouth.org, www.ed.gov, and www.secretservice.gov/). These schoolwide programs and Web sites are all designed to develop students who are socially competent and faculty, parents and guardians, and staff members who use proactive interventions to prevent violent behaviors.

Culturally Responsive Violence Prevention Instructional Programs

Flannery (1997) identified the need for culturally responsive violence prevention instructional programs in schools by describing school as "a place where children from diverse racial and cultural backgrounds come together and spend a great part of their day together. This can contribute to incidents of violence due to racial tension, cultural differences in attitudes and behavior, or an admixture of children from diverse neighborhoods (e.g., busing children to school from a different part of town)" (p. 37). These factors emphasize the need for "an integration of a staff culture that emphasizes nonviolent means of conflict resolution with the student culture. Student culture reflects normative adolescent developmental issues, such as the important influence of the peer group, increased need for independence and autonomy, and the struggle to establish a personal or ethnic identity, as well as recognition of culture-specific priorities like maintaining personal racial or ethnic identity" (Regulus, 1995, cited in Flannery, 1997, p. 37). Culturally responsive pedagogy is an absolute within all school contexts and is the scaffold for successful and effective school programs. Culturally responsive school faculty and staff will have the ability to acknowledge the importance of race and cultural issues and recognize "that schools do not operate in a social or cultural vacuum" (Flannery, 1997, p. 37). U.S. demographic information describing students, teachers, and administrators indicate the incongruence between school personnel and the students they serve, and they are "increasingly isolated from the students and neighborhoods they serve, particularly in urban areas" (p. 38). This cultural chasm is fueled by media portrayals of school violence and inner-city youth and their communities. Teachers who are unfamiliar with the cultural backgrounds and behaviors of these students may be intimidated and, thus, apprehensive about maintaining disciplinary rules and regulations.

If teachers do not make a concerted effort to establish a rapport with their students and are fearful of them, "teaching becomes almost impossible, and concerns about safety and control take precedence over concerns about learning and teaching" (Flannery, 1997, p. 38). The following scenario highlights one teacher's commitment to establish a rapport that may have saved a student's life.

In Florida, Ms. Brewer, a new high school teacher was troubled by a student with whom she had made every effort to establish a positive rapport. Zakia, the African American female student, made it very clear that she was not going to listen to the teacher who was White and she did "not like her." Zakia, who was an unofficial class leader, negatively influenced the behavior of the rest of the class. Ms. Brewer considered herself to be a culturally responsive educator and decided that she would try something new each time Zakia came to her classroom. After weeks of trying to make a positive connection, Ms. Brewer spoke about a television program that many of the students of color watched each week. Zakia was so impressed that she stayed behind after class to tell Ms. Brewer that she now "liked her."

One afternoon, Zakia came by Ms. Brewer's room and confided in her. She told her that her stepfather had been sexually molesting her. She explained that she had contemplated suicide and did not think that she could go on. Ms. Brewer talked Zakia into seeing the school counselor and the proper authorities were notified. A few weeks later, Zakia's mother came to the school and thanked Ms. Brewer for not "giving up on Zakia."

Guidelines for Violence Prevention

In schools, violence prevention strategies need to be taught to all faculty, staff, students, administrators, parents and guardians, and community partners. These strategies must be included in the schoolwide management policy and integrated into every area of the school environment.

In general, school factors that are conducive to disorder, crime, and violence include (a) overcrowding, (b) high student/teacher ratios, (c) curricular content that does not relate to student interests, (d) low expectations for student academic achievement and behavior, (e) poor facilities design that both increase isolation and hinder internal communication, and (f) adult failure to act because they believe nothing will work or they simply do not know what to do (Rossman & Morley, 1996; Sautter, 1995; Watson, 1995). In addition, the perception of a pervasive climate of fear of violence makes it difficult to attract and retain good teachers, particularly in inner-city schools, and thus to attain educational objectives. School discipline may suffer as teachers hesitate to confront misbehaving students because they fear for their own safety.

Schoolwide Strategies

Safe school environments require a school culture and climate that demonstrates respect for, communication with, and responsibility to teachers and faculty on a day-to-day basis. A positive school environment provides students with high expectations for their own behavior and strategies that encourage them to manage conflict in nonviolent ways. A positive school environment also provides teachers with the training needed to be effective behavioral managers and a climate conducive to high expectations for behavior for everyone in the school. Here are some ways to facilitate such an environment:

- Violence prevention programs
- Mediation and conflict resolution programs
- Training opportunities for parents and community partners
- Training for all faculty on managing aggressive students
- A schoolwide shared vision for behavioral management
- Zero tolerance policies
- A commitment to implementing culturally responsive classroom management plans

SUMMARY

For students who represent diverse cultural and linguistic backgrounds, the amount of successful school interactions must be increased and include more comprehensive culturally responsive methods. These methods should consider the student's learning, behavioral, linguistic, and cultural history and, in order to be effective, educators must increase the depth and breadth of their knowledge about culturally and linguistically diverse students and their families. Educators should also actively explore and implement strategies that level the playing field for all students in accessing daily instructional material in the classroom and be cognizant of the fact that teachers should gather information about a student from multiple sources, contexts, and procedures.

Finally, to enhance a teacher's effectiveness in meeting the needs of culturally and linguistically diverse students, the chapter emphasized the following: (1) know the cultural values and orientations of all students; (2) accept students as individuals and celebrate both the similarities and differences that are present across cultures; (3) respect, relate, and build relationships with all students; (4) require high expectations of all students; (5) examine teacher behaviors and antecedent conditions in the classroom that may promote inappropriate behaviors; (6) be aware of culture-specific behaviors with regard to communication styles, social taboos, and motivational systems; and (7) redesign classrooms to accommodate cultural differences and style via a relevant curriculum and cooperative learning structures.

Discussion Questions

1. How do multicultural competence and culturally responsive management strategies affect student success and achievement?
2. What are some basic strategies for working with students who exhibit challenging behaviors?
3. What is the role of teachers in supporting behavior management programs?
4. What method for teaching social competence and self-management strategies could be used with very young children?
5. Though violence in schools is not extensive, why are prevention strategies necessary and in what ways do these strategies impact student behavior?

References

Addressing Diversity in Schools: Culturally Responsive Pedagogy. (2004). *Practitioner Brief Series.* National Center for Culturally Responsive Educational Systems (NCCRESt).

Anderson, M., Beard, K., Delgado, B., Kea, C., Raymond, E., Singh, N., Sugai, G., Townsend, B., Voltz, D., & Webb-Johnson, G. (1998). *Working with culturally and linguistically diverse children, youth, and their families: Promising practices in assessment, instruction, and personnel preparation. A white paper.* Reston, VA: CCBD, a division of the Council for Exceptional Children.

Artiles, A. (1998). The dilemma of difference: Enriching the disproportionality discourse with theory and context. *Journal of Special Education, 32,* 32–36.

Artiles, A., & Trent, S. (1994). Overrepresentation of minority students in special education: A continuing debate. *Journal of Special Education, 27,* 410–437.

Asmus, J., Vollmer, T., & Borrero, J. (2002). Functional behavioral assessment: A school based model. *Education and Treatment of Children, 25*(1), 67–90.

Bacon, E., & Kea, D. (1998). Crossing the continental divide: Connecting African American and Appalachian students through paraprofessional conferences. *North Carolina Journal of Teacher Education, 9,* 86–108.

Bandura, A. (1977). *Social learning theory.* Upper Saddle River, NJ: Prentice Hall.

Blake, C., Wang, W., Cartledge, G., & Gardner, R. (2000). Middle school students with serious emotional disturbances serve as social skills trainers and reinforcers for peers with SED. *Behavioral Disorders, 25,* 280–298.

Bos, C. S., & Vaughn, S. (1994). *Strategies for teaching students with learning and behavior problems* (3rd ed.). Needham Heights, MA: Allyn & Bacon.

Bowman, L. (2000). Juvenile delinquency among African American males: Implications for special education. *Multiple Voices for Ethnically Diverse Exceptional Learners, 4,* 62–72.

Carr, E., Taylor, J., & Robinson, S. (1991). The effects of severe behavioral problems in children on the teaching behavior of adults. *Journal of Applied Behavior Analysis, 24*(3), 523–535.

Cartledge, G. (n.d.). *President's commission on excellence in special education assessment and identification task force: Minority overrepresentation and misidentification,* pp. 1–22.

Cartledge, G., Kea, C., & Simmons-Reed, E. (2002). Serving culturally diverse children with serious emotional disturbance and their families. *Journal of Child and Family Studies, 11,* 113–126.

Cartledge, G., & Kleefeld, J. (1994). *Working together: Building children's social skills through folk literature.* Circle Pines, MN: American Guidance Service.

Cartledge, G., & Loe, S. A. (2001). Cultural diversity and social skill instruction. *Exceptionality (9),* 1&2, 33–46.

Cartledge, G., Wang, W., Blake, C., & Lambert, M. (2002). Middle school students with behavior disorders acting as social skill trainers for peers. *Beyond Behavior,* 14–18.

Children's Defense Fund. (2001). *The state of America's children yearbook, 2001.* Washington, DC: Author.

Chinn, P., & Hughes, S. (1987). Representation of minority students in special education classes. *Remedial and Special Education, 8,* 41–46.

Courson, F., & Heward, W. (1988). Increasing active response through the effective use of paraprofessionals. *Pointer, 33*(1), 27–31.

Daniels, V. I. (1998) How to manage disruptive behavior in inclusive classrooms. *Teaching Exceptional Children, 30*(4), 26–31. (ERIC Journal Reproduction Service No. EJ562668).

Davey, B. (1989). Active responding in content classrooms. *Journal of Reading, 33*(1), 44–46.

Davis, J., & Jordan, W. (1995). The effects of school context, structure, and experience on African American males in middle and high school. *Journal of Negro Education, 63*, 570–587.

DuPaul, G., & Hoff, K. (1998). Reducing disruptive behavior in general education classrooms: The use of self-management strategies. *School Psychology Review, 27*, 290–314.

Evans, J. (1998). Culturally responsive pedagogy: Making cultural transitions during student teaching: A placement model. *North Carolina Journal of Teacher Education, 2*, 110–117.

Flannery, D. J. (1997). *School violence: Risk, preventive intervention, and policy.* New York: ERIC Clearinghouse on Urban Education Institute for Urban and Minority Education.

Frith, G. H., & Armstrong, S. W. (1986). Self-monitoring for behavior disordered students. *Teaching Exceptional Children, 18*(2), 144–148.

Gallup Poll. (2000). *Poll Release, April, 2000, on School Safety.*

Gallup Poll. (2001). *Poll Release, March, 2001, on School Safety.*

Gardner, R., Heward, W., & Grossi, T. (1994). Effects of response cards on student participation and academic achievement: A systematic replication with inner-city students during whole-class science instruction. *Journal of Applied Behavior Analysis, 27*(1), 63–71.

Gartin, B., & Murdick, N. (2001). The use of functional assessment of behavior and positive behavior supports. *Remedial & Special Education, 22*(6), 344–360.

Gay, G. (2000). *Culturally responsive teaching: Theory research and practice.* New York: Teachers College Press.

Gay, G. (2002). Preparing for culturally responsive teaching. *Journal of Teacher Education, 53*, 106–116.

Goodwin, A. (1997). Multicultural stories: Preservice teachers' conceptions of and responses to issues of diversity. *Urban Education, 32*, 117–145.

Goodwin, M. (1999). Cooperative learning and social skills: What skills to teach and how to teach them. *Intervention in School and Clinic, 25*, 29–33.

Gresham, F. M. (1998). Social skills training with children: Social learning and applied behavior analytic approaches. In T. S. Watson & F. M. Gresham (Eds.), *Handbook of child behavior therapy* (pp. 475–497). New York: Plenum.

Gunter, P., & Coutinho, M. (1997). Negative reinforcement in classrooms: What we're beginning to learn. *Teacher Education and Special Education, 20*(3), 249–264.

Heckaman, K., Conroy, M., Fox, J., & Chair, A. (2000). Functional assessment-based intervention research on students with or at risk for emotional and behavioral disorders in school settings. *Behavioral Disorders, 25*(3), 196–210.

Heward, W. (2006). *Exceptional children: An introduction to special education* (8th ed.). Upper Saddle River, NJ: Merrill/Prentice Hall.

Heward, W., Gardner, R., Cavanaugh, R., Courson, F., Grossi, T., & Barbetta, P. (1996). Everyone participates in this class: Using response cards to increase active student response. *Teaching Exceptional Children, 28*(2), 4–10.

Horner, R., Sugai, G., & Horner, H. (2000). A schoolwide approach to student discipline. *The School Administrator, 57*(2), 20–23.

Irvine, J. J. (1990). *Black students and school failure: Policies, practices, and prescriptions.* New York: Greenwood.

Kamps, D., Kravits, T., Stolze, J., & Swaggert, B. (1999). Prevention strategies for at-risk students and students with EBD in urban elementary schools. *Journal of Emotional and Behavioral Disorders, 7*, 178–189.

Kirk, S., Gallagher, J., & Anastasiow, N. (2006). *Educating exceptional children.* Boston, MA: Houghton Mifflin.

Korinek, L., & Popp, P. (1997). Collaborative mainstream integration of social skills with academic instruction. *Preventing School Failure, 41*, 148–152.

Kravetz, S., Faust, M., Lipshitz, S., & Shalhav, S. (1999). LD, interpersonal understanding, and social behavior in the classroom. *Journal of Learning Disabilities, 32*, 248–256.

Lewis, T. J., & Sugai, G. (1999). Effective behavior support: A systems approach to proactive schoolwide management. *Focus on Exceptional Children, 31*(6), 24–47.

Lewis, T., Sugai, G., & Colvin, G. (1998). Reducing problem behavior through a school-wide system of effective behavior support: Investigation of a school-wide social skills training program and contextual interventions. *School Psychology Review, 27*, 446–459.

Lo, Y., Loe, S., & Cartledge, G. (2002). The effects of social skills instruction on the social behaviors of students at risk for emotional or behavioral disorders. *Behavioral Disorders, 27*, 371–385.

Lopez, E. (1995). Best practices in working with bilingual children. In A. Thomas & J. Grimes (Eds.), *Best practices in school psychology* (Vol. 3, pp. 1111–1121). Washington, DC: National Association of School Psychologist.

Maag, J. (1994). Promoting social skills training in classrooms: Issues for school counselors. *School Counselor, 42*, 100–114.

Maag, J., & Webber, J. (1995). Promoting children's social development in general education classrooms. *Preventing School Failure, 39*, 13–20.

Maag, J. W. (1999). *Behavior management: From theoretical implications to practical applications*. San Diego, CA: Singular.

Mahar, S., & Lyndall, S. (2002). *Social competence: A whole school approach to linking learning and well-being*. Melbourne, Australia: Social Competencies Unit, Department of Education & Training.

Maheady, L., Mallette, B., Harper, G., & Sacca, K. (1991). Heads together: A peer-mediated option for improving the academic achievement of heterogeneous learning groups. *Remedial & Special Education, 12*(2), 25–33.

Mayer, G. (1995). Preventing antisocial behavior in the schools. *Journal of Applied Behavior Analysis, 28*, 467–478.

Mayer, G. R. and Sulzer-Azaroff, B. (1990). Interventions for vandalism. In G. Stoner, M. R. Shinn, and H. M. Walker (Eds.), *Interventions for achievements and behavior problems*. Washington, DC. National Association of School Psychologists.

McCray, A., & Neal, L. (2003). The disproportionality of American Americans in special education. In R. Henderson & C. Yeakey (Eds.), *Surmounting all odds: Education, opportunity, and society in the new millennium*. Greenwich, CT: Information Age Publishers (pp. 455–485).

McIntyre, T. (1991). Understanding and defusing the street corner behaviors of urban black socially maladjusted youth. *Severe Behavior Disorders Monograph*, 85–97.

Meadows, N., Neel, R., Scott, C., & Parker, G. (1994). Academic performance, social competence, and mainstream accommodations: A look at mainstreamed students with serious behavioral disorders. *Behavioral Disorders, 19*(3), 170–180.

Mitchem, K. (2001). Adapting self-management programs for classwide use. *Remedial and Special Education, 22*, 75–89.

Mitchem, K., Young, K., West, R., & Benyo, J. (2001). CWPASM: A classwide peer-assisted self-management program for general education classrooms. *Education and Treatment of Children, 24*, 111–141.

Narayan, J., Heward, W., Gardner, R., Courson, F., & Omness, C. (1990). Using response cards to increase student participation in an elementary classroom. *Journal of Applied Behavior Analysis, 23*(4), 483–490.

National Center for Educational Statistics (NCES). (2003). *The condition of Education 2003* (NCES 2003–067). Washington, DC: US. Government Printing Office.

National Collaborative on Diversity in the Teaching Force. (2004). *Assessment of diversity in America's teaching force: A call to action*. National Education Association.

Neal, L., Webb-Johnson, G., & McCray, A. (2003). Movement matters: The need for culturally responsive teaching. *Journal of the New England League of Middle Schools*, 28–33.

Nieto, S. (2002). *Language, culture, and teaching: Critical perspectives for a new century* (Vol. 1). Mahwah, NJ: Lawrence Erlbaum.

Obiakor, F. E. (2001). Transforming teaching and learning to improve minority student achievement in inclusive setting. *Journal of Special Education Leadership, 14*(2), 81–88.

Obiakor, F., Utley, C., Smith, R., & Harris-Obiakor, P. (2002). The comprehensive support model for culturally diverse exceptional learners: Intervention in an age of change. *Intervention in School and Clinic, 28*, 14–28.

Reitz, A. (1994). Implementing comprehensive classroom-based programs for students with emotional and behavioral problems. *Education and Treatment of Children, 17*, 312–332.

Rossman, S. B. & Morley, E. (1996, August). Introduction. *Education and Urban Society, 28*(4), 395–411. (EJ 431 783).

Ruhl, K., & Berlinghoff, D. (1992). Research on improving behaviorally disordered students' academic performance: A review of the literature. *Behavioral Disorders, 17*(3), 178–190.

Salend, S. (1999). Facilitating friendships among diverse students. *Intervention in School and Clinic, 35*, 9–16.

Sasso, G., Melloy, K., & Kavale, K. (1990). Generalization, maintenance, and behavioral conversation associate with social skills training through structured learning. *Behavioral Disorders, 16*, 9–22.

Sautter, R. C. (1995, January). Standing up to violence. *Phi Delta Kappan, 76*(5), K1-K12. (EJ 494 715).

Shin, J., Deno, S., Robinson, S., & Marston, D. (2000). Predicting classroom achievement from active responding on a computer-based groupware system. *Remedial & Special Education, 21*(1), 53–60.

Shores, R., Gunter, P., & Jack, S. (1993). Classroom management strategies: Are they setting events for coercion? *Behavior Disorders, 18*(2), 92–102.

Skiba, R. J., & Peterson, R. L. (1999). The dark side of zero tolerance: Can punishment lead to safe schools? *Phi Delta Kappan, 80*, 372–382.

Stein, M., & Davis, C. (2000). Direction instruction as a positive behavioral support. *Beyond Behavior, 10*(1), 7–12.

Sugai, G., Horner, R. H., Dunlap, G., Hienenman, M., Lewis, T. J., Nelson, C. M., Scott, T., Liaupsin, C., Sailor, W., Turnbull, A. P., Turnbull H. R. III, Wickham, D., Wilcox, B., & Ruef, M. (2000). Applying positive behavioral support and functional behavioral assessment in schools. *Journal of Positive Behavioral Interventions 2*(3): 131–43.

Sutherland, K., & Wehby, J. (2001). Exploring the relationship between increased opportunities to respond to academic requests and the academic and behavioral outcomes of students with EBD. *Remedial & Special Education, 22*(2), 113–121.

Tam, B., & Scott, M. (1996). Three group instructional strategies for students with limited English proficiency in vocational education. *Journal for Vocational Special Needs Education, 19*(1), 31–36.

Thornton, N., & Gerlach, V. (1989). A model for designing responsive instruction. *Performance Improvement Quarterly, 2*(2), 13–27.

Thurlow, M., Graden, J., Greener, J., & Ysseldyke, J. (1983). LD and non-LD students opportunities to learn. *Learning Disability Quarterly, 6*, 172–183.

U.S. Department of Health and Human Services. (1999). *Mental health: A report of the Surgeon General.* Washington, DC: Author.

Van Acker, R., & Talbott, E. (1999). The school context and risk for aggression: Implications for school-based prevention and intervention efforts. *Preventing School Failure, 44*, 12–20.

Villegas, A. M., & Lucas, T. (2002). Preparing culturally responsive teachers: Rethinking the curriculum. *Journal of Teacher Education, 53*(1), 20–32.

Vincent, C. G., Horner, R. H., & Sugai, G. (2002). *Developing social competence for all students.* (ERIC/OSEP Digest #E626). The ERIC Clearinghouse on Disabilities and Gifted Education (ERIC EC). (ERIC Document Reproduction Service No. ED99CO0026)

Walker, H. M., Nishiok, V. M., Zeller, R., Bullis, M., & Sprague, J. R. (2001). School-based screening, identification, and service-delivery issues. *Report on Emotional & Behavioral Disorders in Youth, 1*(3), 51–52, 67–70.

Watson, R. (1995, February). A guide to violence prevention. *Educational Leadership, 55*(5), 57–59. (EJ 497 539).

Wehby, J., Symons, F., & Canale, J. (1998). Teaching practices in classrooms for students with emotional and behavioral disorders: Discrepancies between recommendations and observations. *Behavioral Disorders, 24*(1), 51–56.

Weinstein, C. S., Tomlinson-Clarke, S., & Curran, M. (2004). Toward a conception of culturally responsive classroom management. *Journal of Teacher Education, 55*(1), 25–38.

Wood, S., & Cronin, M. (1999). Students with emotional/behavioral disorders and transition planning: What the follow-up studies tell us. *Psychology in the Schools, 36*(4), 327–345.

PART III

Culturally Responsive Instructional Methods in Reading and the Content Areas

Chapter 7

Helping Culturally and Linguistically Diverse Exceptional Students Learn to Read

With Contributions by Jennifer Urbach

Chapter Objectives

Upon completion of this chapter the reader will be able to:

1. Describe the characteristics of CLD students with reading disabilities and understand how struggling readers differ from more proficient readers.
2. Explain the differences between first- and second-language reading.
3. List the key principles involved in teaching CLDE students to read.
4. Explain what it means for literacy instruction to be culturally responsive.
5. Describe the essential components of reading instruction.
6. Briefly summarize research-based instructional practices for teaching CLDE students how to read.
7. Explain multicomponent instructional practices for teaching CLDE students how to read.

VIGNETTE

Ms. Ruiz and Mrs. Buell co-teach for 2 hours a day during the literacy block in an inclusive third-grade transitional bilingual classroom at La Frontera, a large, urban elementary school. Ms. Ruiz is the general education teacher. She speaks Spanish as her first language and is bilingual. Ms. Buell is the special education teacher. She speaks a little conversational Spanish, but is not fluent. Last year she began working on a master's degree and endorsement in bilingual/ESL special education. It is now April, and the class recently finished taking the state's mandated high-stakes tests in English and Spanish.

Let's meet three of their students, all of whom have LD labels and struggle with reading: Carlos is a 9-year-old who was retained the previous year. He speaks Spanish in his home with his parents and three younger siblings. Carlos was born in Mexico, but his family moved to the United States when he was one; his younger siblings were all born in the United States. During kindergarten and first grade, Carlos attended bilingual classes and was instructed primarily in Spanish, though he also received some English as a second language instruction. Although slightly below grade level in reading, he seemed to be progressing satisfactorily and by the end of first grade, he could read at a primer level in Spanish. In second grade, he again was placed in a bilingual class, but this year his teacher began teaching him to read in English. He struggled, and his teacher suspected that his lack of success could be attributed to what she considered to be a poor home environment and a lack of parental support. In consultation with the school's administrators, she determined that he needed more time learning in English and that he should be retained and placed in an English-only classroom. His new second-grade teacher was alarmed at his low skills in English and apparent lack of progress, and so referred him for a special education evaluation. Because by now Carlos could speak close-to-fluent oral English and his classroom teacher and the psychologist assumed he was English dominant, he was tested exclusively in English. He qualified for placement as having LD because of a discrepancy between his IQ score of 89 on a WISC-III and even lower scores on an English reading test (standard score = 60, pre-primer grade level). The psychologist also noted that he had difficulty following oral directions in English and added that he was weak in auditory processing. When Carlos began attending the special education resource room for an hour a day for help with English reading, Ms. Buell soon became frustrated with his lack of responsiveness to the intensive, individualized instruction she provided. She had recently begun to take classes at a nearby university in bilingual/ESL special education, and wondered if Carlos had been transitioned to English instruction too soon, before he had been able to build a strong foundation in his native language. She advocated for a change in placement so that he could receive native language support. This is where we find Carlos today, in Ms. Ruiz's third-grade bilingual classroom receiving in-class rather than pull-out support from Ms. Buell. The results have been astounding; once Carlos again began reading in Spanish, he progressed rapidly and made almost 2 years' growth in less than a year. He is reading fluently in Spanish and seems to comprehend well. Recently his teachers began reintroducing English reading, while still maintaining some instruction in Spanish. Carlos still has an LD label, but Mrs. Buell questions the accuracy of this and is pushing to have him reevaluated by a bilingual multidisciplinary team.

Elva is an 8-year-old, second-generation Mexican American student. Her development has been normal with no notable delays. Elva lives with her parents and two older siblings. Her mother is bilingual and her father speaks primarily Spanish but can communicate in English at a basic conversational level. The family speaks both Spanish and English in the home. Although the children speak Spanish with their father, and usually with their mother, more and more often they are using English to communicate with one another. Elva has been in bilingual classes since kindergarten. Her progress has been marginal from the beginning but her teachers have never recommended retention. She now reads at an upper first-grade level in Spanish and has only emergent writing skills. She functions close to grade level in math and other content areas. Her social skills are well developed and she has a consistent friendship network within the classroom. Although Elva was supposed to begin transitioning to English reading this year, her teacher has been reluctant to start this process. After consulting with Mrs. Buell, Ms. Ruiz referred Elva for a special education assessment in September. Ms. Ruiz had also been Elva's sister's third-grade teacher, and she was concerned about the differences in their progress and Elva's low oral and written skills in Spanish as well as English. Elva also seemed to be struggling in comparison with her bilingual peers. Her Spanish Language Proficiency score on the LAS was a 3 and her oral proficiency in English was a 2. Based on scores on the Woodcock-Muñoz and the Woodcock-Johnson Psychoeducational Battery, as well as conversations with her parents and teachers, the school's multidisciplinary team concluded that Elva had learning disabilities that manifested in both English and Spanish. In January the two teachers started introducing English reading while continuing to support Elva's Spanish reading development. Elva's reading is slow and laborious and her word identification skills are quite low. She relies on picture and context cues to figure out words rather than knowledge of sound-symbol correspondence. She lacks phonological awareness. This is where Mrs. Buell has decided to focus her initial efforts.

Manny is a third-generation Mexican American. He is 8 years old and lives with both parents and two older half-brothers. His father is bilingual and his mother understands some Spanish, but is more comfortable with English. His two half-brothers speak only English, and the family speaks mostly English in the home. However, Manny spends a lot of time with his paternal grandmother, and she prefers Spanish. Manny began school in an English-only kindergarten at another school and was identified as LD in first grade because of concerns about his struggles learning to read as well as his problematic behavior. He recently moved to La Frontera and was placed in Ms. Ruiz's transitional bilingual class at his parents' request. They reasoned that because he had struggled in the English-only classrooms in his previous school (where that had been the only option), he might do better in a class with a bilingual teacher. Over the years, Manny has tended to fool around during any kind of literacy-related activity rather than focus on the task at hand (in contrast to his behavior during math, at which he excels). Manny approaches a literacy-related task expecting to fail it. Mrs. Buell's goals are not only to help Manny become a more proficient reader by developing comprehension strategies, but also to improve his confidence and enjoyment of reading by building on his interests and knowledge. He seems to have a great deal of difficulty monitoring his own performance and has little awareness of when he has understood an assignment or something he has read. Miscues have little to do with the story he is reading. Manny needs to learn how to self-monitor when comprehension has broken down and how to take steps to improve his understanding. Manny also exhibits difficulty with memory, and in particular has trouble remembering decontextualized information. His teachers are helping him make connections between previously learned and new information and link information across subjects and settings. The thematic unit approach is proving to be helpful with Manny for this reason, as is allowing him to select his own reading materials that cover topics about which he is interested and has some background knowledge.

Reflective Questions

1. What instructional practices in literacy would you implement with Carlos?
2. What practices would you try with Manny? With Elva?

INTRODUCTION

Culturally and linguistically diverse students with reading disabilities are a heterogeneous group that includes students from different ethnic backgrounds, different socioeconomic levels, and different countries of origin, with different prior school experiences, different levels of language proficiency, and different kinds of strengths and struggles (Baca, 2002; Klingner, Artiles, & Méndez Barletta, 2006). Some may be refugees; others may be considered "illegal" immigrants. Some subpopulations of ELLs are particularly vulnerable to identification as LD. For example, Artiles, Rueda, Salazar, and Higareda (2005) conducted research on subpopulations of ELLs in 11 urban districts in California. They found that ELLs who tested as limited in their native language as well as in English showed the highest rates of identification in special education. They also found that ELLs in English immersion classrooms were more likely to receive special education than their peers in modified English immersion or bilingual programs. Artiles et al. (2005) raised questions about the validity of the districts' subgroups and noted that we need to know more about the specific characteristics of ELLs who are most vulnerable for placement in special education, especially those students who test as "limited" in multiple languages.

We know that some CLD students are misidentified as LD or as having other disabilities. For example, Schiff-Myers, Djukic, McGovern-Lawler, and Perez (1994) described a student misclassified as having a language-learning disability who seemed to have arrested development in both her primary language and English. Yet the child's difficulties turned out to be temporary and she eventually mastered English. Determining whether a child's struggles are primarily caused by learning in a language in which he or she is not fluent or whether a child has had an adequate opportunity to learn is indeed challenging. Of the students in Ms. Ruiz's class, it is most likely that Carlos does not have a disability, but that Elva and Manny do. Elva and Manny are quite different, however, in many ways. For instance, Elva has trouble identifying words, whereas Manny can decode, but struggles with comprehension and focusing.

Differences Between More and Less Proficient Readers in a Second Language

ELLs with LD seem to differ from more proficient readers in that they focus more on surface aspects of reading, apply fewer comprehension strategies, tap into background knowledge less, and have more limited vocabularies (Ammon, 1987; Hardin, 2001; Langer, Bartholome, Vasquez, & Lucas, 1990). They are less able to monitor their understanding and notice when comprehension has broken down. When they do not understand, they are less able to take steps to improve their comprehension. Yet, importantly, they do seem to be able to transfer strategies from their native language to English reading.

In their analyses of students' oral reading miscues, Miramontes (1987, 1990) and Avalos (2003) found that ELL readers with LD exhibited areas of strength, yet generally were perceived by their teachers to be similar and weak in all skills. Students' profiles varied depending on their language dominance, with students with greater English proficiency more likely to do better comprehending English texts.

Yet studies in which students were asked to "think aloud" while reading paint a more complex picture. In two separate studies, Hardin (2001) and Langer et al. (1990) found that students' level of second language proficiency played a less prominent role in second language reading than did their level of their strategy usage in their first language. In other words, ELLs' comprehension of both English and Spanish texts depended on their ability to use comprehension strategies. Better readers were distinguished more by their use of strategies than their fluency in English and students who

---

TABLE 7.1 Differences Between More and Less Proficient Readers in a Second Language

ELLs with LD or who struggle with reading:

- Focus more on surface aspects of reading.
- Apply fewer and less appropriate comprehension strategies.
- Tap into background knowledge less.
- Have more limited vocabularies.
- Are less able to monitor their understanding.
- Are less able to resolve comprehension difficulties in either language.

Sources: Ammon (1987); Hardin (2001); Jiménez, García, & Pearson (1995, 1996); Langer, Bartholome, Vasquez, & Lucas (1990); Miramontes (1987, 1990).

did well in one language generally did well in the other. In their comparison of the reading strategies of successful bilingual Latina/o readers, successful monolingual English readers, and less successful Latina/o readers, Jiménez, García, and Pearson (1995) and Jiménez, García, and Pearson (1996) achieved similar results. The less successful Latina/o readers used fewer strategies and were less effective resolving comprehension difficulties in either language. When they encountered unknown vocabulary items they had difficulty constructing plausible interpretations of the text (see Table 7.1).

Similarities and Differences in First and Second Language Reading

There are important differences between learning to read in one's first and a second language. Second language readers tend to focus more on word meanings than native language readers (Jiménez et al., 1995; Jiménez et al., 1996). Translation, cognate awareness, and information transfer (across languages) are all strategies that seem to be unique to bilingual reading. Similarly, unknown vocabulary seems to be an obstacle for bilingual readers in a way that it was not for the monolingual reader. Also, the cultural and linguistic familiarity of reading passages in one's first language seems to facilitate comprehension for the monolingual reader. English-only readers seldom need to overtly monitor their comprehension in the way second language readers do because they rarely encounter unknown vocabulary and generally have well-developed background schema relevant to the text they are reading. Knight, Padrón, and Waxman (1985) found that the third- through fifth-grade ELLs in their study selected strategies with different relative frequencies than native English readers. Padrón and Waxman (1988) noted that ELLs' use of counterproductive strategies negatively affected their English reading comprehension. The authors concluded that this might be one reason ELLs generally score lower than English monolingual students on reading achievement tests. This finding is similar to those of studies contrasting more and less proficient second language readers described in the previous section (see Table 7.2).

TABLE 7.2 Differences Between Reading in a First or Second Language

In comparison with first language readers, second language readers are more likely to:

- Focus on word meanings (and focus at the word level when monitoring their comprehension).
- Struggle with figurative language and idiomatic expressions.
- Translate text to their native language to assist with comprehension.
- Apply knowledge of cognates.
- Transfer information across languages.
- Stumble on unknown vocabulary.
- Encounter unfamiliar cultural referents.
- Come across unknown text structures.
- Lack relevant background schema.
- Experience differences across languages in sound/symbol correspondence.

Sources: Carrell & Grabe (2002); Jiménez et al. (1995); Jiménez et al. (1996); Knight, Padrón, & Waxman (1985); Padrón & Waxman (1988).

Relationships Among First and Second Language Oral Proficiency, Native Language Reading, and Reading in English as a Second Language

English second language oral proficiency, native language reading, and English second language reading are all related (Fitzgerald, 1995; Garcia-Vasquez, 1995; Gottardo, 2002). Yet just how these factors affect one another varies by grade level and whether students are proficient readers in their first language. The strongest predictors of English word reading among first-graders were native language proficiency and English phonological processing, native language reading, and English vocabulary (Gottardo, 2002). Variation in students' vocabularies seems to be an important predictor, yet one that is often overlooked. Carlisle, Beeman, Davis, and Spharim (1999) found that a significant portion of the variance in the reading comprehension of the ELL struggling readers in their study was explained by the extensiveness of students' vocabularies in both English and Spanish, as well as by their phonological awareness. Carlisle et al. (1999) concluded that vocabulary development in both the native language and English should be important priorities because of their effects on English reading comprehension.

Teaching Implications: We still need to better understand how CLD students with and without disabilities differ as they become literate. We also need to know more about how to distinguish between those who have actual disabilities from those who may be struggling for other reasons. As noted in the Executive Summary of the National Symposium on Learning Disabilities in ELLs (2003, p. vi), we must learn to "identify impediments to normal development for those who are not disabled" as well as develop a better understanding of the normal trajectory for language acquisition among ELLs in the United States. This is essential before students with LD can reliably be identified.

In addition, we need to learn much more about the role of cultural variables, as well as affective and motivational factors, in influencing learning (Klingner et al., 2006; National Symposium on Learning Disabilities in ELLs, 2003). This is an area about which we have little research, although work by scholars such as Trueba (1988) has shed light on the central role that cultural conflict and other sociocultural factors play in learning. LD identification, assessment, and instruction must be grounded in a cultural theory of human learning and development (Rogoff, 2003).

TEACHING CULTURALLY AND LINGUISTICALLY DIVERSE EXCEPTIONAL STUDENTS HOW TO READ

What makes bilingual/ESL special education "special" for CLDE students (Klingner & Bianco, 2006)? Optimal programs for CLD students with disabilities are based on supportive, culturally responsive learning environments that include validated instructional practices (Ortiz, 1997, 2001). In such programs, students' native languages and cultures are valued and English language development is nurtured. It is a heightened focus on *language* and *culture* that makes bilingual/ESL special education "special" in comparison with generic special education. Below we list key principles of instruction grounded in research with culturally and linguistically diverse populations with special needs. Next we describe culturally responsive literacy instruction. We then discuss research-based instructional practices.

Key Principles

What do experts recommend as best practice for CLD students with disabilities? In compiling the list in Table 7.3, we drew from various research syntheses (August & Hakuta, 1997; Gersten & Baker, 2000; Müller & Markowitz, 2004; Ortiz, 2001) as well as observational studies of schools and classrooms in which CLD students excel (including those with disabilities) (Graves, Gersten, & Haager, 2004; Pressley, Allington et al., 2001; Pressley, Wharton-McDonald et al., 2001; Taylor, Pearson, Clark, & Walpole, 2000). Although not all of these principles are unique to literacy instruction, they have clear implications for how best to teach reading (see Table 7.3).

Culturally Responsive Literacy Instruction

Researchers have only conducted a few observational studies in bilingual special education classrooms (Lopez-Reyna, 1996; Ruiz, 1989, 1995). Yet these studies illustrate the importance of providing a nurturing, supportive environment as a backdrop for

TABLE 7.3 Key Principles of Effective Instruction for CLDE Students

The most effective instruction:

- Incorporates the student's native language in strategic ways.
- Builds on students' home cultures.
- Helps students access their prior knowledge, make connections, and build new knowledge.
- Helps students apply concepts to the tasks at hand as well as in their own lives.
- Provides students with frequent opportunities to use language for both conversational and academic purposes.
- Promotes vocabulary as a "curricular anchor."
- Preteaches and reinforces key vocabulary.
- Uses visuals, realia, and graphic organizers to support concepts and teach vocabulary.
- Focuses on higher order thinking and active problem solving.
- Incorporates collaborative learning activities (e.g., cooperative learning and peer tutoring).
- Provides multiple and varied opportunities to review and apply previously learned concepts.
- Includes formal and informal opportunities to practice throughout the day.
- Promotes active engagement.
- Includes explicit phonics instruction with an emphasis on applications during real reading (e.g., with connected text).
- Provides explicit feedback that is appropriate for the learner's level.
- Includes opportunities for independent reading of authentic texts.
- Provides a balance between skills and holistic instruction.

The most effective environments:

- Are warm and supportive, with much positive reinforcement.
- Are well managed.
- Are safe.
- Are cooperative and collaborative.
- Include parental and community involvement.
- Ensure high levels of student engagement (e.g., lots of time spent reading and writing).

The most effective teachers:

- Enact sophisticated knowledge of reading instruction as well as of bilingual and/or second language instruction.
- Make sure students are involved in tasks matched to their competency level.
- Know how to make learning relevant and meaningful.
- Know how to accelerate demands on students as their competencies improve.
- Have high expectations for students and know how to help students meet expectations.

(continued)

TABLE 7.3   (continued)

- Monitor the cognitive and language demands on ELLs.
- Carefully watch students' progress and provide scaffolded support as needed.
- Encourage students to self-regulate.
- Understand that second language acquisition takes time and that ELLs can follow different learning trajectories than their mainstream peers.
- Know how to distinguish between language acquisition and learning disabilities.
- Develop positive relationships with students.
- View families as valued partners.
- Learn about and connect with their students' cultures and communities.
- Bridge borders between home and school cultures.
- Demonstrate care, respect, and commitment to each student's learning abilities, desires, and potentialities.
- Feel a strong sense of responsibility for all of their students, including those in special education.

Sources: Au & Kawakami (1994); August & Hakuta (1997); Burke, Hagan, & Grossen (1998); Cardelle-Elawar (1990); Cummins (1984, 1989); Gay (2000); Gersten & Baker (2000); Graves, Gersten, & Haager (2004); Henderson & Landesman (1995); Jiménez (2001); Jiménez & Gersten (1999); Klingner & Vaughn (1996, 2000); Ladson-Billings (1994); Lopez-Reyna (1996); McGroarty (1989); Miniccuci et al. (1995); Muñiz-Swicegood (1994); Ortiz & Wilkinson (1991); Padrón & Waxman (1988); Pressley, Allington et al. (2001); Pressley, Wharton-McDonald et al. (2001); Reyes & Bos (1998); Rousseau, Tam, & Ramnarain (1993); Saunders, O'Brien, Lennon, & McLean (1998); Taylor, Pearson, Clark, & Walpole (2000); Tikunoff et al. (1991); Villegas & Lucas (2002); Willig, Swedo, & Ortiz (1987).

instruction. Both Lopez-Reyna and Ruiz noted that student performance varied depending on the learning context. It was only in supportive, culturally responsive learning environments in which teachers stressed meaning-making through active engagement in authentic learning activities that students were able to demonstrate the upper range of their academic, linguistic, and social skills.

All children deserve to receive literacy instruction that is responsive to and builds on their culture, prior knowledge, interests, motivation, and home language (August & Hakuta, 1997; Au, 2000; Rueda, MacGillivray, Monzó, & Arzubiaga, 2001; Ruiz, 1998; Wiley, 1996). What does it mean for literacy instruction to be culturally responsive? Culture is involved in all learning; it is part of who we are and affects everything we do. Therefore, all instruction is culturally responsive to someone—the question is, "To whom?" Is the instruction responsive only to the White, mainstream students in the classroom, or to everyone? Moje and Hinchman (2004) noted, "All practice needs to be culturally responsive in order to be best practice" (p. 321). Culture is not a unitary construct, but rather is complex and dynamic. It is much more than holidays, foods, and customs, but rather is represented in how we learn, what we value, and the ways we interact with others. What does it mean to account for culture when teaching children to read (Klingner et al., 2005)? It means recognizing that when young children begin school, their experiences with print may not have been the same as those of their mainstream peers, but they still have had valuable experiences on which their teachers can and should build. "Literacy learning begins in the home, not the school, and instruction should build on the foundation for literacy learning established in the home" (Au, 1993, p. 35). Even in conditions of poverty, homes can be rich in print and family members engage in literacy activities of many kinds on a daily basis (Anderson & Stokes, 1984; Heath, 1983; Purcell-Gates, 1996; Taylor & Dorsey-Gaines, 1988; Teale, 1986). Accounting for culture means understanding that even when students' discourse and behavioral styles do not match school-expected ways, they still should be validated (Heath, 1983; Cazden, 1988). It means realizing that bilingualism and multiculturalism are assets and that learning should be an additive rather than a subtractive process (August & Hakuta, 1997). It means explicitly connecting home, community, and school literacy practices. Finally, it means making sure students are motivated and engaged in meaningful reading activities (Guthrie & Wigfield, 2000; Rueda et al., 2001).

Culturally responsive teachers respect students' values and learn what they can about their students' cultures (Alvermann, 2005; Gay, 2000; Ladson-Billings, 1994). They work to understand their own assumptions and stereotypical views well enough to catch themselves from making unwarranted judgments about students and their families. They genuinely want to know more about their students and the communities in which they teach. They value the many "funds of knowledge" among their students' families and strive to bring these into the classroom (Moll & González, 1994). "As educators we must not assume that we can only teach the families how to do school, but that we can learn valuable lessons by coming to know the families, and by taking the time to establish the social relationships necessary to create personal links between households and classrooms" (Moll, 1999, p. xiii).

Culturally responsive literacy programs develop partnerships and tap into community resources. For example, they enlist volunteers to serve as reading tutors (Baker, Gersten, & Keating, 2000; Fitzgerald, 2001; Invernizzi, Juel, & Rosemary, 1997; Wasik, 1998; Wasik & Slavin, 1993). In one effective model, local elders participate in the schooling of American Indian students (Aguilera, 2003). Other efforts focus on developing partnerships with parents and other caregivers to enhance home literacy experiences (Arnold, Lonigan, Whitehurst, & Epstein, 1994; Dickinson & Smith, 1994; Valdez-Menchaca & Whitehurst, 1992; Whitehurst et al., 1994).

Culturally responsive literacy programs incorporate relevant multicultural literature into daily instruction (Bieger, 1995/1996; Godina & McCoy, 2000). Multicultural literature should go beyond portraying holidays and stereotypical images and viewpoints. It should be used in transformative ways that enable students to view concerns, themes, problems, and concepts from the perspectives of diverse groups (Banks & Banks, 1997). Literature should also allow students to identify real social problems and to read about how characters take action to solve problems (Bieger, 1995/1996).

In culturally responsive literacy programs, students also learn skills (Delpit, 1995). Teachers should not only provide multiple opportunities for students to engage with authentic text in meaningful ways, in a supportive environment, but also provide explicit instruction in the building blocks of reading. We discuss these essential components next.

Essential Components of Reading Instruction

Research indicates that within a culturally responsive, supportive learning environment, specific practices facilitate learning to read. Five of these are often described as "the big ideas" of reading, and are the foundation of the No Child Left Behind Act: phonemic awareness, word study (or phonics), vocabulary, fluency, and comprehension (National Reading Panel, 2000). In addition, we emphasize the importance of motivation and oral language. We describe each of these below.

Oral Language (Oracy). Oracy instruction links language development and literacy learning by emphasizing teacher–child interactions (Geisler, in press). Advocates for oracy programs emphasize the importance of explicit teaching of both TALK and TEXT (Gentile, 2004). For ELLs, the challenge is not just how to provide explicit instruction in reading and writing, but also how to link oral language and literacy instruction. The teacher emphasizes daily oral language activities and considers these critical to students' development as readers and writers. This focus on oral language development includes not only vocabulary, but also common language structures. When students' oral language improves, so do their reading fluency and comprehension. Ideally, children learning to read in a second language are initially taught in their first language (Gentile, 2004). Of the students in Ms. Ruiz's class, Elva is the one most in need of a focus on oracy.

Phonemic Awareness. Phonemic awareness is the ability to identify and manipulate the phonemes or sounds in spoken words. It is also the understanding that, when put together, the sounds of spoken language make words. Phonemic awareness does not involve written text—it refers only to the ability to manipulate *sounds.* Phonologi-cal awareness is the ability to manipulate the sounds in spoken words. This ability has been found to be predictive of ELLs' reading achievement in English (Chiappe, Siegel, & Gottardo, 2002) and Spanish (Lindsey, Manis, & Bailey, 2003). In fact, Spanish phonological awareness may be a better predictor of English word reading than English or Spanish oral proficiency or English word recognition (Durgunoglu, Nagy, & Hancin-Bhatt, 1993). Thus, developing native language phonological awareness appears to be a way to improve reading in English.

For ELLs learning to read in English, phonemic awareness (in English) can present special challenges (Antunez, 2002). Some phonemes may not be present in the student's native language and, therefore, might be difficult for a student to pronounce and, even more importantly, distinguish auditorily from similar sounds. For example, Spanish-speaking children may confuse *ch* and *sh,* because most dialects in Spanish do not include "sh." Teachers can help ELLs with phonemic awareness by finding out which phonemes exist and do not exist in the student's native language. Many activities that work well with all students should also help ELLs, such as word plays, songs, poems, language games, and word walls (Hiebert et al., 1998). Rhymes exist in every language. Antunez (2002) suggests that teachers ask students or their parents to share these culturally relevant and teachable rhymes with the class, and build phonemic awareness activities around them. Antunez (2002) offers one example in Spanish:

> Bate, bate, chocolate,
>
> tu nariz de cacahuate.
>
> Uno, dos, tres, CHO!
>
> Uno, dos, tres, CO!
>
> Uno, dos, tres, LA!
>
> Uno, dos, tres, TE!
>
> Chocolate, chocolate!
>
> Bate, bate, chocolate!
>
> Bate, bate, bate, bate,
>
> Bate, bate, CHOCOLATE!

Interventions in phonemic or phonological awareness may be particularly important for ELLs who are struggling to acquire literacy skills. For example, Nag-Arulmani, Reddy, and Buckley (2003) evaluated whether ELLs with reading difficulties would respond better to a phonological intervention or one that addressed oral proficiency. Students who received explicit phonological instruction showed significantly better gains in reading than oral language proficiency and control groups. Most notable was that the intervention was most effective for the children who began the study with the lowest levels of single-word reading, phonological awareness, and decoding skills. Of the students in Ms. Ruiz's class, Elva is the one who can most benefit from this type of support. She is receiving daily supplemental instruction in phonological awareness from Mrs. Buell.

Phonics. Phonics is the understanding of sound-symbol correspondence, or, in other words, which letters make which sounds. It generally is much more difficult for ELLs to learn phonics in English when they have not already acquired this understanding in their first language. The process becomes much more abstract and less meaningful (Peregoy & Boyle, 2000). When students have learned to read in another language first, the process of learning to read in English is facilitated when the orthographic systems of the two languages are similar, and much more challenging when they are not (such as Chinese or Japanese). Spanish and English share many similarities. For instance, the sounds represented by the letters *b, c, d, f, l, m, n, p, q, s,* and *t* are similar enough that they usually transfer to English (Antunez, 2002). On the other hand, vowels look the same in Spanish and English but represent different sounds. Therefore, English vowel sounds and their various spellings can be very challenging for ELLs (Peregoy & Boyle, 2000). Again, of the students in Ms. Ruiz's class, Elva is most in need of explicit instruction in phonics. Her teachers have opted to use a Language Experience Approach with her so that they can make sure this instruction is meaningful and relevant for her, rather than disconnected and abstract (Dixon & Nessel, 1983; Hudelson, 1984; Peregoy & Boyle, 2001). We describe this approach later in this chapter.

Vocabulary. Vocabulary development is one of the greatest challenges for ELL teachers (Antunez, 2002). Students' understanding of vocabulary affects their fluency as well as their comprehension. Some ELLs are able to read phonetically (word calling) and yet do not understand what they have read because they have not acquired the necessary vocabulary. Teachers should provide explicit instruction in key vocabulary, with multiple and frequent opportunities to practice (see Chapter 9; also, see Beck, McKeown, & Kucan, 2002; Peregoy & Boyle, 2001). Students should also learn how to use prefixes and suffixes to figure out word meanings, how to use context clues, and how to use resources such as dictionaries and glossaries. Figurative language (e.g., "funny bone," "raining cats and dogs") and idioms (e.g., "a little bird told me," "shoot yourself in the foot") can be quite problematic for ELLs. By skimming students' text beforehand looking for challenging expressions, the teacher can anticipate these difficulties and engage students in a discussion about literal and figurative meanings of different words and phrases (Antunez, 2002; Hiebert et al., 1998). All of the students in Ms. Ruiz's class are benefiting from their teachers' emphasis on vocabulary. Mrs. Buell often provides extra support in key terms through pre-teaching and follow-up review activities.

Fluency. Fluency is the ability to read quickly and accurately. Repeated oral reading and independent silent reading are two common ways of improving fluency—in other words: practice, practice, practice. Opportunities to hear a more expert reader model fluent, expressive reading are important. Struggling ELL readers can read along with a teacher or a more proficient peer, or they might listen to and follow along with books on tape or on CD. This practice does not need to occur exclusively during independent reading. Shared reading activities, such as the reading aloud of big books, can help ELLs improve their fluency (Boyle & Peregoy, 2001; Hiebert et al., 1998). Antunez (2002) points out that fluency should not be confused with accent. Many ELLs will read and speak English with an accent as they are beginning to learn English, and others will have one throughout their lives. Students can read fluently in English with a native language accent. Ms. Ruiz and Mrs. Buell have made fluency a high priority for all of their students, but have especially targeted fluency as important for Carlos, who seems to be "taking off" with his literacy skills.

Reading Comprehension. Reading comprehension is the "sine qua non of reading" (Beck & McKeown, 1998). Although fundamental skills such as phonics and fluency are important building blocks of reading, knowing how to read words ultimately has little value if comprehension is missing. Reading comprehension is a complex process of constructing meaning by coordinating a number of processes including skills related to decoding, word reading, and fluency and the integration of background knowledge, vocabulary, and previous experiences (O'Shea, Sindelar, & O'Shea, 1987; Snow, 2002). Many factors affect the reading comprehension of ELLs, whether they are reading in their native language or in English. As already noted, these include language proficiency, vocabulary knowledge, and use of comprehension strategies. Numerous instructional practices have been developed to help students with LD improve their reading comprehension, such as:

- Creating graphic organizers.
- Modeling or "thinking aloud" a strategic approach to reading.
- Predicting what a story or passage will be about or what will happen next.
- Monitoring understanding and using fix-up strategies when comprehension breaks down.
- Finding the main idea.
- Generating questions.
- Summarizing.

We discuss some of these below, and some in Chapter 9 (also, see Klingner, Vaughn, & Boardman, in press). Of course, comprehension instruction is important and relevant for all students, but it is particularly critical and timely for students who are adequate word readers but lack understanding of what they read. For this reason, Mrs. Buell and Ms. Ruiz are prioritizing comprehension strategy instruction for Manny.

Motivation. Snow, Burns, and Griffin (1998) emphasized the importance of student motivation in the precursor to the National Reading Panel report, *Preventing Reading Difficulties in Young Children*. They noted that "motivation is crucial" (p. 50 of Executive Summary) and that one of the principle reasons students struggle to learn to read is a loss of motivation. Rueda et al. (2001) investigated the role of context and sociocultural factors in affecting reading engagement and motivation for ELLs. They noted that motivation is not just in the learner, but also in the task and in the setting. Some of the characteristics of instructional contexts that promote intrinsic motivation include:

- Opportunities for social interaction.
- Choices about reading materials and tasks.
- Real-world literacy tasks.
- Learning strategies.
- Instruction that is at an appropriate level and provides students with many opportunities for success.

- Meaningful, interesting, engaging tasks that connect with outside-of-school experiences.
- Home–school partnerships.

We must not forget that reading "is an active process to which the reader brings his or her individual attitudes, interests, [and] expectations" (Irwin, 1991, p. 7). Instructional programs must take into account the importance of motivation if they are to provide an optimal learning environment. Ms. Ruiz and Mrs. Buell think about this aspect of literacy instruction every day and are very aware of its importance. They consider it especially important for students such as Manny who seem to dislike reading.

RESEARCH–BASED INSTRUCTIONAL PRACTICES FOR STRUGGLING ELL READERS

In recent years, numerous researchers have focused their efforts on examining the efficacy of reading interventions for English language learners with reading difficulties (De La Colina, Parker, Hasbrouck, & Lara-Alecio, 2001; Denton, Anthony, Parker, & Hasbrouck, 2004; Escamilla, Loera, Ruiz, & Rodriguez, 1998; Linan-Thompson, Vaughn, Hickman-Davis, & Kouzekanani, 2003; Linan-Thompson, Vaughn, Prater, & Cirino, 2006; Nag-Arulmani, Reddy, & Buckley, 2003; Vaughn, Mathes, Linan-Thompson, & Francis, 2005). In some of these studies, students were instructed in their native language, whereas in others they received instruction in English only. Some practices focus on specific aspects of reading, and others are packages or programs that cover multiple components. We first describe individual approaches and then multi-component models. For each of these instructional approaches, we provide a brief overview, a summary of research, and a description of how it is implemented.

Descubriendo la Lectura

Descubriendo la Lectura is a Spanish version of Reading Recovery (Clay, 1985). Both provide short-term interventions of one-to-one tutoring for first graders who show signs of struggling. The goal of Descubriendo la Lectura is to drastically reduce the number of bilingual first-grade students who experience difficulty learning to read and write in bilingual classrooms. Students are targeted for assistance using a Spanish Observation Survey. Like the English version, the survey includes six observational tasks that provide a profile of a student's reading and writing skills. Those students scoring in the lowest 20 percent are recommended for participation in the program. Students participate in daily half-hour lessons for 12 to 20 weeks. As soon as students can read as well as their classmates who have been making adequate progress, lessons are discontinued. Hudson and Smith (2001) describe it as "a good first step" for supporting struggling readers (p. 39).

Research suggests that Descubriendo la Lectura works well for students who are somewhat behind their peers but do not have severe delays. Those students who do not respond are dropped from the program. Escamilla et al. (1998) found that outcomes for Descubriendo la Lectura students were comparable to outcomes for Reading Recovery students. About 8 of 10 students who received the full series of Descubriendo la Lectura lessons were able to read and write with the average range of performance of their class. The few students who were still having difficulty were referred for further evaluation and possible special education placement. Neal and Kelly (1999) found that one-fourth of the English language learners who participated in Reading Recovery or Descubriendo la Lectura in their study (i.e., the group of students with the lowest skills prior to intervention) did not make sufficient progress and were dropped from the program.

Descubriendo la Lectura lessons are 30 minutes long. Each lesson consists of five components (adapted from Hudson & Smith, 2001):

1. *Rereading two or more familiar books to build fluency.* The student reads two familiar books aloud. These books are from previous lessons. While the student is reading, the tutor notes strategies used correctly and independently.

2. *Taking a running record.* The student reads aloud independently from the book introduced the previous day while the tutor takes a running record of the text, marking words read correctly and noting miscues. After the child reads, the tutor highlights strategies used during the reading and discusses the story to reinforce comprehension. The tutor may also use magnetic letters to reinforce words missed.

3. *Writing a story.* The student writes in a notebook that includes a practice page and a "perfect page" for the final story. The discussion of the story read for the running reading record often provides material for the daily story writing. Student and tutor work together to figure out the spellings of words and practice them on the practice page before writing them onto the story page.

4. *Putting together the cut-up story.* As the student writes in the journal, the teacher writes the previous day's story on a sentence strip and cuts it into separate words. The student then reassembles the sentence, rereading it several times. This sentence is put in an envelope to be reassembled and read at home.

5. *Attempting a new story with coaching.* In the last part of the lesson, the tutor introduces a new book by previewing the story, modeling new words and phrases orally, and asking the student to predict what will happen. The student and tutor then read the book together, discussing the story and working on new strategies for reading the print.

Teachers must participate in specialized training to become Descubriendo la Lectura tutors.

Read Naturally

Read Naturally is an intensive reading intervention that combines repeated reading of connected text, vocabulary and comprehension instruction, and progress monitoring. The goal of Read Naturally is to improve students' fluency (i.e., speed, accuracy, and proper expression). Read Naturally is meant to be implemented for a minimum of three 30-minute sessions each week.

De La Colina et al. (2001) investigated the effectiveness of Read Naturally using Spanish text and found that it improved the fluency and, to a lesser extent, the comprehension of first- and second-grade English language learners considered low achieving and at risk. Those students who were highly engaged improved the most. Denton et al. (2004) examined the effectiveness of Read Naturally, though in English. Their participants included second- through fifth-grade English language learners identified by their teachers as having difficulty learning to read. Denton et al. found no statistically significant differences and only minimal effect sizes favoring Read Naturally over a control condition on word identification, word attack, and passage comprehension measures.

Read Naturally can be implemented by a teacher, a paraprofessional, or a parent volunteer (although the teacher must oversee its use). The first step is to assess a student's oral reading fluency level using curriculum-based measurement procedures. Next, the student chooses a story at his or her reading level, and based on the title and the picture, predicts what the story will be about. Then the student thinks about what he or she already knows about the topic and writes it down. The student then times him- or herself for a one-minute unpracticed reading of the story, marking difficult words, recording the words correct per minute, and graphing them. Following this, the tutor reads the story, modeling correct pronunciation, expression, and phrasing, while the student follows along, tracking the print. This is repeated twice, each time a little more quickly. Next the student tries reading the story independently again. Once the student has reached a predetermined goal for number of words read, he or she answers questions about the story. Then the student writes a retell. The last step is to read the story again for one minute while the teacher listens for expression and notes any errors (Hasbrouck, Ihnot, & Rogers, 1999).

Read Well

Read Well is a published program that combines systematic, explicit phonics instruction with practice in decodable text and contextualized vocabulary and comprehension instruction. It was designed for first-, second-, and third-grade students who are not fluent readers, though it can also be used with kindergarten students with age-appropriate modifications. Students are tutored individually or in small groups.

Denton et al. (2004) investigated the effectiveness of Read Well with second- through fifth-grade ELLs who were struggling readers. Tutors worked with students in

English reading three times a week in 40-minute periods for 10 weeks. In comparison with matched students who did not receive this extra intervention, the Read Well students showed significantly more growth in word identification, but not in word attack (nonword reading) or comprehension. The authors speculated that students' lack of growth in comprehension could have been due to a lack of emphasis on helping students learn English vocabulary. In Read Well, vocabulary instruction is informal rather than systematic.

Read Well comes in a complete package that includes 38 units, each with lessons for three to four days. Just how much students cover depends on how quickly they progress. Each Read Well unit includes a decoding practice folder and theme-related student reader with narrative and expository texts. The teacher guides the students through the decoding practice folder using explicit instructional strategies. Then skills that have been previously introduced and mastered by the students are put into practice through the reading of connected text. Students then read their stories, reading decodable parts on their own and more challenging parts with the teacher. Every unit also includes comprehension activities and an assessment.

MULTICOMPONENT APPROACHES FOR TEACHING CLDE STUDENTS HOW TO READ

A few researchers have tested the effectiveness of multicomponent approaches for improving the reading comprehension of CLD students with disabilities. This work has been conducted on reciprocal teaching and classwide peer tutoring. For other approaches to improving students' reading comprehension, see Chapter 8.

Reciprocal Teaching[1]

For over 20 years, reciprocal teaching has been acknowledged as a collaborative, comprehension-fostering instructional technique that emphasizes the importance of equipping students with the ability to use comprehension strategies (Rosenshine & Meister, 1994). In this model, a group of students and the teacher collaboratively examine a paragraph of text through dialogue. Students are guided in how to use four comprehension strategies: questioning, summarizing, clarifying, and predicating. At first the teacher helps the students with these strategies by modeling and scaffolding the students' implementation of the strategies, but gradually reduces assistance. The premise is that teaching students to collaboratively use the four strategies in a dialogue will help them bring meaning to the text while helping them internalize the use of the strategies, thus, ultimately improving their reading comprehension.

Reciprocal teaching was developed to support struggling readers. Although it was not originally designed for ELLs, it has been suggested as a viable instructional method

---

[1]Contributed by Jennifer Urbach.

for ELL students. In their national research report regarding schooling for language-minority children, August and Hakuta (1997) state:

> Those whose skill with word recognition is limited can improve their comprehension by employing strategies such as reading the whole text for gist; self-monitoring for understanding; and using cues from titles, pictures, headings, and the like. Explicit instruction in comprehension strategies such as prediction, summarization, and questioning—for example, the widely used "reciprocal teaching" (Palincsar and Brown, 1984) . . . has been shown to be useful with poor first-language readers, and some evidence suggests it would also be useful with second-language readers who have comprehension difficulties. (p. 61)

Recent research has also supported this claim (Fung, Wilkinson, & Moore, 2003; Klingner & Vaughn, 1996). Yet, even though reciprocal teaching has been proven effective it is not simply the teaching of the four strategies that make it valuable. In fact, sometimes reciprocal teaching has been implemented ineffectively because the goal of reciprocal teaching—to improve students' comprehension monitoring and comprehension of the text—and the basic theories that underlie reciprocal teaching are misunderstood. One result of not understanding these concepts is "lethal mutations," resulting in a less effective technique (Seymour & Osana, 2003; Brown & Campione, 1996).

Theoretical Bases for Reciprocal Teaching. Brown and Palincsar (1989) state that three related theories on guided learning help to explain reciprocal teaching's effectiveness: Vygotsky's zone of proximal development, scaffolding, and proleptic teaching. Vygotsky's (1978) zone of proximal development (ZPD) is central to reciprocal teaching. Brown and Campione (1996) state that "reciprocal teaching was designed to provoke zones of proximal development" (p. 296). In the zone, the focus is not on what students can do independently, but on how students' developing knowledge can be enhanced through guidance and social interaction.

For Brown and Palincsar, instruction in the zone of proximal development was conceptualized by drawing on theories of scaffolding (Wood, Bruner, & Ross, 1976) and proleptic teaching (Rogoff & Gardner, 1984). Using the metaphor of a construction scaffold, they believed that scaffolding instruction meant providing "adjustable and temporary supports" that help the expert guide the learner to solve a problem that they could not do on their own (Brown & Palincsar, 1989, p. 411). To be successful, the expert must be aware of where the child's abilities lay in the typical development of the skill and adjust instruction accordingly. Proleptic teaching, also drawn on by Brown and Palincsar, sets high expectations for all learners no matter where they are in development. In proleptic teaching the teacher acts as the expert while the child takes on an apprentice role. The expert begins by modeling the tasks and slowly releases control to the apprentice.

Research Support for Reciprocal Teaching. Reciprocal teaching was originally designed to help small groups of junior high students who were adequate decoders but poor comprehenders (Palincsar & Brown, 1984). Modeling and guided practice in the cognitive strategies occurred through dialogue (Palincsar & David, 1991). A second form of reciprocal teaching eventually evolved after reciprocal teaching expanded to meet the needs of larger groups and younger students. The only difference between the two forms is that the latter included explicit instruction in the cognitive strategies before the dialogues took place (Rosenshine & Meister, 1994). Rosenshine and Meister (1994) reviewed 16 studies on reciprocal teaching and found that both types of reciprocal teaching demonstrated significant findings on an experimenter developed comprehension test and on a standardized comprehension test.

Research focusing on the use of reciprocal teaching with ELLs has found that when the use of the native language was included or encouraged the method seemed to be successful (Fung et al., 2003; Klingner & Vaughn, 1996). Fung et al. (2003) modified reciprocal teaching by using both L1 and L2 as a medium of instruction on alternating days. The researchers argued that the use of L1 helped facilitate the "internalization of the comprehension fostering and monitoring strategies by using the students' stronger language" and L2 was used to "encourage knowledge and strategy transfer and to improve students' comprehension of English expository text" (p. 6).

Klingner and Vaughn (1996) studied 26 seventh- and eighth-grade students with learning disabilities who were English language learners. Students learned a modified version of reciprocal teaching that included an emphasis on accessing background knowledge. In this study students read English text but were encouraged to use both L1 and L2 in their discussions. An important finding was that a continuum of students benefited from reciprocal teaching rather than just a narrow profile of students. Although the original studies targeted only students who were adequate decoders but poor comprehenders, Klingner and Vaughn found that students who had comprehension levels higher than their decoding levels also benefited.

Implementing Reciprocal Teaching. As stated before, there are two forms of reciprocal teaching, the original reciprocal teaching model and one in which explicit instruction is provided before dialogue starts. Besides this difference the two forms are identical, centralizing the dialogue, the comprehension strategies, and the implementation procedures.

Dialogue is essential to reciprocal teaching and begins after the group reads a paragraph from the classroom text. The "dialogue leader" then begins a discussion structured around the four reading strategies. The dialogue leader is responsible for starting the discussion by asking questions. Answering the questions, elaborating or commenting on participants' answers, and asking new questions become the work of the entire group. The dialogue leader then provides a summary of the paragraph and again the group can elaborate or comment on the summary. If appropriate, the dialogue leader may give or ask for predictions for the upcoming paragraph. Clarification is used when a group member is unclear about a word or concept. Through this process the group is able to move beyond merely regurgitating the words of the text and actually bring a collective meaning to the passage. After the dialogue is finished, the process begins again with a new section of text and a new leader.

At the heart of the dialogue are the four strategies: questioning, clarifying, summarizing, and predicting. The strategies were selected because they are the strategies good readers use and because they improve comprehension monitoring and comprehension (Palincsar & David, 1991).

1. *Questioning.* Questioning is usually the first strategy used. The goal of questioning is for the leader (and possibly other participants) to ask questions about the paragraph to help illuminate the main idea of the passage.
2. *Clarifying.* Clarifying is a self-monitoring strategy that helps a student identify unknown words or unclear concepts in a paragraph.
3. *Summarizing.* Summarizing is explaining the general ideas of the paragraph. Students learn that if they cannot formulate a good summary they do not understand the text.
4. *Predicting.* Predicting is simply formulating guesses about what will happen next based on the clues in the previously read paragraph.

The teacher's job in reciprocal teaching is to guide students in their ability to use the strategies. This guidance is mainly provided through dialogue. The first role the teacher must fulfill is to model the strategies through "think alouds" and being the first dialogue leader. This sets up high expectations for all the students, a basic feature of proleptic teaching. Then the teacher must be adept at assessing the students' ZPD and adjusting support through scaffolding techniques such as prompts, elaborations, modifications, praise, and feedback. Finally the teacher must make a "conscious attempt to release control of the dialogue" as students become more "expert" in the use of the strategies (Palincsar & David, 1991, p. 129). In Ms. Ruiz's class, she and Mrs. Buell take turns facilitating reciprocal teaching while the other teacher works with other students. Reciprocal teaching is proving to be especially helpful for Manny. The teachers have noticed improvement in his motivation as well as comprehension.

Teaching Implications: Studies of reciprocal teaching's use with English language learners have shown that it is effective when students are encouraged to access both L1 and L2. Yet even when teachers do encourage students' native language use, reciprocal teaching can be ineffective if the goals and theories behind reciprocal teaching are not understood. Therefore it is important to stress the importance of the process; that is, a dialogue where all students are given temporary support so that they can participate in constructing a collective understanding of the text via the use of strategies. Through continued use of these dialogues, even the most novice students need less support because they have begun to internalize the strategies.

Classwide Peer Tutoring[2]

Classwide peer tutoring (CWPT), an intraclass, reciprocal peer tutoring strategy, is an effective, time-tested instructional tool (Greenwood et al., 2001; Arreaga-Mayer, 1998a). CWPT is conducted in a systematic, gamelike format where students are

[2]Contributed by Jennifer Urbach.

assigned both to a tutor-tutee dyad and to one of two classroom teams. Through a question-and-answer peer tutoring system, the tutor-tutee dyads work to accumulate points that ultimately help their team. This format increases students' active engagement and motivates them to learn the material.

Originally developed by the Juniper Gardens Children's Project at the University of Kansas, CWPT has been used for students from kindergarten to high school in areas such as reading, spelling, math, and social studies. Although it has been an effective strategy for students with mild disabilities, autism, and even typical students, it was originally developed for elementary students who were culturally and linguistically diverse and English language learners (Greenwood et al., 200l). For ELLs, CWPT provides active opportunities to converse in English, retrieve knowledge and skills in their native language (Arreaga-Mayer, 1998b), and, if necessary, continue practice based on the immediate feedback from their tutors. Arreaga-Mayer (1998a) contends that CWPT is consistent with Gersten and Jimenez's (1994) eight constructs for effective instruction for ELLs: challenge, involvement, success, scaffolding/cognitive strategies, collaborative/cooperative learning, feedback, techniques for second language acquisition, and respect for cultural diversity.

Theoretical Bases of CWPT. In response to research indicating that students at risk in traditional classroom settings are rarely actively engaged, the researchers at the Juniper Gardens Children's Project sought to design a system that would increase students' "opportunity to respond" (Greenwood et al., 1989; Delquadri et al., 1986). This opportunity to respond has been defined as "environmental factors (e.g., time allocated for instruction, curriculum, tasks presented to students, and teacher behaviors) and the amount of active student responding (e.g., reading aloud, writing, and talking academic)" (Delquadri et al., 1986, p. 536).

Opportunity to respond is crucial for ELL students. In their synthesis on effective instructional practices for ELL students, Baker and Gersten (2000) stated that "English-Language Learners need frequent opportunities to use oral language in the classroom. Active, daily language use should be structured to include both conversational and academic discourse. Techniques such as class-wide peer tutoring seem promising" (p. 461). CWPT increases the opportunity to respond by assigning students to tutor-tutee dyads. In each dyad, students have a chance to be both the tutee and the tutor in the same session. Thus, all students are actively engaged in teaching and learning the day's skills or content.

Research Support for CWPT. There has been a significant amount of research regarding the effectiveness of CWPT. Greenwood and colleagues (2001) noted that "at least 25 published CWPT intervention studies report CWPT's superiority to conventional forms of teacher-mediated instruction for accelerating reading fluency/comprehension and mastery of other basic academic skills" (p. 35). Arreaga-Mayer (1998a) noted that research studies focusing on CLD students found that "English language use and academic engagement, as well as achievement gains, increased significantly in CWPT classrooms compared to traditional teacher-mediated instruction" (p. 94).

Most recently, Saenz, Fuchs, and Fuchs (2005) assessed the effects of peer-assisted learning strategies (PALS), a reciprocal classwide peer tutoring strategy, on the reading performance of native Spanish-speaking students with learning disabilities and their low-, average-, and high-achieving classroom peers in grades 3 through 6. Students who participated in PALS outgrew contrast students on reading comprehension. The authors noted that the clearest conclusion from their research was that "PALS improves the reading comprehension of ELL with and without LD in transitional bilingual education classrooms" (p. 243).

Implementing CWPT. Although the opportunity to respond is the theoretical underpinning of this instructional method, there are many other elements that make CWPT so effective. CWPT offers a systematic approach to peer tutoring that can be broken down into four essential procedures: set up, training, implementation, and monitoring.

For any program to run well, the teacher must give forethought to the set up of instruction on a weekly basis. Each week the teacher selects and prepares materials that can be used in CWPT sessions. The teacher also assigns the students to dyads. Pairs can be matched randomly or by ability level. Arreaga-Mayer (1998b) and Greenwood et al. (2001) suggest that ELL students should be paired with other students who speak their same language but who are more proficient in English. The dyads are then placed on a team with other dyads. By restructuring the teams on a weekly basis students are more likely to have a chance to be on a winning team.

Prior to the actual implementation of CWPT, students need to receive training in CWPT procedures (i.e., how to administer the questions, correct mistakes, award points, and give feedback). Arreaga-Mayer (1998b) recommends that teachers not only model the procedures but also allow students to role-play the sessions. Because of the prominence of positive feedback and success in CWPT, extra emphasis on the importance of teamwork and fair play is vital as well (Arreaga-Mayer, 1998a; King-Sears & Cummings, 1996). After students are trained in the procedures, teachers can begin the implementation of CWPT.

At the beginning of the week, teachers usually prepare a mini-lesson of the material. Arreaga-Mayer (1998b) contends that this is especially important for ELLs. During these mini-lessons, she recommends that teachers allow students to access their native language to help them with new concepts. Students gain the most optimal effects from CWPT when it is implemented 4 to 5 days a week (Arreaga-Mayer, 1998a). Typically, CWPT lasts for 30 minutes; however, Arreaga-Mayer (1998b) argues that 40 minutes are necessary for reading activities. Each student should experience 10 to 15 minutes of tutoring during the session and generally 10 minutes are needed to award, tally, and post points.

Typical tutoring sessions begin with the tutor presenting a question either verbally or visually. The tutee then responds in either an oral or visual manner. If the tutee is correct, the tutor can award the tutee two points. If the student is incorrect the tutor provides the tutee with the correct answer. The tutee then must either write or say the answer three times. If the tutee is able to correctly state the answer three times, they are awarded one point. If they are unable to say it correctly all three times, they do not receive a point.

This procedure does change slightly when students are reading. In this case students read passages and are awarded points based on the tutee's reading accuracy. After reading the passage for 10 minutes, tutors ask questions about the passage. These typically follow a "who, what, where, and why" format (Arreaga-Mayer, 1998b). Again, points are distributed based on the correctness of the tutee's answers.

Because all the students are engaged in their dyads at the same time, the teacher is free to move about and listen to the groups. At this point, the teacher can provide an incentive for the dyads to implement CWPT correctly by randomly awarding bonus points to dyads that present the material appropriately, are clearly and consistently awarding points and correcting errors, and give positive feedback to their partners.

Although teachers do not directly administer the questions, CWPT enables teachers to closely monitor students' work in several ways. As teachers move about the classroom awarding points, they can also informally assess students' progress by listening to the answers students are giving. Teachers are also able to gauge individual student achievement by the points they accumulate at the end of each session. Finally, monitoring of the students' progress is also completed more formally. Typically teachers using CWPT administer a weekly pre- and posttest that allows them to monitor the students' gains each week. When CWPT is used for reading, Arreaga-Mayer (1998b) suggests either doing more in-depth monitoring of a few students on a weekly basis or administering a one-minute reading rate check and questions to all students.

Teaching Implications: The effectiveness of CWPT (and variations such as PALS) with students at various grade levels and with various learning characteristics makes it an invaluable tool in inclusive CLD classrooms. Through these strategies, students are able to read, retell, identify the main idea, and predict information in forthcoming paragraphs while still receiving structured feedback and points from their tutor. Both CWPT and PALS allow the teacher to provide students with structured opportunities to respond and grow as learners and therefore can be effective in any classroom. Additional discussions about peer tutoring in general are presented in Chapter 9.

OTHER INSTRUCTIONAL APPROACHES

The methods we describe next have not necessarily been researched with CLD students with disabilities. But they have been recommended for diverse populations and do have some research support that suggests they would be appropriate for CLD classrooms that include students with disabilities. Yet further research is needed. The first of these is the language experience approach, followed by reader response journals, and then literature response groups. These approaches are just a sampling of the many promising approaches available (see Peregoy & Boyle, 2001, for others).

The Language Experience Approach

The language experience approach (LEA) is a reading method based on students' own language. Students as authors dictate a story about an actual experience to a scribe, who may be a teacher, a teaching assistant, a parent or community volunteer, or a tutor. Next they copy the story (or trace it), illustrate it, and read it again and again. Thus, children's own language becomes their reading material. This has several advantages: The students are familiar with all of the vocabulary and content used in the story, as well as the context for the story. It is based on their interests and prior knowledge. They are motivated to read the story silently as well as to others. In so doing, they develop awareness of the connection between reading and writing and the understanding that written words are recorded speech intended to convey meaning that can be read by others. Many students who have experienced difficulty learning letters and sounds in isolation (going from part to whole, or letters to words) excel when they use this approach. Students are able to memorize their own story words, and then learn that a certain letter makes the sound at the beginning of a favorite word (e.g., "b" for "*bicicleta*"). When students see the letter, they are reminded of the word and are then able to make the association between symbol and sound. Although LEA is generally seen more frequently in kindergarten and first-grade classrooms, Ms. Ruiz and Mrs. Buell have found that it is very helpful with the students in their class transitioning from Spanish to English reading. They also use LEA with the few students in the class who are still at an emergent reading level, such as Elva.

LEA has been used successfully with emergent readers for many years (Ashton-Warner, 1963; Allen, 1976; Sulzby & Barnhart, 1992). It is a whole-to-part approach recommended for ELLs of many ages (Dixon & Nessel, 1983; Hudelson, 1984; Peregoy & Boyle, 2001; Rigg, 1987) and for ELLs with LD (Haager & Klingner, 2005; Klingner & Nares, 1984). LEA can be implemented with an individual child, a small group of children, or an entire class.

In a one-to-one setting, the teacher and child follow these steps:

1. *Discuss the child's ideas.* First, the teacher engages the child in a discussion about his or her experiences and asks the child to select a topic. Possible topics include any aspect of the child's experiences away from or in school (e.g., an outing over the weekend, a new pet, a favorite sport). Some children start with a list of "Things I Like." This becomes an easy-to-read first story with a predictable format (i.e., "I like to play soccer." "I like to ride my bike." "I like to play video games.").

2. *Record the story.* Second, the teacher records what the child says, verbatim, resisting the temptation to correct grammar or change vocabulary (at least at this point). The child reads each word as it is recorded, and then, with assistance as necessary, rereads the story.

3. *Copy and illustrate the story.* Third, the teacher asks the child to trace or copy the story onto chart paper or butcher paper, or type it into the computer, and then

illustrate it. At this point, the child might wish to underline or circle favorite words in the story. Again, the student rereads the story to the teacher, a partner, and/or a small group of students at the center. A mask or "word window" made by cutting a slot out of a piece of lightweight cardboard can help the child isolate words as he or she reads.

4. *Practice sentences.* Fourth, the child (with assistance if appropriate) makes sentence strips that correspond to the story. These are practiced daily. The child matches them with his or her story, puts them in the proper order in the pocket chart, identifies patterns in sentence structure, and looks for sets of the same or similar words in different sentences.

5. *Learn words.* Fifth, when the student can read the story and individual sentences independently, he or she cuts the sentence strips into words or phrases and uses these in a variety of activities to help him or her learn to identify the individual words in the story (similar to Clay's cut-up sentences technique from Reading Recovery, 1985, or Descubriendo la Lectura, Escamilla et al., 1998). Students typically memorize their stories, and even though they can "read" each sentence accurately, they cannot necessarily read each word separately or recognize words in different contexts. Students can practice flashcards with a partner and match them with the story. The child may want to draw little picture cues on the flashcards, in pencil so that they can later be erased. When the student is ready, he or she can re-create the entire story using the word cards. Additional sets of flashcards can be used in games such as Lotto, Memory, or Bingo. Other activities include grouping word families together in the pocket chart and, to help with transference, looking for story words in other contexts, such as in trade books or newspapers. Children are often quite excited when they recognize one of their "own" words written elsewhere—they seem to develop quite a sense of ownership for the words in their stories. Once students have mastered their words, they can put them in their word bank in a little recipe or file box, or in a personal dictionary. A motivating way to determine when a child has mastered a word is for the partner who is helping to write a tally mark on a word card each time it has been read correctly—when 10 tally marks have accumulated, the word has been mastered and is ready to be filed. These words can also become spelling words.

6. *Learn letter sounds.* Sixth, LEA words can be used to reinforce phonics skills. The teacher may ask the student to find all of the words that begin with a particular sound (e.g., "Can you find another word that begins with 'b' like in 'bike'?") or exhibit a certain pattern (e.g., "Can you find any words that rhyme with 'bike'?"). The student can also think of and list words not in the story that begin or end with a target sound, or have the same vowel sound (e.g., "Can you think of any other words that start with the same sound as 'bike'?"). Once students have mastered flashcards, they can be cut into individual letters and kept in business-size envelopes with the word written on the back of the envelope. A pocket can be formed on the outside of the envelope by folding up the bottom of the envelope

and stapling it on both sides. The student's task is then to assemble the letters to spell the word, putting them in the pocket. You might wish to have students mark vowels to differentiate them from consonants, or even to indicate the kind of sound they make (e.g., by marking short vowel sound with a curved line or "smile" on top, and long vowel sounds with a straight line). Letters and words can also be used to form anagrams or crossword puzzles.

Wordless picture books (Peregoy & Boyle, 2001; Perry, 1997) provide another motivating, effective way to help struggling ELL students (of any age). They can be used much like LEA, except that the class or individual students dictate a story about the pictures they are seeing in the wordless picture book. The pictures in the book provide the prompts for the dictated story. The teacher and student(s) first look at the book and discuss the pictures. Then the teacher and the student(s) go through the book a second time while the student(s) dictate a story. The teacher photocopies the book, glues or tapes the new story onto the appropriate pages in the book, adds the children's or child's name(s) below the author's name on the title page, and presents the book to the student(s). The no-longer-wordless picture book then can be read and reread and used for a variety of instructional purposes.

Reader Response Journals

Reader response journals provide a place for students to record their feelings, reactions, and impressions of the books they read (Atwell, 1998; Berger, 1996; Hancock, 1993; Handloff & Golden, 1995). Doing so deepens their involvement in the story, improves their understanding, and preserves those special transactions with books that make reading a rewarding, personal journey (Hancock, 1993). Reader response journals are based on reader response theory—the view of reading that emphasizes the role of the reader in interpreting and creating meaning from text (Flood & Lapp, 1988; Rosenblatt, 1978).

Whenever students read they should respond by writing in their journals. Ms. Ruiz gave her class the following directions for keeping a reader response journal:

Each day, you should enter the date of your response. The journal is **not** intended to be a summary of the book. You don't need to prove to me you are reading the book by telling me the entire plot. Rather, it is a place for you to record your reflections, reactions, and impressions. Learn to listen to yourself while you are reading and then you will be able to describe the effect the book is having on you. Most of all, have fun! Here are some ideas you might want to include in your response journal (at this point she displayed a poster board with the underlined key words listed and left it in the front of the room for the students to refer to as needed):

1. *Share experiences and memories.* Comment on how the reading passage relates to your own experiences. What does it remind you of?
2. *Connect.* How does what you are reading relate to other things you have read or learned or discussed in class?

3. *Ask questions.* What confuses you? What don't you understand? What do you disagree with?

4. *React.* How do you respond emotionally? Does something make you feel angry, happy, or sad? How do you feel about the characters?

5. *Highlight.* Quote or point out parts of the book you think are really important, or that you want to be sure to remember.

Once Ms. Ruiz finished giving instructions, Mrs. Buell began the task of providing individualized support and making modifications for certain students. Sometimes Elva dictated her responses to her and drew pictures that illustrated her favorite parts of the passages they had just read. Manny might draw a concept map rather than write a narrative. Carlos wrote his response on the computer (he preferred the computer not only because typing was easier than handwriting, but also because he liked having the spell-checker readily available). By providing these supports for individual students, Mrs. Buell enabled the students with disabilities to participate fully in subsequent discussions or dialogues.

Journal entries can serve as a springboard for discussions with peers in literature response groups or become like dialogue journals and shared with the teacher or peers in a written conversation. Atwell (1998) used student-to-teacher as well as student-to-student writing in her classes and found differences in the ways students wrote, depending on their intended audience. With peers, students tended to be more open with their feelings and to more frequently ask for recommendations.

Similar to the reader response journal, the response sheet provides students with additional guidelines that can help them use their reactions to what they are reading as a catalyst for group discussions. The following response sheet and directions are adapted from Peregoy and Boyle (2001):

Response Sheet

You may begin your discussions with the questions listed on this sheet, or you may develop your own questions. Be ready to accept the opinions of others in your group. You may expect the same from them with regard to your views. Your job is to help one another understand the story and to share your views of the story. Remember, there is no one single interpretation of any story you read.

1. If you did (or didn't) like the book, was there one event or character that caused this reaction? What? Why?

2. Do your response group members share your reaction to this book? What reactions are the same? Different?

3. If you were faced with the same problem as the character(s) in the book, would your reaction have been the same? Why or why not?

4. Have you ever felt like the main character in the story? If so, how?

5. Do any of the characters remind you of anyone you know? If so, how?

6. Would you change the ending of the book? If so, how?

7. Which character would you most like to meet? What would you say, or ask, if you could meet this character?

8. If you could step inside this book in one place, where would that be? Why? What would you do?

9. Do you think the author was trying to teach us something? If so, what?

10. Did any part of the book make you very mad, sad, or happy? If so, explain.

Literature Response Groups

Literature response groups provide students with the opportunity to discuss with their peers the work of published authors (Peregoy & Boyle, 2001). The books they discuss might be associated with a theme that is of interest to them and related to instruction in other subject areas. Similar versions of this are called literature circles (Bos, 1991; Short & Klassen, 1993) or book clubs (Raphael & McMahon, 1994). They are another method for facilitating full participation of students who have reading difficulties and providing opportunities for ELLs to communicate with their peers in small, supportive groups. They provide all students with the opportunity to engage in meaningful dialogue with their peers and to think deeply and critically about what they read.

Small groups of three to six students who have read (or listened to) the same book meet at least once a week to exchange their impressions and reactions. It is important to model the discussion process for students, asking open-ended questions and making encouraging, supportive comments. Students who are accustomed to hearing only one point of view (e.g., the teacher's) and thinking that there is one "correct" interpretation may take awhile before they recognize that there can be several ways to interpret an event (e.g., what motivates a character to act in a certain way). Literature response groups help children learn to be flexible in their thinking and tolerant of multiple viewpoints. The following steps prepare students to work effectively in literature response groups (adapted from Peregoy & Boyle, 2001, pp. 265–266):

1. Read good literature to children daily and ask for individual responses informally.

2. Share your own responses to characters' dilemmas.

3. Encourage different points of view, including views that differ from your own.

4. Share your enthusiasm and enjoyment of stories and literary language.

5. Help children connect events in a story with circumstances in their own lives.

One student begins by sharing his or her reaction to an aspect of the story, and other students then share their impressions or interpretations. Students may wish to use their reader response journals and/or response sheets to guide their conversations.

At the conclusion of a literature response group session, members might decide what they would like to discuss the next time they meet and what they need to do to prepare for their next discussion (e.g., by rereading a relevant passage). Students might also present a synopsis of their discussion to their classmates in a brief sharing session.

After finishing a book, students can extend their interpretations through such activities as creating dramas, readers' theater, big books, story maps, puppet shows, animated films, dioramas, songs, murals, book jackets, radio scripts, timelines, rebus books, board games, collages, mobiles, posters, costumes, videos (Peregoy & Boyle, 2001), pop-up books, accordion books, fold-up books, upside-down books, or picture books (Yopp & Yopp, 2001). Such activities allow students to demonstrate their various strengths (e.g., students with visual spatial strengths might choose to make a diorama or a board game; students with verbal-linguistic strengths might tape themselves reading a story, play, or poem they have written).

SUMMARY

In summary, what is the best way to help CLDE children learn how to read? Students are most likely to thrive in a warm, supportive environment, with skillful, knowledgeable, culturally responsive teachers who implement instructional approaches that reinforce and build on students' native language and cultures and are meaningful, motivating, differentiated, and promote high levels of academic achievement. Students benefit from explicit instruction in phonological awareness, phonics (the "code"), vocabulary, comprehension, fluency. Students with reading disabilities should have frequent opportunities to read books and other materials at their instructional level, but also need access to grade-level reading materials and the general education curriculum (e.g., through cooperative learning and peer-assisted learning). Those students who struggle require additional assistance in a one-to-one or small group setting. This instruction should be tailored to students' needs (in other words, support should focus on phonological awareness if that is what the student needs or comprehension strategy instruction if that would be more appropriate).

Discussion Questions

1. You have just been hired as an adjunct instructor at the local university to teach a course on teaching reading to CLDE students.

   a. What will you teach your students about the characteristics of CLD students with reading disabilities?

   b. What will you teach them about differences between learning to read in one's first or a second language?

2. Your school district is moving to a response to intervention model (see Chapter 1) and you have been invited to be on your school's planning team as an expert in literacy instruction for CLDE students. The school has been directed to make sure that all literacy instruction is research-based. You want to make sure that the instruction is appropriate and is responsive to the needs of CLD students.

a. What key principles will you emphasize?

b. In what ways will the literacy instruction be culturally responsive?

c. What essential components of reading instruction will you make sure are included?

3. You are a special education teacher. Three of your third-grade students, Amy, John, and Marvin, seem not to be making any progress learning how to read. Amy and John are both ELLs (Amy speaks Vietnamese as her first language; John speaks Portuguese), and Marvin is African American. You have discussed your concerns with their classroom teacher and previous teachers, and have concluded that they have "turned off to reading" after experiencing failure too many times. You decide that your number-one goal with them will be to increase their motivation. How will you go about doing this?

References

Aguilera, D. E. (2003). *Who defines success: An analysis of competing models of education for American Indian and Alaskan Native students.* Unpublished doctoral dissertation, University of Colorado, Boulder.

Allen, R. V. (1976). *Language experiences in communication.* Boston: Houghton Mifflin.

Alvermann, D. (2005). Exemplary literacy instruction in grades 7–12: What counts and who's counting? In J. Flood and P. Anders (Eds.), *Literacy development of students in urban schools: Research and policy* (pp. 187–201). Newark, DE: International Reading Association.

Ammon, M. S. (1987). Patterns of performance among bilingual children who score low in reading. In S. R. Goldman & H. T. Trueba (Eds.), *Becoming literate in English as a second language* (pp. 71–105). Norwood, NJ: Ablex.

Anderson, A. B., & Stokes, S. J. (1984). Social and institutional influences on the development and practice of literacy. In H. Goelman, A. Oberg, & F. Smith (Eds.), *Awakening to literacy* (pp. 24–37). Exeter, NH: Heinemann.

Antunez, B. (2002). Implementing Reading First with English language learners. *Directions in Language and Education, 15.* Retrieved May 9, 2006, from http://www.ncela.gwu.edu/pubs/directions/15.pdf

Arnold, D. H., Lonigan, C. J., Whitehurst, G. J., & Epstein, J. N. (1994). Accelerating language development through picture book reading: Replication and extension to a videotape training format. *Journal of Educational Psychology, 86,* 235–243.

Arreaga-Mayer, C. (1998a). Increasing active student responding and improving academic performance through classwide peer tutoring. *Intervention in School & Clinic, 34,* 89–94.

Arreaga-Mayer, C. (1998b). Language-sensitive peer-mediated instruction for culturally and linguistically diverse learners in the intermediate elementary grades. In R. M. Gersten & R. T. Jimenez (Eds.), *Promoting learning for culturally and linguistically diverse students* (pp. 73–90). Belmont, CA: Wadsworth.

Artiles, A. J., Rueda, R., Salazar, J., & Higareda, I. (2005). Within-group diversity in minority disproportionate representation: English language learners in urban school districts. *Exceptional Children, 71,* 283–300.

Ashton-Warner, S. (1963). *Teacher.* New York: Simon & Schuster.

Atwell, N. (1998). *In the middle: New understanding about writing, reading, and learning* (2nd ed.). Portsmouth, NH: Heinemann.

Au, K. H. (1993). *Literacy instruction in multicultural settings.* Forth Worth, TX: Harcourt Brace Jovanovich.

Au, K. H. (2000). A multicultural perspective on policies for improving literacy achievement: Equity and excellence. In M. L. Kamil, P. B. Mosenthal, P. D. Pearson, & R. Barr (Eds.), *Handbook of reading research* (Vol. 3, pp. 835–851). Mahwah, NJ: Erlbaum.

Au, K., & Kawakami, A. (1994). Cultural congruence in instruction. In E. Hollins, J. King, & W. Hayman (Eds.), *Teaching diverse populations* (pp. 5–23). New York: SUNY Press.

August, D., & Hakuta, K. (1997). *Improving schooling for language minority children: A research agenda.* Washington, DC: National Academy Press.

Avalos, M. A. (2003). Effective second-language reading transition: From learner-specific to generic instructional models. *Bilingual Research Journal, 27*(2), 171–205.

Baker, S., & Gersten, R. (2000). What we know about effective instructional practices for English-language learners. *Exceptional Children, 66,* 454–470.

Baker, S., Gersten, R., & Keating, T. (2000). When less may be more: A 2-year longitudinal evaluation of a volunteer tutoring program requiring minimal training. *Reading Research Quarterly, 35,* 494–519.

Banks, J., & Banks, C. (Eds.). (1997). *Multicultural education: Issues and perspectives* (3rd ed.). Boston: Allyn & Bacon.

Beck, I. L., & McKeown, M. G. (1998). Comprehension: The sine qua non of reading. In S. Patton & M. Holmes (Eds.), *The keys to literacy* (pp. 40–52). Washington, DC: Council for Basic Education.

Beck, I. L., McKeown, M. G., & Kucan, L. (2002). *Bringing words to life: Robust vocabulary instruction.* New York: Guilford Press.

Berger, L. R. (1996). Reader response journals: You make the meaning . . . and how. *Journal of Adolescent & Adult Literacy, 39,* 380–385.

Bieger, E. M. (1995/1996). Promoting multicultural education through a literature-based approach. *The Reading Teacher, 49*(4), 308–312.

Bos, C. S. (1991). Reading-writing connections: Using literature as a zone of proximal development for writing. *Learning Disabilities Research & Practice, 6,* 251–256.

Brown, A. L., & Campione, J. C. (1996). Theory and design of learning environments. In L. Schauble & R. Glaser (Eds.), *Innovations in learning: New environments for education* (pp. 289–325). Mahwah, NJ: Lawrence Erlbaum Associates.

Brown, A. L., & Palincsar, A. S. (1989). Guided, cooperative learning and individual knowledge acquisition. In L. B. Resnick (Ed.), *Knowing, learning, and instruction: Essays in honor of Robert Glaser* (pp. 393–451). Hillsdale, NJ: Lawrence Erlbaum Associates.

Burke, M., Hagan, S., & Grossen, B. (1998). What curricular design and strategies accommodate diverse learners? *Teaching Exceptional Children, 31*(1), 34–48.

Cardelle-Elawar, M. (1990). Effects of feedback tailored to bilingual students' mathematics needs on verbal problem solving. *The Elementary School Journal, 91,* 165–175.

Carlisle, J. F., Beeman, M., Davis, L. H., & Spharim, G. (1999). Relationship of metalinguistic capabilities and reading achievement for children who are becoming bilingual. *Applied Psycholinguistics, 20,* 459–478.

Carrell, P., & Grabe, W. (2002). Reading. In N. Schmitt (Ed.), *An introduction to applied linguistics* (pp. 233–250). New York: Oxford University Press.

Cazden, C. B. (1988). *Classroom discourse: The language of teaching and learning.* Portsmouth, NH: Heinemann.

Chiappe, P., Siegel, L. A., & Gottardo, A. (2002). Reading-related skills of kindergartners from diverse linguistic backgrounds. *Applied Psycholinguistics, 23,* 95–116.

Clay, M. M. (1985). *The early detection of reading difficulties.* Portsmouth, NH: Heinemann.

Cummins, J. (1984). *Bilingualism and special education: Issues in assessment and pedagogy.* San Diego, CA: College Hill.

Cummins, J. (1989). A theoretical framework for bilingual special education. *Exceptional Children, 56,* 111–119.

De La Colina, M. G., Parker, R. I., Hasbrouck, J. E., & Lara-Alecio, R. (2001). Intensive intervention in reading fluency for at-risk beginning Spanish readers. *Bilingual Research Journal, 25,* 503–538.

Delpit, L. (1995). *Other people's children.* New York: The New Press.

Delquadri, J. C., Greenwood, C. R., Whorton, D., Carta, J. J., & Hall, R. V. (1986). Classwide peer tutoring. *Exceptional Children, 52,* 535–542.

Denton, C. A., Anthony, J. L., Parker, R., & Hasbrouck, J. (2004). Effects of two tutoring programs on the English reading development of Spanish-English bilingual students. *The Elementary School Journal, 104,* 289–305.

Dickinson, D. K., & Smith, M. W. (1994). Long-term effects of preschool teachers' book readings on low-income children's vocabulary and story comprehension. *Reading Research Quarterly, 29,* 104–122.

Dixon, C. N., & Nessel, D. (1983). *Language experience approach to reading (and writing)*. Hayward, CA: Alemany.

Durgunoglu, A. Y., Nagy, W. E., & Hancin-Bhatt, B. J. (1993). Cross-language transfer of phonological awareness. *Journal of Educational Psychology, 85*, 453–465.

Escamilla, K., Loera, M., Ruiz, O., & Rodriguez, Y. (1998). An examination of sustaining effects in Descubriendo La Lectura programs. *Literacy Teaching and Learning: An International Journal of Early Reading and Writing, 3*(2), 59–81.

Fitzgerald, J. (1995). English-as-a-second-language learners' cognitive reading processes: A review of research in the United States. *Review of Educational Research, 65*, 145–190.

Fitzgerald, J. (2001). Can minimally trained college student volunteers help young at-risk children to read better? *Reading Research Quarterly, 36*, 28–47.

Flood, J., & Lapp, D. (1988). A reader response approach to the teaching of literature. *Reading Research and Instruction, 27*, 61–66.

Fung, I. Y. Y., Wilkinson, I. A. G., & Moore, D. W. (2003). L1-assisted reciprocal teaching to improve ESL students' comprehension of English expository text. *Learning and Instruction, 13*, 1–31.

Garcia-Vazquez, E. (1995). Acculturation and academics: Effects of acculturation on reading achievement among Mexican-American students. *Bilingual Research Journal, 19*, 305–315.

Gay, G. (2000). *Culturally responsive teaching*. New York: Teachers College Press.

Geisler, D. (in press). Linguistically and culturally responsive literacy instruction. In J. Klingner, J. Hoover, A. Artiles, & L. Baca (Eds.), *English language learners who struggle with reading: Language acquisition or learning disabilities?* Thousand Oaks, CA: Corwin.

Gentile, L. (2004). The *Oracy Instructional Guide*. Carlsbad, CA: Dominie Press.

Gersten, R., & Baker, S. (2000). What we know about effective instructional practices for English-language learners. *Exceptional Children, 66*(4), 454–470.

Gersten, R. M., & Jimenez, R. T. (1994). A delicate balance: Enhancing literature instruction for students of English as a second language. *The Reading Teacher, 47*, 438–449.

Godina, H., & McCoy, R. (2000). Emic and etic perspectives on Chicana and Chicano multicultural literature. *Journal of Adolescent & Adult Literacy, 44*, 172–179.

Gottardo, A. (2002). The relationship between language and reading skills in bilingual Spanish-English speakers. *Topics in Language Disorders, 22*(5), 46–71.

Graves, A., Gersten, R., & Haager, D. (2004). Literacy instruction in multiple-language first-grade classrooms: Linking student outcomes to observed instructional practice. *Learning Disabilities Research & Practice, 19*, 262–272.

Greenwood, C. R., Arreaga-Mayer, C., Utley, C. A., Gavin, K. M., & Terry, B. J. (2001). Class wide peer tutoring learning management system: Applications with elementary-level English language learners. *Remedial & Special Education, 22*, 34–47.

Greenwood, C. R., Delquadri, J. C., & Hall, R. V. (1989). Longitudinal effects of classwide peer tutoring. *Journal of Education Psychology, 81*, 371–383.

Guthrie, J. T., & Wigfield, A. (2000). Engagement and motivation in reading. In M. L. Kamil, P. B. Mosenthal, P. D. Pearson, & R. Barr (Eds.), *Handbook of reading research* (Vol. III, pp. 403–424). Mahwah, NJ: Lawrence Erlbaum.

Haager, D., & Klingner, J. K. (2005). *Differentiating instruction in inclusive classrooms: The special educators' guide*. Boston, MA: Allyn & Bacon.

Hancock, M. R. (1993). Exploring and extending personal response through literature response journals. *The Reading Teacher, 46*, 466–474.

Handloff, E., & Golden, J. M. (1995). Writing as a way of "getting to" what you think and feel about a story. In N. L. Roser & M. G. Martinez (Eds.), *Book talk and beyond: Children and teachers respond to literature* (pp. 201–207). Newark, DE: International Reading Association.

Hardin, V. B. (2001). Transfer and variation in cognitive reading strategies of Latino fourth-grade students in a late-exit bilingual program. *Bilingual Research Journal, 25*, 539–561.

Hasbrouck, J. E., Ihnot, C., & Rogers, G. (1999). "Read Naturally": A strategy to increase oral reading fluency. *Reading Research and Instruction, 39*(1), 27–38.

Heath, S. B. (1983). *Ways with words: Language, life, and work in communities and classrooms*. New York: Cambridge University Press.

Henderson, R. W., & Landesman, E. W. (1995). Effects of thematically integrated mathematics instruction on students of Mexican descent. *Journal of Educational Research, 88*, 290.

Hiebert, E. H., Pearson, P. D., Taylor, B. M., Richardson, V., Paris, S. G. (1998). *Every child a reader: Applying reading research to the classroom.* Center for the Improvement of Earl Reading Achievement. Ann Arbor, MI: University of Michigan School of Education.

Hudelson, S. (1984). Kan yu ret an rayt en ingles: Children become literate in English as a second language. *TESOL Quarterly, 18*, 221–238.

Hudson, R. F., & Smith, S. W. (2001). Effective reading instruction for struggling Spanish-speaking readers: A combination of two literatures. *Intervention in School and Clinic, 37*, 36–39.

Invernizzi, M., Juel, C., & Rosemary, C. A. (1997). A community tutorial that works. *The Reading Teacher, 50*, 304–311.

Irwin, J. W. (1991). *Teaching reading comprehension processes* (2nd ed.). Upper Saddle River, NJ: Prentice Hall.

Jiménez, R. T. (2001). "It's a difference that changes us": An alternative view of the language and literacy needs of Latina/o students. *The Reading Teacher, 54*, 736–742.

Jiménez, R. T., Garcia, G. E., & Pearson, P. D. (1995). Three children, two languages, and strategic reading: Case studies in bilingual/monolingual reading. *American Educational Research Journal, 32*(1), 67–97.

Jiménez, R. T., Garcia, G. E., & Pearson, P. D. (1996). The reading strategies of bilingual Latina/o students who are successful English readers: Opportunities and obstacles. *Reading Research Quarterly, 31*(1), 90–112.

Jiménez, R. T., & Gersten, R. M. (1999) Lessons and dilemmas derived from the literacy instruction of two Latina/o teachers. *American Educational Research Journal 3612*, 265–301.

King-Sears, M. E., & Cummings, C. S. (1996). Inclusive practices of classroom teachers. *Remedial & Special Education, 17*, 217–225.

Klingner, J., & Bianco, M. (2006). What is special about special education for culturally and linguistically diverse students with disabilities? In B. Cook & B. Schirmer (Eds.), *What is special about special education?* Austin, TX: PRO-ED.

Klingner, J. K., Artiles, A. J., Kozleski, E., Harry, B., Tate, W., Zion, S., Durán, G. Z., & Riley, D. (2005). Addressing the disproportionate representation of culturally and linguistically diverse students in special education through culturally responsive educational systems. *Educational Analysis and Policy Archives, 13*(38), 1–39.

Klingner, J. K., Artiles, A. J., & Méndez Barletta, L. (2006). English language learners who struggle with reading: Language acquisition or learning disabilities? *Journal of Learning Disabilities, 39*, 108–128.

Klingner, J. K., & Nares, I. (1984, January). *Intervention strategies for working with LEP/NEP students with learning disabilities.* Paper presented at the annual meeting of the California Association for Bilingual Education, San Francisco, CA.

Klingner, J. K., & Vaughn, S. (1996). Reciprocal teaching of reading comprehension strategies for students with learning disabilities who use English as a second language. *Elementary School Journal, 96*, 275–293.

Klingner, J. K., Vaughn, S., & Boardman, A. (in press). *Teaching reading comprehension to students with learning disabilities.* New York: Guilford.

Knight, S. L., Padrón, Y. N., & Waxman, H. C. (1985). Cognitive strategies used by ESL students. *TESOL Quarterly, 19*, 789–792.

Ladson-Billings, G. (1994). *The dreamkeepers: Successful teachers of African American children.* San Francisco: Jossey-Bass.

Langer, J. A., Bartholome, L., Vasquez, O., & Lucas, T. (1990). Meaning construction in school literacy tasks: A study of bilingual students. *American Educational Research Journal, 27*, 427–471.

Linan-Thompson, S., Vaughn, S., Hickman-Davis, P., & Kouzekanani, K. (2003). Effectiveness of supplemental reading instruction for second-grade English language learners with reading difficulties. *Elementary School Journal, 103*, 221–238.

Linan-Thompson, S., Vaughn, S., Prater, K., & Cirino, P. T. (2006). The response to intervention of English language learners at-risk for reading problems. *Journal of Learning Disabilities, 39*(5), 390–398.

Lindsey, K. A., Manis, F. R., & Bailey, C. E. (2003). Prediction of first-grade reading in Spanish-speaking English-language learners. *Journal of Educational Psychology, 95*, 482–494.

Lopez-Reyna, N. A. (1996). The importance of meaningful contexts in bilingual special education: Moving to whole language. *Learning Disabilities Research & Practice, 11,* 120–131.

McGroarty, M. (1989). The benefits of cooperative learning arrangements in second language instruction. *The Journal for the National Association for Bilingual Education, 13,* 127–143.

Miniccuci, C., Berman, P., McLaughlin, B., McLeod, B., Nelson, B., & Woodworth, K. (1995). School reform and student diversity. *Phi Delta Kappan, 77*(1), 77–80.

Miramontes, O. (1987). Oral reading miscues of Hispanic students: Implications for assessment of learning disabilities. *Journal of Learning Disabilities, 20*(10), 627–632.

Miramontes, O. (1990). A comparative study of English oral language reading skills in differently schooled groups of Hispanic students. *Journal of Reading Behavior, 22,* 373–394.

Moje, E. B., & Hinchman, K. (2004). Culturally responsive practices for youth literacy learning. In T. L. Jetton & J. A. Dole (Eds.), *Adolescent literacy research and practice* (pp. 321–350). New York: Guilford Press.

Moll, L. (1999). Forward. In J. Paratore, G. Melzei, & B. Krol-Sinclair (Eds.), *What should we expect of family literacy? Experiences of Latino children whose parents participate in a intergenerational literacy project* (p. xiii). Chicago, National Reading Conference.

Moll, L. C., & González, N. (1994). Critical issues: Lessons from research with language-minority children. *JRB: A Journal of Literacy, 26,* 439–456.

Müller, E., & Markowitz, J. (2004, March). *English language learners with disabilities.* Alexandria, VA: Project FORUM.

Muñiz-Swicegood, M. (1994). The effects of metacognitive reading strategy training on the reading performance and student reading analysis strategies of third grade bilingual students. *Bilingual Research Journal, 18,* 83–97.

Nag-Arulmani, S., Reddy, V., & Buckley, S. (2003). Targeting phonological representations can help in the early stages of reading in a non-dominant language. *Journal of Research in Reading, 26,* 49–68.

National Reading Panel. (2000). *Teaching children to read: An evidence-based assessment of the scientific research literature on reading and its implications for reading instruction: Summary report.* Washington, DC: National Institute of Child Health and Development.

National Symposium on Learning Disabilities in English Language Learners. (2003). *Symposium summary.* Washington, DC: U.S. Department of Education and the National Institute of Child Health and Human Development.

Neal, J. C., & Kelly, P. R. (1999). The success of reading recovery for English language learners and descubriendo La lectura for bilingual students in California. *Literacy Teaching and Learning, 2,* 81–108.

O'Shea, L. J., Sindelar, P. T., & O'Shea, D. J. (1987). The effects of repeated readings and attentional cues on the reading fluency and comprehension of learning disabled readers. *Learning Disabilities Research, 2,* 103–109.

Ortiz, A., & Wilkinson, C. (1991). Assessment and intervention model for the bilingual exceptional student (AIM for the BEST). *Teacher Education and Special Education, 14,* 35–42.

Ortiz, A. A. (1997). Learning disabilities occurring concomitantly with linguistic differences. *Journal of Learning Disabilities, 30,* 321–332.

Ortiz, A. A. (2001). *English language learners with special needs: Effective instructional strategies.* Washington, DC: ERIC Education Reports.

Padrón, Y. N., & Waxman, H. C. (1988). The effect of ESL students' perceptions of their cognitive strategies on reading achievement. *TESOL Quarterly,* 146–150.

Palincsar, A. S., & Brown, A. L. (1984). The reciprocal teaching of comprehension-fostering and comprehension-monitoring activities. *Cognition and Instruction, 1,* 117–175.

Palincsar, A. S., & David, Y. M. (1991). Promoting literacy through classroom dialogue. In E. H. Hiebert (Ed.), *Literacy for a diverse society: Perspectives, practices and policies* (pp. 122–139). New York: Teachers College Press.

Peregoy, S. F., & Boyle, O. F. (2000). English learners reading English: What we know, what we need to know. *Theory into Practice, 39*(4), 237–247.

Peregoy, S. F., & Boyle, O. F. (2001). *Reading, writing, and learning in ESL* (3rd ed.). New York: Longman.

Perry, L. A. (1997). Using wordless picture books with beginning readers (of any age). *Teaching Exceptional Children, 29,* 68–69.

Pressley, M., Allington, R., Wharton-McDonald, R., Block, C. C., & Morrow, L. M. (2001). *Learning to read: Lessons from exemplary first grades.* New York: Guilford.

Pressley, M., Wharton-McDonald, R., Allington, R., Block, C. C., Morrow, L., Tracey, D., Baker, K., Brooks, G., Cronin, J., Nelson, E., & Woo, D. (2001). A study of effective grade-1 literacy instruction. *Scientific Studies of Reading, 5*, 35–58.

Purcell-Gates, V. (1996). Stories, coupons, and the TV Guide: Relationships between home literacy experiences and emergent literacy knowledge. *Reading Research Quarterly, 31*, 406–428.

Raphael, T. E., & McMahon, S. I. (1994). Book club: An alternative framework for reading instruction. *The Reading Teacher, 48*, 102–116.

Reyes, E., & Bos, C. (1998). Interactive semantic mapping and charting: Enhancing content area learning for language minority students. In R. Gersten & R. Jiménez (Eds.), *Promoting learning for culturally and linguistically diverse students: Classroom applications from contemporary research* (pp. 133–152). Belmont, CA: Wadsworth.

Rigg, P. (1987). Using the language experience approach with ESL adults. *TESL Talk, 20*(1), 188–200.

Rogoff, B. (2003). *The cultural nature of human development.* New York: Oxford University Press.

Rogoff, B., & Gardner, W. P. (1984). Adult guidance of cognitive development. In B. Rogoff & J. Lave (Eds.), *Everyday cognition: Its development in social context* (pp. 95–116). Cambridge, MA: Harvard University Press.

Rosenblatt, L. M. (1978). *The reader, the text, the poem: The transactional theory of the literary work.* Carbondale, IL: Southern Illinois University Press.

Rosenshine, B., & Meister, C. (1994). Reciprocal teaching: A review of the research. *Review of Educational Research, 64*, 479–530.

Rousseau, M. K., Tam, B. K. Y., & Ramnarain, R. (1993). Increasing reading proficiency of language minority students with speech and language impairments. *Education and Treatments of Children, 16*, 254–271.

Rueda, R., MacGillivray, L., Monzó, L., & Arzubiaga, A. (2001). *Engaged reading: A multilevel approach to considering sociocultural factors with diverse learners.* Ann Arbor, MI: Center for the Improvement of Early Reading Achievement.

Ruiz, N. (1998). Instructional strategies for children with limited-English proficiency. *Journal of Early Education and Family Review, 5*, 21–22.

Ruiz, N. T. (1989). An optimal learning environment for Rosemary. *Exceptional Children, 56*, 130–144.

Ruiz, N. T. (1995). The social construction of ability and disability: II. Optimal and at-risk lessons in a bilingual special education classroom. *Journal of Learning Disabilities, 28*, 491–502.

Saenz, L., Fuchs, L. S., & Fuchs, D. (2005). Peer-assisted learning strategies for English language learners with learning disabilities. *Exceptional Children, 71*, 231–247.

Saunders, W., O'Brien, G., Lennon, D., & McLean, J. (1998). Making the transition to English literacy successful: Effective strategies for studying literature with transition students. In R. Gersten & R. Jiménez (Eds.), *Effective strategies for teaching language minority students* (pp. 99–132). Belmont, CA: Wadsworth.

Schiff-Myers, N. B., Djukic, J., McGovern-Lawler, J., & Perez, D. (1994). Assessment considerations in the evaluation of second-language learners: A case study. *Exceptional Children, 60*(3), 237–248.

Seymour, J. R., & Osana, H. P. (2003). Reciprocal teaching procedures and principles: Two teachers' developing understanding. *Teaching and Teacher Education, 19*, 325–344.

Short, K., & Klassen, C. (1993). Literature circles: Hearing children's voices. In B. Cullinan (Ed.), *Children's voices: Talk in the classroom* (pp. 66–85). Newark, DE: International Reading Association.

Snow, C. E. (2002). *Reading for understanding. Toward an R&D program in reading comprehension.* Santa Monica, CA: RAND.

Snow, C. E., Burns, M. S., & Griffin, P. (1998). *Preventing reading difficulties in young children.* Washington, DC: National Academy Press.

Sulzby, E., & Barnhart, J. (1992). The development of academic competence: All our children emerge as writers and readers. In J. W. Irwin & M. A. Doyle (Eds.), *Reading/writing connections: Learning from research* (pp. 120–144). Newark, DE: International Reading Association.

Taylor, B. M., Pearson, P. D., Clark, K., & Walpole, S. (2000). Effective schools and accomplished teachers: Lessons about primary-grade reading instruction in low-income schools. *Elementary School Journal, 101*, 121–165.

Taylor, D., & Dorsey-Gaines, C. (1988). *Growing up literate: Learning from inner-city families.* Portsmouth, NH: Heinemann.

Teale, W. H. (1986). Home background and literacy development. In W. H. Teale & E. Sulzby (Eds.), *Emergent literacy: Writing and reading.* Norwood, NJ: Ablex.

Tikunoff, W. J., Ward, B. A., van Broekhuizen, L. D., Romero, M., Castaneda, L. V., Lucas, T., & Katz, A. (1991). *Final report: A descriptive study of significant features of exemplary special alternative instructional programs.* Los Alamitos, CA: The Southwest Regional Educational Laboratory.

Trueba, H. T. (1988). English literacy acquisition: From cultural trauma to learning disabilities in minority students. *Linguistics and Education, 1,* 125–152.

Valdez-Menchaca, M. C., & Whitehurst, G. J. (1992). Accelerating language development through picture book reading: A systematic extension to Mexican day care. *Developmental Psychology, 28,* 1106–1114.

Vaughn, S., Mathes, P. G., Linan-Thompson, S., & Francis, D. J. (2005). Teaching English language learners at risk for reading disabilities to read: Putting research to practice. *Learning Disabilities Research & Practice,* 20, 58–67.

Villegas, A. M., & Lucas, T. (2002). Preparing culturally responsive teachers: Rethinking the curriculum. *Journal of Teacher Education, 53,* 20–32.

Vygotsky, L. S. (1978). *Mind in society.* Cambridge, MA: Harvard University Press.

Wasik, B. A. (1998). Using volunteers as reading tutors: Guidelines for successful practices. *The Reading Teacher, 51*(7), 562–570.

Wasik, B. A., & Slavin, R. E. (1993). Preventing early reading failure with one-to-one tutoring: A review of five programs. *Reading Research Quarterly, 28,* 178–200.

Whitehurst, G. J., Epstein, J. N., Angell, A. L., Payne, A. C., Crone, D. A., & Fischel, J. E. (1994). Outcomes of an emergent literacy intervention in Head Start. *Journal of Educational Psychology, 86,* 542–555.

Wiley, T. G. (1996). Literacy and language diversity in sociocultural contexts. *Literacy and language diversity in the United States.* Washington, DC: Center for Applied Linguistics and Delta Systems.

Willig, A., Swedo, J., & Ortiz, A. (1987). *Characteristics of teaching strategies which result in high task engagement for exceptional limited English proficient students.* Austin: University of Texas at Austin, Handicapped Minority Research Institute on Language Proficiency.

Wood, P., Bruner, J., & Ross, G. (1976). The role of tutoring in problem solving. *Journal of Child Psychology and Psychiatry, 17,* 89–100.

Yopp, R. H., & Yopp, H. K. (2001). *Literature-based reading activities* (3rd ed.). Boston, MA: Allyn & Bacon.

Chapter 8

Teaching Written Expression to Culturally and Linguistically Diverse Exceptional Learners

Anne W. Graves, Ph.D.
San Diego State University

Chapter Objectives

Upon completion of this chapter the reader will be able to:

1. Describe the unique writing instruction needs of CLDE students and the close link between learning to read and write.
2. List and give examples of the four principles for guiding writing instruction and practice.
3. Create a community of learners for enhanced writing instruction.
4. Describe the writing-as-a-process model of instruction and provide examples of successful implementation.
5. Allocate adequate instructional and practice time for writing.
6. Summarize research-based student strategies for learning to write, select from this array of strategies, and implement appropriate instruction when needed.

VIGNETTE

Dalisay is a Spanish- and English-speaking sixth grader who entered school in kindergarten speaking only Spanish. The primary language spoken at home is Spanish as her parents speak little English. Soon after Dalisay began formal schooling she began to be taught in English-only classrooms. She struggled in learning as she attempted to acquire and learn in English. After three years of formal schooling in English, Dalisay continued to struggle and was referred to her school's child study team for possible special education evaluation and placement. A formal battery of assessments was completed and the assessment team concluded that Dalisay had a learning disability. When tested in reading, Dalisay was able to retell a story within the proper sequence; however, her vocabulary and grammar were significantly below grade level. In regards to her writing abilities, Dalisay exhibited difficulties with writing sequence and text structure skills. Her difficulties with writing also contributed to the identification of a learning disability and she avoids writing and admits that she does not like to write.

Devon is an African-American individual who is in the fourth grade. Throughout formal schooling, Devon exhibited overactive behavior often leading to behavior problems in the classroom. He also has had significant problems attending to tasks and remaining focused on his learning through-out school. In first grade, Devon was identified as having Attention Deficit Hyperactivity Disorder (ADHD) and by grade three he was labeled as a student with conduct disorders. Although Devon's behavioral problems interfered with much of his academic and social development, he experienced particular problems remaining on task and completing written assignments. His written work is replete with run-on sentences, often beginning with the word "And," along with numerous spelling and punctuation errors.

The combination of Devon's behavior and writing needs and the inability of Dalisay to properly sequence written language suggests the importance of implementing a highly structured and organized approach to teaching writing for both students.

Reflective Questions

1. What cultural and linguistic considerations must be addressed to best understand the writing needs of Dalisay?
2. What additional information about Devon's writing needs should be gathered to best establish an effective writing program for this student?

INTRODUCTION

Dalisay and Devon are examples of culturally and linguistically diverse exceptional (CLDE) learners who have written expression difficulties. About half of fourth graders score above "basic" in overall reading and writing skills. By eighth grade, this number drops to about one in three. Nationally, one in four adults demonstrate proficiency at the lowest level. These data appear to indicate that we are in "crisis" in the schools in the United States, particularly in urban centers.

The recent No Child Left Behind (NCLB) Act mandates that states prove all students are proficient in basic skills through competency exams (Lewis, 2003). Writing is being assessed by state and district exams; sometimes passing these exams is necessary for graduation and promotion to higher grades (Chalk, Hagan-Burke, & Burke, 2005). Though more theory and research are undoubtedly needed to solve our modern problems related to education, existing data consistently suggest a strong connection between reading comprehension and writing (Graham & Harris, 2005). From a logical perspective, school-age individuals are rarely better writers than readers. For CLDE learners, and all students in school for that matter, writing and reading comprehension are closely linked.

Teachers face the daunting task of simultaneously building literacy or content knowledge, developing writing ability, and enhancing English language growth (Baca & Cervantes, 2004). Complicating matters is the fact that many students are from families where the adults in the household have varying levels of English language proficiency and literacy. This can limit the opportunities that are available for practicing the English language or for providing assistance with writing activities in the context of homework.

The purpose of this chapter is to recommend practices for writing instruction in both elementary and secondary school. Four guiding principles (see Figure 8.1) for designing instruction and practice are critical: (1) create a community of learners; (2) engage in writing as a process, which includes reading comprehension development; (3) allocate adequate instructional and practice time; and (4) implement strategy instruction when needed.

CREATING A COMMUNITY OF LEARNERS FOR ENHANCED WRITING INSTRUCTION

When students struggle with writing tasks in school, their *affective*, or socioemotional, reactions are often counterproductive. Disabilities combined with challenges in learning English or membership in a traditionally underrepresented group can often produce intensification of racial and ethnic tensions (Baca & Cervantes, 2004; Artiles, Rueda, Salazar, & Higareda, 2002; Jiménez, 2003; Gay, 2000; Obi, Obiakor, & Algozzine, 1999; August & Hakuta, 1997). One of the critical elements of effective writing instruction is the creation of a community of learners in which these tensions are lessened.

FIGURE 8.1 Four Guiding Principles for Writing Instruction

1. Create a community of learners.
2. Engage in writing as a process, which includes reading comprehension development.
3. Allocate adequate instructional and practice time.
4. Implement strategy instruction when needed.

Creating a community of learners can be defined as creating a learning environment that promotes emotional and intellectual fairness and security. A good learning environment can enhance self-esteem in all learners (Fitzgerald, 2003; Ruiz, 1995a, 1995b). English learners and students of color are in a cultural setting established by the school that is different from the cultural systems in their homes (Haager & Klingner, 2005; Faltis & Hudelson, 1994). These students are in a survival mode; they are unable simultaneously to consider others' feelings, plan for their own future, and function outside an egocentric concern for their own survival (Baca & Cervantes, 2004; Walker de Felix, Waxman, Paige, & Huang, 1993). These students typically encounter new information or processes in school that are unfamiliar and therefore difficult to learn (Harry, 1996; Harry & Klingner, 2006). When facing these challenges, students may resist learning basic skills such as writing and may experience emotional blocks or trauma when trying to speak English or participate in school tasks (Cummins, 1992). CLDE students are likely to feel a greater sense of belonging, feel more supported emotionally, and have higher self-esteem in a community of learners in the classroom setting (for a full description of each step, see Echevarria & Graves, 2007). To foster a community of learners for enhanced writing instruction:

1. Provide activities that promote success in reading and writing.
2. Focus on writing activities that are meaningful to students.
3. Create roles in the classroom for family and community members.
4. Hold high expectations for *all* learners.
5. Be responsive to cultural and personal diversity.

Provide Activities That Promote Success in Reading and Writing

In one third-grade classroom, with approximately 85 percent English learners, the teacher had weekly conferences with students individually. In these conferences she would ask the student to either retell part of a narrative students were reading or retell part of a content area chapter. The words spoken by the student were written in the student's notebook by the teacher. The student was then asked to read that text to a peer, all the while editing and revising with peer input. Though the teacher wrote the words the students were aware of their own intellectual ownership of the text. The teacher was just a scribe in that situation. The students could edit and revise the text and would confer with a peer to "fix it up." Once a week students would read aloud their summaries or stories and post them on the "work this week" bulletin board. This teacher kept a portfolio of each child's work and each week a new piece was added. At the end of the year the students had an impressive book of their own writing to take home (Graves, Gersten, & Haager, 2004; Graves, Plasencia-Peinado, Deno, & Johnson, 2005). In their recent book entitled, *Scaffolding Reading Experiences for English-Language Learners*, Fitzgerald and Graves (2004) asserted that when students read their own words and have an opportunity to edit and revise, language learning is intensified.

In another class, this one in a middle school, 97 percent of the eighth-grade students were Latino. The majority were not born in the United States. The students were at varying levels of English and Spanish proficiency. The teacher used English reading materials not consistent with the cultures of the students and far above their reading levels; some of the writing tasks were incomprehensible to the students. One young man in the class sat with a scowl on his face and constantly sought attention from his peers through inappropriate behavior. The teacher reported that this student and many others were frustrated. Further, parents were concerned about their lack of progress. It was recommended that this teacher start to use a more meaningful approach by providing activities relevant to the students' lives.

The teacher devised practice exercises to develop vocabulary, spelling, reading comprehension, and writing based directly on student-generated ideas. When the teacher used this approach, the behavior problems virtually vanished and the troubled students became happier and more cooperative. Providing meaningful activities can enhance feelings of belonging at school because students are able to bring their own ideas to the task. These types of activities can cause students to begin to take pride in their work and to experience success. Journal writing stands out as a meaningful activity. Writing at the beginning of each class day or at the beginning of each unit may be critical for the development of secondary students' writing skills, and it can also reinforce positive feelings toward school (Guthrie & Wigfield, 2000; Peyton, Jones, Vincent, & Greenblatt, 1994).

Literature-based instruction in reading and writing is a way to provide rich and exciting activities for students in the early grades. As students move to middle school the same type of language experience approaches are increasingly important (Anderson & Roit, 1996). Abundant information is now available regarding this type of instruction for secondary students (Graves & Liang, 2005; Waldschmidt, Kim, Kim, Martinez, Hale, 1999). For example, one middle school math teacher had students use a binder as a journal. The teacher assigned various types of writing throughout the year. For 3 minutes at the start of each math period, the students made journal entries about their thoughts and feelings concerning the math homework. At other times, the students wrote for 3 minutes about how the concepts they were learning applied to their lives. The students were asked to share their writing in small groups or to read journal entries to the class without disclosing the student writer. Each week, the teacher collected the writing, read the entries, and provided written comments in the journals. The comments promoted success by providing a written interaction, or dialogue, with each student and established an opportunity for language development, even in a math class.

Focus on Writing Activities That Are Meaningful to Students

Theories about language acquisition generally support native language instruction to facilitate underlying academic proficiency. Skills learned in the native language can later be "transferred" and applied to English language learning (Baca & Cervantes, 2004; Chang, 2004; Jiménez, 2003; Cummins, 1992; Krashen, 1985). However, native language instruction is not always available in schools. To help native language speakers, teachers can create a nonthreatening atmosphere where students can share information about their own cultural and ethnic backgrounds (Franklin & Thompson, 1994). For example, the teacher can arrange partner sharing and cooperative group activities to facilitate feelings of safety and comfort. The students in each group can learn how problems are solved or how stories are told within each unique cultural and linguistic perspective.

Moll (1988) writes extensively about the value of the "funds" of knowledge that students bring to the classroom. These funds of knowledge can be tapped through daily journal entries. The knowledge gained by the teacher about the students should be incorporated into other writing tasks as well. For example, in an American history lesson on the design of the first American flag, students can be instructed to draw a picture of any flag with which they are familiar and describe that flag. Often this will be a flag from their native country. They can be asked to investigate the country and flag on the Internet with family members, write a summary of what they find, draw flags, and share their work. This might also be a good parent-involvement activity; parents might be asked to bring in real flags or to draw pictures of the flags of countries of origin.

Create Roles in the Classroom for Family and Community Members

The celebration of cultural and linguistic diversity in schools is not likely to feel real to parents and community members until a comfortable place is created for the families of all students (Goldenberg, Gallimore, Reese, & Garnier, 2001; Baca & Cervantes, 2004; Gay, 2000; Gonzalez et al., 1993; Chang, 2004). Teachers must establish relationships with family members and should invite families to serve in the classroom. Families of students with disabilities can find common ground and often assist one another in finding roles and responsibilities in the context of school activities.

Family members in the classroom might help students learn about native cultures and can serve as role models for all students. In one class, a parent who claimed to have made over one hundred piñatas was asked to guide a piñata art project. On the other hand, classroom service does not have to be culturally specific. It is designed to bring parents and community members into the class on a regular basis to provide a multiplicity of cultural leadership. For example, any parent could be asked to share life experiences or job-related experiences (Hildebrand, Phenice, Gray, & Hines, 2000) and students could write paragraphs or summaries about what the parents report. "Special visits" provide excellent opportunities for engaging in a written and verbal dialogue more meaningful to students.

Parents and family members can be encouraged to volunteer for many different roles in the classroom. Volunteers can read stories to students and have students write daily summaries or work in small groups on developing a group summary. They can also help students with written science or social studies projects. Parents or community members with special skills can occasionally teach classes. For example, one teacher invited a father who works on a fishing boat to speak to the class about ocean animals. The student assisted his father with English and they worked together to present fish stories and pictures to the class. Students made a book about the topic, writing various sections that had been described by the boy's father.

In another example, a fifth-grade teacher planned a family-friendly unit entitled *Viva San Diego*. The teacher invited parents to participate. Each student was asked to pick an area of the city he or she wanted to learn more about, such as Balboa Park or San Diego State University. Students and parents were asked to do research and to visit their chosen areas to learn as much as they could about them. In the end, each student wrote a report and made a model of the area selected. All of these models and reports were displayed in the school's showcase.

A recent publication by Chang (2004) describes a research project that aimed to establish an after-school support group for low-achieving Asian American English learners in middle school, some of whom were students with disabilities. This serves as another example of creating family and community roles. Teachers and parents participated together to assist students in the "sheltered instruction program" by attending workshops and forming a support team. The teams were composed of parents, general education, special education, and English language development teachers. After a year of in-services, *Family Literacy Nights* were launched. The goals and results of the project were as follows (Chang, 2004):

- Classroom strategies and knowledge were transferred to home practices.
- Teachers, parents, and students formed productive activity teams to complete assignments similar to those given in school.
- Teams explored multiple paths to teaching and learning through questioning, strategies, role-plays, vocabulary development, and written book projects.
- Parents made "what-to-do" lists for supervising students at home and discussed home practices that were likely to improve student work.

Parents were taught to follow strategies for home use developed by Chang (2004) in her work at the Center for Research on Education, Diversity & Excellence (available: http://www.cal.org/crede/pubs/ResBrief9.htm). Paraphrased, the strategies are:

1. Help your child produce what she really knows.
2. Model language used at home and in school.

3. Provide opportunities to use new vocabulary words at home.
4. Help your child relate what was learned in school to home each day.
5. Give positive feedback.
6. Help your child think of questions and see how ideas or concepts are related.
7. Talk about lifelong learning.
8. Value your child's abilities in multiple ways; help your child learn through multiple paths (e.g., writing projects or summaries of content).

Hold High Expectations for All Learners

Treuba, Jacobs, and Kirton's research (1990) showed that high school English teachers had low expectations of Latino students. The teachers interviewed felt that Latino students were incapable of completing higher level projects. As part of an experiment, the teachers assigned students higher level written projects with topics relevant to their own lives. The students conducted authentic research from their own experiences and from the community. The results of the experiment indicated that they could complete high-quality projects. Trueba and colleagues (1990) concluded that Latino students could produce relatively high-level work when they understood the connection between schoolwork and out-of-school experiences. Teachers need to have high expectations.

A fourth-grade teacher wanted to ask each student a higher order question at least once a week. The teacher composed at least six higher order questions for each 50-minute period. He kept a box containing each student's name on a piece of paper and drew five names from the box each day. He wrote those names on the board and checked off the names as he asked one of the higher order questions of each student. The names drawn one day were taken from the box so that the remaining names for the next days of the week were those students who had not yet received questions. The questions were not necessarily asked in succession but were spread throughout the period, coupled with different parts of the plan for the day. All students were expected to answer questions.

Students are more likely to perform well when asked and expected to prepare written answers to higher order questions (Henze & Lucas, 1993). For example, one middle school science teacher designated a student as a weekly problem solver for the classroom. Any class problem during the week was assigned to the problem solver. The problem solver could work independently or use a self-selected committee to compose a written answer to the problem. Students responded well to the responsibility and to their new roles in the classroom. One week, the student problem solver was faced with a situation in which the teacher had scheduled a field trip to the beach as part of a marine biology unit, but the school could not supply enough adult supervision. The field trip was not approved. The principal told the teacher that if adult supervision was obtained by the class members the class could still make the trip. The student of the week proposed sending notes home to all the parents and to community members asking for support supervising the field trip. The effort was entirely student initiated; the notes were written by the problem solver and her committee. The students were successful in obtaining enough adult supervision, and the field trip was approved. The students were pleased with their efforts and their new responsibilities in the classroom. Teachers can create challenging environments for students by arranging activities in which the students form collaborative or cooperative problem-solving groups such as this. During the same unit on marine biology, the science teacher asked a student group to list how they thought an oil spill had affected sea life. The teacher then had the students pair off and write reports on how an oil spill would affect the grey whales.

Be Responsive to Cultural and Personal Diversity

What does it mean to be culturally responsive in the context of teaching writing? A few examples are provided here to assist you in thinking about writing instruction (see Chapter 2 for more information on this topic). A sixth-grade teacher of students who were English learners was also the faculty advisor for the Homework Club. Approximately 25 percent of the students in the club had various types of disabilities. The teacher encouraged students from all cultural and linguistic groups to join the Homework Club. During the daily lunchtime meeting, the students were allowed to eat lunch, play music, and receive help with their homework. The teacher created a safe atmosphere for fun and learning. Parents could attend the meetings, as well.

Across grade levels from elementary to high school, teachers figure out ways to empower students and to motivate them when developing effective writing instruction strands. Again, Moll (1988) writes extensively about the value of the "funds" of knowledge that students bring to the classroom. These funds of knowledge can be tapped through daily journal writings and a culture of sharing daily writings in the classroom. The knowledge gained regarding students' lives can then be incorporated into lessons and content for coursework (Gonzalez et al., 1993). For example, a second-grade teacher provided each student with a spiral notebook in which pages cannot tear out easily. In the beginning of the year the students personalized their notebooks by decorating them. The teacher wrote a sentence stem on the board: "Today the weather is . . . " Students were asked to write for 2 minutes. Then students immediately turned to their partner and read the entry. Each day during the week the teacher asked four of the students to read their entries, keeping track each day of who had already participated that week. As the year progressed students were asked to make entries about various events and personal entries as well.

A high school English teacher had a three-times-a-week journal entry assignment in which students selected a job application from an array the teacher had in the classroom, filled it out, and then wrote a paragraph about what tasks the job would entail. The students shared their journal entries in small groups at the end of the session. The teacher read each entry and worked with students on developing self-promotion skills and professional approaches to job applications. The teacher also became an advocate for the students, encouraging them to apply for summer jobs or after-school jobs. When the students learned that the teacher was their ally, students were more motivated to learn from this teacher. Students also developed a respect for one another through multiple sessions together where journal entries were shared.

In another example, a high school teacher of students who were in sheltered English classes spent time in class explaining campus activities and assisting the students in filling out applications for campus programs and activities. The teacher became an advocate for the students by ensuring that decisions about campus clubs, programs, and after-school activities were fairly made all the while working with students on improving their written expression. This seemed to help students feel as much a part of school as everyone else. From time to time in class, this teacher would raise questions about school issues that may have involved prejudice or stereotyping and encouraged students to write about such issues.

Teaching Implication: Building a community of learners is accomplished when students are writing for a common purpose such as a class or school newsletter and situations in which students collaborate on projects and problem solving. Students feel part of a "community" when each student feels involved and plays an active role. Teachers can build this atmosphere and this community of learners gradually and progressively throughout the year. For example, one teacher created a sharing time at the beginning of the year in which students had 2 minutes to share something they had learned about the thematic unit on whales. Later in the year, as students grew more and more comfortable with one another and with sharing, the teacher changed it to "author's sharing" and students read what they had written about how a local grocery store was operated. As part of a thematic unit on community businesses, students were creating a book. Building a community of writers means that teachers serve as coaches and guides in student progress.

Building a community of learners also involves the provision of abundant mechanisms for student recognition. All forms of sharing and publishing assist students in receiving attention and recognition for their work. Of course, the sharing and publishing that give writers a purpose for their work is essential in building a community of writers.

WRITING-AS-A-PROCESS INSTRUCTION FOR CLDE LEARNERS

There is a growing body of research on writing instruction provided to general education and special education students (Graham & Harris, 2005; De La Paz & Graham, 2002; Baker, Gersten, & Graham, 2003; Ferreti, MacArthur, & Graham, 2003). Results indicate that writing-as-a-process instruction with strategy instruction is effective in improving both the quality and amount written in student compositions (Deno, 1985; Espin, De La Paz, Scierka, & Roelofs, 2005; Rapp, 1997; Wong, Butler, Ficzere, & Kuperis, 1996). In addition, a few studies of writing instruction for special education students who speak a first language other than English indicate similar results (Ruiz, 1995a, 1995b; Ruiz & Figueroa, 1995; Graves, Valles, & Rueda, 2000).

Echevarria and Graves (2007) describe writing-as-a-process instruction, originally developed by Donald Graves (1983). This type of instruction has been shown to be

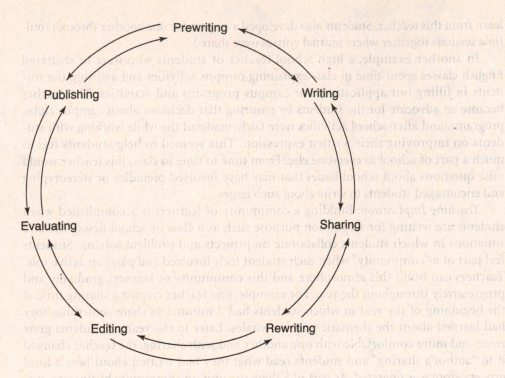

FIGURE 8.2 Writing as a Process

effective for CLDE learners as well (Englert et al., 2005; Graves et al., 2000; Graves et al., in press). The writer's workshop format (see Figure 8.2) typically includes situations in which the teacher provides prewriting, writing, sharing, rewriting, editing, evaluating, and publishing activities for students.

Prewriting is typically defined as brainstorming and planning. Writing is the act of composing. Rewriting is changing content to reflect more clearly stated and meaningful text. Editing is changing spelling, handwriting, punctuation, and grammar to conform to established standards. Sharing occurs in publishing as students share a story with classmates or create books for the class. Sharing in publishing also occurs by creating formal newsletters, putting books in the school library, or writing letters to prospective employers. Evaluation exists as students review or reread their work prior to publishing. As illustrated in this double circle with arrows going both ways to represent counter-clockwise thinking and clockwise thinking all in the same written work, the writing process is thought to be recursive and nonlinear. The writer starts with prewriting and progresses on to writing, but then may go back to prewriting to change the plan during revision and on to editing before returning to writing. Publishing can occur but changes in the written efforts could even occur after publication if the author wishes.

Journal writing activities, prewriting, and writing without an immediate focus on "editing" can build fluency. Once students have developed basic fluency, a mini-lesson segment each day focusing on various aspects of form and correctness is important. A focus on "form" might involve strategic instruction on narrative and expository text. A focus on "correctness" would be the development of revising and editing strategies for learning to proofread and fine-tune written expression.

The write-as-a-process instructional model should be contextualized with integrated writing activities including listening, speaking, reading, and writing with a focus on real audiences. For example, in one high school class students created a school newspaper each week with photographs, captions, and a few stories about school that week. The paper was well received by students in the school and by the end of the year the demand for the weekly publication was approximately 200 copies per week. Students were involved in the planning, writing, revising, editing, and publishing week in and week out; all the while perfecting the process. Students took various roles in the process and discussed ideas throughout the week. Every contributor was listed as an author for each issue.

The following are a few more examples of using the writing-as-a-process instruction model in the classroom:

- **A Seventh-Grade Class.**   A seventh-grade science teacher had students construct freshwater and saltwater aquariums for a unit on ecosystems. The students wrote reports about the aquariums before constructing them and were integrally involved in the planning and building of each aquarium. After the aquariums were completed, the students wrote about their observations and formulated hypotheses about observed changes in the aquariums. Students shared observations and reports throughout the process. Students had weekly conferences with peers or the teacher to discuss revising and editing their own work. In the end, the students prepared "perfect final copies" of the various pieces of their reports. The perfect copies were placed in a book about the project. Students took photographs and drew pictures to illustrate the book. The book was placed on display in the school foyer and students each received a copy to take home. Throughout the process each student had an important contribution to make. Emphasis was placed on listening to the work of others, speaking about plans and revisions, reading their own work and work of others, and the writing itself. Students were encouraged to establish ownership of their writing, including decisions about content and revisions and self-evaluation.

- **A Second-Grade Class.**   Students who are just beginning writing as a process or who are nonwriters may follow a modified writing-as-a-process model (see Figure 8.3). Students might share after every phase of their work, and the phases and segments might be shorter depending on the initial writing abilities of the learners. For example, students might do a prewriting activity and a quick write on whales. They might share their ideas and in sharing talk about different types of whales. The teacher might extend these ideas and build on them by setting up an activity the next day that focuses on orcas. Extensions are student driven and activities add to a writing or language arts program based on the work of students.

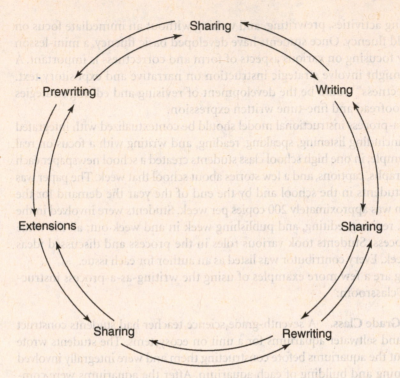

FIGURE 8.3 Writing as a Process (Early Stages)

- **A Fourth-Grade Class.** In a fourth-grade class, a teacher used explicit strategy instruction in writing. After teaching the students each step of the writing process overtly, the teacher used different colored paper to represent the stages of writing. Planning was completed on yellow paper, first draft on orange paper, and the final draft was completed on the computer or on white paper. Revising was accomplished on the orange paper by marking through and correcting spelling and punctuation. Students engaged in the process at least once a week. The students learned to start the writing process by expressing ideas. The writing process occurred in predictable stages.

ALLOCATING ADEQUATE TIME FOR CLDE LEARNERS

Research in many content areas supports the notion that allocated instructional and practice time during the school day improves performance (Woolfolk, 2006). This remains one of the critical considerations for special education teachers because students with learning challenges often need intensive instruction and practice to achieve written expression improvements (Graham & Harris, 2005).

One year-long study of the effects of technology on writing performance in students with learning disabilities indicated that one hour of writing time per week will *not* produce significant writing quality or quantity improvements (Lewis, Graves, Ashton, & Kieley, 1997). Therefore, teachers need to allocate more than one hour of writing time per week to develop an awareness in students of the amount of time and the number of drafts that it takes to write something of high quality (see Figure 8.4).

One suggestion for thinking about how to manage time is to determine the amount of time through instruction and homework that can be devoted to writing. Once this amount of time is determined, students should spend one-third of that time on writing, one-third on prewriting and teacher-directed instruction or mini-lessons, and one-third on sharing and revising. With this model the students are engaged in writing for essentially half of the time allotted because revising time is writing time.

In middle and high school learning resource settings (i.e., room or setting where student spends 1-3 hours per day working on individual needs), when students are working in content areas, they should spend at least one-third of the time on writing. The writing could be focused entirely on the content immediately at hand. For example, if the students are working on ecosystems in science and some of the students need

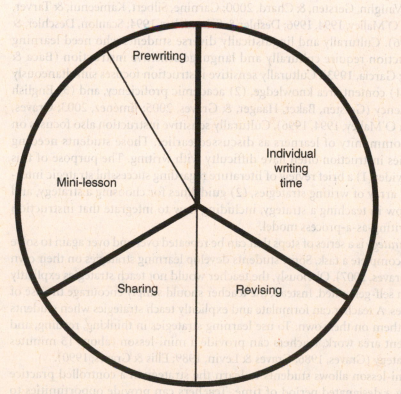

FIGURE 8.4 Time Management Model for CLDE Learners

abundant practice on writing, the teacher could set up a writers' workshop in which students generate a paragraph about the contrasting characteristics of two ecosystem models present in the class (e.g., freshwater and saltwater ecosystems).

WRITING INSTRUCTION STRATEGIES FOR CLDE LEARNERS

Teachers must be sensitive to the fact that CLD learners may have extraordinary cognitive burdens when learning new information due to potential unfamiliarity with academic language and text structures. Students can be so overwhelmed in attempting to derive meaning from English or technical school language that they may not spontaneously generate the strategies needed for efficient and effective learning (Ortiz & Graves, 2001; Yang, 1999).

Teachers can facilitate learning by directly teaching strategies (see Chapter 11). Explicit instruction of learning strategies can increase the comfort and learning potential of students needing support and has a long history of research supporting its efficacy in educational psychology, special education, and general education including English learners (Woolfolk, 2006; Graham & Harris, 2005; Fitzgerald, 2003; Fitzgerald & Graves, 2004; Vaughn, Gersten, & Chard, 2000; Carnine, Silbert, Kameenui, & Tarver, 2004; Chamot & O'Malley, 1994, 1996; Deshler & Schumaker, 1994; Scanlon, Deschler, & Schumaker, 1996). Culturally and linguistically diverse students who need learning strategies instruction require culturally and language sensitive instruction (Baca & Cervantes, 2004; García, 1993). Culturally sensitive instruction focuses simultaneously on developing (1) content area knowledge, (2) academic proficiency, and (3) English language proficiency (Gersten, Baker, Haager, & Graves, 2005; Jiménez, 2003; Graves, 1998; Chamot & O'Malley, 1994, 1996). Culturally sensitive instruction also focuses on establishing a community of learners as discussed earlier. Those students needing learning strategies instruction often have difficulty with writing. The purpose of this section is to provide: (1) a brief review of literature regarding successful strategic interventions and an array of writing strategies, (2) guidelines for choosing a strategy, and (3) steps to follow in teaching a strategy, including how to integrate that instruction back into the writing-as-a-process model.

A *learning strategy* is a series of steps that can be repeated over and over again to solve a problem or to complete a task. Some students develop learning strategies on their own (Echevarria & Graves, 2007). Obviously, the teacher would not teach strategies explicitly if they have been self-generated. Instead, the teacher should simply encourage the use of effective strategies. A teacher can formulate and explicitly teach strategies when students do not develop them on their own. To use learning strategies in thinking, reading, and writing in content area work, teachers can provide a mini-lesson (about 15 minutes daily) on the strategy (Graves, 1986; Graves & Levin, 1989; Ellis & Graves, 1990).

Using a mini-lesson allows students to learn the strategy in a controlled practice situation during a designated period of time. Teachers can provide opportunities to memorize and use the strategy during a practice session before requiring strategy use in a content area application. Learning strategies can be developed not only for academics but for language acquisition and many other areas, such as social skills and vocational skills.

Learning strategies are not a curriculum. Instead, strategies are used as a part of the curriculum to enhance access to content, academic, or life-skills proficiency. Strategies enhancing access to content are used in literature, science, social studies, and math classes and facilitate gaining knowledge. For example, the "steps for writing about an experiment" is a science strategy taught at the beginning of the school year. It should increase the knowledge a student gains from science lessons if the steps of an experiment are automatic for the learner. The science strategy can be reused throughout the year and for future science work. Such learning strategies provide a series of steps to integrate language knowledge and content knowledge (Fitzgerald & Graves, 2004; Jiménez, 2003; Gersten, Taylor, & Graves, 1999; Jiménez, García, & Pearson, 1996; Chamot & O'Malley, 1994, 1996).

Many studies have been published showing the effectiveness of learning strategies with CLDE students (Chamot & O'Malley, 1996; De La Paz, 1999, 2001; Englert, 2005; Echevarria & Graves, 2007; Genesee, Lindholm-Leary, Saunders, & Christian, 2005). Related to writing instruction, the self-regulated strategy development (SRSD) model for teaching writing was originally developed by Graham and Harris at the University of Maryland (Graham & Harris, 1989). The SRSD model is an approach in which students learn specific strategies and procedures for using the strategies in writing. This model also encourages students to self-regulate their behavior while engaged in a task. Teachers model the use of the strategies and provide scaffolding while the student develops the skills.

Studies at the Elementary Level. In several investigations of the effects of planning on writing for upper elementary students (Graves, Montague, & Wong, 1990; Montague & Graves, 1991; Montague, Graves, & Leavell, 1991), urban students with mild disabilities were taught to plan for narrative writing by using a checklist. Students were taught to plan by filling in the following sections: Character, Setting, Problem, Plan, and Ending. Approximately 90 percent of the students were from diverse backgrounds in these studies. Results indicated that students who received the planning instruction outperformed those who did not.

Graham and Harris and their colleagues at the University of Maryland have conducted many studies over the past 20 years investigating the effects of strategy instruction on the writing of students with learning disabilities. In all cases, strategy instruction was added as a supplement to writing-as-a-process instruction (Graham & Harris, 1989, 2005). Three types of strategies were studied: for planning and goal setting (Graham & Harris, 1989; Harris & Graham, 1996), for framing text (Graham & Harris, 1989), and for revising (MacArthur, Schwartz, & Graham, 1991). Results indicated that both the quality and structure of compositions improved with strategy instruction. Typically the length of compositions increased and, in some studies, the improvements brought students with learning disabilities to the level of functioning of their general education peers (Danoff, Harris, & Graham, 1993).

Graham and Harris (1989) developed the TREE strategy for writing an opinion essay. When planning, students learn to:

- Generate a *Topic* (T).
- Record *Reasons* (R).
- Add *Examples* (E).
- Finish with an *Ending* (E).

Sexton, Harris, and Graham (1998) conducted a study that used the SRSD model to develop planning and writing strategies for writing essays. Participants in the study included six students with learning disabilities in the fifth and sixth grades. The students used the TREE mnemonic to help them form a topic for their essay and supporting ideas (TREE: Topic, Reason, Explain, Ending). The mnemonic also encouraged students to evaluate the effectiveness of their ideas. Students used the plan they made to write persuasive essays. Scaffolding and support by teachers were given during the writing process. Results suggested that strategy instruction may be effective at the secondary level. Students improved in writing performance and also indicated more comfort and confidence in the writing process.

Troia and Graham (2002) also evaluated the effectiveness of explicit, teacher-directed strategy instruction in writing on the performance of elementary students. Participants included fourth- and fifth-grade students with learning disabilities. Students in the intervention group received advance *planning* strategy instruction that focused on:

- Goal setting (What is the purpose of your writing? Who is your audience?)
- Brainstorming (Create a web or a list of ideas)
- Organizing ideas before writing a story (Teach about text structure)

Data from the study revealed that the one-month instructional program helped students improve the quality and length of their story writing. The results also showed that students did not transfer the skills to other genres of writing that were not part of the instructional focus, indicating specific instruction in different genres or structures of writing is needed to ensure student success in a variety of types of writing.

Studies at the Secondary Level. Studies examining the use of this model in teaching writing to students with mild disabilities at the secondary level support its effectiveness. De La Paz (1999, 2001) conducted two studies that used the SRSD model to teach strategies for planning and writing expository essays to students with and without learning disabilities. The participants of the study were seventh- and eighth-grade students in an urban setting with and without learning disabilities. In both of the studies, a general education teacher delivered instruction while a special education teacher supported the students. These studies showed that students with and without disabilities made progress in their writing skills in the inclusive setting, indicating that strategy instruction is an effective instructional technique to use with inclusive classes when teaching writing. The intervention lasted for 12 to 16 full class periods. Teachers modeled the PLAN and WRITE strategy (De La Paz, 1999). The mnemonic PLAN and WRITE helps students to remember the steps in planning and writing an essay (see Figure 8.5).

Pay Attention to the Prompt
List Main Ideas
Add Supporting Ideas
Number Your Ideas
Work from Your Plan to Develop Thesis Statement
Remember Your Goals
Include Transition Words for Each Paragraph
Try to Use Different Kinds of Sentences
Exciting, Interesting, $100,000 Words

FIGURE 8.5 PLAN and WRITE
Strategy
Source: De La Paz (1999).

Students were then guided through writing practice and given support as they achieved mastery. After the intervention, students made plans for their essays, increased essay length, increased the number of functional elements in their essays, and improved the quality of their essays.

De La Paz (2001) conducted another study using the participants and design of the above-mentioned study. Rather than examining the effectiveness of the SRSD approach to teach the PLAN and WRITE strategy for students with learning disabilities, this study focused on students with attention deficit disorders and specific language impairment. Results for this study were consistent with the previous study. Students with attention deficit disorders and specific language impairment also increased their use of plans for essay writing, increased essay length, produced more quality content, and better structured their writing (De La Paz, 2001).

The effectiveness of the SRSD model on the writing performance of students with learning disabilities in high school was also examined in a study by Chalk, Hagan-Burke, and Burke (2005), furthering the support for the use of this model for teaching writing. Students were taught the DARE strategy through teacher modeling. DARE stands for (Chalk, Hagan-Burke, & Burke, 2005):

- *Develop* topic sentence.
- *Add* supporting detail.
- *Reject* arguments from the other side.
- *End* with a conclusion.

Students memorized the strategy and then applied it in collaborative practice with the teacher. Finally, students wrote essays independently. A repeated measure design was used to assess the effects of the SRSD model. Results showed that the students improved their word production and the quality of their essays.

Barry and Moore (2004) conducted a study with 20 eighth-grade students with learning disabilities who needed to pass a competency exam to advance to the next grade. An SRSD model was used to teach the students how to write expository and persuasive essays like the one used for the competency exam. After 12 weeks of instruction, all the students in the study passed the exam. The findings also showed that students with learning disabilities who received the SRSD training performed comparable to general education students of about the same age from across the state.

Another instructional model, cognitive strategy instruction, aims to shape behavior through the teaching of strategy steps, cognitive modeling, guided instruction, and self-regulation (Hallenbeck, 2002). The Cognitive Strategy Instruction in Writing (CSIW) model draws on cognitive strategy instruction and emphasizes collaboration and teacher modeling during the writing process. This approach was used to teach expository writing to students with learning disabilities in the seventh grade in a study by Hallenbeck (2002). Two student pairs were instructed using the CSIW method. The results showed that three out of the four students made improvements in their writing ability. Students increased the number of total words in their essays and improved their ability to collaborate with other students. Earlier strategy instruction studies in written expression yielded similar results.

Strategy Instruction in Diverse Inclusive Settings. General education placements give students access to rigorous, standards-based curriculum. Effective teaching methods are needed to meet the unique needs of all the diverse learners found in an inclusive setting. McLesky, Henry, and Axelrod (1999) examined data from *Reports to Congress* that dealt with the placement of students with learning disabilities. Although states differed in their placement practices, the results of the study show that students with learning disabilities are being instructed in less restrictive settings at an increasing rate. This signifies the need for general education teachers to use effective practices for instructing students with learning disabilities. In addition, collaboration between special education teachers and general education teachers is needed to meet students' unique needs (McLesky, Henry, & Axelrod, 1999). Strategy instruction is a method that can be used in the inclusive setting to meet the needs of all students. The implications of these studies, and other research in strategy instruction, show that across content areas and differing student needs, strategy instruction is effective. The benefits of strategy instruction can help all students to learn. When strategy instruction is used in the inclusive classroom, it can lead to positive outcomes for students with and without disabilities.

Strategy Instruction and High-Stakes Testing. High-stakes testing has become an increasing concern in public education, especially with mandates from the federal government for the use of these types of assessments. NCLB requires that students with mild disabilities participate in high-stakes testing. Yet, students from diverse backgrounds often perform poorly on these measures (Harry & Klingner, 2006).

Carter (2004) conducted a study with high school students from diverse backgrounds and examined the use of test-taking strategy instruction and its effect on the test performance of the students. The participants of the study included 38 students with learning disabilities, mild mental retardation, and language impairment. The intervention included a series of six lessons that taught students test-taking strategies they could use in multiple-choice language arts and math exams. Pre- and posttest measures were taken using a simulated Tennessee Competency Achievement Program (TCAP) math test and Test Anxiety Inventory (TAI). The findings indicate that test-taking strategy instruction resulted in decreased student test anxiety and slightly increased student performance on the simulated TCAP math test. Although the students increased their scores on the TCAP, these increases were not significant enough to give most of the students taking the exam a passing score. The researchers recommend that to be more effective, strategy instruction in test-taking skills be taught to students early in their academic careers and should persist over time. Additionally, strategies taught should be aligned with the specific type of problems students will encounter on the tests (Carter, 2004).

More promising results were shown in the study by Barry and Moore (2004) outlined earlier. This study used strategy instruction to teach writing to a group of diverse students for the writing component of the competency exam required for a high school graduation diploma. This 12-week intervention was specific to the essay the students would take in the state competency exam. After the intervention, all 20 students with learning disabilities included in the study passed the state writing competency exam. The results of this study are encouraging and call for teachers to use strategy instruction to prepare students for high-stakes exams, especially those that determine eligibility for a diploma.

Guidelines for Selecting Strategies

Research indicates that several guidelines for selecting strategies are important. First, choose strategies that are highly useful across many situations. Second, choose to teach strategies given a history of difficulty in an area. CAUTION: Students who have already spontaneously generated *effective* strategies should not be discouraged from using them or forced to replace them with other strategies. Third, compare strategies to a scope and sequence and teach the strategies in an order that is logical and fits into the framework of the writing program. Fourth, make language and examples simple and comprehensible. Fifth, adapt to individual differences as students begin to use the strategy.

Steps for Teaching a Strategy

There are four recommended steps for teaching any strategy:

1. Examine the strategy for necessary preskills (i.e., concepts and rules/principles) that must be taught for successful mastery of the strategy.

2. Model the strategy for students and think aloud to demonstrate each step.

3. Practice the strategy many times and monitor progress before having students practice independently.

4. Provide abundant practice and opportunities for student to apply the strategy in many different situations.

STEP ONE: Examine the strategy to identify prerequisite skills (i.e., concepts and rules) for successful and efficient mastery of the strategy. Students must be taught each of these prerequisite concepts and rules before attempting to learn the strategy.

Students who have mastered each preskill will be able to automatically and quickly employ the strategy using all of the concepts and rules combined.

STEP TWO: Model the strategy for students and think aloud through each step. Different strategies may have different numbers of substeps, but each should be modeled in succession and in detail. For example, a three-step paragraph writing strategy might be: (1) Think about a topic and write a sentence; (2) write two to three sentences that expand or explain your topic; and (3) write a sentence to sum up the paragraph's main point. Think aloud for students demonstrating each step.

STEP THREE: Use the strategy with students and monitor progress before having them use it on their own. Monitor the use of the strategy carefully and correct all errors. If the student doesn't know the strategy or isn't using it properly, go back to step 2.

STEP FOUR: Provide abundant practice and opportunities for students to use the strategy in many different practical situations. Infuse the use of the strategy into the meaningful activities and into the work used to build a community of learners. Build collaborative and cooperative activities so that students can apply the strategies.

Teaching Implications: Use of the above process provides a more organized and structured approach for assisting diverse learners with writing tasks. Below are two examples—one for a sixth and one for a ninth grade class—illustrating the application of various writing components to assist diverse learners.

- **A Sixth-Grade Class**   A sixth-grade social studies teacher devoted 20 of her 50 minutes per class to writer's workshop. The teacher consistently used about one-third of the time for writing; one-third for sharing, presenting, revising, or editing; and one-third for mini-lessons or teacher-directed learning. The teacher did not accomplish all three aspects each day, but spent at least one hour each week on writing. The teacher asked the students to pretend they lived at the time of the California gold rush and to write a story about their adventures. The class kicked off the new assignment with a teacher-led student brainstorming activity. Next, each student created a story web or outline, sketched out illustrations, and finally moved onto writing drafts. The students had 20 minutes each day during the week to complete the assignment. The teacher chose the narrative genre because students are usually comfortable with story structure. When writing in a new language students must be comfortable with the genre. Story writing often makes history come alive for students.

For students floundering on the narrative story structure, the teacher used the *story grammar cueing system* (Graves et al., 1990; Montague, Graves, & Leavell, 1991). The cueing system is a list of the story grammar parts (setting, characters, problem, resolution, ending). The students were instructed to think about the parts as they wrote and revised their stories; students were to make a check by each part as they incorporated it (Graves & Montague, 1991). The cueing system required the students to reflect on the steps and encouraged self-regulated learning because eventually students would internalize the steps and use the system on their own.

During the next lesson, the students formed peer pairs and made corrections and changes in their stories. The peer revision provided each student with abundant feedback. The teacher provided a revision format during several mini-lessons. The revision strategy included four questions for students to ask themselves about their stories: Does the story make sense? What do I like about the story? Does the story have characters, a setting, a problem, a resolution, and an ending? Is the capitalization, overall appearance, punctuation, and spelling correct? The students needed a significant amount of time to complete the assignment, and teacher guidance was necessary to ensure accomplishment. At the end of the week, the students wrote final drafts on the computer and created a class book. The book was given to another sixth-grade class as a gift.

- **A Ninth-Grade Class**   A ninth-grade English teacher noted that her students were struggling with writing expository material. The teacher decided to use a think-aloud modeling procedure to teach report writing. As the teacher read to the students about the colonial tradition of Thanksgiving, the note-taking process was modeled on the overhead projector. After the reading and note-taking lesson, the teacher taught the five-paragraph essay strategy and gave the students a handout with the format of that strategy specified. The format called for an introductory paragraph, three supporting paragraphs, and a concluding paragraph. The teacher then modeled essay writing by using the format to think aloud about a topic. The students were encouraged to make comments and suggestions as the outline was constructed on the overhead projector. Finally, the teacher talked with students about the accuracy and logic of the outline.

After the outlining process on the topic of Thanksgiving, the teacher used the overhead projector again and wrote a report on it in concert with student participation. At another time, the students worked together in table groups and wrote reports about famous people in colonial history, such as Pocahontas, John Smith, and Miles Standish. For 20 minutes each day over the course of a week, each group completed five tasks: (1) reading together while taking notes on orange paper, (2) preparing an outline on pink paper, (3) preparing a first draft on yellow paper, (4) editing the first draft, and (5) entering a final draft into the computer at the end of the week. During the next week, the groups shared their reports with the rest of the class. The students' writing quality was good compared to work done before exposure to the essay strategy and the writing-as-a-process strategy.

Sharing. Individualized sharing opportunities, such as talking, reading, and role-playing, contribute to language development in students (Englert & Mariage, 1992). Teachers can use segments of time for individualized sharing. For example, in a high school class of 30, three students a day were asked to present 3-minute oral reports on their written work. Within 2 weeks, each student in the class had presented a report and the teacher had used only 10 minutes of the 50-minute period each day.

TWO PROJECTS THAT INCORPORATE THE FOUR PRINCIPLES OF A GOOD WRITING INSTRUCTION PROGRAM

For students like Dalisay and Devon who were mentioned at the outset, research and examples from expert teachers yield specific teaching practices that will improve written expression skills in CLDE students based on the four principles of a successful writing instruction (see Figure 8.1).

The Early Literacy Project (ELP) developed by Englert and her colleagues (Englert, Garmon, Mariage, Rozendal, Tarrant, & Urba, 1995; Englert & Mariage, 2003) and the Optimal Learning Environment (OLE) developed by Ruiz (1995a, 1995b) are examples of comprehensive writing instruction programs that have incorporated all four guiding principles. Each of these projects, *first*, built a community of learners including a focus on meaningful activities, the creation of roles for family and community members, the ability to hold high expectation for all learners, and responsiveness to cultural and personal diversity. *Second*, each project required a specific allocation of time for writing each day. *Third*, each used writing-as-a-process instruction by including requirements for planning, writing, revising, editing, sharing, and publishing. *Fourth*, each provided think-aloud modeling and strategy instruction when needed.

The Early Literacy Project

In the reported research on the ELP by Englert and colleagues, about one-third of the participants were African American. The program includes some of the following elements: thematic units; unsupervised silent reading; partner reading and writing; sharing chair, which provides students with opportunities to ask questions and act as informants to peers and teachers; story discussions; author's center for writing-as-a-process projects; and morning news, which provides students with a language experience activity in which the teacher writes about students' personal experiences as the student dictates. The ELP includes an emphasis on the following five principles:

1. Using meaningful and purposeful writing activities.
2. Teaching self-regulated learning. Students ask a series of questions to learn to engage more actively in the editing and revising process.
3. Using what Englert and colleagues have called POWER: Plan, Organize, Write, Edit, and Revise. This includes using Plan-Think Sheets for each of these steps by which students engage in every aspect of writing as a process on a different colored page. For example, yellow is planning, light blue is organizing, light red is writing, orange is editing and revising, and finally a white sheet is often used for perfect final copy.

4. Incorporating responsive instruction. Students who need assistance may receive direct instruction, strategy instruction, or less explicit instruction, but students who are working successfully are encouraged and allowed to work independently.

5. Building communities of learners through collaborative learning and problem solving among students (discussed in the first half of this chapter).

The Optimal Learning Environment

The OLE program is very similar to the ELP in that it is based on creating a contextualized environment for learning with a focus on thematic units. The rationale for such a learning environment is particularly compelling for students who are Spanish speakers with learning disabilities. First, Spanish is a language that is 99 percent phonologically consistent. Therefore, students are likely not to have the difficulty with decoding that students with learning disabilities experience in English and less likely to need direct instruction in decoding. In addition, English immersion is the predominant model for Spanish speakers in the schools, hence, students who are labeled are often students who have not had Spanish language learning opportunities. If students are to be able to salvage their potential for becoming literate, native language work could provide a bridge toward learning to read and write. A meaningful and purposeful use of the language has the potential to resurrect their motivation and their appreciation for language and literacy.

The OLE program, not unlike the ELP program, includes an integration of oral, listening, speaking, reading, and writing in authentic activities, such as "Why do you think recess should be a part of the school day?" Both programs require abundant active involvement of students. The goal in OLE is for students to develop communicative competence (Ruiz, 1995a). The learning environment is designed to facilitate this development by including the following strategies:

1. Interactive journals, in which the teacher responds to students' daily entries in writing each day to provide modeling of written dialog

2. Writer's workshop, based on writing as a process in which students go through planning, drafting, editing, revising, final drafting, and publishing each time they produce a written product

3. Patterned writing and reading, in which students read and copy key phases, such as "Brown bear, brown bear what do you see? I see a red bird looking at me. Red bird, red bird what do you see? I see a yellow duck looking at me" (Carle, 1970). A Spanish example is: "¡Arañas, arañas por todas partes! Hay diez arañas en la telaraña. ¡Arañas, arañas por todas partes! Hay nueve arañas en la telaraña" (Williams, 1996)

4. Student-created text for wordless books

5. Shared reading with predictable text, literature conversation with read-alouds

6. Literature study with response journals
7. Student-made alphabet wall charts
8. Drop everything and read (D.E.A.R.) time

Both the OLE program and the ELP program are focused on student experiences and background knowledge providing much direction for the content of literacy activities, including an emphasis on authentic purposes for reading and writing. Research results indicate that the use of OLE improves the writing performance of these individuals and provides a mechanism for nonwriters and readers in English and Spanish to develop improved English and Spanish performances (Ruiz, 1995a, 1995b).

OLE Project Study of CLDE Learners. A study of Spanish-speaking youngsters with learning disabilities was conducted and provide information about the OLE project and its effects on writing outcomes (Graves et al., 2000). The study was a descriptive case-study comparison of writing instruction in four bilingual special education settings (Graves et al., 2000). Results from the study indicated significant progress for students who were taught as part of the OLE project.

In the study, the research included self-reports of teachers' instructional choices, observations of the teachers and their students, and an analysis of the compositions of the students in each setting at the beginning of a 10-week period, at the end of a 10-week period, and one year later. After 10 weeks students in each writing instruction situation demonstrated higher quality based on the Montague and Graves Writing Quality Scale (Graves & Montague, 1991). Interactive journal writing, Writer's Workshop, OLE, and a combination of journal writing, brainstorming/planning, and spelling practice all yielded improved written compositions after 10 weeks. The commonalties among classrooms were that teachers spent at least one hour per week teaching writing, were teaching students to write for real audiences, provided direct instruction on mechanics, and tried to create a community of learners in the classroom. After one year, the use of the OLE program (Case Two) produced more dramatic results than the writing instruction in the other three classrooms. OLE is a formal program with requirements for activities and time spent with students each week. Apparently, over the course of the year, the quality of the instruction that students received was higher than when a less regimented system was in place. This study affirms strong effects found in results from earlier studies (Ruiz, 1995a, 1995b; Ruiz & Figueroa, 1995). In follow-up interviews, teachers voiced concerns about whether students were ready to transition to English. Pressure for students in general education to use English in school can force teachers to make instructional decisions that they might not make otherwise. OLE provided a system by which instruction and practice in the native language could continue until the teacher thought that students were ready for the transition to English.

The ELP and OLE are two examples of the use of the four guiding principles (see Figure 8.1) for successful writing instruction. Together these principles form a set of promising teaching practices for improving the written expression of all CLDE students.

SUMMARY

Based on NCLB, school systems are assessing all learners to determine proficiency in various academic skill areas, including writing. To best facilitate the development of writing for diverse learners, communities of learners should be developed within which a variety of strategies may be implemented. These include scaffolding, parent and community involvement, learning strategies, maintaining high learning expectations, as well as being responsive to cultural and linguistic diversity. In addition, the chapter presented a process for teaching writing as a process to facilitate writing production and improve the quality of writing generated by diverse learners. The Early Literacy and the Optimal Learning Environment Projects were also presented as effective programs for teaching writing to CLDE learners.

Discussion Questions

1. What are the four guiding principles for writing instruction?
2. What are the primary writing needs of CLDE learners?
3. Why is a community of learners important for teaching writing to CLDE learners?
4. What steps should be followed when teaching a writing strategy?
5. How might the writing-as-a-process model be used to meet the needs of CLDE learners?

References

Artiles, A., Rueda, R., Salazar, J., & Higareda, I. (2002). English-language learner representation in special education in California urban school districts. In D. Losen & G. Orfield (Eds.), *Racial inequity in special education* (pp. 117–136). Cambridge, MA: Harvard Education Press.

August, D., & Hakuta, K. (Eds.). (1997). *Improving schooling for language minority children: A research agenda.* Washington, DC: National Academy Press.

Baca, L., & Cervantes, J. (2004). *The bilingual special education interface.* Boston, MA: Merrill.

Baker, S., Gersten, R., & Graham, S. (2003). Teaching expressive writing to students with learning disabilities: Research-based applications and examples. *Journal of Learning Disabilities, 36*(2), 109–123.

Barry, L. M., & Moore, W. E. (2004). Students with specific learning disabilities can pass state competency exams: Systematic strategy instruction makes a difference. *Preventing School Failure, 48*(3), 10–15.

Carle, E. (1970). *Brown bear, brown bear what do you see?* New York, NY: Henry Holt.

Carnine, D., & Silbert, J., Kameenui, E. J., & Tarver, S. G. (2004). *Direct Instruction reading* (4th ed.). Upper Saddle River, NJ: Merrill/Prentice Hall.

Carter, E. W. (2004). Preparing adolescents with high-incidence disabilities for high stakes testing with strategy instruction. *Preventing School Failure, 49*(2), 55–62.

Chalk, J. C., Hagan-Burke, S., & Burke, M. D. (2005). The effects of self-regulated strategy development on the writing process for high school students with learning disabilities. *Learning Disability Quarterly, 28*, 75–87.

Chamot, A. U., & O'Malley, J. M. (1994). *The CALLA handbook: Implementing the cognitive academic language learning approach*. Reading, MA: Addison-Wesley.

Chamot, A. U., & O'Malley, J. M. (1996). The cognitive academic language learning approach (CALLA); A model for linguistically diverse classrooms. *Elementary School Journal, 96*, 259–274.

Chang, J. M. (2004). *Family literacy nights: Building the circle of supporters within and beyond school for middle school English language learner* (Educational Practice Report No. 11). Santa Cruz, CA and Washington, DC: Center for Research on Education, Diversity & Excellence.

Cummins, J. (1992). Bilingual education and English immersion: The Ramirez report in theoretical perspective. *Bilingual Research Journal, 16*, 91–104.

Danoff, B., Harris, K. R., & Graham, S. (1993). Incorporating strategy instruction with the writing process in the regular classroom: Effects on the writing of students with and without learning disabilities. *Journal of Reading Behavior, 25*, 295–322.

De La Paz, S. (1999). Self-regulated strategy instruction in regular education settings: Improving outcomes for students with and without learning disabilities. *Learning Disabilities Research & Practice, 14*(2), 92–106.

De La Paz, S. (2001). Teaching writing to students with attention deficit disorders and specific language impairment. *The Journal of Educational Research, 95*(1), 37–47.

De La Paz, S., & Graham, S. (2002). Explicitly teaching strategies, skills, and knowledge: Writing instruction in middle school classrooms. *Journal of Education Psychology, 94*, 291–304.

Deno, S. L. (1985). Curriculum-based measurement: The emerging alternative. *Exceptional Children, 52*, 219–232.

Deshler, D., & Schumaker, J. (1994). Strategy mastery by at-risk students: Not a simple matter. *The Elementary School Journal, 94*, 153–167.

Echevarria, J., & Graves, A. (2007). *Sheltered content instruction: Teaching students with diverse needs* (3rd ed.). Los Angeles, CA: Allyn & Bacon.

Ellis, E. S., & Graves, A. (1990). Teaching rural students with learning disabilities a paraphrasing strategy to increase comprehension of main ideas. *Rural Special Education Quarterly, 10*(2), 2–10.

Englert, C. S., Garmon, A., Mariage, T., Rozendal, M., Tarrant, K., & Urba, J. (1995). The early literacy project: Connecting across the literacy curriculum. *Learning Disability Quarterly, 18*, 253–277.

Englert, C. S., & Mariage, T. V. (1992). Shared understandings: Structuring the writing experience through dialogue. In D. Carnine & E. Kameenui (Eds.), *Higher order thinking* (pp. 107–136). Austin, TX: Pro-Ed.

Espin, C. A., De La Paz, S., Scierka, B. J., & Roelofs, L. (2005). The relationship between curriculum-based measures in written expression and quality and completeness of expository writing for middle school students. *The Journal of Special Education, 38*, 208–217.

Faltis, C. J., & Hudelson, S. (1994). Learning English as an additional language in K–12 schools. *TESOL Quarterly, 28*(3), 457–468.

Fitzgerald, J. (2003). New directions in multilingual literacy research: Multilingual reading theory. *Reading Research Quarterly, 38*, 118–122.

Fitzgerald, J., & Graves, M. F. (2004). *Scaffolding reading experiences for English-language learners*. Norwood, MA: Christopher-Gordon.

Franklin, E., & Thompson, J. (1994). Describing students' collected works: Understanding American Indian children. *TESOL Quarterly, 28*(3), 489–506.

García, E. (1993). Project THEME: Collaboration for school improvement at the middle school for language minority students. *Proceedings of the Third National Research Symposium on Limited English Proficient Issues: Focus on Middle and High School Issues* (pp. 323–350). Washington, DC: U.S. Department of Education, Office of Bilingual Education and Minority Language Affairs.

Gay, G. (2000). *Culturally responsive teaching: Theory, research, & practice*. New York: Teacher's College Press.

Genesee, F., Lindholm-Leary, K., Saunders, W., & Christian, D. (2005). English language learners in U.S. schools: An overview of research findings. *Journal of Education for Students Placed At Risk, 10*(4), 363–385.

Gersten, R., Baker, S., Haager, D., & Graves, A. W. (2005). Exploring the role of teacher quality in predicting reading outcomes for first grade English learners: An observational study. *Remedial & Special Education, 26*(4), 190–200.

Gersten, R. M., Taylor, R., & Graves, A. W. (1999). Direct instruction and diversity. In R. Stevens (Ed.), *Teaching* in American schools: A tribute to Barak Rosenshine. Upper Saddle River, NJ: Merrill/Prentice Hall.

Goldenberg, C., Gallimore, R., Reese, L., & Garnier, H. (2001). Cause or effect? A longitudinal study of immigrant Latino parents' aspirations and expectation, and their children's school performance. *American Educational Research Journal, 38,* 547–582.

Gonzalez, N., Moll, L. C., Floyd-Tenery, M., Rivera, A., Rendon, P., Gonzales, R., & Amonti, C. (1993). *Teacher research on funds of knowledge: Learning from households* (Educational Practice Report: 6). Santa Cruz, CA: National Center for Research on Cultural Diversity and Second Language Learning.

Graham S., & Harris, K. (1989). Improving learning disabled students' skills at composing essays: Self-instructional strategy training. *Exceptional Children, 56,* 201–214.

Graham S., & Harris, K. (2005). Self-regulated strategy development: Helping students with learning problems develop as writers. *Elementary School Journal, 105,* 169–181.

Graves, A., & Montague, M. (1991). Using story grammar cueing to improve the writing of student with learning disabilities. *Learning Disabilities Research and Practice, 6,* 246–251.

Graves, A., Montague, M., & Wong, Y. (1990). The effects of procedural facilitation on story composition of learning disabled students. *Learning Disabilities Research, 5*(4), 88–93.

Graves, A., Valles, E., & Rueda, R. (2000). Variations in interactive writing instruction: A study of four bilingual special education settings. *Learning Disabilities Research and Practice, 15,* 1–10.

Graves, A. W. (1986). The effects of direct instruction and metacomprehension training on finding main ideas. *Learning Disabilities Research, 1*(2), 90–100.

Graves, A. W. (1998). Instructional strategies and techniques for students who are learning English. In R. Gersten & R. Jiménez (Eds.), *Promoting learning for culturally and linguistically diverse students: Classroom applications from contemporary research.* Belmont, CA: Wadsworth.

Graves, A. W., Gersten, R., & Haager, D. (2004). Literacy instruction in multiple-language first-grade classrooms: Linking student outcomes to observed instructional practice. *Learning Disabilities Research & Practice, 19*(4), 262–272.

Graves, A. W., & Levin, J. R. (1989). Comparison of monitoring and mnemonic text-processing strategies in learning disabled students. *Learning Disability Quarterly, 12,* 232–236.

Graves, A. W., Plasencia-Peinado, J., Deno, S., & Johnson, J. (2005). Formatively evaluating the reading progress of first-grade English learners in multiple language classrooms. *Remedial & Special Education, 26*(4), 215–225.

Graves, D. (1983). *Writing: Teachers and children at work.* Portsmouth, NH: Heinemann.

Graves, M. F., & Liang, L. A. (2005). On-line resources for fostering understanding and higher-level thinking in senior high school students. *Fifty-first National Reading Conference Yearbook.* Chicago: National Reading Conference.

Guthrie, J. T., & Wigfield, A. (2000). Engagement and motivation in reading. In M. Kimil, P. Mosenthal, P. D. Person, & R. Barr (Eds.), *Handbook of reading research* (Vol. 3, pp. 403–422). Mahway, NJ: Lawrence Erlbaum.

Haager, D., & Klinger, J. K. (2005). *Differentiating instruction in inclusive classrooms: The special educator's guide.* Boston, MA: Pearson.

Hallenbeck, M. J. (2002). Taking charge: Adolescents with learning disabilities assume responsibility for their own writing. *Learning Disabilities Quarterly, 25,* 227–246.

Harris, K., & Graham, S. (1996). *Making the writing process work: Strategies for composition and self-regulation* (2nd ed.). Cambridge, MA: Brookline Books.

Harry, B. (1996). These families, those families: The impact of researcher identities on the research act. *Exceptional Children, 62,* 292–300.

Harry, B., & Klingner, J. (2006). *Why are so many minority students in special education? Understanding race and disability in schools.* New York: Teachers College Press.

Henze, R. C., & Lucas, T. (1993). Shaping instruction to promote the success of language minority students: An analysis of four high school classes. *Peabody Journal of Education: Trends in Bilingual Education at the Secondary Level, 69*(1), 54–81.

Hildebrand, V., Phenice, L. A., Gray, M. M., & Hines, R. P. (2000). *Knowing and serving diverse families* (2nd ed.).Upper Saddle River, NJ: Merrill/Prentice Hall.

Jiménez, R. T. (2003). Literacy and Latino students in the United States: Some considerations, questions, and new directions. *Reading Research Quarterly, 38*, 122–128.

Jiménez, R. T., García, G. E., & Pearson, E. P. (1996). The reading strategies of bilingual Latina/o students who are successful English readers: Opportunities and obstacles. *Reading Research Quarterly, 31*, 90–112.

Krashen, S. D. (1985). *The input hypothesis: Issues and implications.* New York: Longman.

Lewis, A. C. (2003). Holes in NCLB. *The Education Digest, 68*(6), 68–69.

Lewis, R. B., Graves, A., Ashton, T., & Kieley, C. (1997). Text entry strategies for improving writing fluency of students with learning disabilities. *Learning Disabilities Research and Practice, 13*, 95–108.

MacArthur, C., Schwartz, S., & Graham, S. (1991). Effects of a reciprocal peer revision strategy in special education classrooms. *Learning Disability Research and Practice, 6*, 201–210.

McLesky, J., Henry, D., & Axelrod, M. I. (1999). Inclusion of students with learning disabilities: An examination of data from reports to Congress. *Exceptional Children, 66*, 55–66.

Moll, L. C. (1988). Some key issues in teaching Latino students. *Language Arts, 65*, 465–472.

Montague, M., Graves, A., & Leavell, A. (1991). Planning, procedural facilitation, and narrative compositions of junior high school students with learning disabilities. *Learning Disabilities Research and Practice, 6*, 219–224.

Obi, S. O., Obiakor, F. E., & Algozzine, B. (1999). *Empowering culturally diverse exceptional learners in the 21st century: Imperatives for U.S. educators* (Report No. EC307730). Washington, DC: National Institute of Education. (ERIC Document Reproduction Service No. ED439551).

Ortiz, A., & Graves, A. W. (2001). English language learners with literacy-related learning disabilities. *International Dyslexia Association Commemorative Booklet Series, 52*, 31–36.

Peyton, J. K., Jones, C., Vincent, A., & Greenblatt, L. (1994). Implementing writing workshop with ESOL students: Visions and realities. *TESOL Quarterly, 28*(3), 469–488.

Rapp, W. H. (1997). Success with a student with limited English proficiency: One teacher's experience.

Multiple Voices for Ethnically Diverse Exceptional Learners, 2, 21–37.

Ruiz, N. T. (1995a). The social construction of ability and disability I: Profile types of Latino children identified as language learning disabled. *Journal of Learning Disabilities, 28*, 476–490.

Ruiz, N. T. (1995b). The social construction of ability and disability II: Optimal and at-risk lessons in a bilingual special education classroom. *Journal of Learning Disabilities, 28*, 491–502.

Ruiz, N. T., & Figueroa, R. A. (1995). Learning-handicapped classrooms with Latino students: The optimal learning environment (OLE) project. *Education and Urban Society, 27*, 463–483.

Scanlon, D., Deshler, D. D., & Schumaker, J. B. (1996). Can a strategy be taught and learned in secondary inclusive classrooms? *Learning Disabilities Research and Practice, 11*(1), 41–57.

Sexton, M., Harris, K. R., & Graham, S. (1998). Self-regulated strategy development and the writing process: Effects on essay writing and attributions. *Exceptional Children, 64*, 295–311.

Troia, G. A., & Graham, S. (2002). The effectiveness of a highly explicit, teacher-directed strategy instruction routine: Changing the writing performance of students with learning disabilities. *Journal of Learning Disabilities, 35*, 290–305.

Trueba, H. T., Jacobs, L., & Kirton, E. (1990). *Cultural conflict and adaptation: The case of Hmong children in American society.* London: Falmer Press.

Vaughn, S., Gersten, R., & Chard, D. (2000). The underlying message in LD intervention research: Findings from research syntheses. *Exceptional Children, 67*, 99–114.

Waldschmidt, E. D., Kim, Y. M., Kim, J., Martinez, C., & Hale, A. (1999). *Teacher stories: Bilingual playwriting and puppetry with English language learners and students with special needs* (Report No. FL026293). Montreal, Quebec, Canada: ERIC Clearinghouse on Languages and Linguistics. (ERIC Document Reproduction Service No. ED442288).

Walker de Felix, J., Waxman, H., Paige, S., & Huang, S. Y. (1993). A comparison of classroom instruction in bilingual and monolingual secondary school classrooms. *Peabody Journal of Education: Trends in Bilingual Education at the Secondary School Level, 69*(1), 102–116.

Williams, R. L. (1996). *Aranas, aranas por todas partes!* Cypress, CA: Creative Teaching Press.

Wong, B. Y. L., Butler, D. L., Ficzere, S., & Kuperis, S. (1996). Teaching low achievers and students with learning disabilities to plan, write, and revise opinion essays. *Journal of Learning Disabilities, 29*, 197–212.

Woolfolk, A. (2006). *Educational psychology* (10th ed.). Boston: Allyn & Bacon.

Yang, N. D. (1999). The relationship between English as a foreign language learners' beliefs and learning strategy use. *System 27*, 515–535. Available online: <www.elsevier.com/locate/system>.

Chapter 9

Supporting Learning in the Content Areas

With a Contribution by Shanan Fitts

Chapter Objectives

Upon completion of this chapter the reader will be able to:

1. Describe various ways to increase students' participation in content area learning.
2. Explain inquiry-based and activity-oriented learning approaches.
3. Briefly summarize collaborative approaches, such as cooperative learning and peer or cross-age tutoring.
4. Describe different methods of reading comprehension strategy instruction for the content areas (e.g., Collaborative Strategic Reading, Cognitive Academic Language Learning Approach).
5. Tell different ways of helping students learn new vocabulary.
6. Explain different adaptations and modifications that facilitate learning for CLDE students.

VIGNETTE

Lucille Sullivan was a superb fifth-grade teacher who managed her class of bilingual students and English language learners with kindness and a firm hand. She never was heard to raise her voice. Mutual respect was paramount in her classroom; teacher and students alike seemed to share a calm sense of purpose. It was in this classroom environment she implemented Collaborative Strategic Reading (CSR) with her students on a regular basis. There were 37 students in her class, all but 2 of whom spoke Spanish as their first language or learned both Spanish and English in their homes. The class included 16 students who were English language learners (i.e., were not yet considered proficient in English), 2 students with learning disabilities, 5 high-achieving students, 6 average-achieving students, and 8 low-achieving students. Ms. Sullivan did not speak Spanish.

Students used CSR two or three times a week while reading their science textbooks, for 30 to 40 minutes a day, working together in cooperating learning groups. Each group included at least two high-achieving or average-achieving students who were proficient in Spanish and English and at least two ELL students. Students read their textbooks in English, but translated vocabulary and key concepts into Spanish for their ELL peers. Discussions about text content took place in English and Spanish. Students had been learning how to implement CSR for several weeks and had become quite proficient at it; ELL students had received reinforcement in Spanish in how to use CSR in their pull-out home language classes. Let's listen in while three different groups help each other understand what "wrinkle" means while using CSR's "click and clunk" strategy. Group 1 also gets the gist (i.e., figures out the main idea, another CSR strategy).[1]

Group 1

Mario: *Que cosa quiere decir* wrinkle? (What does wrinkle mean?)

Maribel: *Es lo que cubre el cerebrum.* (It is what covers the brain.)

Gloria: *No, es cuando tu tienes que planchar y tiene arrugas. Son arrugas.* (It is when you have to iron and it has wrinkles. They are wrinkles.)

Frank: OK, can someone get the gist? Gloria?

Gloria: It is talking about the cerebrum and its surface is like wrinkled and folded . . .

---

[1] *Elsewhere we share many different CSR excerpts (Klingner & Vaughn, 2000). These examples are shared here for the first time.*

Group 2

Roland: Wrinkles?

Tasha: Wrinkles *son como tu abuela siempre esta arrugada.* (Wrinkles are like how your grandmother always is wrinkled.)

Group 6

Susana: Did everyone understand what we read?

Maria: Does anybody know what wrinkle is?

Ruben: It's like folding something.

Denis: Reread the sentence with the clunk before or after the clunk looking for clues.

Ruben: It's like a paper that you are going to throw away and it is all wrinkled. It is like a paper that you fold it and it is all wrinkled up.

In the next two examples, students get the gist (i.e., figure out the main idea of what they have just read):

Group 3

Marcos: What is the most important idea we have learned about the topic so far? José?

José: That when drugs are abused, drugs can be dangerous and very harmful.

Sylvia: That when drugs are taken as directed they can help.

José: But, drugs can also be misused or used improperly.

Group 1

Paul: Who would like to get the gist?

Luis: I think it is talking about how the bones connect together and how they couldn't slide off. How they could be twisted and not slide off.

Paul: OK, does anybody want to add more to that? Does anybody have another opinion? *Que es tu opinion? Si quieren agregar algo a lo que el digo? Que es la idea principal de este pedacito de lo que leemos?*

Luis: *Bueno, la idea principal de lo que leemos es de los cartilagos, de los huesos y como se unen.* (OK, the main idea of what we read is about the cartilage, about the bones and how they join.)

Paul: *Muy bien.* Frank?

Frank: *Yo creo que la idea principal es como los huesos se unen, como ellos se envuelven uno a otros. Como el* joint *ayuda a los huesos moverse.* (I think the main idea is how the bones join, how they are involved with each other. How the joint helps the bones move.)

Finally, in these last two examples, students generate and answer questions after they have finished reading the day's passage:

Group 5

Pablo: My question is, "How can drugs be harmful to you?"

Albert: OK, Jessica, can you answer that?

Jessica: It can harm you by taking it wrong.

Julia: OK, which means it is by taking a medicine wrong or improper.

Pablo: OK, that's it exactly.

Group 4

Carolina: What does the spinal chord do?

Juan: The spinal chord? The spinal chord is a thick chord on a nerve in the middle of the back bone.

Carolina: I'm sorry, but you didn't answer the question.

Juan: The spinal chord carries messages to and from the brain.

Carolina: OK, now that's more like it.

These examples illustrate the high level of involvement typical of all groups. Students appeared to take seriously their responsibility to help one another while working together in cooperative learning groups. They had internalized CSR's comprehension strategies and applied them skillfully while learning content. The examples also indicate the unstilted quality of students' discussions. Although students were engaged in teacher-like behaviors, they also used language that was clearly their own.

Reflective Questions

1. Why would CSR, or other approaches like it, be useful and appropriate for helping CLDE students learn in content area classes?
2. What are important considerations when planning content area instruction for CLDE students?

INTRODUCTION

Students with learning disabilities and other high-incidence disabilities who are also English language learners face numerous challenges. They must not only struggle to overcome their disability, but typically are taught in a language that is not their first language and in which they lack full proficiency. To complicate matters, content area textbooks are not written with English language learners in mind (Richard-Amato & Snow, 1992; Peregoy & Boyle, 1997). The vocabulary and text structure can be confusing, and textbook authors often assume background knowledge that is not shared by students from culturally and linguistically diverse backgrounds.

The best programs for English language learners with disabilities incorporate supportive, culturally responsive learning environments as well as validated instructional practices (Ortiz, 1997, 2001). Optimal programs include native language instruction and a focus on English language development in addition to research-based practices in the content areas. It is this heightened focus on *language* that makes bilingual/ESL special education different than generic special education. Each of the approaches we describe in this chapter support students' language development as well as their content learning. First we discuss the importance of background knowledge, and then we explain ways to increase students' participation in content classrooms. In subsequent sections of the chapter we describe inquiry-based and activities-oriented instruction, collaborative grouping structures, comprehension strategies, content vocabulary instruction, and adaptations and modifications.

The Role of Background Knowledge

All students benefit from help retrieving background knowledge as they learn a new topic, but this is especially true for English language learners. When students can make connections between what they already know and what they will be learning, they are more likely to understand and remember the new information. In some cases students may lack sufficient prior knowledge about a topic in the curriculum, and then it is the teacher's role to help students develop this knowledge. In other words, the teacher should help students access what they already know, develop new knowledge, and build bridges between the two. Moll (1990) suggests bringing in experts from the local community to help connect students' home and school cultures and reinforce the value of what students already know and can do.

Similarly, in discussing science learning, Lee and Luykx (2006) note, "*Equitable learning opportunities* occur when school science values and respects the experiences culturally and linguistically diverse students bring from their home and community environments, (and) articulates their linguistic and cultural knowledge with science disciplines" (p. 4, italics added). When they are provided with opportunities to apply their prior knowledge, CLD students can capitalize on their linguistic and cultural experiences as intellectual resources for learning science.

Echevarria and Graves (2003) recommend several approaches for enhancing students' background knowledge:

- Ask students to brainstorm about their own relevant experiences before beginning a unit or lesson. Have all students jot down a few ideas to share with their classmates as part of this process. This gives them time to reflect and form their thoughts, increasing the likelihood that students will contribute to a class discussion.

- Provide students with opportunities to expand their experiential knowledge base through videos, Websites, live demonstrations, supplemental books, direct experiences through hands-on learning, other multimedia presentations, and guest speakers.
- Take students on field trips. This is a great way to provide students with shared experiences that can provide the foundation for extension activities in the classroom (e.g., a trip to a farm before beginning a unit about farm animals).
- Supplement instruction with pictures, real objects, and other visual aids.

INCREASING PARTICIPATION

Although little research has been conducted with CLD students with and without disabilities on ways to increase their participation in content area classes, related research indicates that this is a promising area. Traditional approaches to whole-class instruction generally do not effectively involve all students. When asking questions, most teachers tend to call on high-achieving students most likely to know the correct answers (Maheady, Mallete, Harper, & Saca, 1991). Whether it is because they feel pressure to cover content, try to maintain a fast pace in the classroom to limit discipline problems, or for some other reason, teachers generally do not adequately check for understanding by all of their students. Three errors teachers typically make during whole-class lessons are (a) asking a general question such as "Does everyone understand?" and then assuming that everyone does when no one raises a hand; (b) calling only on volunteers, who typically know the correct answers to questions, and then assuming everyone else knows the answers as well; and (c) asking only a few questions before continuing (Rosenshine & Stevens, 1986).

Yet there are many more effective and efficient ways to involve all students in learning. These include response cards, increased wait time, Think-Pair-Share (and other share-with-a-partner methods), Numbered Heads Together (and other cooperative learning techniques, described later in this chapter), choral responses, and hands-on or activities-oriented instruction (described in the next section).

Response Cards

Response cards are not necessarily "cards," though they can be. They are anything that students hold up simultaneously in response to questions posed by the teacher or another student (Cavanaugh, Heward, & Donelson, 1996; Heward et al., 1996). They might be index cards, signs, small dry-erase boards or chalkboards, or other items. The use of response cards can appreciably increase student participation (Heward, 1994). They offer several advantages to traditional forms of eliciting student feedback in that they (a) provide teachers with the means to immediately assess students' understanding, (b) give students visual cues that reinforce learning and serve as prompts that can help them formulate a response, and (c) enable students to learn accurate responses by observing others. Response cards are quite adaptable and can be used with any curriculum area or type of content. There are several types (Heward et al., 1996).

1. *Preprinted response cards.* Students select and hold up a card from their own individual set in response to a question. These can be generic, such as yes/no and true/false cards, or related to a specific topic in the curriculum, such as science terms, the names of the planets, or the names of historical figures.

2. *Preprinted "pinch" response cards.* Each student has a single card with different answers listed. In response to a question, the student holds up the card with the thumb and forefinger pinching the portion of the card that displays his or her answer (e.g., math operations).

3. *Preprinted response cards with built-in moveable pointers.* Students move the pointer so that it points to an answer (e.g., a clock with moveable hands, a wheel and a pointer for displaying the names of the seasons).

4. *Write-on response cards.* Students mark or write on blank index cards, small chalkboards, or individual dry-erase boards (e.g., key vocabulary terms).

5. *Hand signals.* Rather than holding up response cards, students can signal "thumbs up" or "thumbs down" for yes/no, true/false, and other dichotomous questions. Or they can hold up one, two, or three fingers to indicate their choice of responses to multiple-choice questions.

Heward and colleagues (1996) offered several useful suggestions for using response cards. They recommended providing clear signals to let students know when they are to hold up and put down their cards (e.g., "Cards up" and "Cards down"). Then they suggested that teachers vary their responses depending on how many students answer questions correctly. When all students are correct, the teacher can provide quick, positive feedback and move on to the next question. If only a few students answer incorrectly, the teacher should state the correct answer (e.g., "Yes, copper is a pure element") and move to the next question. When more than a few students answer incorrectly, the teacher should provide the correct response and then repeat the same question later.

Wait Time

"Wait time" refers to the practice of allowing students more time to frame their responses to questions before calling on anyone to answer. Typically 3 to 5 seconds is sufficient. This simple but effective technique increases participation and improves learning outcomes, especially for English language learners and students with learning disabilities who benefit from the additional time to form their ideas before responding (Brice & Roseberry-McKibben, 1999; Echevarria & Graves, 2003; Tobin, 1987; Watson, Northcutt, & Rydele, 1989). In a review of wait time research, Tobin (1987) found that increasing wait time improved achievement in all content areas with all levels of students, from kindergarten through 12th grade. Students tended to respond with longer answers, volunteer answers more often, and ask more questions.

Think-Pair-Share

Think-Pair-Share is an easy-to-implement, effective technique that provides students with wait time as well as the opportunity to discuss their ideas with peers (Lyman, 1981; McTighe & Lyman, 1988). The teacher poses a question and then provides students with time to think about their responses ("think"). Then the teacher directs students to discuss their ideas with a partner ("pair"). Finally, the teacher asks selected students to share their responses with the larger group or class ("share"). A worthwhile adaptation is to have students jot down their ideas in learning logs during the "think" period. This prevents students from sitting idly, provides notes the students can refer to when sharing their ideas, and offers a tangible record of learning.

Choral Responses

Choral responses are when a pair of students or a small group responds in unison. For example, the teacher might ask a group of students to read a portion of the social studies textbook aloud rather than asking for volunteers or for just one student to read. This practice can reduce students' anxiety and enhance their involvement in class activities. It is a way to scaffold or support the participation of students who might not be confident enough to contribute on their own. This approach has been recommended for English language learners (Tam & Scott, 1996) as well as students with disabilities (Courson & Heward, 1988; Kamps, Dugan, & Leonard, 1994).

INQUIRY-BASED AND ACTIVITIES-ORIENTED INSTRUCTION

Inquiry-based and activities-oriented science and mathematics instruction facilitate active engagement and promote learning among students with LD (Mastropieri, Scruggs, & Magnusen, 1999), English language learners (Lee, 2002; Lee & Fradd, 1996), and linguistically diverse students with disabilities (Echevarria & Graves, 2003). "Science education professionals generally agree that hands-on, inquiry-based science potentially benefits all students, yet there are few specific guidelines for helping students with LD achieve success in general education science classrooms" (Dalton, Morocco, Tivnan, & Mead, 1997, p. 670). Dalton et al. suggest the following guidelines for supporting students' inquiry-based learning:

1. Provide a safe environment for expressing different viewpoints.
2. Design curricula and instruction using thematic teaching and integrative instruction to help students develop a deeper understanding of concepts than is possible when knowledge is accumulated in bits and pieces (this is especially important for CLD students and students with LD).
3. Provide students with opportunities to examine conflicting evidence through hands-on learning experiences.

4. Use teaching/coaching and instructional conversations to help students revise and elaborate their understandings.

5. Integrate opportunities for students to work with new material in collaboration with their peers.

6. Use multiple modalities to help students explore and examine science concepts and engage in science processes.

7. Assess students' learning at key points during the instructional cycle to inform the instructional decision-making process; include hands-on performance tasks as well as questions that students can respond to by drawing or writing.

COLLABORATIVE GROUPING

Cooperative Learning

Cooperative learning can be a powerful technique to use in diverse classrooms that include English language learners with learning disabilities and other special needs (Klingner & Vaughn, 2000). It has been found to be effective with students with learning disabilities (McMaster & Fuchs, 2002; Putnam, 1993), English language learners (Kagan & High, 2002; Richard-Amato, 2003), and culturally diverse populations (Cohen, Lotan, Scarloss, & Arellano, 1999). In a cooperative setting, all participants benefit from diversity; it is the differences among members—differences in their talents, skills, perceptions, and thoughts—that make a cooperative group powerful (Johnson & Johnson, 1993). ELLs with and without disabilities can benefit from native language support from their peers (Klingner & Vaughn, 1996, 2000).

Cooperative learning is the instructional use of small groups so that students work together to maximize their own and each other's learning. Unlike with individualistic approaches, students work together to accomplish shared goals and learn collaborative skills at the same time they are mastering content material (Johnson & Johnson, 1989). Later in this chapter we describe an instructional approach that includes cooperative learning as a core element, CSR (Klingner et al., 2001). But first we talk about the benefits of cooperative learning, elements of cooperative learning, and some of the challenges that can occur when implementing cooperative learning in diverse classrooms.

Benefits of Cooperative Learning. Numerous academic and social benefits are associated with cooperative learning:

1. Students at low, average, and high achievement levels benefit academically (Johnson & Johnson, 1993). Klingner, Vaughn, and Schumm (1998) found that it was the high-achieving students in heterogeneous, inclusive classrooms who showed the greatest gains when using cooperative learning.

2. English language learners are more likely to receive comprehensible input because their peers can adjust their language output to make sure they are understood (Kagan & High, 2002).

3. Students encourage and support each other's language use and tend to be more motivated than with other structures (Kagan & High, 2002).

4. English language learners have more opportunities to contribute to discussions than when using whole-class formats, providing valuable practice (Kagan & High, 2002).

5. Students tend to be better adjusted psychologically and have more positive self-concepts when they are part of a cooperative classroom structure (Johnson & Johnson, 1993).

6. Students are less likely to stereotype students from other ethnic backgrounds or with disabilities and seem to accept differences more readily when they are members of the same cooperative team (Johnson & Johnson, 1993).

Elements of Cooperative Learning. Cooperative learning is much more than simply asking a group of students to work together on a project. Cooperative learning group activities are most effective when they are planned, well-organized, and well-structured, with a clear purpose and well-defined responsibilities (Gillies & Ashman, 2000; Klingner & Vaughn, 2000). Johnson and Johnson (1989) describe the following five basic requisites for cooperative learning:

1. *Positive interdependence.* Students believe that their work benefits others in the group and that others' work benefits them. Everyone is responsible for helping everyone else learn.

2. *Face-to-face, promotive interaction among students.* Group members encourage, support, help, and assist each other's efforts to learn. They learn to explain their reasoning to each other.

3. *Individual accountability.* Student performance is assessed regularly, both individually and as a group. Frequent assessments help group members know who may need more assistance and promote motivation.

4. *Social skills.* Cooperative learning groups are most productive when members are skilled in how to work together and support one another. These skills, including leadership, decision making, trust building, communication, and conflict resolution, should be taught.

5. *Evaluation.* At the end of a session, students assess their group's functioning by answering two questions:
   a) What is something each member did that was helpful for the group?
   b) What is something each member could do to make the group even better tomorrow?

Students should each have a role that is important to the functioning of the group. These roles can rotate on a daily basis, or less often. Possible roles include:

Leader: Guides the group in the implementation of the assignment.

Reporter: Reports the main ideas discussed during a group session to the whole class.

Reader: Reads a passage aloud to the group.

Encourager: Encourages all group members to participate, to share their ideas, and to seek others' ideas.

Clarifier: Makes sure that everyone in the group understands, and paraphrases or restates as necessary.

Challenger: Stirs up thinking by offering a different point of view.

Time keeper: Keeps track of time; informs the group when time is nearly up.

Runner: The only group member allowed to request assistance from the teacher or communicate with other groups.

Potential Problems with Cooperative Learning and Possible Solutions. Three of the most common challenges associated with cooperative learning are (a) the fears and anxieties of students who may be lower achieving, shy, in special education, and/or English language learners; (b) higher achieving students' concerns that their grades will be negatively affected; and (c) passive uninvolvement by students. Suggestions for dealing with these difficulties follow (adapted from Haager & Klingner, 2005).

When some students are fearful and anxious about participating in a cooperative learning group, the following steps may help alleviate their anxiety:

1. Clearly explain the procedures groups will follow, and check for understanding. Provide tape-recorded and/or written versions of directions to which students can refer.

2. Assign structured roles to students, with clear expectations, so that they understand their responsibilities. Cooperative learning roles are designed to provide "something for everyone" (e.g., even if a student cannot read the assigned text, he or she can listen carefully and summarize what the group is saying, provide leadership, or help keep the group on task).

3. Coach students in the behaviors and social skills needed during cooperative group work. Pre-training in social skills and monitoring how well students are implementing the skills can increase their confidence.

4. Pre-teach a few students the academic skills needed to complete the group's work. Try to give students a source of expertise that the group will need (e.g., a few key vocabulary words).

When higher achieving students are anxious that other students will lower the overall performance of their group, these procedures might alleviate their concerns:

1. Coach higher achieving students in helping, tutoring, teaching, and sharing skills. Many teaching skills can easily be taught to students (e.g., the use of praise and prompting).

2. Make sure that the academic requirements for students are reasonable. Ways in which lessons can be adapted so that students at different achievement levels, students with disabilities, and English language learners can participate in the

same cooperative groups are to (a) use different criteria for success for each member; (b) vary the amount each group member is expected to master; (c) give group members different assignments, (e.g., lists of spelling words, or math problems), and then use the average percentage worked correctly as the group's score; (d) let students demonstrate what they have learned in different ways (e.g., an English language learner might draw a diagram rather than write an essay); and (e) use improvement scores rather than total correct scores.

3. Emphasize that everyone is different, and that the group's success depends on utilizing the unique abilities and viewpoints of everyone in the group. Prior to initiating group work, teachers should explicitly state and convey their conviction that, "No one will be good at everything; everyone is good at something."

When some students are not paying attention to the group's work and are rarely participating, the teacher may wish to:

1. Teach other group members strategies for actively involving the student.

2. Find out why the student is unengaged; do not assume that the student is uninterested. The student may be having difficulty understanding or may not get along with one or more other students in the group. Once you have a better understanding of the reason for the student's lack of participation, take steps to alleviate whatever problems there may be (e.g., for an English language learner who might not understand, make sure a bilingual classmate is in the group who can provide support).

3. Find out what motivates the student and choose activities that match the students' interests.

4. Select activities that draw on different students' abilities and match task requirements to students' competencies.

5. Assign a role to the passive, uninvolved student that is essential to the group's success (such as "Leader").

6. Implement a system such as "talking chips" to encourage participation (or to inhibit domination by other students) (Kagan & High, 2002). Each student in the group is provided with the same amount of chips. When a student contributes to the group's discussion, he or she spends a chip. Each group member is expected to spend all of his or her chips (but not more). Chips can be redistributed once they have all been spent.

7. Use a "Jigsaw" approach (Slavin, 1988). This method is useful for learning new material. In their heterogeneous small groups, each student selects or is assigned a different topic to be studied. Students then regroup, forming "expert groups" of students all studying the same topic. After a designated period of time, students return to their original groups in order to teach group members about their topics.

8. Try "Numbered Heads Together" (Kagan & High, 2002). This technique is used for review and for checking understanding. Each student in a group is assigned a number. The teacher asks a question and students then consult in their groups to make sure everyone knows the answer (i.e., putting "their heads together"). The teacher then rolls a die and calls out the number that appears. The student in the group with that number then answers the question on behalf of his or her group.

9. Implement "Send-A-Problem" (Kagan, 1990). This is another approach that involves everyone in a group and is useful for review and checking for comprehension. Each student writes a review problem on a flashcard and asks group members to solve it. Review questions are then passed to another group.

Peer and Cross–Age Tutoring

Peer tutoring is another useful collaborative technique for culturally and linguistically diverse classrooms that include students with disabilities. Tutoring provides academic, social, and linguistic benefits and helps tutors as well as tutees (Cook, Scruggs, Mastropieri, & Casto, 1986; Goodlad & Hirst, 1989; Jenkins & Jenkins, 1987). Same-age classmates, older students, and community volunteers can all serve as tutors. For a specific application of peer tutoring the reader is referred to Chapter 7, specifically the section discussing classwide peer tutoring (CWPT).

Tutoring has been implemented effectively in classrooms with CLD students with disabilities (Harper, Maheady, Mallette, & Karnes, 1999), students with learning disabilities (Cook et al., 1986; Fuchs, Fuchs, Hamlett, & Appleton, 2002; Fuchs, Fuchs, Mathes, & Simmons, 1997; Mastropieri et al., 2001; Scruggs & Richter, 1988; Woodward, Monroe, & Baxter, 2001), students with mental retardation (Mastropieri et al., 2001; Mortweet et al., 1999), and students with behavior disorders (Coleman & Vaughn, 2000). Students with disabilities and English language learners can successfully serve as tutors as well as tutees (Klingner & Vaughn, 1996; Scruggs & Richter, 1988; Vaughn, Gersten, & Chard, 2000).

Perhaps the potential of tutoring is most powerful when older students with disabilities assist younger students, as in Klingner and Vaughn (1996). Eighth-grade English language learners with learning disabilities tutored younger English language learners with disabilities, teaching them how to use comprehension strategies while reading content area texts. Students very much valued being in a helping role, some "for the first time ever" in school. Cross-age tutoring when implemented in this way becomes a "source of power for the powerless" (Malamuth, Turcotte, & Fitz-Gibbon, 1981, p. 118). Because tutors feel needed by the students they are helping, they gain a sense of purpose and meaningful participation they may otherwise lack. Students who previously seemed unmotivated and uncooperative have developed more positive self-concepts and improved attitudes toward school when placed in responsible roles (Allen, 1976; Goodlad & Hirst, 1989). In a study in which truant junior high students with LD tutored younger students with LD, tutors' truant behaviors decreased and they demonstrated significant gains on a measure of locus of control (i.e., an individual's ability to understand the relationship between his or her own behavior and the outcome of events) (Lazerson, Foster, Brown, & Hummel, 1988).

As with cooperative learning, it is important to teach students the skills they need to work together successfully. Tutors can be taught how to establish rapport, ways to provide support, and how to praise and encourage their tutees. Tutees should be taught how to ask questions or ask for clarification, or convey when they do not understand.

COMPREHENSION STRATEGIES FOR CONTENT AREA LEARNING
Teaching Reading Comprehension Embedded within Content Instruction

As students progress through the elementary grades, they transition from "learning to read" to "reading to learn." The ability to understand what is read in content area textbooks becomes increasingly important. Yet many students with learning disabilities are weak in comprehension. They lack the metacognitive skills to monitor their understanding or to repair breakdowns when they occur (Torgesen & Licht, 1983). English language learners also struggle to make sense of their textbooks, particularly given unknown vocabulary, unfamiliar text structure, and topics for which they lack background knowledge. Thus, challenges with comprehension are compounded for English language learners who also have disabilities.

Yet students with poor comprehension skills can be taught to apply the reading comprehension strategies that good comprehenders seem to use automatically, thereby improving their reading comprehension. Students with learning disabilities (Gersten, Fuchs, Williams, & Baker, 2001), ELLs (Echevarria & Graves, 2003; Hernandez, 1991), ELLs who are low readers (Jiménez, 1997), and CLD students with learning disabilities (Klingner & Vaughn, 1996) have all successfully learned to apply comprehension strategies. Comprehension strategies are helpful for *all* readers, but are especially important for students who struggle with reading. Many different strategies can help improve reading comprehension. We next describe multiple-strategy instructional approaches that have been found to be effective with CLD students with and without disabilities.

Interactive Instructional Model

Bos and Anders (1990, 1992) developed the interactive instructional model for improving text comprehension and facilitating content area learning. Although they designed the model primarily for students with learning disabilities, it can benefit other students as well, particularly ELLs (Echevarria & Graves, 2003). The model emphasizes the importance of activating students' background knowledge and uses semantic feature analysis, relationship maps, and relationship charts to help students learn new concepts and understand how ideas are connected. The interactive instructional model also incorporates interactive strategic dialogues. To implement the interactive instructional model, teach students to:

1. *Brainstorm* what they already know about the topic.
2. Make a *clue list* using what the text says about the topic.
3. *Predict* how the concepts are related and make a *relationship map* or *relationship chart*.
4. *Read* to confirm and integrate understandings about the concepts and the relationships among them.
5. *Review* and *revise* the relationship map or chart.
6. Use the map or chart to *study* for a test or *write* about what was learned.

Students work together in cooperative discussion groups to work through these steps and apply the strategies. As with Reciprocal Teaching (Palincsar & Brown, 1984) and Collaborative Strategic Reading (described next; Klingner et al., 2001), the role of the teacher changes as students become increasingly proficient using the strategies. At first the teacher must take a more active role in teaching students how to use the strategies, but as students become more proficient and can scaffold and support each other while working in their cooperative learning groups, the teacher's role becomes more that of a facilitator (Bos & Anders, 1992).

Collaborative Strategic Reading (CSR)[2]

Collaborative Strategic Reading (CSR) combines cooperative learning strategies (e.g., Cohen, 1986; Johnson & Johnson, 1989; Kagan, 1991) and reading strategy instruction (Palincsar & Brown, 1984) to enhance student engagement with and comprehension of grade-level, content area texts (Klingner & Vaughn 1999, 2000; Klingner, Vaughn, Dimino, Schumm, & Bryant, 2001). Originally developed to help English language learners with learning disabilities become more confident, competent, and successful readers in heterogeneous "mainstream" classrooms, CSR has also proven to be a valuable approach for other students who can decode a text, but have difficulties with comprehension. CSR provides the students with a more independent way to interact with grade-level textbooks and learn important content than, for example, the whole-class, teacher-led, read-the-text-and-answer-the-questions-at-the-end-of-the-chapter approach. CSR has been used successfully in classrooms with CLD students at all achievement levels, ELLs who have learning disabilities, students with disabilities, as well as other students who are reading on or above grade level at both the elementary and middle school levels.

In CSR, students work in academically and/or linguistically heterogeneous cooperative groups to read a text with each student in the group in charge of a specific role.

---

[2]Contributed by Shanan Fitts.

Hence, with CSR, all students are included and everyone has the opportunity to contribute to the group's learning and the comprehension of the text. The reading strategies included in CSR are (a) previewing the text and engaging prior knowledge of the topic; (b) monitoring comprehension (i.e., identifying "clicks" and "clunks") and taking steps to improve understanding when comprehension breaks down; (c) summarizing the main points of passages (i.e., "getting the gist"); and (d) generating questions about the important ideas in the passage and reviewing what was learned (i.e., "wrapping up"). Each of these aspects will be treated in more depth below.

Theoretical Bases of CSR. CSR is based primarily on theories and research on reading strategy instruction, specifically reciprocal teaching (Palincsar & Brown, 1984) and transactional strategy instruction (TSI) (Pressley et al., 1992; Pressley & Wharton-McDonald, 1997). Both of these approaches take a constructivist approach to reading and reading comprehension, as does CSR. Constructivists, very generally, believe that learning how to read and interpret texts requires more than the acquisition of discrete skills. Rather, reading comprehension is a complex and active process, which takes place within a sociohistorical context, in which the reader engages with the text and with other students to construct meaning. Constructivists believe that students construct meaning and knowledge, and that the meaning of any particular text is open to interpretation. What children take away from a text will be influenced by their background knowledge, prior experiences, the current context, as well as their self-concept as a reader.

The Vygotskian concepts of scaffolding and the zone of proximal development (ZPD) are also central to CSR. Vygotsky (1978) envisioned learning as an integral aspect of the ZPD, a mental, physical, conceptual, and emotional space cocreated by the teacher and the students. The ZPD is usually described as the distance between the problem-solving abilities of the learner working alone versus the problem-solving abilities when assisted by a more expert other (Lave & Wenger, 1991). Teachers initially scaffold student learning by modeling the metacognitive skills employed by good readers through think-alouds and role-playing. As students become more expert at identifying the strategies that they are using and deciding when and how to use them, they can support one another through their work in cooperative groups.

Research Support for CSR. Klingner, Vaughn, and colleagues, the developers of CSR, have studied the effectiveness of the approach for approximately 10 years (Klingner & Vaughn, 1996; Klingner, Vaughn, & Schumm, 1998; Klingner et al., 2001). Their research has demonstrated that CSR improves reading comprehension scores in comparison with other approaches and enhances student engagement for a wide variety of students (Klingner, Vaughn, & Schumm, 1998; Klingner, Vaughn, Argüelles, Hughes, & Ahwee, 2004). CSR research demonstrates that children can help each other to improve their reading comprehension skills, since students made gains even when they were not receiving direct instruction from the teacher (Klingner & Vaughn, 1996). In a study that included an examination of student discourse, students were found to be implementing the strategies, assisting one another in the application of strategies, and working cooperatively to comprehend content (Klingner & Vaughn, 2000). Fifth-grade

Spanish-speaking English language learners used CSR to help them read and understand their science textbook. The researchers found that the use of CSR enhanced students' reading comprehension, content learning, and vocabulary acquisition. CSR is an approach that provides teachers with a more productive way to utilize content area textbooks in the classroom than traditional teacher-focused instructional techniques.

How CSR Works. Science and social studies texts can be especially difficult for novice readers as they contain specialized and often unfamiliar vocabulary. Furthermore since students often have less experience with expository texts, the unfamiliar structure can be an additional stumbling block. CSR helps students identify what they know about a topic and a text and build off of that knowledge base. In CSR, students are asked to employ four reading strategies (Klingner et al., 2001):

1. *Preview.* The purpose of previewing the text is to help students identify what the text will be about, to engage the students' prior knowledge and experiences with the topic, and to generate questions and interests about the topic. Students are given about 8 minutes to preview the text. The teacher helps the students with the preview by reminding them to use all of the visual clues in the text, such as picture, charts, or graphs, and to look at the headings used throughout the chapter.

2. *Click and clunk.* Click and clunk is the process students use to monitor their comprehension of the text. As suggested intuitively by this rather clever onomatopoeia, when students "get" the information, it clicks, and when they don't get it, it clunks. Students work together to identify clunks in the text and then use "fix-up" strategies such as looking for context clues to "declunk" the word or concept. Students record their clunks in their learning logs to share with their teacher and peers later.

3. *Get the gist.* When getting the gist, students are asked to state the main ideas in their own words as succinctly as possible. In this way students learn how to synthesize information, taking a larger chunk of text and distilling it into a key concept or idea. For example, one teacher who worked with Klingner and Vaughn (1999) would ask her students to read a paragraph or two and construct the main point of the paragraphs in 10 words or less. She would then ask different members of the class for their version of the gist and request feedback on these contributions from the class. Finally, the students would be asked to write the gist in their own words.

4. *Wrap up.* To wrap up students are asked to create questions about the text and summarize the main points of the text as a whole. Whereas getting the gist focuses on smaller chunks of text, the wrap-up is meant to help students tie it all together and reflect on what they have learned. Students formulate questions and use these to discuss what they have learned with their peers. Finally, students record what they learned in their learning logs.

Instructional Guidelines and Implementation. At the outset, the teacher uses whole-class explicit instruction to teach students the reading comprehension strategies. The teacher reads a passage aloud and talks about the different strategies he or she employed to comprehend that passage. After the class has been introduced to the strategies and has practiced using them as a class with the teacher, they can use the strategies in cooperative groups.

Using cooperative groups with CSR effectively incorporates struggling readers and more advanced readers within the same group and with the same text and thereby maximizes the learning and participation of all students in a heterogeneous classroom. As previously discussed, according to Johnson and Johnson (1989), cooperative learning should encourage and include (a) positive interdependence, (b) considerable face-to-face interaction among students, (c) individual accountability, (d) positive social skills, and (e) self- and group evaluation or reflection. In cooperative groups, students aren't just working-together at the same table on the same assignment, rather each person has a key role to play and everyone is responsible for the success of the group. In the case of CSR, students discuss what they have read, assist one another in the comprehension of the text, and provide both academic and affective support for their group members.

Roles. Research on cooperative learning has demonstrated that cooperative groups function best when everyone has a meaningful way to contribute to the group (Cohen, 1986). Some students are used to taking the lead and others may be used to following, but with CSR everyone has a chance to try out all of the roles. Klingner and Vaughn have designed a cue sheet to help students when they are in charge of leading the group.

CSR roles include (Klingner et al., 2001):

1. *Leader.* Leads the group in the implementation of CSR by saying what to read next and what strategy to apply next. Asks the teacher for assistance if necessary.

2. *Clunk Expert.* Uses clunk cards to remind the group of the steps to follow when trying to figure out a difficult word or concept.

3. *Gist Expert.* Guides the group toward the development of a gist and determines that the gist contains the most important idea(s) but no unnecessary details.

4. *Announcer.* Calls on different group members to read or share an idea. Makes sure everyone participates and only one person talks at a time.

5. *Encourager.* Watches the group and gives feedback. Looks for behaviors to praise. Encourages all group members to participate in the discussion and assist one another. Evaluates how well the group has worked together and gives suggestions for improvement.

Students do need training to be able to work in cooperative learning groups productively and effectively. If working in cooperative learning groups is new for students, it may be helpful for them to practice the skills necessary to function successfully in groups. Those skills include listening attentively, asking for feedback, asking others for their opinion, taking turns, asking clarifying questions, and using conflict resolution skills.[3]

---

[3]For ideas on activities designed to develop and practice these skills with your students, a good place to start is Spencer Kagan's (1992) book entitled *Cooperative Learning.*

The Cognitive Academic Language Learning Approach (CALLA)[4]

CALLA was developed as an instructional program for English language learners preparing to participate in mainstream academic content instruction in English (Chamot & O'Malley, 1996; O'Malley & Chamot, 1990). CALLA was developed in the 1980s and early 1990s when traditional ESL classrooms focused on skills-based instruction rather than content-based instruction. CALLA integrated "content area instruction with language development and explicit instruction in learning strategies" (Chamot & O'Malley, 1996, pp. 259–260). The authors emphasized their belief that content-based ESL classes were more worthwhile and effective for second language learners because they tend to offer learners more authentic and interactive learning environments.

ESL classrooms that focus solely on literacy instruction may neglect to develop students' skills to read, understand, and apply discipline specific texts and information. Students need to be able to read, write, and analyze nonfiction texts as well as fictional ones. Science, for example, is a language-rich discipline, but the vocabulary and text structures used in science are distinct from those used in fictional stories and language arts texts. Furthermore, Chamot and O'Malley noted that research conducted in the 1980s demonstrated that students in content-based classes outperformed their peers enrolled in skills-based programs (for example, see Mohan, 1986).

Theoretical Bases of CALLA. CALLA is based on a theoretical framework called cognitive learning theory. The key premise of this theoretical framework is that "learning occurs through active, dynamic mental processes" (Chamot & O'Malley, 1996, p. 262) and that individuals are active participants in the learning process. In the development of CALLA, Chamot and O'Malley applied Anderson's (1983, 1985) theories regarding the cognitive processes involved in learning complex cognitive skills such as language to second language acquisition and learning strategies. The CALLA approach seeks to empower students by teaching them to recognize the usefulness of their own prior knowledge and experiences, and by teaching skills to identify and use specific strategies to help them learn challenging and unfamiliar material.

Another important aspect of cognitive learning theory is the idea that learning occurs within social contexts and within communities of learners. Students who are learning a second language need extra support, scaffolding, and many opportunities for practice in order to become effective members of a perhaps unfamiliar learning community. People acquire knowledge through the application of knowledge in authentic contexts and actively use their prior understandings to build and produce new understandings.

The authors asserted that language learning is goal oriented and that students learn best when they have many opportunities to use language for a variety of purposes. They described CALLA as based on a "social-cognitive theory of motivation" (Chamot & O'Malley, 1996, p. 263), where motivation refers to a student's sense of self-efficacy or belief in his or her own abilities to learn successfully.

---

[4]Contributed by Shanan Fitts.

Research Support for CALLA. Although programs and classrooms implementing CALLA have not received a lot of attention from educational researchers, Chamot and her colleagues have conducted many studies to examine the ways in which strategy instruction raises the achievement of English language learners in the content areas (Chamot, 1995; Chamot, Barnhardt et al., 1993; Chamot, Dale et al., 1993; Chamot & Küpper, 1989; O'Malley & Chamot, 1990). CALLA was implemented in the Arlington Public Schools in Virginia in math beginning in 1988, with science added in 1991. The goals of the program were to develop curricula and materials that would support higher level thinking skills and be accessible to ELLs, to train and support teachers as they learned how to implement CALLA, and to increase parent involvement in math and science. In an article published in the *Bilingual Research Journal,* Chamot noted that both programs were completely supported by the Arlington Public Schools as of 1995 (Chamot, 1995). The evaluation of the CALLA math program and the assessment of student achievement included student self-evaluations, as well as both criterion-referenced and norm-referenced tests. According to the program evaluation completed by Thomas (1992), students were achieving at above-average levels and were making greater gains than students in a comparison group. Chamot (1995) noted that assessing the science program was a greater challenge, but that a longitudinal study conducted by Galland (1995) demonstrated that students in the CALLA program were "accelerating their learning in both content subjects as well as developing academic language proficiency. Classroom observations and teacher reports also indicated that students were motivated and actively involved in the learning process" (Chamot, 1995, p. 12).

How CALLA Works. According to Chamot and O'Malley (1996) the CALLA model incorporates the following aspects: "high priority content topics, academic language development based on content, and explicit instruction in learning strategies" (p. 263). CALLA is similar to sheltered content instruction, but was originally developed as a model for ESL classrooms—CALLA instruction in math, science, and social studies is meant to complement but not replace mainstream content area instruction (Chamot & O'Malley, 1992). Many of the techniques and suggestions the authors give will be familiar to many teachers. What is unique about this approach (and less easily understood or implemented) is the emphasis on the explicit instruction of learning strategies. O'Malley and Chamot define learning strategies as "special thoughts or behaviors that individuals use to help them comprehend, learn or retain new information" (1990, p. 1). Some examples of learning strategies are clarifying, summarizing, guessing, predicting, and memorization. More learning strategies are delineated below.

Learning strategies taught in the CALLA model include metacognitive strategies, cognitive strategies, and social and affective strategies (Chamot & O'Malley, 1996):

- **Metacognitive Strategies**
- Advance organization (previewing the text)
- Advance preparation (rehearsing the language needed for an oral or written task)
- Selective attention (focusing on key information)

- Self-monitoring (checking one's own comprehension while listening or reading)
- Self-evaluation (judging how well one has accomplished a task)
- Self-management (seeking or arranging conditions that facilitate one's learning)
- **Cognitive Strategies**
  - Grouping (classifying words and concepts)
  - Note-taking (writing down key words and concepts)
  - Summarizing (making a mental or written summary of key information)
  - Imagery (using visual images to understand and remember information)
  - Auditory representation (rehearsing a sound, phrase, or fact to assist with recall)
  - Elaboration (relating new information to prior knowledge)
  - Transfer (applying what is already known)
  - Inferencing (using text information and prior knowledge to guess meanings)
- **Social and Affective Strategies**
  - Clarification (eliciting an explanation or verification from a teacher or peer)
  - Cooperation (collaborating with peers to solve problems)
  - Self-talk (thinking positive and talking oneself through a difficult task) (pp. 265–266)

Chamot and O'Malley (1992) stated that four general assertions justify the need for learning strategy instruction for CLD students:

1. Mentally active learners are better learners.
2. Strategies can be taught.
3. Learning strategies transfer to new tasks.
4. Academic language learning is more effective with learning strategies. (p. 50)

Instructional Guidelines and Implementation. CALLA is a student-centered approach meant to empower students and make them more confident and independent learners. The teacher models use of strategies for the students through think-alouds and provides students with the opportunity to reflect on which strategies were used and what worked. The instructional sequence suggested by Chamot and O'Malley is familiar and includes:

1. *Preparation.* Preparing the students to engage with the new material through accessing and engaging prior knowledge. The authors emphasize the need to attend to the content rather than the form of students' responses. For example, if students are able to offer input in their native language, the teacher should accept this.

2. *Presentation.* Teacher presents the new material in a context rich fashion using contextual clues, visuals, and hands-on activities. The authors suggest that teachers model their own thought processes and learning strategies during this phase.

3. *Practice.* Students actively engage in applying the new information through reading, writing, oral, and hands-on activities. The practice phase is typically collaborative. The teacher acts as a facilitator, helping students to assimilate new information and apply learning strategies.

4. *Evaluation.* Evaluations can focus on content, language use, or learning strategies. The teacher and students check the level of students' performance and understanding. Students are also encouraged to evaluate what kinds of learning strategies they used and which ones worked well for them.

5. *Expansion Activities.* Students are asked to relate what they have learned to other contexts and situations outside school. The authors note that this is a great opportunity for teachers and students to make connections to students' cultures and communities.

Teaching implications: Research demonstrates that teaching students strategies to assist them in the reading and comprehension of text, and therefore content, helps CLD students to become more confident and independent learners. As stated by Allen (2003), "it is evident from the volume and quality of research published that the teaching of learning strategies, by whatever method chosen, enhances the learning of reading and other language skills" (p. 333). As with any program or reform, the successful implementation of CALLA in a school depends on strong leadership and institutional support for ongoing teacher training and curriculum development. Chamot (1995) noted that "ongoing professional development opportunities for teachers are critical in successful program implementation, and these activities are most beneficial when both content specialists and language teachers are involved" (p. 392).

Instructional Conversations

Instructional conversations (ICs) are ideal for culturally and linguistically diverse classrooms that include ELLs and students with disabilities (Echevarria & McDonough, 1995; Goldenberg, 1992/1993; Goldenberg & Patthey-Chavez, 1995; Rueda, Goldenberg, & Gallimore, 1992; Tharp & Gallimore, 1991). An IC is an interactive teaching approach that does more than impart knowledge and teach skills as in traditional lesson formats. Students learn new knowledge and strategies, and then apply these as they try to understand, appreciate, and grapple with important ideas about a wide variety of topics. ICs focus on an issue or concept that is meaningful and relevant for students. The teacher encourages students to share their own ideas and build on their prior knowledge while guiding them to increasingly complex levels of understanding. The dialogue between the teacher and the students is the means by which support is provided and adjusted. In contrast to instruction that assumes that all knowledge resides in the head of the teacher whose job it is to pass along this knowledge to students who are like empty vessels waiting to be "filled up" with new information, ICs assume that students play an important role in constructing new knowledge as they add their own perspectives. ICs have been used successfully with students with learning disabilities, students with mild mental retardation, and limited English proficient (LEP) students with disabilities (Echevarria & McDonough, 1995). Students who have previously experienced failure and feel a sense of helplessness can thrive in an environment where their opinions are valued. ICs help validate students with special needs as individuals with something important to contribute, and help them develop a sense of themselves as thinkers. Table 9.1 presents elements of ICs.

CONTENT VOCABULARY

Content area classes in science, social studies, and mathematics all require the understanding of key discipline-specific vocabulary terms (Echevarria & Graves, 2003). Yet many ELLs (Qian, 1999) and students with high-incidence disabilities (Simmons & Kameenui, 1990) have limited vocabularies, as well as inefficient strategies for learning and remembering new words and concepts. The difference between the numbers of words known by students with poor vocabularies and students with extensive vocabularies is quite large and grows over time (Simmons & Kameenui, 1998). For example, Simmons and Kameenui (1990) found that 10- and 12-year-old students with learning disabilities had less extensive vocabularies than peers of the same age without disabilities. Not only do students with disabilities and English language learners typically know fewer words, their understanding of concepts may lack depth (Graves, 1989; Qian, 1999). This is important because vocabulary size and academic achievement are linked (Baumann & Kameenui, 1991; Graves, Brunetti, & Slater, 1982; Graves, 1989).

Numerous instructional methods can enhance students' vocabulary learning and have helped students with various types of learning difficulties (Beck, McKeown, & Kucan, 2002; Irvin, 2001) as well as English language learners (Echevarria & Graves, 2003). Students learn the majority of new words through *incidental* learning, such as while reading, being read to, in conversations, or by watching television (Blachowicz & Fisher, 1996; Elley, 1988; Eller, Pappas, & Brown, 1988). Yet many students with disabilities are less likely to pick up words incidentally and benefit from explicit instruction or through *intentional* learning (Simmons & Kameenui, 1998). Similarly, Jiménez, García, and Pearson (1996) recommend explicit instruction for those ELLs who struggle with reading. Explicit instruction can speed up the process of vocabulary acquisition, and help students learn concepts in greater depth. This kind of systematic instruction can be particularly helpful for students who struggle with the many difficult vocabulary terms in their content area classes. Students also benefit from instruction in strategies that can help them figure out the meanings of words on their own.

Figuring Out the Meaning of Unknown Words While Reading

Instructional time focused on helping students learn strategies to figure out the meanings of unknown words while they are reading is time well spent. These are skills that last a lifetime and are useful in various settings, including when students take high-stakes

TABLE 9.1 Elements of Instructional Conversations

1. **Thematic focus.** The teacher selects a theme to focus the discussion that is considered to be relevant and meaningful for the students. The teacher has a general plan for how instruction will unfold. For students with special needs, the theme should not be too abstract (Echevarria & McDonough, 1995).

2. **Activation of background knowledge.** The teacher stimulates students to make connections between their prior knowledge and the topic they are discussing. This background knowledge is then woven into the discussion that follows.

3. **Direct teaching.** When necessary, the teacher provides direct teaching of a skill or concept.

4. **Promotion of increasingly complex language and expression.** The teacher uses a variety of techniques to elicit extended responses from students, such as invitations to expand (i.e., "Tell me more about _____"), requests for clarification (i.e., "What do you mean by _____"), restatements (i.e., "In other words, _____"), and pauses (i.e., increased "wait time"). The teacher does not dominate the discussion, but rather guides it along.

5. **Elicitation of rationale for viewpoints.** The teacher encourages students to explain their reasoning in support of an argument or position. The teacher probes for the bases of students' statements (e.g., "How do you know?" "What makes you think that?" "Show me where it says _____.").

6. **Fewer known-answer questions.** Although the teacher might do some quizzing of students' recall of basic factual information, much of the discussion focuses on questions and answers for which there can be more than one correct answer. The teacher is genuinely interested in what students think.

7. **Responsivity to student contributions.** While having an initial plan and maintaining the focus and coherence of the lesson, the teacher is also responsive to the opportunities for additional instruction provided by students' statements.

8. **A challenging but nonthreatening atmosphere.** The teacher creates a warm and accepting atmosphere where students feel comfortable sharing multiple viewpoints and taking risks. Students with special needs might need more prompting and encouraging to feel confident enough to share their ideas (Echevarria & McDonough, 1995). Students are challenged to negotiate and construct the meaning of text, each within his or her own "zone of proximal development" (Vygotsky, 1978; Englert & Mariage, 1996). The goal is to help students move from incomplete thought and expression to complete and articulate thought and expression. In an inclusion classroom, students' levels will vary a great deal, thus an appropriately challenging question for one student could be too abstract for another student.

9. **General participation, including self-selected turns.** The teacher uses a variety of strategies to encourage students to participate, and does not hold the exclusive right to determine who talks. Students are encouraged to volunteer to talk as in a natural conversation.

Source: Adapted from Goldenberg (1992/1993) and Saunders, Goldenberg, & Hamann (1992).

tests. All readers come across unknown words while reading. It is what they do when they come across difficult vocabulary that distinguishes more and less successful readers.

Successful bilingual and monolingual readers apply different strategies for figuring out the meanings of words (Jiménez, García, & Pearson, 1995, 1996). Jiménez, García, and Pearson (1996) compared the strategic reading processes of eight sixth- and seventh-grade bilingual Latina/o children who were considered successful English readers with the reading processes of three successful English readers and three less successful bilingual

Latina/o readers. The successful Latina/o readers actively translated from one language to another and were able to access cognates (i.e., words that are similar in spelling and meaning in more than one language, such as "dentist" in English and "*dentista*" in Spanish). When the successful Latina/o readers encountered unknown words while reading, they were able to use different strategies to figure out the meanings of these words. The less successful Latina/o readers used fewer strategies and were less effective resolving comprehension difficulties. When they encountered unknown vocabulary items they did not know how to proceed. Similarly, the middle school English language learners with learning disabilities in Klingner and Vaughn's (1996) investigation of comprehension strategies previously had been told "to skip" the words they do not know. This approach left them feeling confused and frustrated, without the skills they needed to become independent readers. It was when they learned strategies for figuring out unknown words that their vocabulary knowledge and comprehension improved.

Context Clues. The first step in helping students figure out unknown words while reading is to teach them the ways in which content textbook authors provide definitions in context. Readence, Bean, and Baldwin (1998) described three (adapted from Haager & Klingner, 2005):

1. *Definition.* Textbook authors often define key terms in the same sentence in which they are introduced, although sometimes definitions appear in previous or subsequent sentences. Embedded definitions are the most common type of context clue in content textbooks (Readence, Bean, & Baldwin, 1998). For example:
   a) **Photosynthesis** is the process by which plants turn sunlight into energy.
   b) National Parks were established partially in order to provide a **refuge** for flora and fauna of that region. In the parks, the creatures were kept safe from civilization.

2. *Description.* Although an explicit definition for the word is not provided, the word is described in such a way that a good guess can be made about its meaning. For example:
   a) Many families lived crowded together in cheaply built **tenements**.

3. *Contrast.* The word is compared with another word or concept, often its opposite. For example:
   a) The only light in the dark swamp was provided by the **luminescence** of the fireflies.

Key vocabulary words are often written in boldface (as in the above examples), underlined, or italicized to emphasize their importance. Therefore, students should be alerted to look for context clues when they see a word highlighted in one of these ways.

Morphemic Analysis. Another useful strategy for helping students figure out unknown words is morphemic analysis, or, put more simply, breaking a word into smaller parts. These smaller parts are known as *morphemes*. Students are taught to look for a prefix or suffix in the word as well as the word's root (e.g., *librarian* = library + ian or *renewable* = re + new + able). Students can also look for smaller words they know, as in compound words (*aircraft* = air + craft).

External Reference. Dictionaries, glossaries, and thesauruses are all excellent sources of information about unknown words (Readence, Bean, & Baldwin, 2004). Glossaries at the back of textbooks are generally the easiest form of external reference to use because the definitions provided match the ways the words are used in the book. When the textbook does not include a glossary, a dictionary may be the next best choice. However, dictionaries can be difficult to use and can lead to confusion. When the target word has many possible definitions, even those students without disabilities can easily select the wrong definition. For these reasons, it is important to provide students with guided practice in how to use external sources of information to their maximum benefit. Increasingly, perhaps because of their availability with word processors, students are turning to thesauruses rather than dictionaries to help them figure out what words mean. Thesauruses can provide a quick indication of a word's general meaning, but also can lead to mix-ups and incomplete understandings.

We recommend encouraging English language learners with and without disabilities to try to figure out unknown words using context clues and morphemic analysis while reading rather than stopping to check an external source for a word's definition. Students become more proficient at figuring out words with practice (Klingner et al., 2001). We suggest asking students to keep a log of the difficult words they encounter while reading, similar to the process followed with CSR. Once students have completed a chapter (or section of a chapter), they can then check their understandings of challenging words using a glossary, dictionary, and/or a thesaurus. This follow-up verification might be done as homework. Or it could be accomplished with support from the ESL or special education teacher.

Teaching Word Meanings

When teachers explicitly pre-teach key vocabulary terms, it helps all students by providing them with background knowledge that can help them understand the topic they will be studying, but it especially helps English language learners and students with learning disabilities (Echevarria & Graves, 2003; Bos & Anders, 1990). Pre-teaching also draws students' attention to important information for which they should be alert. There are many ways to introduce new words. In this chapter we focus on ways to help students learn content vocabulary. Graphic organizers are one valuable technique for this purpose.

Graphic Organizers. Graphic organizers provide students with a visual diagram of the relationships among key vocabulary terms that facilitates their understanding and retention of new words. By making the connections among concepts explicit, students are better able to link new information to their prior knowledge. Graphic organizers are an effective approach for supporting the vocabulary learning of students with LD, including English language learners with LD (Bos & Anders, 1992; Kim, Vaughn, Wanzek, & Wei, 2004). Software programs such as Kidspiration and Inspiration (Inspiration, 2004) can aid in this process. Types of graphic organizers include tree diagrams, semantic maps or webs, concept maps, word maps, and semantic feature analysis.

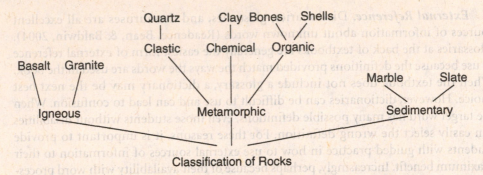

FIGURE 9.1 Tree Diagram

Tree Diagram. Just like the name sounds, tree diagrams consist of a "trunk" and "branches." The "trunk" is the overarching concept to be learned, and the branches are the vocabulary terms that serve as examples (Konopak, 1991) (see Figure 9.1).

Semantic Map or Web. Semantic mapping involves diagramming related concepts from a reading passage or oral lesson (Heimlich & Pittelman, 1986). It is a highly recommended strategy for improving the content area learning of English language learners (Reyes & Molner, 1991; Echevarria & Graves, 2003; O'Malley & Chamot, 1990) and has been used effectively with English language learners with disabilities (Bos, Allen, & Scanlon, 1989; Bos & Anders, 1992; Gallego, Durán, & Scanlon, 1990). Webs can be completed at the beginning of a lesson as a way to pre-teach or introduce key concepts, or at the end as a review. Webs can be used with individual students or with the entire class to assist students in organizing and understanding the relationships among concepts.

Semantic maps can be written on a chalkboard or whiteboard, using an overhead projector, or on chart paper (Readence et al., 2004). First, write the topic or key concept in the center of the board. Then ask students to brainstorm and share either orally or in writing different words related to the topic. They might do this individually, in pairs, or in small groups. The words they generate can be from their own experiences, from the lesson, or from their reading of the text. List students' words on the chalkboard or overhead projector, and then organize them into an octopus-like diagram, with students' input. A helpful variation of this is to have students jot their words down on sticky notes (Ellis, 1997). That way it is easy to move the words around on the web, reorganizing them at will. Label each of the various categories and add new categories or subcategories and related words as they come up. It is perhaps the discussion and questioning activities that accompany the development of the map or web that are the most valuable aspects of the activity (see Figure 9.2).

Concept Maps. Concept maps are similar to semantic maps in that they provide a visual representation of the connections among various concepts (Konopak, 1991; Martin, 1996). However, they are different in that they include additional information specifying how the concepts are related. For instance, in the previous example, we could add descriptions that would clarify the relationships among categories. Our solar system

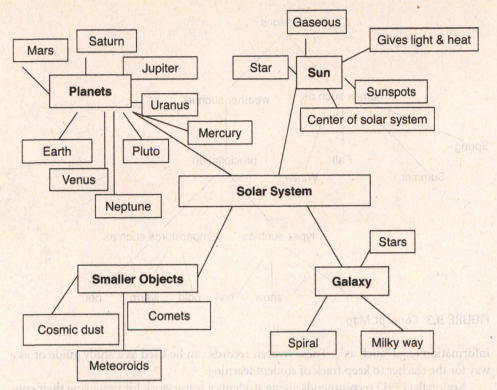

FIGURE 9.2 Semantic Web

includes a sun, planets, and smaller objects, but is *part of* a larger galaxy, the Milky Way. Concept maps can take different forms. A common approach is to present concepts hierarchically, with the broadest term at the top, the most specific terms at the bottom, and lines in between connecting them, with text indicating how they are related. To teach students how to prepare concept maps, Martin (1996) suggests giving students small cards (made by cutting 3 x 5 index cards into thirds) and asking them to write a set of words on the cards, one per card. Using the example presented in Figure 9.3, these words would be SEASONS, CLIMATE, FALL, HOT, NAMES, WINTER, PRECIPITATION, SPRING, RAIN, SUMMER, SNOW, COLD, HAIL, TEMPERATURES, WARM, and TYPES. Working individually or with a partner, students then arrange the cards, placing the most general topic at the top, the names for categories within this topic underneath the general topic, and examples underneath the category cards. The organization and placement of cards can vary, depending on how students perceive the relationships among concepts. There can be more than one "right" way to sort them. Once students have completed this activity, they can compare their different categorization schemes and make adjustments by moving their cards around. When they are satisfied with the organization of their maps, they can record them on paper and draw lines to connect concepts, adding clarifying

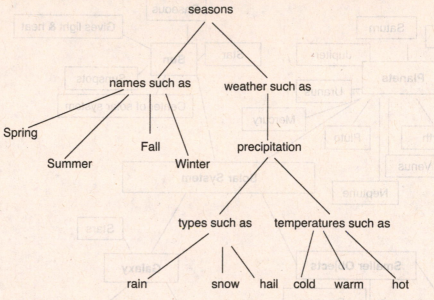

FIGURE 9.3 Concept Map

information (e.g., "such as"). These written records can be used as a study guide or as a way for the teacher to keep track of student learning.

Konopak (1991) recommends giving students a framework for preparing their concept maps (see Figure 9.4). Again, the general topic, or overarching concept, is placed at the top. Students then answer questions to guide their thinking about the topic.

Word Maps. Word maps are similar to concept and semantic maps except that they are less elaborate (Blachowicz & Fisher, 1996). The directions are relatively simple: For

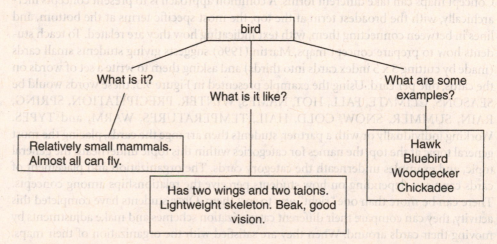

FIGURE 9.4 Concept Map Framework

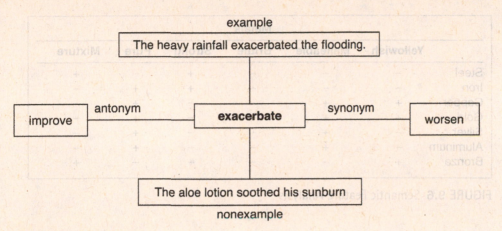

example

| The heavy rainfall exacerbated the flooding. |

| improve | antonym | **exacerbate** | synonym | worsen |

| The aloe lotion soothed his sunburn |

nonexample

FIGURE 9.5 Word Map

any given target vocabulary word, students think of a synonym, an antonym, an example, and a nonexample. They arrange these in boxes or circles with the target word in the middle (see Figure 9.5).

Semantic Feature Analysis. This type of graphic organizer is somewhat different than the webs and maps we have already described. Students analyze important concepts from their text or a lesson by indicating how they are similar and different, or by contrasting them according to whether they possess or do not possess certain critical attributes. To complete a semantic feature analysis, students prepare a table or grid and list a set of concepts or names down the left side (e.g., kinds of animals, trees, elements, foods, or famous historical characters). Next they list a set of criteria or possible features across the top. Students then determine whether each concept listed down the side is associated with each of the features listed across the top. If the feature applies, students record a + (plus sign) in the grid where that column and row intersect. If the feature is not one associated with the concept, students write a − (minus sign) in the corresponding box on the grid. Every space on the grid must have a plus or a minus for every feature. Once students have completed a semantic feature analysis, they should be guided in making observations about category items. A semantic feature analysis can be completed in combination with a semantic map, or as an activity by itself (see Figure 9.6). It has been used successfully to help English language learners and students with disabilities understand concepts (Bos & Anders, 1992).

Computer Software. Various computer software programs are available to help students organize their ideas and create graphic organizers. Perhaps the best-known products are Inspiration and Kidspiration (Inspiration, 2004). Kidspiration was designed for students in kindergarten through the fifth grade, whereas Inspiration was developed for students in grades six and up. Both programs help students organize their thoughts, categorize information, understand concepts, integrate new and prior knowledge, clarify their thinking, and express their ideas while creating graphics such as outlines, diagrams, and visual maps.

	Metals					
	Yellowish	Malleable	Brittle	Strong	Pure	Mixture
Steel	−	−	−	+	−	+
Iron	−	−	+	+	+	−
Copper	+	+	−	−	+	−
Gold	+	+	−	−	+	−
Silver	−	+	−	−	+	−
Aluminum	−	+	−	−	+	−
Bronze	+	−	−	+	−	+

FIGURE 9.6 Semantic Feature Analysis

ADAPTATIONS AND MODIFICATIONS

The 1997 and 2004 amendments to IDEA specify that students with disabilities must be provided opportunities to progress in the general education curriculum as part of their Individualized Education Plan. *Accommodation, adaptation,* and *modification* are terms used to describe adjustments teachers make for individual students. Although educators often use these terms synonymously, they are not equivalent (e.g., Bradley, King-Sears, & Tessier-Switlick, 1997; Vallecorsa, deBettencourt, & Zigmond, 2000). *Accommodation* is the umbrella term and refers to the process of making sure learning activities are appropriate and are accessible to students with disabilities as needed, as stipulated by IDEA 2004. Accommodations might require changing the school building, such as adding wheelchair ramps or special bathroom equipment, or they might entail some type of curricular or instructional adjustment. An *adaptation* is a type of accommodation and can be a change to the curriculum, instruction, textbooks, or learning environment (Haager & Klingner, 2005). For example, a classroom teacher might adapt a test for an individual student by letting the student take the test orally in a one-to-one situation with the teacher, by reading the questions to the student, by permitting the student to demonstrate understanding in a different way, or by allowing the student to take extra time to complete the exam. The student participates in the same activity as classmates and uses the same materials but with slight adaptations. The student is held accountable to the same learning standards as the other students, must learn the same content, and must obtain the same scores to earn passing grades. However, when a student's disability is such that the general education learning expectations are not realistic, the adaptations become *modifications*. Modifications involve not only adapting assignments and assessment procedures, but also adjusting learning expectations so that they are realistic and appropriate for an individual student. Examples of this might be assigning easier vocabulary words or requiring the student to learn fewer concepts. Vocabulary assessments might consist of simple fill-in-the-blank questions, with very literal and concrete wording, rather than requiring open-ended responses. Adaptations and modifications are also appropriate for ELLs. Although the terms used to describe them are different, they are much like many of the practices used in sheltered English instruction (Becijos, 1997; Echevarria, Vogt, & Short, 1999). Whether the student has a learning disability, is an ELL, or both, the goal is to make sure instruction is comprehensible and at the appropriate level (Fletcher, Bos & Johnson, 1999). The objective, however, is not to water down the curriculum, but to make it accessible.

Types of Adaptations

There are many different ways to adapt lessons, learning activities, and assessment procedures. Teachers should consider various options for what could be adapted, and how, and then make their decisions based on the likelihood of student success as well as the feasibility of the adaptation (Vallecorsa et al., 2000). A general rule of thumb is that teachers should select adaptations that are the least obtrusive and disruptive to the teaching routine while still maximizing the possibility of student success and enabling the student to develop independence (Haager & Klingner, 2005). For example, given a choice of using a peer buddy to read a written assignment to a student with a reading disability or rewriting a worksheet so that it is easier for the student to read, the teacher would have to weigh the effort involved and the student's needs. Though rewriting is more time consuming, the teacher might decide to make the investment because it would allow the student to work independently. However, using a peer buddy could also be a good choice because it is easier and a peer would provide a model. We list several examples of different types of adaptations to accommodate individual learners in Table 9.2.

It can be challenging for general education and special education or bilingual/ESL special education teachers to know just when and how to make adaptations for students. Schumaker and Lenz (1999) developed the following guidelines to assist teachers with this process:

1. *Create a plan.* Develop both short-term and long-term plans. Planning is best done collaboratively by everyone responsible for supporting a student, including the general education or bilingual teacher, the special education or bilingual special education teacher, and a language development specialist, as appropriate. Parents and students might also participate in the planning process.
2. *Identify and evaluate the demands on the student.* Observe the student and evaluate the curriculum and textbooks to determine their level of difficulty and how appropriate they are for the student in their current form. Consider the student's strengths as well as learning needs. Determine how to tailor instruction to the individual's specific needs.
3. *Establish the purpose of possible adaptations.* Consider whether the student will be able to fully and successfully participate in class activities if adaptations are provided. Decide whether some adaptations would be more conducive than others for achieving this goal.
4. *Determine the type and number of adaptations needed.* Decide whether to adapt the content, evaluation criteria or expectations, materials or textbook,

TABLE 9.2 Adaptation Choices to Meet Individual Student Needs

Types of Adaptations and Examples

Adapt the Content

- Ask the student to learn fewer vocabulary words or concepts, for example, 12 vocabulary words instead of 25.
- Emphasize key events and their causes rather than details, for example, battles and causes of conflicts in social studies without requiring details such as dates.
- Test the student on textbook material section by section rather than on an entire unit.
- Teach a related, similar unit of study, such as simple machines in physical science, parallel to the whole-class unit on simple and complex machines.

Adapt the Evaluation Criteria or Expectations

- Teach basic subtraction facts while the class learns subtraction with regrouping.
- Score a writing sample based on student's targeted needs, such as punctuation or paragraph structure, rather than the grade-level criteria.
- Require a lesser number of problems or items on an assignment or test.

Adapt the Materials or Textbook

- Eliminate some math problems or chapter questions in a social studies text.
- Provide a study guide or outline emphasizing key points.
- Use a highlighter to mark key concepts.
- Substitute materials, textbooks, or videotapes for assigned text.
- Use audiotaped textbooks or peer readers.
- Use assistive technology, such as the Kurzweil Reader, that will read scanned text.
- Simplify materials by rewriting or restructuring.
- Eliminate superfluous material to shorten reading tasks.

Adapt Instructional Delivery

- Provide additional pre-teaching, or previewing, of concepts to be covered such as vocabulary words.
- Identify key concepts and make them explicit to students (e.g., by pointing them out and using visual reinforcements), and review them often.
- Teach the same concept with multiple presentations or modes of instruction.
- Use consistent routines and prompts.
- Check for understanding frequently and reteach for students who need further instruction (e.g., teaching in a different way rather than repeating the same approach).
- Provide samples of finished products when giving assignments.
- Provide written versions of directions for assignments, with visual cues when possible.

(continued)

Adjust the Timing or Pacing of Instruction

- Provide additional time for students to read or complete assignments and assessments.
- Slow the pace of instruction or provide additional explanations.

Adjust the Physical Environment

- Seat students so that one or more peers who can provide assistance are close by (e.g., a bilingual student who can help with translating).
- Provide visual cues or prompts on the wall or taped on a student's desk.
- Provide a table for small group work with a teacher, a classmate, or other support provider.
- Provide a listening area for audiotaped books and directions for assignments.

Adjust the Type of Support Provided

- Provide individual support from the classroom teacher, a special education teacher, a second language specialist, or other support provider.
- Provide opportunities for peer support such as peer tutoring or partner reading.
- Work with students who may need extra assistance in a small group following a whole-group presentation to check for understanding.
- Provide concept maps, outlines, and study guides as advance organizers and for test preparation.
- Allow students to use a word bank or dictionary of words for writing tasks.
- Go over directions and model tasks individually with students who need additional help.
- Check frequently on individual students who may need more help.

Adjust Grouping Procedures

- Place students in heterogeneous groups for peer assistance and modeling.
- Pair students with a knowledgeable and supportive peer.
- Place students in skills-based groups for direct instruction.

Source: Adapted from Haager & Klinger (2005).

instructional delivery, the timing or pacing of instruction, the physical environment, type of support, or grouping procedures for an individual student. It is likely that multiple adaptations will be appropriate.

5. *Discuss the adaptation(s) with students and parents.* Meet with the student and his or her parents to discuss the adaptations and the plan for implementing them. This is particularly important if the student and his or her parents have not been part of the planning process up to this point. Parents may be able to provide reinforcement at home. Also, consider sharing information with classmates about the importance of accommodating individual student needs.

6. *Implement, evaluate, and adjust the adaptations.* Try the adaptations and assess their effectiveness. Adjust implementation as necessary. The student's teachers and support personnel

should meet periodically so that everyone involved can evaluate their role and whether any changes are needed.

7. *Record information about adaptations in the student's IEP.* Keep a written record of adaptations and how they are intended to support students' progress toward meeting learning objectives. Note when they will start, who is responsible for implementing them, and when they will be evaluated.

SUMMARY

In this chapter, we described various ways to support CLDE students' learning in the content areas. We emphasized that the best programs for English language learners with disabilities are those in which teachers implement validated instructional practice in supportive, culturally responsive learning environments. We discussed various ways to increase students' participation in content area learning and explained inquiry-based and activity-oriented methods. We also portrayed collaborative approaches, including cooperative learning and peer or cross-age tutoring. We described different methods of reading comprehension strategy instruction for the content areas (e.g., Collaborative Strategic Reading, Cognitive Academic Language Learning Approach), and stressed the need to help students learn new vocabulary. Finally, we explained different adaptations and modifications that facilitate learning for CLDE students. It is our hope that through such approaches, CLDE students will no longer be faced with watered down and washed out instruction. Rather, they will experience frequent opportunities to learn through meaningful, challenging, engaging, appropriate instruction that truly helps them achieve to their potential.

Discussion Questions

1. You are concerned that not all of the students in your diverse sixth-grade class seem to be participating during large group content area lessons. Some students seem to drift off and daydream or engage in off-task behaviors. What can you do to increase participation?

2. You have been asked by your school to conduct an after-school workshop for your colleagues on cooperative learning and peer tutoring. You will have one hour. What will you emphasize? Prepare an outline of what you will cover.

3. You have just been contacted by a social studies textbook publisher who knows of your expertise in teaching CLDE students. They are developing a new series and would like you to advise them on how best to teach and reinforce key vocabulary. Currently, their teachers' guides suggest having students read new words and their definitions and using the words in sentences. What else would you recommend?

4. You and the other teachers at your grade level have decided to teach your students a multicomponent reading comprehension strategy instruction model for the content areas. Which approach would you suggest, and why?

5. You have been hired as a special education teacher in a school with an inclusion model. This year the school has prioritized making sure all teachers know different adaptations and modifications that facilitate learning for CLDE students. It is part of your job to help with this effort. What would you focus on? How will you support teachers in learning about adaptations and modifications?

References

Allen, S. (2003). An analytic comparison of three models of reading strategy instruction. *IRAL: International Review of Applied Linguistics in Language Teaching, 41*, 319–339.

Allen, V. L. (1976). *Children as teachers: Theory and research on tutoring.* New York: Academic.

Anderson, J. R. (1983). *The architecture of cognition.* Cambridge, MA: Harvard University Press.

Anderson, J. R. (1985). *Cognitive psychology and its implications* (2nd ed.). San Francisco, CA: Freeman.

Baumann, J. F., & Kameenui, E. J. (1991). Research on vocabulary instruction: Ode to Voltaire. In J. Flood, J. Jensen, D. Lapp, & J. Squire (Eds.), *Handbook of research on teaching the English language arts* (pp. 604–632). New York: Macmillan.

Becijos, J. (1997). *SDAIE: Strategies for teachers of English learners.* Bonita, CA: Torch Publications.

Beck, I. L., McKeown, M. G., & Kucan, L. (2002). *Bringing words to life: Robust vocabulary instruction.* New York: Guilford.

Blachowicz, C., & Fisher, P. (1996). *Teaching vocabulary in all classrooms.* Englewood Cliffs, NJ: Merrill.

Bos, C. S., Allen, A. A., & Scanlon, D. J. (1989). Vocabulary instruction and reading comprehension with bilingual learning disabled students. *National Reading Conference Yearbook, 38*, 173–179.

Bos, C. S., & Anders, P. L. (1990). Effects of interactive vocabulary instruction on the vocabulary learning and reading comprehension of junior-high learning disabled students. *Learning Disability Quarterly, 13*, 31–42.

Bos, C. S., & Anders, P. L. (1992). A theory-driven interactive instructional model for text comprehension and content learning. In B. Y. L. Wong (Ed.), *Contemporary intervention research in learning disabilities: An international perspective* (pp. 81–95). New York: Springer-Verlag.

Bradley, D. F., King-Sears, M. E., & Tessier-Switlick, D. M. (1997). *Teaching students in inclusive settings: From theory to practice.* Boston: Allyn & Bacon.

Brice, A., & Roseberry-McKibben, C. (1999). Turning frustration into success for English language learners. *Educational Leadership, 56*(7), 53–55.

Cavanaugh, R. A., Heward, W. L., & Donelson, F. (1996). Effects of response cards during lesson closure on the academic performance of secondary students in an earth science course. *Journal of Applied Behavior Analysis, 29*(3), 403–406.

Chamot, A. U. (1995). Implementing the Cognitive Academic Language Learning Approach: *CALLA* in Arlington, Virginia. *Bilingual Research Journal, 19*, 379–394.

Chamot, A. U., Barnhardt, S., El-Dinary, P. B., Carbonaro, G., & Robbins, J. (1993). *Methods for teaching learning strategies in the foreign language classroom and assessment of language skills for instruction: Final report.* Available from ERIC Clearinghouse on Languages and Linguistics.

Chamot, A. U., Dale, M., O'Malley, J. M., & Spanos, G. A. (1993). Learning and problem solving strategies of ESL students. *Bilingual Research Journal, 16*(3&4), 1–38.

Chamot, A. U., & Küpper, L. (1989). Learning strategies in foreign language instruction. *Foreign Language Annals, 22*(1), 13–24.

Chamot, A. U., & O'Malley, J. M. (1992). The cognitive academic learning approach: A bridge to the mainstream. In Richard-Amato, P. A. & Snow, M. A. (Eds.), *The multicultural classroom: Readings for content-area teachers* (pp. 39–56). Reading, MA: Addison-Wesley.

Chamot, A. U., & O'Malley, J. M. (1996). The cognitive academic language learning approach (CALLA): A model for linguistically diverse classrooms. *Elementary School Journal, 96*(3), 259–273.

Cohen, E. G. (1986). *Designing groupwork: Strategies for the heterogeneous classroom.* New York: Teachers College Press.

Cohen, E. G., Lotan, R. A., Scarloss, B. A., Arellano, A. R. (1999). Complex instruction: Equity in cooperative learning classrooms. *Theory into Practice, 38*(2), 80–86.

Coleman, M., & Vaughn, S. (2000). Reading interventions for students with emotional/behavioral disorders. *Behavioral Disorders, 25*, 93–104.

Cook, S. B., Scruggs, T. E., Mastropieri, M. A., & Casto, G. C. (1986). Handicapped students as tutors. *The Journal of Special Education, 19*, 483–492.

Courson, F. H., & Heward, W. L. (1988). Increasing active student response through the effective use of paraprofessionals. *Pointer, 33*(1), 27–31.

Dalton, B., Morocco, C. C., Tivnan, T., & Mead, P. L. R. (1997). Supported inquiry science: Teaching for conceptual change in urban and suburban science classrooms. *Journal of Learning Disabilities, 30*, 670–684.

Echevarria, J., & Graves, A. (2003). *Sheltered content instruction: Teaching English-language learners with diverse abilities* (2nd ed.). Needham Heights, MA: Allyn & Bacon.

Echevarria, J., & McDonough, R. (1995). An alternative reading approach: Instructional conversations in a bilingual special education setting. *Learning Disabilities Research and Practice, 10*(2), 108–119.

Echevarria, J., Vogt, M., & Short, D. (1999). *Making content comprehensible for English language learners: The SIOP model.* Boston, MA: Allyn & Bacon.

Eller, R. G., Pappas, C. C., & Brown, E. (1988). The lexical development of kindergartners: Learning from written context. *Journal of Reading Behavior, 20*, 5–24.

Elley, W. B. (1988–89). Vocabulary acquisition from listening to stories. *Reading Research Quarterly, 24*, 174–187.

Ellis, E. S. (1997). Watering up the curriculum for adolescents with learning disabilities. *Remedial and Special Education, 18*, 326–346.

Englert, C. S., & Mariage, T. V. (1996). A sociocultural perspective: Teaching ways-of-thinking and ways-of-talking in a literary community. *Learning Disabilities Research and Practice, 11*(3), 157–167.

Fletcher, T. V., Bos, C. S., & Johnson, L. M. (1999). Accommodating English Language Learners with language and learning disabilities in bilingual education classrooms. *Learning Disabilities Research & Practice, 14*(2), 80–91.

Fuchs, L. S., Fuchs, D., Hamlett, C. L., & Appleton, A. C. (2002). Explicitly teaching for transfer: Effects on the mathematical problem-solving performance of students with mathematics disabilities. *Learning Disabilities Research & Practice, 17*, 90–106.

Fuchs, D., Fuchs, L. S., Mathes, P. G., & Simmons, D. C. (1997). Peer-assisted learning strategies: Making classrooms more responsive to diversity. *American Educational Research Journal, 34*, 174–206.

Galland, P. A. (1995). *An evaluation of the Cognitive Academic Language Learning Approach (CALLA) in the High Intensity Language Training (HILT) Science Program in Arlington Public Schools.* Unpublished master's research paper, Georgetown University.

Gallego, M. A., Durán, G. Z., & Scanlon, D. J. (1990). Interactive teaching and learning: Facilitating learning disabled students' progress from novice to expert. In J. Zutell & S. McCormick (Eds.), *Literacy theory and research: Analyses from multiple paradigms. Thirty-ninth yearbook of the National Reading Conference* (pp. 311–319). Chicago: National Reading Conference.

Gersten, R., Fuchs, L. S., Williams, J. P., & Baker, S. (2001). Teaching reading comprehension strategies to students with learning disabilities: A review of research. *Review of Educational Research, 71*, 279–320.

Gillies, R. M., & Ashman, A. F. (2000). The effects of cooperative learning on students with learning difficulties in the lower elementary school. *Journal of Special Education, 34*, 19–27.

Goldenberg, C. (1992/1993). Instructional conversations: Promoting comprehension through discussion. *The Reading Teacher, 46*, 316–326.

Goldenberg, C., & Patthey-Chavez, G. (1995). Discourse processes in instructional conversations: Interactions between teacher and transition readers. *Discourse Processes, 19*, 57–73.

Goodlad, S., & Hirst, B. (1989). *Peer tutoring: A guide to learning by teaching.* New York: Nichols.

Graves, M. F. (1989). A quantitative and qualitative study of elementary school children's vocabularies. *Journal of Educational Research, 82*, 203–209.

Graves, M. F., Brunetti, G. J., & Slater, W. H. (1982). The reading vocabularies of primary grade children of varying geographic and social backgrounds. In J. A. Niles & L. A. Harris (Eds.), *New inquiries in reading research and instruction* (pp. 99–104). Rochester, NY: National Reading Conference.

Greenwood, C. R., Delquadri, J. C., & Hall, R. V. (1989). Longitudinal effects of Classwide Peer Tutoring. *Journal of Education Psychology, 81*, 371–383.

Haager, D., & Klingner, J. K. (2005). *Differentiating instruction in inclusive classrooms: The special educators' guide.* Boston, MA: Allyn & Bacon.

Harper, G. F., Maheady, L., Mallette, B., & Karnes, M. (1999). Peer tutoring and the minority child with disabilities. *Preventing School Failure, 43*(2), 45–51.

Heimlich, J. E., & Pittelman, S. V. (1986). *Semantic mapping.* Newark, DE: International Reading Association.

Hernandez, J. S. (1991). Assisted performance in reading comprehension strategies with non-English proficient students. *Journal of Educational Issues of Language Minority Students, 8*, 91–112.

Heward, W. L. (1994). Three "low-tech" strategies for increasing the frequency of active student response during group instruction. In R. Gardner III, D. M. Sainato, J. O. Cooper, T. E. Heron, W. L. Heward, J. Eshleman, & T. A. Grossi (Eds.), *Behavior analysis in education: Focus on measurably superior instruction* (pp. 283–320). Monterey, CA: Brooks/Cole.

Heward, W. L., Gardner III, R., Cavanaugh, R. A., Courson, F. H., Grossi, T. A., & Barbetta, P. M. (1996). Everyone participates in this class: Using response cards to increase active student response. *Teaching Exceptional Children, 28*, 4–10.

Inspiration Software. (2004). *Inspiration.* Retrieved on April 25, 2004, from http://www.inspiration.com/home.cfm

Irvin, J. L. (2001). Assisting struggling readers in building vocabulary and background knowledge. *Voices from the Middle, 8*(4), 37–43.

Jenkins, J. R., & Jenkins, L. M. (1987). Making peer tutoring work. *Educational Leadership, 44*, 64–68.

Jiménez, R. T. (1997). The strategic reading abilities and potential of five low-literacy Latina/o readers in middle school. *Reading Research Quarterly, 32*, 224–243.

Jiménez, R. T., Garcia, G. E., & Pearson, P. D. (1995). Three children, two languages, and strategic reading: Case studies in bilingual/monolingual reading. *American Educational Research Journal, 32*, 31–61.

Jiménez, R. T., Garcia, G. E., & Pearson, P. D. (1996). The reading strategies of bilingual Latina/o students who are successful English readers: Opportunities and obstacles. *Reading Research Quarterly, 31*, 90–112.

Johnson, D. W., & Johnson, R. T. (1989). Cooperative learning: What special educators need to know. *The Pointer, 33*, 5–10.

Johnson, D. W., & Johnson, R. T. (1993). Foreword. In J. W. Putnam (Ed.), *Cooperative learning and strategies for inclusion* (pp. xiii, xiv). Baltimore, MD: Brookes.

Kagan, S. (1990). *Cooperative learning resources for teachers.* San Juan Capistrano, CA: Resources for Teachers.

Kagan, S. (1991). *Cooperative learning.* San Diego, CA: Kagan Cooperative Learning.

Kagan, S., & High, J. (2002). Kagan structures for English language learners. *ESL Magazine, 5*(4), 10–12.

Kamps, D. M., Dugan, E. P., & Leonard, B. R. (1994). Enhanced small group instruction using choral responding and student interaction for children with autism and developmental disabilities. *American Journal on Mental Retardation, 99*(1), 60–73.

Kim, A., Vaughn, S., Wanzek, J., & Wei, S. (2004). Graphic organizers and their effects on the reading comprehension of students with LD: A synthesis of research. *Journal of Learning Disabilities, 37*(2), 105–118.

Klingner, J. K., & Vaughn, S. (1996). Reciprocal teaching of reading comprehension strategies for students with learning disabilities who use English as a second language. *Elementary School Journal, 96*, 275–293.

Klingner, J. K., & Vaughn, S. (1999). Promoting reading comprehension, content learning, and English acquisition through collaborative strategic reading (CSR). *The Reading Teacher, 52*, 738–747.

Klingner, J. K., & Vaughn, S. (2000). The helping behaviors of fifth-graders while using collaborative strategic reading (CSR) during ESL content classes. *TESOL Quarterly, 34*, 69–98.

Klingner, J. K., Vaughn, S., Argüelles, M. E., Hughes, M. T., & Ahwee, S. (2004). Collaborative strategic reading: "Real world" lessons from classroom teachers. *Remedial and Special Education, 25*, 291–302.

Klingner, J. K., Vaughn, S., Dimino, J., Schumm, J. S., & Bryant, D. P. (2001). *From clunk to click: Collaborative Strategic Reading.* Longmont, CO: Sopris West.

Klingner, J. K., Vaughn, S., & Schumm, J. S. (1998). Collaborative strategic reading during social studies in heterogeneous fourth-grade classrooms. *Elementary School Journal, 99*, 3–21.

Konopak, B. C. (1991). Teaching vocabulary to improve science learning. In C. M. Santa & D. E. Alvermann (Eds.), *Science learning: Processes and applications* (pp. 134–146). Newark, DE: International Reading Association.

Lave, J., & Wenger, E. (1991). *Situated learning: Legitimate peripheral participation.* Cambridge, UK: Cambridge University Press.

Lazerson, D. B., Foster, H. L., Brown, S. I., & Hummel, J. W. (1988). The effectiveness of cross-age tutoring with truant, junior high school students with learning disabilities. *Journal of Learning Disabilities, 21*, 253–255.

Lee, O. (2002). Science inquiry for elementary students from diverse backgrounds. In W. G. Secada (Ed.), *Review of Research in Education* (Vol. 26, pp. 23–69). Washington, DC: American Educational Research Association.

Lee, O. (2005). Science education and English Language Learners: Synthesis and research agenda. *Review of Educational Research, 75*, 491–530.

Lee, O., & Fradd, S. (1996). Literary skills in science learning among linguistically diverse students. *Science Education, 80*(6), 651–671.

Lee, O., & Luykx, A. (2006). *Science education and student diversity: Synthesis and research agenda.* Cambridge: Cambridge University Press.

Lyman, R. (1981). The responsive classroom discussion. In A. S. Anderson (Ed.), *Mainstreaming digest.* College Park, MD: University of Maryland.

Maheady, L., Mallete, B., Harper, G. F., & Saca, K. (1991). Heads together: A peer mediated option for improving the academic achievement of heterogeneous learning groups. *Remedial and Special Education, 12*(2), 25–33.

Malamuth, N. M., Turcotte, S. J. C., & Fitz-Gibbon, C. T. (1981). Tutoring and social psychology. *The Journal of Educational Thought, 15*, 113–123.

Martin, D. J. (1996). *Elementary science methods: A constructivist approach.* Albany, NY: Delmar.

Mastropieri, M. A., Scruggs, T. E., & Magnusen, M. (1999). Activities-oriented science instruction for students with disabilities. *Learning Disability Quarterly, 22*, 240–249.

Mastropieri, M. A., Scruggs, T. E., Mohler, L. J., Beranek, M. L., Spencer, V., Boon, R. T., & Talbott, E. (2001). Can middle school students with serious reading difficulties help each other and learn anything? *Learning Disabilities Research & Practice, 16*, 18–27.

McMaster, K. N., & Fuchs, D. (2002). Effects of cooperative learning on the academic achievement of students with learning disabilities: An update of Tateyama-Sniezek's review. *Learning Disabilities Research & Practice, 17*, 107–117.

McTighe, J., & Lyman, F. T., Jr. (1988). Cueing thinking in the classroom: The promise of theory-embedded tools. *Educational Leadership, 45*, 18–24.

Mohan, B. A. (1986). *Language and content.* Reading, MA: Addison-Wesley.

Moll, L. C. (Ed.). (1990). *Vygotsky and education: Instructional implications and applications of sociohistorical psychology.* Cambridge, MA: Cambridge University Press.

Mortweet, S. L., Utley, C. A., Walker, D., Dawson, H. L., Delquadri, J. C., Reddy, S. S., Greenwood, C. R., Hamilton, S., & Ledford, D. (1999). Classwide peer tutoring: Teaching students with mild mental retardation in inclusive classrooms. *Exceptional Children, 65*, 524–536.

O'Malley, J. M., & Chamot, A. U. (1990). *Learning strategies in second language acquisition.* Cambridge: Cambridge University Press.

Ortiz, A. A. (1997). Learning disabilities occurring concomitantly with linguistic differences. *Journal of Learning Disabilities, 30*, 321–332.

Ortiz, A. A. (2001). *English language learners with special needs: Effective instructional strategies.* Washington, DC: ERIC Education Reports.

Palincsar, A. S., & Brown, A. L. (1984). The reciprocal teaching of comprehension-fostering and comprehension-monitoring activities. *Cognition and Instruction, 1*, 117–175.

Peregoy, S. F., & Boyle, O. (1997). *Reading, writing, and learning in ESL* (2nd ed.). White Plains, NY: Longman.

Pressley, M., Beard El-Dinary, P., Gaskins, I., Schuder, T., Bergman, J., Almasi, J., & Brown, R. (1992). Beyond direct explanation: Transactional instruction of reading comprehension strategies. *The Elementary School Journal, 92*, 513–555.

Pressley, M., & Wharton-McDonald, R. (1997). Skilled comprehension and its development through instruction. *School Psychology Review, 26*(3), 448–466.

Putnam, J. W. (1993). *Cooperative learning and strategies for inclusion: Celebrating diversity in the classroom.* Baltimore, MD: Brookes.

Qian, D. D. (1999). Assessing the roles of depth and breadth of vocabulary knowledge in reading comprehension. *Canadian Modern Language Review, 56,* 282–307.

Readence, J. E., Bean, T. W. & Baldwin, S. (1998). *Content area literacy: An integrated approach* (6th ed.). Dubuque, IA: Kendall/Hunt.

Readence, J. E. Bean, T. W., & Baldwin, S. (2004). *Content area literacy: An integrated approach* (8th ed.). Dubuque, IA: Kendall/Hunt.

Reyes, M. L., & Molner, L. A. (1991). Instructional strategies for second-language learners in the content areas. *Journal of Reading, 35,* 96–103.

Richard-Amato, P. (2003). *Making it happen: From interactive to participatory language teaching* (3rd ed.). Upper Saddle River, NJ: Pearson ESL.

Richard-Amato, P. A., & Snow, M. A. (Eds.).(1992). *The multicultural classroom: Readings for content-area teachers.* White Plains, NY: Longman.

Rosenshine, B., & Stevens, R. (1986). Teaching functions. In M. Wittrock (Ed.), *Third handbook of research on teaching* (pp. 376–391). New York: Macmillan.

Rueda, R., Goldenberg, C., & Gallimore, R. (1992). *Rating instructional conversations: A guide* (Educational Practice Report 4). Santa Cruz, CA: The National Center for Research on Cultural Diversity and Second Language Learning, University of California, Santa Cruz.

Saunders, W., Goldenberg, C., & Hamann, J. (1992). Instructional conversations beget instructional conversations. *Teaching and Teacher Education, 8*(2), 199–218.

Schumaker, J. B., & Lenz, B. K. (1999). *Adapting language arts, social studies, and science materials for the inclusive classroom.* Reston, VA: The Council for Exceptional Children.

Scruggs, T. E., & Richter, L. (1988). Tutoring learning disabled students: A critical review. *Learning Disability Quarterly, 11,* 274–286.

Simmons, D. C., & Kameenui, E. J. (1990). The effect of task alternatives on vocabulary knowledge: A comparison of students with and without learning disabilities. *Journal of Learning Disabilities, 23,* 291–297.

Simmons, D. C., & Kameenui, E. J. (1998). *What reading research tells us about children with diverse learning needs: Bases and basics.* Mahwah, NJ: Lawrence Erlbaum.

Slavin, R. E. (1988). *Students team learning: An overview and practical guide* (2nd ed.). Washington, DC: National Education Association.

Tam, B. K. Y., & Scott, M. L. (1996). Three group instructional strategies for students with limited English proficiency in vocational education. *Journal for Vocational Special Needs Education, 19*(1), 31–36.

Tharp, R., & Gallimore, R. (1991). *The instructional conversation: Teaching and learning in social activity* (Research Report 2). Santa Cruz, CA: The National Center for Research on Cultural Diversity and Second Language Learning, University of California, Santa Cruz.

Thomas, W. P. (1992). *County of Arlington (VA) ESEA Title VII program: The Cognitive Academic Language Learning Approach (CALLA) project for mathematics, 1991–1992.* Evaluation report submitted to the Office of Bilingual Education, U.S. Department of Education.

Tobin, K. (1987). The role of wait time in higher cognitive level learning. *Review of Educational Research, 57*(1), 69–95.

Torgesen, J. K., & Licht, B. (1983). The learning disabled child as an inactive learner: Retrospect and prospects. In J. D. McKinney & L. Feagans (Eds.), *Current topics in learning disabilities* (Vol. 1, pp. 3–32). Norwood, NJ: Ablex.

Vallecorsa, A. L., deBettencourt, L. U., & Zigmond, N. (2000). *Students with mild disabilities in general education settings: A guide for special educators.* Upper Saddle River, NJ: Merrill/Prentice Hall.

Vaughn, S., Gersten, R., & Chard, D. J. (2000). The underlying message in LD intervention research: Findings from research syntheses. *Exceptional Children, 67,* 99–114.

Vygotsky, L. S. (1978). *Mind in society.* Cambridge, MA: Harvard University Press.

Watson, D. L., Northcutt, L. & Rydele, L. (1989). Teaching bilingual students successfully. *Educational Leadership, 46*(5), 59–61.

Woodward, J., Monroe, K., & Baxter, J. (2001). Enhancing student achievement on performance assessments in mathematics. *Learning Disability Quarterly, 24,* 33–46.

PART IV

Related Skills and Strategies

Chapter 10

Collaborative Consultation and Parent Involvement

Chapter Objectives

Upon completion of this chapter the reader will be to:

1. Provide a rationale for improving parent and community involvement.
2. Discuss some of the barriers to effective parental involvement.
3. Offer solutions to overcoming these barriers.
4. Provide strategies for improving parent and community involvement.
5. Present models and best practices of parent involvement.

VIGNETTE

In preparing to begin the new school year, second-grade teacher Teresa Rodriguez and bilingual special education consultant Jesse Alaniz decided to schedule an orientation for the parents and guardians of their students. Although Teresa and Jesse recognized that collaborating with the parents and guardians of their culturally and linguistically diverse exceptional (CLDE) students was essential, they also believed that collaboration with their other students' parents and guardians would enhance the learning opportunities for all students. In planning the orientation, Teresa and Jesse first contacted all of the parents by either e-mail or phone to find out what time of day would be most convenient for them to meet. Jesse assisted Teresa in making the phone calls and composing e-mails in both English and Spanish, and because the availability of parents seemed to be split between those able to meet during the day and those available in the evening, Teresa and Jesse decided to schedule both a day and an evening orientation.

Teresa and Jesse opened the orientation by welcoming the parents and guardians and introducing themselves, their backgrounds, and their roles in the school. Conducting the orientation in both Spanish and English, Teresa and Jesse emphasized how much they valued the parents as partners in their children's education and explained that the major goal of this initial meeting was to become familiar with the parents' goals and desires for their children's education and the parents' areas of expertise. Teresa and Jesse invited the parents to complete a written survey (either an English or Spanish version, both designed using clear and simple language) to gather background information on what the parents and guardians value most in their child's education and life, what they believe are their child's academic and nonacademic strengths and weaknesses, activities the child participates in at home, any hobbies or sports, and areas the parents and guardians would identify as areas of expertise for themselves. Teresa and Jesse invited those parents willing to share any of their responses with the group to do so and then concluded the meeting by providing parents with a pamphlet that included their contact information, the contact information of other resource people in the school, a list of ways the parents could become involved at school and with their child's schoolwork at home, opportunities to participate in the school's advisory council, and a schedule of PTA meetings. They also welcomed the parents to schedule a visit to the classroom at any time. Finally, Teresa and Jesse encouraged all of the parents and guardians to schedule a conference

The authors wish to acknowledge Amy Saks for her assistance in developing this vignette.

with them and their child during the first month of school to design an individual plan to best meet their child's learning needs.

Following the meetings, Teresa and Jesse compiled the data from the surveys, using that data to design a classroom environment conducive to meeting the goals reported by parents. Many parents included in their goals for their child the ability to work well with others in groups, so Teresa and Jesse made collaborative group work a key pedagogical tool, providing for students a structure for such work by first assigning then eventually having students select roles within the group. Another common goal among parents was that their child was self-confident, so Teresa and Jesse designed differentiated learning activities that addressed multiple learning styles and allowed children to feel challenged and experience success. When Teresa and Jesse met with each parent and guardian and their child in the individual conferences, they drew from the initial surveys the parents completed, their observations and anecdotal notes of the child in school, the child's written work, and the parents' observations of the child at home in designing together learning objectives for the student and a plan for the role each member—Jesse, Teresa, the parent/guardian, and the student—will play in the student's learning. At the end of each conference, Jesse and Teresa scheduled their next meeting with the parent, reminded them that they would send home weekly or biweekly progress reports depending on the student's learning needs, and encouraged the parents to contact them at any time they had suggestions, questions, or concerns regarding their child's progress.

Reflective Questions

1. What value do you see in setting up a parent orientation meeting at the beginning of the school year?
2. Implementing a parent involvement plan for every student may seem overwhelming. What suggestions do you have for facilitating this process?
3. Why is collaboration among the regular teacher, the special education consultant, and the parents an important practice?

INTRODUCTION

Historically the teaching profession has promoted independence rather than collaboration. In other words teachers have been socialized to carry out their teaching responsibilities as independent agents. Having one's own classroom has been the goal for aspiring teachers entering into the teaching profession. As schools have been reformed and restructured in recent years, teacher independence has begun to give way to teacher collaboration and interdependence. This has been especially true as schools have tried to better meet the needs of challenging students such as those with special education needs as well as English language learners. In an effort to promote a culture of inclusion in the schools, teachers have had to come together and figure out new ways of working together to better serve the needs of all students.

DEFINING COLLABORATION

The educational literature in recent years has started to put more emphasis on teacher collaboration and consultation. One of the first questions that comes up as we examine this trend is, What is meant by collaboration and consultation? It thus becomes important to define and clarify some of these key terms. Collaboration generally means that two or more people are working together to accomplish a goal. Collaboration assumes that the individuals involved are peers or equal in status and expertise. Consultation, on the other hand, assumes an expert–novice or a more expert–less expert relationship between the collaborators. Harris and Heron (2001) maintain that there are several definitions of consultation and collaboration that vary in substance and content depending on the setting, the target, and the intervention employed. They define collaborative consultation as voluntary, mutual, and interactive engagements that connote parity, reciprocity, and mutual problem solving by sharing resources, responsibility, and accountability.

Idol, Nevin, and Paolucci-Whitcomb (1995) define collaborative consultation as follows:

> Collaborative consultation is an interactive process, which enables people with diverse expertise to generate creative solutions to mutually defined problems. The outcome is enhanced, altered, and produces solutions that are different from those that the individual team members would produce independently. The major outcome of collaborative consultation is to provide comprehensive and effective programs for students with special needs. (p. 133)

The role of the educational consultant is threefold. According to Goldstein and Sorcher (1974), the three dimensions involve the provision of technical assistance, the utilization of effective communication skills, and the coordination of services.

RATIONALE FOR INCREASED COLLABORATION

Given that our goal is to provide the most effective programs possible for students with special needs, it thus becomes imperative for us to explore strategies that will help us attain this goal. Clearly then, an emphasis on collaborative consultation among special education, bilingual/ESL education, and regular education teachers is an essential strategy in meeting this goal. One arena that is ideal for this type of collaborative consultation is at the prereferral stage. All school buildings are now required to have a building-based team that works together to recommend interventions for students who are struggling and falling behind in their learning. These prereferral teams go by many different names. Some focus on the child and call themselves child study teams, others focus on the teacher and call themselves teacher support teams. Some focus on instruction and call themselves instructional support teams. Regardless of the name given these teams, their responsibility is to meet as a group and review the records of individual students who are presented to the team and recommend interventions designed to help that student succeed. The prereferral process is thus an excellent training ground for developing collaborative consultation skills. School districts and building leaders should not only support this activity, but also provide staff development for these teams along with release time for them to meet and do this important work.

The State of Pennsylvania implemented a successful prereferral initiative a few years ago called the Instructional Support Team (IST). This model calls for the following support mechanisms:

1. Strong administrative support
2. Staff development
3. Release planning time
4. A teacher on special assignment to follow up with the implementation of the recommended interventions

Through the implementation of this prereferral model, Pennsylvania has been able to reduce the referrals to special education. A study by the Center for Special Education Finance (Hartman & Fay, 1996) found the IST program to be more cost effective than the traditional special education program. According to Hartman and Fay (1996):

> The strength of the IST lies in providing more and better services to more students. Many more students with learning and behavioral problems were provided services through the IST program than the traditional program. Fewer students in IST schools were referred for evaluation; fewer were placed in special education; fewer were returned to regular education (without additional support in the regular classroom) following evaluation; and fewer were retained in the same grade. Therefore, on all measures, the IST appeared to be more effective in serving students. (p. 31)

Prereferral intervention teams have been more popular at the elementary level. Many secondary schools, however, have also utilized prereferral teams effectively. Myers and Kline (2001) have suggested that the prereferral model needs to be adapted to better fit the context of the secondary school. They suggest that both the parents and the student be included in the process. They also recommend that team membership be voluntary and that ongoing training of the team be provided along with strong support of the school administrators.

Another opportunity to use collaborative consultation is through the inclusion of students with special needs in the regular classroom. In the past, special education was provided in self-contained classrooms or in resource rooms. Today the trend is to keep the student with special needs in the regular classroom and provide support services to the regular teacher through collaborative consultation. This strategy requires the special education teacher to come into the regular classroom and provide both direct services for the student with special needs and supportive services to the regular classroom teacher.

Teaching Implications: If you are a bilingual/ESL or bilingual special education teacher, you can practice collaborative consultation with regular classroom teachers regarding the needs of English language learners (ELLs). For the most part you would share your expertise on how to make lessons more easily comprehensible through the use of visual and contextual support and through the use of sheltered English strategies.

What is needed more than anything else in order to implement collaborative consultation is a change in the professional culture of the school. Collaborative consultation has to become part of the school culture. Teachers have to start seeing collaborative consultation as something that is normal and expected from everyone. Collaborative consultation has to become an everyday practice rather than an occasional strategy. Once the school culture adopts collaborative consultation as a desirable practice, more and more teachers will start engaging in it.

Many different collaborative consultation models have been described in the literature. A school needs to adopt one model and provide training and practice with that model until it becomes second nature to the teachers in the building.

ADOPTING A MODEL

Kurpius (1978) recommends the nine-step procedure shown in Table 10.1 for engaging in collaborative consultation.

STEP ONE: PREENTRY. During this phase the consultant clarifies his or her educational philosophy and orientation toward the process and discusses the relationship between the parties involved. Intervention strategies are discussed. Likewise, the role of the parent is discussed. At the end of this phase, the ground rules and the roles and responsibilities of each person should be clear.

TABLE 10.1 Nine Steps of Collaboration

Step	Procedure
Step 1	Preentry
Step 2	Entry
Step 3	Gathering information
Step 4	Defining the problem
Step 5	Determining solutions
Step 6	Stating objectives
Step 7	Implementing the plan
Step 8	Evaluating the plan
Step 9	Concluding the consultation

STEP TWO: ENTRY. At this point, establishing good rapport and communication is important. This is followed by getting familiar with the overall context of the learning problem being considered. Finally, an agreement is reached regarding the next steps to be taken in an attempt to solve the problem.

STEP THREE: GATHERING INFORMATION. In this stage, the parties agree on what data is needed and how it will be collected. They then work together collecting and sharing the data with one another. This usually involves collecting samples of student work and observing student performance on various tasks.

STEP FOUR: DEFINING THE PROBLEM. At this stage, both parties must come into full agreement regarding what they see as the presenting problem. The problem should be spelled out in behavioral and measurable language. Complex problems should be broken down into subproblems beginning with the most complex first.

STEP FIVE: DETERMINING SOLUTIONS. Several possible solutions should be considered at this point. The least restrictive solution should be tried first. This means that the first solution that is tried is the one that is most straightforward and easily implemented.

STEP SIX: STATING OBJECTIVES. At this stage, it is important to state clear behavioral objectives describing the conditions under which the behavior should occur. Also included should be the criteria for evaluating the accomplishment of the objective.

STEP SEVEN: IMPLEMENTING THE PLAN. Both parties must agree to the implementation strategy and the roles that each will play during the implementation phase. It is important to include a timeline at this stage.

STEP EIGHT: EVALUATING THE PLAN. An objective assessment of the implementation of the plan is now conducted. Both parties need to determine whether the desired change has occurred and, if so, what variables seem to have been responsible for the desired result or failure.

STEP NINE: CONCLUDING THE CONSULTATION. Bringing closure to the collaborative consultation is necessary once the desired outcome has been accomplished. Both parties must agree that the specified goal has been reached. If not, the process is continued until success is attained.

COLLABORATIVE SKILL DEVELOPMENT

Adopting a collaborative consultation model is a good first step that will lead to a more collaborative culture in special education. Much work, however, remains to be done before effective collaboration becomes a meaningful part of the work environment.

According to Heron and Harris (2001) many specific skills are important for professionals using collaborative consultation.

Several specific skills may improve the consultation process. These include the ability to distribute leadership among participants, to manage controversy positively, to communicate without the use of jargon, and to maintain an awareness of and use positive nonverbal language (Idol et al., 1995). Sensitivity to multicultural issues, an understanding of organization, and the ability to summarize important information verbally and in writing are all critical skills (Dougherty, Tack, Fullam, & Hammer, 1996). Additionally, active listening to others, and using nonverbal acknowledgements such as eye contact and nodding. The use of appropriate interview skills is also important, facilitating the exchange of specific information, the expression of feelings, the planning of future courses of action, and an enhancement of problem solving (Idol et al., 1995). A solid knowledge base composed of assessment techniques, instructional and behavioral interventions, potential adaptations to curricular materials, and classroom management skill is essential. Further, a sense of humor, as well as the ability to take risk, respond with integrity, and adapt easily, is helpful (Idol, Nevin, & Paolucci-Whitcomb, (1995). (pp. 11–12)

COLLABORATION SKILLS NEEDED BY TEACHERS OF CLDE STUDENTS

One of the most critical sets of skills needed by collaborative consultants is the ability to engage successfully in mutual and collaborative problem solving. West and Cannon (1998) conducted a national study of 100 experts in the field and identified the following essential collaborative problem-solving skills:

1. Recognize that successful and lasting solutions require commonality of goals and collaboration throughout all phases of the problem-solving process.

2. Develop a variety of data collection techniques for problem identification and clarification.

3. Generate viable alternatives through brainstorming techniques characterized by active listening, nonjudgmental responding, and appropriate reframing.

4. Evaluate alternatives to anticipate possible consequences, narrow and combine choices, and assign priorities.

5. Integrate solutions into a flexible, feasible, and easily implemented plan of action relevant to all persons affected by the problem.

6. Adopt a "pilot problem-solving" attitude, recognizing that adjustments to the plan of action are to be expected.

7. Remain available throughout implementation for support, modeling, and/or assistance in modification.

8. Redesign, maintain, or discontinue interventions using data-based evaluation.

9. Utilize observation, feedback, and interviewing skills to increase objectivity and mutuality throughout the problem-solving process.

Collaborating to Meet CLDE Needs

Harris (1996) maintains that a specific set of multicultural skills are essential for collaborative consultants to have when they are working in a multicultural environment such as bilingual special education. In the area of interpersonal skills she recommends:

1. Making continued and sincere attempts to understand the world from others' points of view.
2. Respecting individuals from other cultures.
3. Having a sense of humor.
4. Tolerating ambiguity.
5. Approaching others with a desire to learn.
6. Being prepared and willing to share information about yourself.
7. Identifying needed multicultural knowledge base.
8. Moving fluidly between the roles of giver and taker of information.

In the area of communication skills she recommends:

1. Working effectively with an interpreter or translator.
2. Using nontechnical language as an aid in equalizing differences between collaborators.
3. Acknowledging cultural differences in communication and relationship building.
4. Using communication to create systems of meaning among collaborators.
5. Identifying language practices that are disabling and change them.
6. Ensuring that problem identification does not conflict with cultural beliefs.
7. Using information regarding socially hidden aspects of power that privilege or silence culturally diverse groups in problem solving.

It is also important to examine the specific roles of the various collaborators (see Table 10.2).

TABLE 10.2 Roles of Professional Collaborators

Position	Role
Principal	Convene group and provide leadership
General education teacher	Describe presenting problem or concern
Special education teacher	Provide disability-related suggestions
Speech pathologist	Discuss speech and language issues
ESL specialist	Present English learning goals
School psychologist	Provide assessment profile

APPLICATIONS OF COLLABORATION: STRATEGIES FOR CLDE LEARNERS

There are numerous opportunities for utilizing collaborative consultation when working with English language learners with disabilities. What follows is an overview of some of the more common opportunities. Perhaps the most critical and important opportunity to engage in collaborative, consultation, as has been stated earlier, is at the prereferral stage.

Prereferral Collaboration

The work of child study teams or instructional support teams is the primary responsibility of general education; nonetheless, special education teachers are often involved. At this stage, students who are falling behind academically are brought to the team to brainstorm interventions that may be useful in their education. English language learners may need native language support, sheltered instruction, and scaffolded instruction. It may be important to consult and involve parents, extended family members, church leaders, and other key individuals who interact with the student on a regular basis.

Assessment Collaboration

Assessment is often an area that requires the collaboration of teachers, parents, psychologist, speech and language specialist, and bilingual/ESL specialist. The classroom teacher is often the first to supply data and information from the instructional perspective. This could include samples of student work in a portfolio format, diagnostic testing results in the content areas, and curriculum-based assessment. The bilingual/ESL specialist frequently provides language proficiency data in both languages. The school psychologist provides IQ test data if needed along with other psychological assessments. Parents can also provide the team with valuable information regarding the student's performance in the home environment.

Instructional Collaboration

Cooperative teaching is another occasion when collaborative consultation can be useful. When working in an inclusive setting, the regular classroom teacher provides the majority of the instruction and the special education teacher comes into the classroom a few times each week to provide a model lesson or work with a small group of students. Another opportunity for collaboration is with team teaching. This could involve the regular teacher working with the special education teacher and/or the bilingual/ESL teacher. If the school uses the coordinated services model, collaboration is required between the special education teacher and the bilingual/ESL teacher. Even a self-contained bilingual special education classroom has a need for collaborative consultation. In this setting, bilingual special education teachers consult with one another to share successful practices and to problem solve mutual problems they are facing.

PARENT AND COMMUNITY INVOLVEMENT

One of the most critical and important responsibilities of teachers of ELLs with special needs is to work closely and in an authentic partnership with the parents of these students. All of the information just covered on collaborative consultation is relevant and applicable to the work that must be done with the parents of ELLs with disabilities. A good deal of research has documented the importance of parent involvement in general education and how it has a positive impact on student achievement (Henderson, Marburger, & Ooms, 1986). If parent involvement is necessary to improve the performance of regular education students, it becomes all the more important for special education students.

Parent partnerships with teachers and schools should include an understanding of the community's attitudes about schooling, cultural influences, socioeconomic environments, and levels of parent education. Parents from Mexico, for example, may view the teacher and the school as totally responsible for the education of their child. They have a high level of respect and trust for the teacher, and they have not been socialized to be actively involved with the teacher in the education of their child.

Rationale for Parent Involvement

Parents are the child's first teacher. It only makes sense that they should continue and extend their teaching responsibility in partnership with teachers and the school. In addition to being the natural and right thing to do, there are other reasons why parental involvement is necessary. The Individuals with Disabilities Education Improvement Act (IDEA) requires that parents be involved and give their informed consent to the placement and the Individualized Education Plan (IEP) that is designed for their child. In addition, the law provides due process procedures that must be provided to parents within the special education process. Subsequent amendments to the law have required an Individualized Family Service Plan (IFSP), which expands the role of the family in planning and implementing the child's educational program (De Mers, Fiorello, & Langer, 1992). An IFSP spells out in detail the active role the parents and family will play in the education of the student. Parent involvement in the special education process can be active and/or passive. Passive involvement would include attending meetings and listening to the recommendations of the school. It also involves giving consent to the placement and the IEP. Passive involvement is sufficient to meet the letter of the law. The ideal form of parental involvement, however, is active and highly engaged participation in a true partnership with the school and the child's teachers. To move from passive compliance to active engagement requires a genuine outreach to parents that includes professional development and training along with the fostering of a responsive and respectful engagement with parents. For this to be accomplished successfully, many schools hire a parent liaison and establish a parent resource center in the school. With these resources in place, parents have access to translation services, child care, transportation, and instructional materials. One obvious example of parental involvement for a CLDE student would be the commitment of the parent to use the native language in the home setting to help stimulate language development. In addition parents of CLDE students can assist with homework assignments and can volunteer to help in the student's classroom.

Barriers and Challenges to Parental Involvement

The most common barriers to parental involvement include time availability, with many parents working long hours and/or two jobs; the lack of targeted resources, such as a parent liaison and a parent resource center; transportation; and child care. Some obstacles are more elusive and involve the belief systems of professionals, including a deficit mentality regarding ELL parents. This is manifested when educators think that parents don't care about their child's education, that they have poor parenting skills, or that they do not have as sophisticated a knowledge of their child as the school does. Another significant obstacle for non-English-speaking parents is the issue of school climate. Oftentimes these parents don't feel welcome in the school because little is done to ease the language barrier or to make them feel welcome and valued in the school. Another barrier or challenge is that not all parents understand the value and importance of active parent involvement in the education of their children and therefore hesitate to get involved.

Changes Needed for Improving Parental Involvement

There is no question that some significant changes must be made by school personnel to improve parental involvement for the parents of ELLs with disabilities. The most important change that must occur is to eliminate the deficit view that many educators have of these parents. These parents love their children as much as any other parent does, and they want the best possible education for them. Their parental attitudes and skills may be different from mainstream parents, but they are not deficient or defective.

For this change in thinking regarding deficit perspective of minority parents to occur, staff development should be planned and carried out. Teachers should be made aware of the cultural diversity in their school community. They should become familiar with the rich cultural capital of the parents of the children they teach. Moll and Amanti (1992) refer to this as "funds of knowledge." Their studies point out that all parents have a great deal of knowledge that is culturally specific. When teachers are exposed to this important resource parents have, they develop a new respect for them as competent members of the community. Once respect for parents is established, teachers can engage with them in a true partnership regarding the education of their children.

In addition to changing the deficit perspective that some teachers may have regarding parents of ELLs with disabilities, it is also necessary to eliminate many of the other basic obstacles that hinder full parental participation in the education of their children. To do this, resources must be provided to support language interpreters, child care, and transportation. Communication should be improved through the hiring of a parent liaison who can make home visits and call parents regularly to keep them informed of important school activities and meetings. Individual teachers must also step forward and contact all the parents of their students and invite them to participate in a range of school activities and encourage them to assist with homework. Once parents see other parents getting involved, they will begin to see how important and normal it is to be actively engaged in their child's education.

A Model for Parental Involvement

Various models for parental involvement have been proposed in the literature. de Valenzuela, Baca, and Baca (2004) have suggested that the ecological model (Bronfenbrenner, 1979) be combined with the critical theory model (Fine, 1993). The ecological model uses a systems approach and stresses the importance of looking at the child and the family within the broader social context of their environment. The systems view takes into account the mutual influencing factors that surround students and families and recognizes that changes in one part of the system affect the whole system. In this model the child is always in the center and is surrounded by the family and community. The critical theory model recognizes and challenges the inequalities of power between parents and schools and thus supports the empowerment of parents and families. Parents are thus made aware of oppression and learn to implement strategies to overcome it (Benett & LeCompte, 1990). Figure 10.1 illustrates the mutual relationships among child, parents, and school that must be acknowledged when implementing parental involvement programs and activities. By adopting this model the school places the child at the center of the educational process and acknowledges the roles played by the parents, family, and the broader social environment. This model focuses on the student's strengths and the strengths of the family. It acknowledges the opportunities as well as the obstacles that exist in the broader social environment, and it supports a genuine partnership with parents and families.

Strategies for Parent Involvement

Having discussed parent and community involvement from a theoretical perspective and having proposed a model from which to start this important work, it is now up to individual schools and teachers to initiate and/or continue the important work of engaging parents to become true partners in the education of their children. The initial strategies and activities should concentrate on the attitudinal changes that are necessary. Teachers and schools need to learn more about the strengths of their parents and

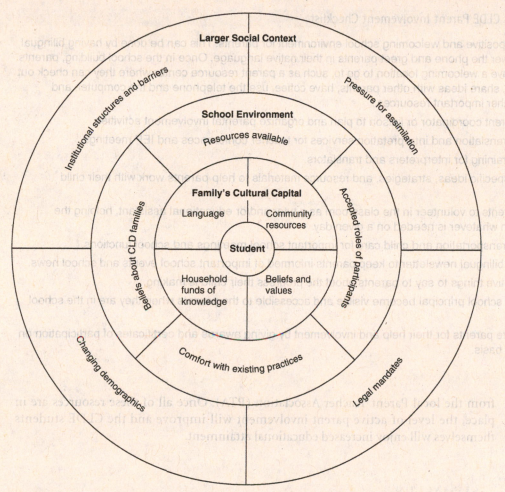

FIGURE 10.1 A Critical-Ecological Model for Family Involvement in Bilingual Special Education

families. They need to view these parents in a more positive light. Teachers must begin to see these parents of students with disabilities as more capable, supportive, and responsible for making important and informed decisions about their children. The checklist in Table 10.3 should help improve the involvement of parents in the education of their special needs child.

Special education teachers who work with CLDE students should meet with their principal and review the checklist in Table 10.3 to ensure that all the necessary resources are in place so that parents will have the support they need to be actively engaged in the education of their child. Some of the suggestions may require additional funding or personnel. If the school budget cannot provide what is needed, support should be requested from the school district special education office as well as

TABLE 10.3 CLDE Parent Involvement Checklist

1. Create a positive and welcoming school environment for parents. This can be done by having bilingual staff answer the phone and greet parents in their native language. Once in the school building, parents should have a welcoming location to go to, such as a parent resource center where they can check out materials, share ideas with other parents, have coffee, use the telephone and the computer, and access other important resources.
2. Hire a parent coordinator or liaison to plan and organize parental involvement activities.
3. Provide translation and interpretation services for teacher conferences and IEP meetings.
4. Provide training for interpreters and translators.
5. Provide specific ideas, strategies, and resource materials to help parents work with their child at home.
6. Invite parents to volunteer in the classroom as a tutor and/or educational assistant, helping the teacher in whatever is needed on a given day.
7. Provide transportation and child care for important school meetings and school functions.
8. Create a bilingual newsletter to keep parents informed of important school events and school news.
9. Find positive things to say to parents about the progress their child is making.
10. Have the school principal become visible and accessible to the parents when they are in the school building.
11. Recognize parents for their help and involvement by giving awards and certificates of participation on a regular basis.

from the local Parent Teacher Association (PTA). Once all of these resources are in place, the level of active parent involvement will improve and the CLDE students themselves will enjoy increased educational attainment.

SUMMARY

In this chapter we have discussed collaborative consultation and parent involvement. The literature on consultation was summarized. The difference between expert consultation and collaborative consultation was stressed. A consultation model was presented and recommended for adoption. A range of consultation skills was reviewed. The most important change needed in schools today is a cultural change that makes collaboration part of the school culture. Collaborative consultation should occur not only with teachers and other educational specialists but with parents as well. Consulting with parents requires additional cross-cultural communication skills. Parental involvement was discussed. Many of the challenges and obstacles to parental involvement were reviewed. An ecological and critical parental involvement model was proposed, and a range of parental involvement strategies was recommended.

Discussion Questions

1. Why is collaborative consultation hard to implement in many schools?
2. What are some of the skills needed to be an effective collaborative consultant?
3. How is collaborative consultation different from expert consultation?
4. How is collaborative consultation used at the prereferral stage?
5. What are some of the major steps in the collaborative consultation model proposed?
6. What is the major attitudinal barrier to effective parental involvement?
7. What can teachers and schools do to improve parental involvement?
8. What would a positive school environment for parental involvement look like?

References

Bennett, K. P., & LeCompte, M. D. (1990). *The way schools work; A sociological analysis of education.* New York: Longman.

Bronfenbrenner, U. (1979). *The ecology of human development: Experiments by nature and design.* Cambridge, MA: Harvard University Press.

De Mers, S. T., Fiorello, C., & Langer, K. L. (1992). Legal and ethical issues in preschool assessment. In E. V. Nuttall, I. Romero, & J. Kalesnik (Eds.), *Assessing and screening preschoolers: Psychological and educational dimensions.* Needham Heights, MA: Allyn & Bacon.

de Valenzuela, J. L., Baca, L., & Baca, E. (2004). *Family involvement in bilingual special education* (4th ed.). Upper Saddle River, NJ: Merrill/Prentice Hall.

Fine, M. (1993). Parent involvement. *Equity and Choice, 9*(3), 4–8.

Goldstein, A. P., & Sorcher, M. (1974). *Changing supervisor behavior.* New York: Pergamon.

Harris, K. C. (1996). Collaboration within a multicultural society: Issues for consideration. *Remedial and Special Education, 17*(6), 335–362.

Harris, K. C., & Heron, T. E. (2001). *The educational consultant: Helping professionals, parents, and students in inclusive classrooms* (6th ed.). Austin, TX: Pro-Ed.

Hartman, W. T., & Fay, T. A. (1996). *Cost-effectiveness of instructional support teams in Pennsylvania* (No. 9). Palo Alto, California: The Center for Special Education Finance.

Henderson, A. T., Marburger, C. L., & Ooms, T. (1986). *Beyond the bake sale: An educator's guide to working with parents.* Columbia, MD: National Committee for Citizens in Education.

Heron, T. E., & Harris, K. C. (2001). *The educational consultant.* Austin, TX: Pro-Ed.

Idol, L., Nevin, A., & Paolucci-Whitcomb, P. (1995). The collaborative consultation model. *Journal of Educational and Psychological Consultation, 6*(4), 347–361.

Kurpius, D. J. (1978). Consultation theory and process: An integrated model. *Personnel and Guidance Journal, 56,* 335–338.

Moll, L. C., & Amanti, L. (1992). Funds of knowledge for teaching: Using a qualitative approach to connect homes and classrooms. *Theory Into Practice, 31*(2), 132–141.

Myers, V. M., & Kline, C. E. (2001). Secondary school intervention assistance teams: Can they be effective? *The High School Journal,* 33–42.

West, J., & Cannon, G. S. (1998). Essential collaborative consultation competencies for regular and special educators. *Journal of Learning Disabilities, 21*(1), 56–63.

Chapter 11

Teaching Study Skills
and Study Strategies

Chapter Objectives

Upon completion of this chapter the reader will be able to:

1. Articulate the significance of study skills in learning.
2. Incorporate major cultural and linguistic factors within the use of study skills.
3. Directly teach study skills necessary for successful learning to occur.
4. Apply various study strategy procedures and methods within a culturally relevant context.
5. Integrate study skills usage within the context of cooperative learning.
6. Select effective strategies for applying classroom and authentic assessment in determining study skill needs of CLDE learners.
7. Direct learners to effectively use and apply various study/learning strategies in the classroom.

VIGNETTE

Mr. Hill told his students that there would be a quiz in the next class period—a quiz that was also listed on the class outline and on the chalkboard. He gave the students a study sheet and told them he would be asking them to define three of the five vocabulary terms on the study sheet. Prior to the quiz, he had discussed all the terms for 4 days in class. The terms were also defined and discussed in the assigned textbook chapter. On the day of the quiz, one-fourth of the class failed the quiz. These five students said that they did not know that they were having a quiz; one student asked where these terms had come from as he had never seen them before. The students that failed the quiz were all culturally and linguistically diverse exceptional (CLDE) learners. Mr. Hill's first response was to ask why these students had not succeeded. "*Was it something I did?*" Or was the failure a result of the students' poor study skills?

In this classroom situation, effective use of several study skills may have assisted these learners to have a better opportunity to succeed with their quiz. These include use of a study guide, note taking from information written on the board, and test studying strategies. All too often, CLDE students' failure to succeed is a direct result of poor study skills. Because classroom teachers like Mr. Hill are so busy focusing on classroom instruction, they are not able to address CLDE students with poor or inadequate study skills. Further, they are not able to teach these students how to develop good study skills as a part of the content they are teaching. However, there are some cultural and linguistic considerations and study skills for CLDE learners that teachers like Mr. Hill can use in their classrooms to assist these students in assuming responsibility for their learning and in becoming more effective learners.

Cultural and linguistic considerations relative to study skills include efforts by Mr. Hill to facilitate student use of study skills consistent with their language proficiency levels in both native language and English and accommodating acculturation levels as students adjust to a new cultural environment. In addition, as Mr. Hill provides opportunities for students to use study skills, he will also be emphasizing the use of higher order thinking, which is essential to effective instruction for CLDE learners. Also, as Mr. Hill attends to the processes associated with various study skills, he will be more cognizant of the connection between teaching styles and students' preferred styles of learning.

Classroom teachers like Mr. Hill want all their students to succeed. However, they may be especially frustrated when students struggle with

The authors wish to acknowledge Michael Orosco for his assistance in developing this vignette.

course content because poor study skills get in the way of their learning. Even though study skills development may not be among the learning objectives for the class, the efforts to emphasize the importance of and to provide resources to help CLDE students in developing better study skills will be reflected in their improved academic performance.

Reflective Questions

1. How might the use of study skills assist a student you have taught better prepare for a class quiz or test?
2. Why do you see the need to ensure that cultural and linguistic factors are addressed when helping students learn and use study skills and study strategies?

INTRODUCTION

Study skills assist students to more successfully acquire, retain, and generalize learning. The importance of study skills to academic learning must be recognized along with the various study skills available to students. Poor academic performance results from many factors, one of which is lack of effective use of study skills to complete educational tasks. Understanding the importance and relevance of study skills for CLD students with special needs is critical to implementing a study skills program in the classroom. Knowledge of study skills is an essential component of successful learning for all students. To a great extent, success or failure in school relates to a student's ability to effectively use study skills in culturally relevant ways. Scruggs and Mastropieri (1992) discussed the importance of study skills preparation for students with learning problems. However, while considered important, Woolfolk (2001) wrote that regular instruction to develop study skills does not usually occur in classrooms. Since study skills are often not an integral part of daily instruction, teachers must purposefully stress the importance of using study skills and study strategies (Good & Brophy, 1995).

STUDY SKILLS AND EFFECTIVE LEARNING

Study skills are "tools" students use in the classroom to facilitate effective learning and include a variety of techniques or strategies (Hoover & Patton, 2007). Overall, study skills assist students to acquire, record, organize, synthesize, remember, and use information and ideas (Hoover, 2004; Devine, 1987). In effect, the accuracy with which students acquire, record, or demonstrate knowledge of content directly relates to their effective or ineffective use of study skills and study strategies. According to Pauk (2000), effective application of study skills represents efficiency in using one's time and mind. Cohen and Spenciner (2005) wrote that "study skills are essential for school and work" (p. 487).

An overarching goal of formal education is to prepare students to lead independent and productive lives. Throughout formal education, the effective use of study skills assists students to complete school as well as acquire a greater sense of independence. The 12 study skills discussed in this chapter along with their significance to learning are presented below:

1. *Reading Rate.* Rates vary with type and length of assignment.
2. *Listening.* This skill is necessary to engage in many learning tasks and requirements.
3. *Note Taking/Outlining.* Students must document critical points for further study.
4. *Report Writing.* This is a method for expressing ideas or reporting on topics of study in writing.
5. *Oral Presentations.* An alternative strategy learners frequently use to share ideas and report information.
6. *Graphic Aids.* Visual depiction of topics can be used to illustrate and share ideas.
7. *Test Taking.* Assessment is an integral part of education, and test-taking skills are essential to ensure reliable and valid results.
8. *Library Usage.* Effective use of the library facilitates learners' easy access to significant amounts of information and research knowledge.
9. *Reference Materials.* Effective use of reference materials facilitates independent learning.
10. *Time Management.* Properly managed time improves the quality of work and increases the number of finished assignments completed in a timely manner.
11. *Self-management.* Learners can become more aware of their behaviors while assuming greater responsibility for own learning and behaviors.
12. *Organizational Skill.* Effective organizational skills are essential to managing increased workloads.

As indicated, a variety of study skills exist and each relates to a specific aspect of learning. Collectively these study skills provide a solid foundation for educational success for CLDE learners. Specifically, the importance of study skills is found in many aspects of teaching and learning, including student abilities to:

1. Efficiently and effectively complete tasks and assignments.
2. Effectively use academic learning time in school.
3. Successfully complete work within established timelines.
4. Complete tasks independently by taking responsibility for own learning.
5. Review, proof, and refine work prior to submission.
6. Develop and implement daily, weekly, or monthly schedules effectively.
7. Structure complex assignments so they are manageable.
8. Complete assigned homework in timely and efficient ways.
9. Successfully interact with others.

Although effective use of study skills is essential to help all students with or without disabilities succeed in school, diversity in the classroom provides an additional dimension that must be valued if teachers are to assist CLDE learners succeed in school.

Cultural and Linguistic Considerations When Teaching Study Skills

According to the National Research Council (Donovan & Cross, 2002) CLD students continue to be at risk for special education placement. Baca and Cervantes (2004) wrote that the inappropriate uses of standardized assessments often underestimate CLD students' academic performance, which contributes to the risk of overidentification for special services. In many situations, poor test results of CLD students reflect lack of proficiency with taking tests or use of other study skills, rather than lack of knowledge, further highlighting the importance of emphasizing study skills development for these students. The needs of CLDE learners challenges all teachers to teach study skills relative to cultural and linguistic values. Ovando, Collier, and Combs (2003), O'Malley and Pierce (1996), and Garcia (2001) all discussed several principles important in the education of CLD students. These principles are applied to the development and teaching of study skills to CLDE learners. As presented below, effective study skills programs for CLDE learners should:

1. Be relevant to students' culture, background, environment and prior experiences.
2. Be reinforced over time and across subject areas.
3. Include both cognitive and academic study skills goals.
4. Maintain high expectations for use of study skills while simultaneously valuing diversity.
5. Facilitate active and inquiry-based learning through use of appropriate study skills.

Expanding on these principles and relating to the six cultural and linguistic factors previously discussed in Chapter 5, Table 11.1 presents suggested considerations for the culturally responsive usage of study skills.

As shown, study skills development and use supports these six factors for effectively educating CLDE students. Considering these six factors when teaching study skills will help teachers ascertain the best study strategies to select, while simultaneously valuing cultural and linguistic diversity. In addition, Hoover and Jacobs (1992) found that American Indian college students' self-perception toward their study skills were only slightly positive. This further highlights the need for ongoing study skills programs throughout elementary and secondary school within a culturally and linguistically relevant context.

TYPES OF STUDY SKILLS

The following subsections provide an overview of each of the 12 study skills along with suggested teaching practices. These are based on author experiences and several sources, including Marzano, Pickering, and Pollack (2001), Hoover (2004),

TABLE 11.1 Cultural and Linguistic Considerations and Study Skills for CLDE Learners

Curricular Factors	Overview	Study Skills Considerations
Language Function	*Communicative*—Routine conversational social language *Academic*—Higher level language usage	Language in the classroom must focus on student's study skills abilities to interpret and convey meaning for authentic purposes (fluency and accuracy)
Acculturation	Process where one cultural group assumes traits of another cultural group	Varied responses to acculturation may be exhibited by the student (anxiety, withdrawal, stress) and must be considered within the learning context when teaching study skills
Conceptual Knowledge	New information is built on existing information/knowledge	Prior and current conceptual knowledge related to the content area provides insight into a student's understanding of hierarchies and connections among concepts, including use of study skills
Thinking Abilities	CLD students should be challenged to use and apply higher order thinking abilities	Determining student study skills in applying their thinking abilities provides valuable insight into how the learner is interacting with and learning a curriculum
Cultural Values/Norms	Students come from a variety of backgrounds possessing varying cultural backgrounds values, norms	Study skill experiences students from diverse backgrounds bring to the classroom must be viewed in relevant ways, to ensure appropriate education and to further develop study skills
Teaching/ Learning Styles	Education of CLD students should focus on how the child learns and under what conditions	Consideration of the interactions between teaching/learning styles is essential for effective study skills use, since oftentimes CLDs may use different reasoning strategies according to their native languages

Adapted from Hoover, J. J., & Patton, J. R. (2005). *Curriculum adaptations for students with learning and behavior problems: Differentiating instruction to meet diverse needs* (3rd ed.). Austin, TX: Pro-Ed. Reprinted by permission.

Pauk (2000), Harris and Sipay (1990), and Mercer and Mercer (2000), to name a few. Specific student study and learning strategies are presented later in this chapter.

Reading Rate

Flexible use of reading rates is important because reading is either directly or indirectly related to academic learning. As students move through the grades different reading rates should be emphasized when teaching study skills to students (Heilman, Blair, & Rupley, 2002). The most common reading rates are skimming, scanning, rapid reading, normal reading, and careful or study-type reading (Harris & Sipay, 1990).

- **Skimming.** Fast-paced rate used to grasp main ideas of printed material (e.g., purposefully glossing over material).
- **Scanning.** Fast-paced rate used to locate specific items in a story (e.g., searching for a specific color, a name in a story, specific location).
- **Rapid Reading.** Fast-paced rate used to grasp main ideas or review previously learned material (e.g., information that is being acquired for temporary use).
- **Normal Reading.** Rate of reading used when more specific comprehension is necessary (e.g., identifying details, connecting main ideas, or responding to a specific question).
- **Careful or Study-type Reading.** Rate used when highly specific comprehension is required (e.g., master details, retain or evaluate material, follow explicit directions).

Appropriate reading rate depends on at least two factors: (1) the purpose of the reading and (2) the nature of the material being read (Harris & Sipay, 1990). In many learning situations, two or more rates are required to successfully complete a task. For example, the learner may be required to *scan* several paragraphs to locate a specific location, and once identified, may need to use a *normal* or *careful* reading rate to determine how activities in that location relate to the overall theme of the story. Collectively, effective use of different reading rates requires guided instruction from the teacher to best help learners succeed.

Effective teaching practices for CLDE learners include:

1. Recognizing that cultural and linguistic background may influence perceived purposes for reading, which affects use of appropriate reading rate.
2. Using the most effective and efficient reading rates for various student learning activities.
3. Clarifying explicit purposes for all reading assignments.
4. Using sheltered instruction principles to teach proper use of each reading rate.

Listening

Similar to reading rate, listening is critical to many classroom tasks. According to Gearheart, Weishahn, and Gearheart (1996) and Devine (1987) much of a student's learning and school day is spent with listening-related tasks. However, according to

Lerner (2005), teaching students the important skill of effective listening is often not undertaken in the classroom. Listening includes both *hearing* someone speak and *comprehending* the message, and relates directly to receiving, applying, and providing evidence of understanding what was heard (Hoover, 2004). Teachers must ensure that conditions exist in the classroom to facilitate effective listening, especially during formal presentations and conversations or when other external auditory stimuli may exist. However, of most importance is the notion that "teachers must teach students how to listen" (Devine, 1987, p. 32).

Effective teaching practices for CLDE learners include:

1. Recognizing that some cultures may place more emphasis on nonverbal communication over verbal interactions, which may affect development of listening skills.
2. Beginning verbal presentations with familiar content and systematically bridge to new material.
3. Repeating important items; emphasizing significant ideas presented.
4. Strategically and periodically summarizing key content during the verbal presentation.
5. Using culturally relevant graphic aids to deliver verbal presentations.
6. Using cue words or signals during listening activities.

Note Taking/Outlining

The combined uses of note taking and outlining assist students to improve their performance in various areas of learning, including listening, reading, vocabulary, and thinking. Through note taking/outlining, learners classify and synthesize information to document main ideas and the more important supporting topics for later use. According to Ekwall and Shanker (1998), effective outlining abilities strengthen note-taking skills. In support, Coman and Heavers (2001) discussed the importance of documenting information in lists (i.e., listing) as a means to support outlining. In reference to CLDE learners, these students require specific skills development and with sufficient practice and systematic instruction effective note taking/outlining skills can be strengthened (Hoover, 2004).

Effective teaching practices for CLDE learners include:

1. Using culturally and linguistically relevant cues to facilitate effective development of note taking or outlining.
2. Following an explicit and culturally appropriate method to keep notes and outline topics.
3. Modeling appropriate and recognizable note taking/outlining formats.
4. Progressing from simple note taking/outlining activities to more complex tasks as students improve their skills.

Report Writing

Report writing requires skills to organize ideas and present them, on paper, in a coherent and meaningful way. A variety of skill sets comprise report writing such as organization, proper spelling and punctuation, topic selection, locating information, and library usage. As a result, report writing, similar to reading and listening, encompasses a variety of interrelated skills. Teachers of CLDE students should provide explicit and consistent instructions when written reports are assigned.

Effective teaching practices for CLDE learners include:

1. Determining academic language proficiency skills since they directly impact writing abilities.
2. Encouraging students to draw upon own cultural experiences when writing.
3. Providing and demonstrating, if necessary, explicit instructions to ensure students understand the purpose for the writing project or assignment.
4. Providing students specific strategies to organize their ideas (see Organizational Skills section).
5. Providing direct guidance to help students with different aspects of writing (e.g., outlines, introductory paragraph, transition sentences, brainstorming ideas).

Oral Presentations

Skills associated with report writing are also relevant to oral presentations. Oral presentations may either supplement a written report or they may be stand-alone assignments, and include activities such as interviews, debates, group discussions, and individual/group presentations. As an alternative method, some students who experience difficulty with written assignments may benefit from different forms of oral presentation. However, this study skill should be introduced thoughtfully and in a supporting, nonthreatening manner to minimize the anxiety often associated with speaking in front of groups of people.

Effective teaching practices for CLDE learners include:

1. Recognizing that acculturation and language proficiency levels affect student oral presentation abilities.
2. Providing students extra time when preparing for and delivering oral presentations.
3. Providing a supportive oral presentation environment in the classroom.
4. Providing flexibility in structuring oral presentation class conditions (e.g., initially make 1-to 2-minute presentations; stand by their desks).
5. Providing students with meaningful and culturally relevant purposes for making their oral presentations.

Graphic Aids

Charts, graphs, maps, models, pictures, and photographs are all graphic aids that support student learning. Graphic aids help students to make complex material more manageable and understandable. In addition, a variety of important concepts and events may be learned effectively through visual material, including topics related to cultural, geographic, and economic diversity. However, some students, especially those with learning disabilities, may experience difficulty with discrimination of visual materials, and these students must be taught what to attend to while reading and interpreting graphic aids. Similar to other study skills, CLDE learners require direct instruction to acquire and use graphic aids accurately.

Effective teaching practices for CLDE learners include:

1. Being certain students from diverse cultural and linguistic backgrounds understand unfamiliar visual material.
2. Encouraging use of graphic aids to supplement oral or written projects.
3. Incorporating graphic aids in teacher verbal presentations to demonstrate proper use to students.
4. Assisting students through explicit questioning to identify and interpret important features of visual material.
5. Providing students sufficient opportunities to develop, use, and integrate graphic aids in their learning.

Test Taking

Few educators would dispute the fact that tests are a major aspect within an educational system. In many schools, standards-based assessment is the prevailing form of evaluation in which all students, including CLDE learners, must participate. Beginning in early elementary school, students are subjected to various forms of testing to document their educational progress. However, as Hoover and Patton (2007) and Good and Brophy (1995) indicated, many students, especially those with learning problems, do not possess sufficient test-taking skills. For example, Kiewra and DuBois (1998) emphasized the importance of test-taking strategies, including testing location in the classroom and being cognizant of significant testing terms (e.g., compare, contrast, evaluate). In addition to acquiring knowledge and information, students must be able to demonstrate their learning in different test-taking situations. *However, without proper test-taking abilities, test results may mistakenly show a lack of student content knowledge, when in reality results only reflect lack of test-taking knowledge.*

Test-taking skills include those abilities needed to prepare and study for tests, take tests, and review graded test results (Hoover, 2004). Although CLDE students are frequently subjected to testing situations, teachers should not automatically assume that these students are familiar with test-taking skills or possess sufficient test-taking skills to yield reliable test results. In a recent research study, Hoover and Trujillo-Hinsch (1999) investigated test-taking abilities of third- and sixth-grade English language learners. This research gathered student self-perceptions of their test-taking abilities. Conclusions relevant to teaching test taking to CLD learners are provided in Table 11.2.

Results from this pilot study provide insight to teachers as they prepare for and teach test taking to CLD learners, including those with disabilities.

Effective teaching practices for CLDE learners include:

1. Recognizing that language proficiency levels directly impact test performance and tests should be given in the most proficient language to obtain the most accurate results.

2. Explicitly and graphically demonstrating to students proper procedures for completing different types of tests.

3. Respecting the fact that some cultures place more emphasis on group rather than individual performance, minimizing the importance of individual testing.

4. Providing students a variety of opportunities to learn about different test-taking strategies and types of materials to assist with test taking.

5. Reviewing graded tests with learners to identify test-taking errors and suggesting strategies to correct those errors.

TABLE 11.2 Test-Taking Self-Perceptions of English Language Learners (ELLs) in Grades 3 and 6

Test-Taking Item	Grade 3 Students	Grade 6 Students
General Use/Application of Test Skills	Perceive themselves using and applying test-taking skills on a consistent basis. Students with lower LAS* scores had lower self-perceptions of test-taking skills	Perceive themselves using and applying test-taking skills on a consistent basis
Test Preparation Skills	Perceived to be weakest test-taking skill	Perceived to be weakest test-taking skill
Test Completion Skills (Essay/Objective Test Mechanics)	Completion skills perceived to be stronger than preparation abilities	Completion skills perceived to be stronger than preparation abilities
Overall Confidence	Perceptions of ELLs taught primarily in Spanish had similar overall perceptions as those taught primarily in English	Lack confidence in overall test preparation abilities (i.e., skills needed to prepare for test)

*Language Assessment Scales (1 = Nonproficient; 5 = Fully Proficient)

Developed from: Hoover, J. J., & Trujillo-Hinsch, J. (1999). *Test-taking skills of English language learners.* Final Research Report, OBEMLA Funded Research Project. Boulder, CO: University of Colorado, Boulder.

Library Usage

The study skill of library usage is concerned with skills needed to locate library resource materials. This includes knowledge of computerized cataloging systems, visual media (e.g., PowerPoint presentations, films, filmstrips, resource guides, curricular materials) as well as knowing the general layout and organization of the library (Wesson & Keefe, 1989). In addition, students should familiarize themselves with the role of the media or resource specialist. Through guided instruction in library usage, teachers can help students to develop and use this important skill gradually and systematically throughout elementary and secondary school.

Effective teaching practices for CLDE learners include:

1. Providing newly acculturated learners specific and direct instruction on how to use a library.
2. Ensuring that students know the location and organization of the school, classroom, and community libraries.
3. Facilitating students' use of library resources through research assignments.
4. Ensuring that students understand the variety of resources within and purposes for using a library.

Reference Material/Dictionary Use

Two additional study skills become important once specific library resources have been located. Specifically, these are using a dictionary and other reference materials in connection with various educational tasks such as library research, report writing, and oral presentations. Harris and Sipay (1990) identified four skills necessary to successfully use reference materials. These include understanding (1) the purposes of an index and table of contents; (2) alphabetical order; (3) how to use chapter headings as a quick overview of the material; and (4) the structure and arrangement found within dictionaries, encyclopedias, and other reference materials. As with the other study skills, CLDE learners require practice in order to effectively master and maintain the use of reference materials.

Effective teaching practices for CLDE learners include:

1. Using culturally appropriate examples to demonstrate use and significance of reference materials.
2. Assigning tasks that periodically require student use of different reference materials to complete assignment.
3. Providing direct instruction to help students acquire and maintain reference materials/dictionary skills.
4. Ensuring that the classroom library contains necessary reference materials to facilitate development and usage for daily assignments.

Time Management

Incorrect or unfinished assignments often reflect difficulty with time management, rather than lack of content knowledge and skills. The study skill of time management helps students to allocate and use their time efficiently. As schools place more demands on students, study time and workloads increase, requiring students to more effectively manage their time. As demands increase, teachers of CLDE learners should structure learning situations and tasks in ways that assist them to manage their time effectively.

Effective teaching practices for CLDE learners include:

1. Respecting the fact that concepts of time may vary by cultures and must be considered when teaching time management.
2. Structuring class situations so students must allocate their own time to successfully complete tasks.
3. Praising students for maintaining on-task behaviors during cooperative and independent work times.
4. Clearly stating, and if needed, posting time allotments allowed for each learning task.
5. Providing students sufficient opportunities to learn time management associated with different types of tasks (i.e., brief assignments, longer reports, studying for a test).

Self–Management of Behavior

Along with time management, students must also learn to manage their own behaviors. Inappropriate and off-task behaviors can interfere significantly with learning, even if students possess other study skills. Effective self-management and self-monitoring of behavior allows students to become more aware of their own behaviors and subsequently change those behaviors that interfere with task completion. The topic of self-management was discussed in detail in Chapter 6; below are suggested examples building on those discussions relative to study skills use.

Effective teaching practices for CLDE learners include:

1. Providing consistent and culturally responsive behavioral expectations.
2. Providing students opportunities to use self-management programs and assist them with behavior progress monitoring.
3. Assisting students to set culturally meaningful self-management goals.
4. Ensuring students possess sufficient language skills to comprehend and apply behavioral expectations.

Organizational Skills

The ability to effectively organize and manage learning consistently challenges most students. Bender (2002) wrote that students with learning problems often experience problems with organization. Additionally, expectations placed on students continue to increase and additional pressure is put on students to complete increased workloads in shorter amounts of time while at the same time achieve higher proficiency levels. Organizational skills will assist CLDE students to more effectively manage their own learning in culturally meaningful ways when less teacher direction is provided. Students who organize themselves to complete tasks within established timelines will be more successful in school as well as with personal and leisure time. Specifically, effective organizational skills help students:

1. Manage multiple tasks.
2. Use multiple study skills simultaneously.
3. Prioritize the proper order for successful completion of tasks.
4. Meet increasingly higher demands in achievement.
5. Monitor own learning efficiency.

Students must understand their learning assignments and timelines in order to make informed decisions to organize their own learning.

Effective teaching practices for CLDE learners include:

1. Emphasizing significance of efficient organization in learning.
2. Recognizing that cultural influences may affect a learner's organizational abilities, which impacts prioritizing tasks.
3. Providing systematic and culturally appropriate opportunities in the classroom for student-directed learning.
4. Developing with the student a structure to organize multiple task completion, timelines, and measures to determining success with the organizational plan.
5. Providing students with numerous opportunities to self-monitor their own organization and effects on learning.

ASSESSING STUDY SKILLS

The assessment of study skills determines those skills students use effectively to successfully learn. Study skill assessment provides answers to several types of questions such as:

1. Does the learner adjust reading rates appropriately to meet the reading task demands?
2. Does the student manage time effectively?
3. Does the student possess and use effective test-studying, test-taking, and test-reviewing strategies?

4. Is the student able to record accurate notes from verbal presentations?

5. Does the student effectively manage and organize own learning?

Hoover and Patton (2007) wrote that assessment of study skills should determine (a) student's current status relative to study skills knowledge and use and (b) how well the student uses specific study strategies in authentic learning situations. For example, learners may be familiar with study skills and how they should be implemented, yet are unable to generalize this knowledge to complete actual classroom tasks. Relevant assessment of study skills should include (1) collection of authentic data on student use of study skills, (2) observation and work sample analysis, and (3) use of assessment devices that specifically reflect targeted study skills. A variety of formal and informal study skill devices exist, including norm- and criterion-referenced instruments as well as classroom-based checklists and forms. The reader is referred to Chapter 5 for a detailed discussion of various assessment procedures for CLDE learners. These discussions here focus specifically on classroom-based assessment of study skills since results from this type of assessment are most relevant to actual classroom learning environments.

Classroom–Based Assessment and Teacher–Made Checklists

Classroom-based assessment of study skills links instruction with assessment, using observations, interviews, work sample analysis as well as checklists/tests to gather information for immediate classroom application (Cohen & Spenciner, 2005). This includes the use of teacher-made devices or formally developed checklists to assess targeted study skills use in the classroom. Various classroom-based checklists have been developed to assess different study skills (Pauk, 2000). However, educators of CLDE learners may find it necessary to create their own checklists, despite the existence of commercial instruments since teachers require more classroom-specific study skill information. McLoughlin and Lewis (2000) wrote that teacher-made instruments provide easy and efficient ways to gather and document information about a learner. Should commercially available study skill devices be inappropriate or too limiting in scope, teachers may use and/or develop their own checklists, such as the one illustrated in Figure 11.1. This instrument may be used within the process outlined below for classroom-based assessment of study skills.

To facilitate classroom-based assessment of study skills, Hoover and Patton (2007) outlined several steps to follow:

1. Identify needed study skills.

2. Locate or construct a teacher's checklist based on the study skill needs identified. (As discussed, published devices may not contain items of immediate importance to the teacher and learner).

3. Construct a student self-analysis checklist reflecting same items on teacher checklist.

4. Provide opportunities for students to use desired study skills in the classroom.

FIGURE 11.1 Study Skills Inventory (continued)

Source: Hoover, J.J., & Patton, J.R. (2007). *Teaching study skills to students with learning problems* (2nd ed.). Austin, TX: Pro-Ed. Reprinted by permission.

Student Name _____ Grade _____

Completed by _____ Date _____

Directions: Rate each item using the scale provided. Base the rating on the individual's present level of performance.

		Rating		
Study Skill	Not Proficient	Partially Proficient	Proficient	Highly Proficient
Reading Rate				
Skims	0	1	2	3
Scans	0	1	2	3
Reads at rapid rate	0	1	2	3
Reads at normal rate	0	1	2	3
Reads at study or careful rate	0	1	2	3
Understands the importance of reading	0	1	2	3
Listening				
Attends to listening activities	0	1	2	3
Applies meaning to verbal messages	0	1	2	3
Filters out auditory distractions	0	1	2	3
Comprehends verbal messages	0	1	2	3
Understands importance of listening skills	0	1	2	3
Graphic Aids				
Attends to relevant elements in visual material	0	1	2	3
Uses visuals appropriately in presentations	0	1	2	3
Develops own graphic material	0	1	2	3
Is not confused or distracted by visual material in presentations	0	1	2	3
Understands importance of visual material	0	1	2	3
Library Usage				
Uses cataloging system (card or computerized) effectively	0	1	2	3
Can locate library materials	0	1	2	3
Understands organizational layout of library	0	1	2	3
Understands and uses services of media specialist	0	1	2	3
Understands overall functions and purposes of a library	0	1	2	3
Understands importance of library usage skills	0	1	2	3
Reference Materials				
Can identify components of different reference materials	0	1	2	3
Uses guide words appropriately	0	1	2	3
Consults reference materials when necessary	0	1	2	3
Uses materials appropriately to complete assignments	0	1	2	3

FIGURE 11.1 (continued)

Study Skill	Rating			
	Not Proficient	Partially Proficient	Proficient	Highly Proficient
Can identify different types of reference materials and sources	0	1	2	3
Understands importance of reference materials	0	1	2	3
Test Taking				
Studies for tests in an organized way	0	1	2	3
Spends appropriate amount of time studying different topics covered on a test	0	1	2	3
Avoids cramming for tests	0	1	2	3
Organizes narrative responses appropriately	0	1	2	3
Reads and understands directions before answering questions	0	1	2	3
Proofreads responses and checks for errors	0	1	2	3
Identifies and uses clue words in questions	0	1	2	3
Properly records answers	0	1	2	3
Saves difficult items until last	0	1	2	3
Eliminates obvious wrong answers	0	1	2	3
Systematically reviews completed tests to determine test-taking or test-studying errors	0	1	2	3
Corrects previous test-taking errors	0	1	2	3
Understands importance of test-taking skills	0	1	2	3
Note Taking and Outlining				
Uses headings (and subheadings) appropriately	0	1	2	3
Takes brief and clear notes	0	1	2	3
Records essential information	0	1	2	3
Applies skill during writing activities	0	1	2	3
Uses skill during lectures	0	1	2	3
Develops organized outlines	0	1	2	3
Follows consistent note-taking format	0	1	2	3
Understands importance of note taking	0	1	2	3
Understands importance of outlining	0	1	2	3
Report Writing				
Organizes thoughts in writing	0	1	2	3
Completes written reports from outline	0	1	2	3
Includes only necessary information	0	1	2	3
Uses proper sentence structure	0	1	2	3
Uses proper punctuation	0	1	2	3
Uses proper grammar and spelling	0	1	2	3
Proofreads written assignments	0	1	2	3
Provides clear introductory statement	0	1	2	3
Includes clear concluding statements	0	1	2	3
Understands importance of writing reports	0	1	2	3
Oral Presentations				
Freely participates in oral presentations	0	1	2	3
Organizes persentations well	0	1	2	3
Uses gestures appropriately	0	1	2	3

Study Skill	Rating			
	Not Proficient	Partially Proficient	Proficient	Highly Proficient
Speaks clearly	0	1	2	3
Uses proper language when reporting orally	0	1	2	3
Understands importance of oral reporting	0	1	2	3
Time Management				
Completes tasks on time	0	1	2	3
Plans and organizes daily activities and responsibilities effectively	0	1	2	3
Plans and organizes weekly and monthly schedules	0	1	2	3
Reorganizes priorities when necessary	0	1	2	3
Meets scheduled deadlines	0	1	2	3
Accurately perceives the amount of time required to complete tasks	0	1	2	3
Adjusts time allotment to complete tasks	0	1	2	3
Accepts responsibility for managing own time	0	1	2	3
Understands importance of effective time management	0	1	2	3
Self-Management				
Monitors own behavior	0	1	2	3
Changes own behavior as necessary	0	1	2	3
Thinks before acting	0	1	2	3
Is responsible for own behavior	0	1	2	3
Identifies behaviors that interfere with own learning	0	1	2	3
Understands importance of self-management	0	1	2	3
Organization				
Uses locker efficiently	0	1	2	3
Transports books and other material to and from school effectively	0	1	2	3
Has books, supplies, equipment, and other materials needed for class	0	1	2	3
Manages multiple tasks or assignment	0	1	2	3
Uses two or more study skills simultaneously when needed	0	1	2	3
Meets individual organizational expectations concerning own learning	0	1	2	3
Understands importance of organization	0	1	2	3

(continued)

FIGURE 11.1 (continued)

Directions: Summarize in the chart below the number of Not Proficient (NP), Partially Proficient (PP), Proficient (P), and Highly Proficient (HP) subskills for each study skill. The number next to the study skill represents the total number of subskills listed for each area.

Study Skill	NP	PP	P	HP
Reading rate (6)				
Listening (5)				
Graphic aids (5)				
Library usage (6)				
Reference materials (6)				
Test taking (8)				

Study Skill	NP	PP	P	HP
Note taking and outlining (9)				
Report writing (10)				
Oral presentations (6)				
Time management (9)				
Self-management (6)				
Organization (7)				

Summary comments about student study skills:

_____

_____

_____

_____

_____

_____

_____

_____

_____

_____

5. Observe the students using the study skills in learning activities, document effects, and complete teacher and student checklists.

6. Summarize teacher and student checklists, compare results, and plan future course of action.

Adhering to this process and using classroom-based assessment instruments ensures that authentic assessment of study skills occurs as well as provides a systematic method for gathering relevant data. Both of these tasks (i.e., following a process and recording results) must be completed in order to develop and implement an effective study skills program for CLDE learners.

TEACHING THE DEVELOPMENT OF STUDY SKILLS

Study skills are best acquired, applied, and generalized within the authentic context of meaningful academic tasks (Hoover & Patton, 2007; Hoover & Rabideau, 1995). As with any area of education, all students, particularly CLDE learners must be provided opportunities to learn and use study skills if they are to be successful in school. Although the development, application, and generalization of each study skill are specific to that study skill's procedures, a general process may be followed to provide students with a structure for learning and applying different study skills and strategies. Discussed below is a classroom-based model that teachers may follow to teach study skills, which is followed by specific guidelines for implementing a study skills program across the grades.

Model for Teaching Study Skills

An effective model for classroom development and usage of study skills for CLDE learners should include at least four elements:

1. Follows a continuous process
2. Yields meaningful and culturally relevant classroom results
3. Provides meaningful, significant, and relevant opportunities to learn
4. Is dynamic so instructional adjustments and differentiations are easily implemented

A five-component process, developed from Hoover (in press), is illustrated in Figure 11.2 and includes assessment, selection, implementation, evaluation, and revisions.

Assessing Study Skills Needs. The initial component in the process of teaching study skills is assessment, in which specific study skill needs are determined (e.g., self-management, oral presentations, note taking during lectures). This process is specific to individual learners and should follow the classroom-based assessment procedures previously discussed using the Study Skills Inventory (Figure 11.1). Once identified, the specific selection of appropriate study strategies is completed.

Selecting Study Strategies to Use. During the second step, two issues are addressed: (1) study skill area(s) to initially learn (based on assessment results), and (2) teaching

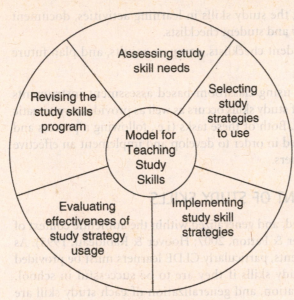

FIGURE 11.2 Study Skills Teaching Model

and study strategies necessary to help the student learn needed study skill(s). In regards to Decision 1, study skill(s) selection should be based on (a) classroom tasks, (b) most pressing socioemotional or academic needs, and (c) student desire and interest to learn the study skill. Once the study skills to be acquired have been identified, Decision 2 is addressed by selecting and using one or more study methods or strategies. Several teaching ideas for each study skill were previously presented. Additional study skill strategies are presented in Table 11.3.

As shown, numerous student strategies containing specific procedures to follow are presented (e.g., SQ3R, PIRATES, GLP, COPS, TOWER, REAP). The teacher and student should select strategies based on student needs related to task completion demands (e.g., organizational skills, reading rate, self-management) and once identified the third component in the process begins.

Implementing Study Skill Strategies. The implementation component emphasizes the use of selected student and teaching strategies in authentic classroom learning contexts. Teaching strategies, related to a study skill, that are incorporated into daily classroom instruction assist learners to apply relevant uses of that study skill as they complete assignments. As shown in Table 11.3, each selected strategy contains several brief steps for students to follow. To ensure success, teachers should initially provide students time for practicing and mastering the study skill steps prior to widespread implementation in learning. Once the learner successfully applies the process of the selected strategy in targeted and directed learning tasks, its use should be applied on a consistent basis in all relevant learning tasks (e.g., if PIRATES is selected it should be

TABLE 11.3 Study Strategies

Strategy	Task Area	Process	Description
CALL-UP	Note taking	Copy ideas accurately Add necessary details Listen and write the question Listen and write the answer Use text to support notes Put response in own words	Helps student to remain focused on what is happening in class during a note-taking task or assignment; helps learners respond more accurately to questions using notes and text to support written responses (Czarnecki, Rosko, & Pine, 1998)
CAN-DO	Acquiring content	Create list of items to learn Ask self if list is complete Note details and main ideas Describe components and their relationships Overlearn main items, followed by learning details	Assists with memorization of lists of items through rehearsal techniques
COPS	Written reports	Capitalization correct Overall appearance Punctuation correct Spelling correct	Provides a structure for proofreading written work prior to submitting it to the teacher
DEFENDS	Written expression	Decide on a specific position Examine own reasons for this position Form a list of points explaining each reason Expose position in first sentence of written task Note each reason and associated points Drive home position in last sentence Search for and correct any errors	Helps learners defend a particular position in a written assignment
EASY	Studying content	Elicit questions (who, what when, where, why) Ask self which information is least difficult Study easy content initially, followed by difficult content Yes—provide self-reinforcement	Helps learners organize and prioritize information by responding to questions designed to identify important content to be learned
FIST	Reading comprehension	First sentence is read Indicate a question based on material in first sentence Search for answer to question	Helps students actively pursue responses to questions related directly to material being read

(continued)

TABLE 11.3 (continued)

Strategy	Task Area	Process	Description
		Tie question and answer together through paraphrasing	
GLP	Note taking	Guided Lecture Procedure	Provides students with a structure for taking notes during lectures; uses group activity to facilitate effective note taking
KWL	Reading comprehension	Know—document what you know Want to know—document what you want to know Learn—list what you have learned	Helps students with reading organization and comprehension and of their thoughts, ideas, and acquired knowledge by relating previous knowledge with desired learning (Ogle, 1986)
MARKER	Time management Organization	Make a list of goals, set the order, set the date Arrange a plan for each goal and predict your success Run your plans for each goal and adjust if necessary Keep records of your progress Evaluate your progress toward each goal Reward yourself when you reach a goal and set a new goal	Helps students to effectively use their time by staying focused on their goals and to reward themselves when goal has been reached (Bos & Vaughn, 2006)
NEAT	Writing	Never hand in messy work Every paper should be readable Always keep your paper clean Try to remember to put your name and the date on every paper	Assists students to double-check their written work for neatness prior to submission
Panorama	Reading	Preparatory stage—identify purpose Intermediate stage—survey and read Concluding stage—memorize material	Includes a three-stage process to assist with reading comprehension
PARS	Reading	Preview Ask Questions Read Summarize	Is used with younger students and with those who have limited experiences with study strategies

Strategy	Task Area	Process	Description
PENS	Sentence writing	Pick a formula Explore different words to fit into the formula Note the words selected Subject and verb selections follow	Is appropriate for developing basic sentence structure and helps students write different types of sentences by following formulas for sentence construction
PIRATES	Test taking	Prepare to succeed Inspect instructions carefully Read entire question, remember memory strategies, and reduce choices Answer question or leave until later Turn back to the abandoned items Estimate unknown answers by avoiding absolutes and eliminating similar choices Survey to ensure that all items have a response	Helps learners to complete tests more carefully and successfully
PQ4R	Reading	Preview Question Read Reflect Recite Review	Helps students to become more discriminating readers
5Rs	Test taking	Record—take notes on right side of paper Reduce—write in key words, phrase, and questions on left side of paper Recite—talk aloud Reflect—question how this relates to what you know Review—read over notes and summarize at bottom of page	Helps students to prepare to take tests; helps students clarify and reflect on what they know and how knowledge relates to potential test items
RAP	Reading comprehension	Read paragraph Ask self to identify the main idea and two supporting details Put main idea and details into own words	Helps students to learn information through paraphasing
RARE	Reading	Review selection questions Answer all questions known	Emphasizes reading for a specific purpose while

(continued)

329

TABLE 11.3 (continued)

Strategy	Task Area	Process	Description
		Read the selection Express answers to remaining questions	focusing on acquiring answers to selection questions not known

RDPE	Underlining	Review entire passage
		Decide which ideas are important
		Plan the underlining to
		  include only main points
		Evaluate results of the
		  underlining by reading only
		  the underlined words
			Helps learners organize and
			remember main points and
			ideas in a reading selection
			through appropriate
			underlining of keywords

REAP	Reading Writing Thinking	Read Encode Annotate Ponder	Helps students combine several skills to facilitate discussion about reading material
ReQuest	Reading questioning	Reciprocal Questioning	Helps students to model teacher questions and receive feedback while exploring the meaning of the reading material

RIDER	Reading
	  comprehension
		Read sentence
		Image (form mental picture)
		Describe how new image
		  differs from previous sentence
		Evaluate image to ensure that
		  it contains all necessary elements
		Repeat process with subsequent
		  sentences
			Cues the learner to form a
			mental image of what was
			previously learned from a
			sentence just read

SCORER	Test taking	Schedule time effectively Clue words identified Omit difficult items until end Read carefully Estimate answers requiring calculations Review work and responses	Provides a structure for completing various tests by helping students carefully and systematically complete test items

SOLVE IT	Math word
	  problems
		Say the problem to yourself
		Omit any unnecessary
		  information in problem
		Listen for key vocabulary
		  terms or indicators
		Vocabulary—change to fit
		  math concepts
			Assists students to
			systematically solve math
			word problems by focusing
			on key vocabulary in the
			problem and relating the
			terms to math concepts and
			solutions

Strategy	Task Area	Process	Description
		Equation—translate problem into a math equation Indicate the answer Translate answer back into context of word problem	
SQRQCR	Math word problems	Survey word problem Question asked is identified Read more carefully Question process required to solve problem Compute the answer Question self to ensure that the answer solves the problem	Provides a systematic structure for identifying the question being asked in a math word problem, computing the response, and ensuring that the question in the problem was answered
SQ3R	Reading	Survey Question Read Recite Review	Provides a systematic approach to improve reading comprehension
SSCD	Vocabulary development	Sound clues used Structure cluers used Contex clues used Dictionary used	Encourages students to remember to use sound, structure, and context clues, as well as a dictionary if needed, to address unfamiliar vocabulary
STOP	Writing	Suspend judgment (brainstorm) Tell thesis Organize ideas Plan moves for effective writing	Helps students remember to brainstorm to document potential ideas, generate a thesis statement, document main and subordinate ideas in outline form, and plan for writing (De la Paz, 1997)
TOWER	Written reports Organization	Think Order ideas Write Edit Rewrite	Provides a structure for completing initial and final drafts of written reports; may be used effectively with COPS
TQLR	Listening	Tuning in Questioning Listening Reviewing	Assists with listening comprehension by reminding students to generate questions and listen for specific statements related to those questions

Source: Hoover, J. J., & Patton, J.R. (2007). *Teaching study skills to students with learning problems* (2nd ed.). Austin, TX: Pro-Ed. Reprinted by permission.

applied in each test-taking situation). Also, selected strategies should be continued for a predetermined amount of time (e.g., next three classroom quizzes or tests) and the effects of using the strategy in the learning task should be observed and documented. For example, if DEFENDS is used for the next three written reports, the teacher should employ work sample analysis procedures to evaluate and document how the reports have improved as a result of using DEFENDS. The implementation activities lead directly to the next component in the process.

Evaluating Effectiveness of Study Strategy Usage. As discussed above, a specified amount of time for using each strategy should be identified (e.g., three written reports, next five classroom tests). In addition, the evaluation of the effectiveness of student use of the study skill or study strategy must be documented. For example, as discussed above, the teacher should record data on how well the student has acquired the desired study skill or strategy, along with the extent to which it was used effectively to complete the learning tasks. Use of simple checklists or guides previously discussed facilitate ongoing evaluation and student response to study skills instruction and use. As teachers observe the study skills used by the learner in actual classroom situations, the effects on classroom performance will become more evident. These effects should be documented to facilitate evaluation of study skills usage. Once use of the strategies for the specified amount of time occurs and results documented, the last component in the process is addressed.

Revising the Study Skills Program. Based on the student's response and progress toward the use of the study skills and associated strategies, the teacher and students collaboratively review the evaluation results and decide on the next appropriate course of action. The use of the study skills and strategies should continue as originally designed if the student makes sufficient progress. If not, other strategies should be identified and attempted to help the student learn and use the study skill, adhering to the procedures outlined in the five-component model described above. As different study skills are needed they can easily be incorporated into the overall study skills program and model through implementation of additional study strategies.

TEACHING STUDY SKILLS THROUGH COOPERATIVE LEARNING AND SEMANTIC WEBS

Two classroom methods appropriate for teaching CLDE learners are cooperative learning and semantic webs. Each of these classroom methods also supports the development and use of study skills as discussed below.

Cooperative Learning and Study Skills Usage

Cooperative learning facilitates students working together to achieve a common goal and acquire academic knowledge and skills (Cohen & Spenciner, 2005). In reference to cooperative learning and diversity, Hallahan and Kauffman (2003) wrote "in cooperative learning, students of different abilities and cultural characteristics work together as a team" (p. 104). The topic of cooperative learning was covered in detail in Chapter 9 and the reader is referred that chapter for a review of this topic.

The processes found within cooperative learning facilitate both the development and the effective use of study skills in learning. Examples of the integration of study skills usage in cooperative learning with CLDE learners are presented in Table 11.4.

TABLE 11.4 Integrating Study Skills and Cooperating Learning for CLDE Learners

Learning Component	Learning Outcome	Relevant Study Skills	Cultural/Linguistic Considerations
Positive Interdependence	Students acquire knowledge/skills themselves and help others with their learning	Reading rate Organizational skills Listening Reference materials Time management Library usage	Teachers must be cognizant that different cultures value group versus individual performance differently. Students not fully acculturated or those with limited English proficiency may experience difficulty acquiring knowledge/skills and therefore have difficulty helping others; *group* sharing is a strength in some cultures.
Face to Face Promotive Interaction	Students share, exchange ideas, engage in group discussions, and encourage others	Listening Self-management Report writing Oral presentations	Linguistic development levels impact a student's ability to verbally share and exchange ideas; CLDE learners may require additional support to fully participate in this aspect of cooperative learning.
Individual Accountability	Students show individual mastery of material	Test taking Report writing Note taking/outlining	Sharing of *individual* accomplishments may not be of significance in some cultures; this should not be viewed as lack of acquisition of knowledge/skills for CLDE learners.
Social Skills	Students receive training to learn how cooperative groups function	Listening Organizational skills Graphic aids Self-management	Use of culturally and linguistically relevant sheltered instructional strategies are necessary to explicitly help CLDE learners acquire necessary group processing and interaction skills, particularly for those in early stages of acculturation or with limited experiential backgrounds.
Evaluation	Students discuss and evaluate their group's functioning and learning process	Listening Self-management Oral presentations Graphic aids	Experiential background, acculturation, and language proficiency influence a CLDE learner's ability to use evaluation skills; group processing skills need to be explicitly taught, practiced, and mastered prior to use in actual cooperative learning situations.

As shown, the table illustrates the five cooperative learning elements previously discussed in Chapter 9, examples of relevant selected study skills, and cultural and linguistic considerations. Overall, student success with various study skills can directly affect successful performance in a cooperative learning group. Cooperative learning and study skills usage provide CLDE learners with another structure for successfully developing and using study skills in education.

Semantic Webs and Study Skills Usage

Semantic webbing also provides learners opportunities to relate new knowledge with existing knowledge, and is an effective practice for improving reading comprehension and other related areas of learning (Polloway, Patton, & Serna, in press; Harris & Sipay, 1990). One related area of learning that may be effectively addressed through semantic webbing is study skills development and use. Drawing on student's prior study skill knowledge, the use of semantic webs can help learners to acquire, apply, and generalize their study skill usage (Hoover, in press). The topic of student use of webbing activities in learning was covered in detail in Chapter 9. Building on those discussions, semantic webbing is also an effective learning tool for developing and effectively using study skills in the classroom. An example of the use of semantic webbing and study skills usage (e.g., note taking/outlining) is illustrated in Figure 11.3.

To develop the completed web, students' existing knowledge of note taking/outlining is activated and shared. As the web is developed, learners add new information to each other's experiences allowing them to see (1) how others use and employ note taking/outlining skills and (2) its significance as a learning tool. Semantic webbing also helps students to see potential problems others may have experienced in note taking and outlining, along with potential strategies for being more efficient with these skills to better deal with lectures and large amounts of printed material. Students can generate other web examples to further develop additional study skills within the context of cultural and linguistic diversity. In regards to use with CLDE learners, a major strength of using semantic webs with these learners is the activation of prior knowledge, which provides a cultural context to the learning tasks.

LEARNING STRATEGIES AND STUDY SKILLS

The topic of learning strategies is applicable to a variety of academic areas. Previously, in Chapter 8, the use of learning strategies was presented in detail, including its use in writing. Throughout this chapter a variety of study skills have been presented along with numerous teaching ideas and student study strategies. Another important teaching method significant to the development of study skills and associated independent learning is the use of learning strategies. As previously discussed, learning strategies are task-specific strategies where students draw on their own existing and prior learning to acquire and learn new material (Polloway, Patton, & Serena, in press). In addition, learning strategies facilitate effective problem solving, achievement of goals, and independent learning (Bender, 2002; Deshler, Ellis, & Lenz, 1996). Similar to study skills, learning strategies facilitate more effective and efficient task completion and retention of content while also developing independence in learning. Also similar to study skills, a primary goal of using learning strategies is to assist students to increase their capacity to learn as well as effectively and efficiently complete learning tasks.

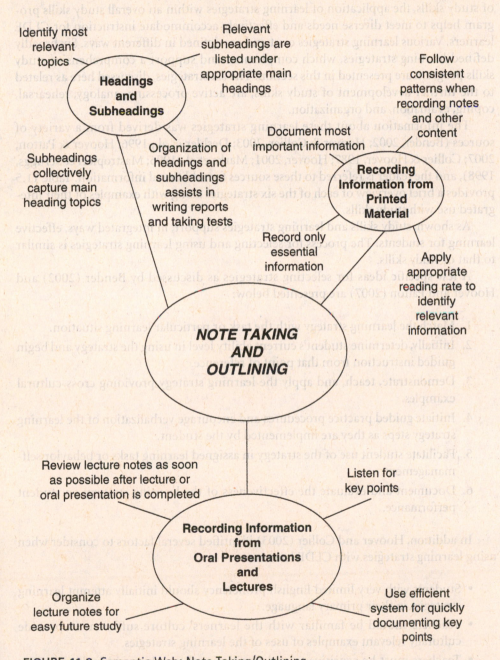

FIGURE 11.3 Semantic Web: Note Taking/Outlining

Source: From "Study Skills" by J. J. Hoover, in E. A. Polloway, J. R. Patton, and L. Serna (Eds.), *Strategies for teaching learners with special needs*, 8th ed. Copyright by Merrill/Prentice Hall. Reprinted with permission.

While the specific scope and purpose of learning strategies may differ from those of study skills, the application of learning strategies within an overall study skills program helps to meet diverse needs and effectively accommodate instruction for CLDE learners. Various learning strategies exist and are defined in different ways. Six broadly defined learning strategies, which complement and support a comprehensive study skills program are presented in this section. The six strategies, discussed here as related to the further development of study skills, are active processing, analogy, rehearsal, coping, evaluation, and organization.

The information about these learning strategies was derived from a variety of sources (Bender, 2002; Hoover & Collier, 2003; Deshler et al., 1996; Hoover & Patton, 2007; Collier & Hoover, 1987; Hoover, 2001; Marks et al., 1996; Mastropieri & Scruggs, 1998), and the reader is referred to these sources for additional information. Table 11.5 provides a brief overview of each of the six strategies along with examples of their integrated use with study skills.

As shown, study skills and learning strategies support, in integrated ways, effective learning for students. The process for selecting and using learning strategies is similar to that of study skills.

A few specific ideas for selecting strategies as discussed by Bender (2002) and Hoover and Patton (2007) are presented below:

1. Match the learning strategy with the task or particular learning situation.
2. Initially, determine student's current ability level in using the strategy and begin guided instruction from that point of reference.
3. Demonstrate, teach, and apply the learning strategy providing cross-cultural examples.
4. Initiate guided practice procedures and encourage verbalization of the learning strategy steps as they are implemented by the student.
5. Facilitate student use of the strategy in assigned learning tasks or behavior self-management.
6. Document and evaluate the effectiveness of the learning strategy on student performance.

In addition, Hoover and Collier (2003) identified several factors to consider when using learning strategies with CLDE learners:

- Students with very limited English proficiency should initially attempt learning strategies in their primary language.
- Teachers should be familiar with the learners' culture sufficient to provide culturally relevant examples of uses of the learning strategies.
- Teachers must be sensitive to and familiarize themselves with cultural views toward problem solving and respect these views as problem-solving learning strategies are employed.

TABLE 11.5 Integrating Study Skills and Learning Strategies

Learning Strategy	Overview	Integrated Study Skills
Active Processing	Use of self-talk/questioning to activate and recall prior knowledge	*Self-management*—Managing self is necessary to successfully use self-questioning *Test taking*—Various test-taking strategies help students recall knowledge and skills *Library usage*—Effective use of library resources supports further development of activated knowledge
Analogy	Relating new knowledge with previously acquired knowledge/skills	*Note taking/outlining*—Skills that help learners integrate new/existing knowledge *Reference materials*—Reference materials provide access to new knowledge building *Reading rates*—Various rates are used to acquire new knowledge based on existing skills
Rehearsal	Reflecting on tasks; thinking through issues prior to beginning assignment	*Listening*—Listening to others' views helps to better reflect on assignment prior to starting task *Self-management*—Skills provide a structure to help students reflect on own learning *Organizational skills*—Organizational skills help learners organize thoughts to think through steps necessary to complete tasks
Coping	Use of problem-solving techniques in learning to address needs, issues	*Test taking*—Test-taking strategies help students break down test items and problem solve to identify solutions to correct test-taking errors *Organizational skills*—Effective organizational skills are needed to help students cope with learning new skills/knowledge *Time management*—Effective time management helps students persevere and persist with learning setbacks
Evaluation	Use of self-monitoring to check work and reflect on solutions	*Self-management*—Self-management facilitates effective evaluation of own learning *Organizational skills*—Students must work in an organized manner to best check and reflect on own learning *Note taking/outlining*—Skills associated with taking notes and creating outlines help with documenting self-monitored progress
Organization	Unique ways that students organize learning and group concepts and skills	*Note taking/outlining*—These abilities contribute to better organized and grouped ideas, concepts, and skills *Test taking*—Test-taking abilities assist learners to organize and group acquired learning while preparing for tests *Graphic aids*—Graphic aids assist learners to better understand and group complex material

- Procedures or steps to use the learning strategies should be explicitly demonstrated by the teacher with subsequent student opportunities for practice.
- Teachers should use cross-cultural strategies to assist learners to develop, apply, and generalize the learning strategies.

Following the above guidelines learning strategies can be effectively used with CLDE learners in conjunction with a comprehensive study skills program. A brief overview of each of the six learning strategies is provided, summarized from information found in the sources identified above. For a more detailed account of learning strategies, the reader is referred to the above sources.

Active Processing

Active processing uses questioning strategies such as self-talk or self-questioning to activate the learner's prior knowledge associated with the content being studied. To use active processing strategies, students use questions to scan, summarize, and predict as their prior knowledge is activated and applied to the tasks at hand. Also, verbalization or self-talk allows learners to reinforce their own learning by stating quietly to themselves what they have just heard or learned (Deshler et al., 1996).

Analogy

Analogy facilitates the recall of previously acquired knowledge and information relevant to the topic being studied. This includes strategies such as schema, cloze, and metaphor procedures. Learning is enhanced as students draw analogies between their culture and the new concepts or materials being learned.

Rehearsal

Rehearsal challenges learners to reflect on what they are doing prior to, during, and after task completion. Through use of rehearsal strategies, students reflect on and think through what they are doing while completing the task. Rehearsal facilitates student use of visualization, recall, and pausing to think prior to, during, and after task completion. Verbal rehearsal is also effective at helping learners access short-term memory (Hughes, 1996).

Coping

Coping facilitates problem solving and helps students to confront issues related to task completion. Coping requires the learner to confront issues, followed by developing solutions, identifying needed assistance, attempting solutions, and persisting until the task is complete. Coping strategies help students to resolve issues that may inhibit completion of learning tasks. Learners are better able to relate solutions to outcomes through structured coping or problem-solving processes (Bos & Vaughn, 2006).

Evaluation

Evaluation strategies help students to know when they have successfully completed their tasks. Evaluation strategies emphasize self-monitoring and self-checking to guide students to evaluate the task and its completion. Through self-monitoring techniques, this strategy helps learners to (1) better analyze their own work, (2) become more cognizant of what they are doing, and (3) know when they have successfully competed the learning task. Self-evaluation also provides students a structure to judge the quality of their completed work (Bos & Vaughn, 2006).

Organization

Organization strategies help students to appropriately categorize and group ideas, skills, and tasks in culturally relevant ways. Through organization strategies, students apply and use patterns, classify content into various groupings, and break down learning into manageable tasks. Overall, organizational learning strategies assist learners to meaningfully differentiate, categorize, cluster, and associate information and knowledge to facilitate successful task completion.

SUMMARY

This chapter has discussed the development and use of study skills for CLDE learners. Twelve study skills critical to success in elementary, secondary, and postsecondary education were presented. These included skills such as test taking, use of different reading rates, listening, note taking, report writing, oral presentations, and time and self-management. A process and associated guidelines for classroom-based assessment of study skills were also presented, along with specific consideration when teaching study skills to CLDE learners. A variety of instructional methods may be incorporated into a comprehensive study skills programs, including semantic mapping, cooperative learning, teaching and student strategies as well as learning strategies. Throughout the chapter, numerous study and learning strategies were presented to assist CLDE learners and their teachers to develop study skills throughout elementary and secondary school.

Discussion Questions

1. What are important cultural and linguistic factors to consider when teaching study skills to CLDE learners?
2. How might a teacher go about teaching test-taking skills to CLDE students?
3. What are some of the more effective practices for assessing student use of study skills?

4. What criteria should be included in the selection of teaching strategies for teaching various study skills to complete classroom tasks?

5. What is the significance of using cooperative learning and semantic webbing to help CLDE learners acquire and use study skills?

References

Baca, L., & Cervantes, H. (2004). *Bilingual special education interface.* Upper Saddle River, NJ: Merrill/Prentice Hall.

Bender, W. N. (2002). *Differentiating instruction for students with learning disabilities.* Thousands Oaks, CA: Corwin Press.

Bos, C. S., & Vaughn, S, (2006). *Strategies for teaching students with learning and behavior problems* (6th ed.). Boston: Pearson.

Cohen, L., & Spenciner, L. J. (2005). *Teaching students with mild and moderate disabilities: Research-based practices.* Upper Saddle River, NJ: Merrill/Prentice Hall.

Collier, C., & Hoover, J. J. (1987). *Cognitive learning strategies for minority handicapped students.* Boulder, CO: Hamilton Publications.

Coman, M., & Heavers, K. (2001). *How to improve your study skills.* New York: Glenco McGraw Hill.

Czarnecki, E., Rosko, D., & Pine, E. (1998). How to call up notetaking skills. *Teaching Exceptional Children, 30,* 14–19.

De la Paz, S. (1997). Strategy instruction in planning: Teaching students with learning and writing disabilities to compose persuasive and expository essays. *Learning Disability Quarterly, 20,* 227–248.

Deshler, D., Ellis, E., & Lenz, K. (1996). *Teaching adolescents with learning disorders: Strategies and methods* (2nd ed.). Denver, CO: Love Publishing.

Devine, T. G. (1987). *Teaching study skills: A guide for teachers* (2nd ed.). Boston: Allyn & Bacon.

Donovan, M. S., & Cross, C. T. (Ed.). (2002). *Minority students in special and gifted education.* Washington, DC: National Academy Press.

Ekwall, E. E., & Shanker, J. L. (1998). *Teaching reading in the elementary school.* Upper Saddle River, NJ: Merrill/Prentice Hall.

Garcia, E. E. (2001). *Hispanic education in the United States: Raices y alas.* Lanham: Rowman & Littlefield Publishers.

Gearheart, B. R., Weishahn, M. W., & Gearheart, C. J. (1996). *The exceptional student in the regular classroom* (6th ed.). Upper Saddle River, NJ: Merrill/Prentice-Hall.

Hoover, J. J. *Management* (CD-ROM). Boulder, CO: University of Colorado at Boulder BUENO Center.

Hoover, J. J. (2004). Teaching students to use study skills. In D. D. Hammill & N. R. Bartel (Eds.), *Teaching students with learning problems* (7th ed, pp. 347–380). Austin, TX: PRO-ED.

Hoover, J. J. (in press). Study skills. In E. A. Polloway, J. R. Patton, & Serna, L. (Eds.), *Strategies for teaching learners with special needs* (8th ed.). Upper Saddle River, NJ: Merrill/Prentice-Hall.

Hoover, J. J., & Collier, C. (2003). *Learning styles* (CD-ROM). Boulder, CO: University of Colorado at Boulder BUENO Center.

Hoover, J. J., & Jacobs, C. (1992). A survey of American Indian college students: Perceptions towards their study skills/college life. *Journal of American Indian Education, 32,* 21–29.

Hoover, J. J., & Patton, J. R. (2005). *Curriculum adaptations for students with learning and behavior problems: Differentiating instruction to meet diverse needs* (3rd ed.). Austin, TX: Pro-Ed.

Hoover, J. J., & Patton, J. R. (2007). *Teaching study skills to students with learning problems: A teacher's guide for meeting diverse needs.* Austin, TX: Pro-Ed.

Hoover, J. J., & Rabideau, D. K. (1995). Teaching skills through semantic webs. *Intervention in School and Clinic, 30,* 292–296.

Hoover, J. J., & Trujillo-Hinsch, J. (1999). *Test-taking skills of English language learners.* Final Research Report, OBEMLA Funded Project. Boulder: University of Colorado, School of Education, BUENO Center.

Hughes, C. A. (1996). Memory and test-taking strategies. In D. D. Deshler, E. S. Ellis, and B. K. Lenz (Eds.), *Teaching adolescents with learning disabilities: Strategies and methods* (2nd ed., pp. 209–266). Denver, CO: Love.

Kiewra, K. A., & DuBois, N. E. (1998). *Learning to learn.* Boston: Allyn & Bacon.

Lerner, J. W. (2005). *Learning disabilities and related disorders: Characteristics and teaching strategies.* Boston, MA: Houghton Mifflin.

Marks, J. W., Laeyes, J. V., Bender, W. N., & Scott, K. S. (1996). Teachers create learning strategies: Guidelines for classroom creation. *Teaching Exceptional Children, 28*(4), 34–38.

Marzano, R. J., Pickering, D. J., & Pollack, J. E. (2001). *Classroom instruction that works: Research-based strategies for increasing student achievement.* Alexandria, VA: Association for Supervision and Curriculum Development.

Mastropieri, M. A., & Scruggs, T. E. (1998). Enhancing school success with mnemonic strategies. *Intervention in School and Clinic, 33*(4), 201–208.

McLoughlin, J. A., & Lewis, R. B. (2000). *Assessing special students: Strategies and procedures.* Upper Saddle River, NJ: Merrill/Prentice Hall.

Mercer, C. D., & Mercer, A. R. (2000). *Teaching students with learning problems.* Upper Saddle River, NJ: Merrill/Prentice Hall.

O'Malley, J. M., & Pierce, L. V. (1996). *Authentic assessment for English language learners.* Boston: Addison-Wesley.

Ogle, D. (1986). A teaching model that develops active reading of expository text. *The Reading Teacher, 39,* 564–570.

Ovando, C. J., Collier, V. P., & Combs, M. C. (2003). *Bilingual and ESL classrooms: Teaching in multicultural contexts.* Boston: McGraw-Hill.

Pauk, W. (2000). *How to study in college.* Boston, MA: Houghton Mifflin.

Polloway, E. A., Patton. J. R., & Serna, L. (in press). *Strategies for teaching learners with special needs* (7th ed). Upper Saddle River, NJ: Merrill/Prentice Hall.

Scruggs, T. E., & Mastropieri, M. A. (1992). Classroom applications of mnemonic instruction: Acquisition, maintenance, and generalization. *Exceptional Children, 58,* 219–229.

Wesson, C. L., & Keefe, M. (1989). Teaching library skills to students with mild and moderate handicaps. *Teaching Exceptional Children, 20,* 29–31.

Chapter 12

Culturally Responsive Transition Planning and Instruction from Early Childhood to Postsecondary Life

Audrey A. Trainor

James R. Patton

Chapter Objectives

Upon completion of this chapter the reader will be able to:

1. Define and explain the concept of transition throughout the developmental stages of life.
2. Define and explain the concept of transition across school settings.
3. Identify important issues relative to transition for students with disabilities from culturally and linguistically diverse backgrounds.
4. Provide a rationale for improving outcomes for CLDE learners via transition planning and instruction.
5. Provide a basis for the consideration of students' cultural identities as an important factor in transition planning and instruction.
6. Identify key culturally responsive practices in transition planning and instruction.

VIGNETTE

Ramón Suárez was a new ninth-grade student on Ms. Medina's special education caseload. Although his father and two adult brothers had lived in the United States for 5 years, Ramón and his mother arrived from Matamoros, Mexico, less than 1 year ago. His records from Mexico indicate that he attended the equivalent of middle school grades in his hometown, so this is Ramón's first experience in U.S. schools. Since his brothers attended school in Mexico, this is also his mother's first experience accessing education services here. Ramón and the other members of his family are all dominant in the Spanish language, but his brothers speak conversational English with teachers and school staff when they bring him to school.

Ramón, who has Down syndrome and several special health care needs, receives special education services. Ms. Medina is preparing for his Individualized Education Plan (IEP) meeting and she intends to address transition-related goals and objectives because Ramón will soon be 16 years old. Her first step has been to talk with Ramón about his interests related to employment. From these discussions, she has ascertained that Ramón spends a great deal of time with his brothers and father on weekends while they work for the family's part-time business of carpet installation. Ramón is interested in spending time with his brothers and going to each installation site. Ms. Medina is not sure if Ramón possesses related employment skills such as being able to measure, calculate measurements, and physical labor required to carry carpet. She has, however, recognized that he has strong people skills. Ms. Medina has identified several informal transition assessment tools that she plans to administer before the meeting. She is also interested in discussing Ramón's parent's expectations of the son for postsecondary employment, education, and living arrangements.

Ramón's mother and father, Mr. and Mrs. Suárez, are preparing for Mrs. Suárez to attend the annual IEP for their son. Ramón's father cannot miss a day of work, so his mother and eldest brother will attend the meeting together. They are not sure what the meeting is about or what will be expected of them. The family wants Ramón to be happy and learn as much as possible at school. Right now, one challenge for the family is getting Ramón to the doctor because he has several medical needs and no health insurance plan. Further, the parents are concerned because neither Ramón nor Mrs. Suárez has residency or citizenship in the United States.

Although his parents have not considered a "transition plan," as there is not an equivalent in Mexican schools, they often discuss Ramón's future as a family. Ramón's parents believe that their eldest son, Juan Carlos, should accept the responsibility of caring for Ramón if anything were to happen to them. They believe Ramón should live with them now and during his adulthood. The Suárezes believe children should live at home with family until marriage, which they do not anticipate Ramón doing.

As Ms. Medina arranges the IEP meeting, she contacts a Spanish-English translator for the school. She thinks one of Ramón's brothers might be able to translate, but she is not sure if they will attend the meeting, or if their fluency is adequate to translate technical and special education language. Ms. Medina plans to address the topic of eligibility for social security benefits and adult service programs such as vocational rehabilitation. She is concerned, however, because Ramón's immigration status, as well as the status of his parents, is not known to school personnel. She considers how to get this information without worrying his parents. She is also unsure about the legal and eligibility implications of citizenship and public assistance programs. For these reasons, she has invited the school's social worker to join the meeting.

Another person who is planning on attending the IEP meeting is the vocational education teacher. This teacher, Mr. Senate, will be the general education teacher in attendance at the meeting. He has not had Ramón in class, but he knows him because he is often in the halls before or after school and Ramón says hello to him. Mr. Senate thinks it would be great to have Ramón join his introductory vocational preparation course. In this class students work on a number of employment skills, including applying and interviewing for jobs, developing work-related interpersonal communication and social skills, and other general employment knowledge and skills.

Ramón knows his mother and brother are coming to meet with his teachers after school tomorrow. Ramón is happy but also a little nervous about the meeting. He asked Mrs. Correa if he was in trouble at school. Mrs. Correa, Ms. Medina's bilingual teaching assistant, told Ramón that he will go to the meeting and talk about school with his family and teachers. Together, they practiced how Ramón can participate at the meeting. Ramón is excited and happy his family will visit his classroom.

The date of the meeting is here. All the members of the IEP team—Mrs. Suárez and her son Juan Carlos, Ramón, Ms. Medina, Mr. Senate, the assistant principal, the school social worker, and the translator—are ready to collaboratively discuss Ramón's educational program, including his transition plan.

Reflective Questions

1. What, if any, is Juan Carlos's role in translating communication between family and school? What other ways might he participate in the meeting?

2. How will Ms. Medina discuss sensitive topics about citizenship that are relevant to transition?

3. How will Mrs. Suárez and Juan Carlos participate in the meeting and interpret its purpose while also addressing the issues of concern to them (e.g., Ramón's medical needs)?

4. How might Ms. Medina or other school personnel prepare the family and other recent immigrant families for these type of interactions?

INTRODUCTION

Formal transition planning and instruction for youth with disabilities are required for young children with disabilities as they transition from early intervention to early childhood programs, and for young adults who are at least 16 years of age as they transition into adulthood and exit from the public school system. Culturally responsive transition planning and instruction, however, includes broad spans of time and change as children grow up. Successful transitions often involve comprehensive planning as well as taking actions that support planning efforts. For youth who are from culturally and linguistically diverse groups, individualized attention to preferences, strengths, and needs of both individuals with disabilities and their families is crucial as youth from these groups often face unique challenges.

TRANSITIONS THROUGHOUT SCHOOLS

Life is made of many transitions from one situation to another. The general notion of any transition is that change is involved as one moves into a new set of circumstances. As illustrated in Figure 12.1, everyone will experience predictable as well as unforeseen changes in their lives. Being able to deal with these transitions is a key element that characterizes handling the demands of life. Figure 12.1 shows both "vertical" (age-related, predictable) and "horizontal" (nonnormative, idiosyncratic) transitions. In our opinion, certain elements contribute to successful transitions, as discussed below, and when these elements are utilized, more positive outcomes are likely.

What is interesting about all of the transitions depicted in Figure 12.1 is that formal transition planning is regularly applied to only two of them. Under the Individuals with Disabilities Education Act (IDEA), transition planning is mandated for infants and toddlers who are exiting services under Part C and for adolescents who are nearing the end of their high school careers (transition planning has to be completed by the time a student reaches age 16).

The school years provide a number of critical, and for the most part, predictable transitions (i.e., vertical transitions). For instance, the transition from a preschool setting to kindergarten is a major transition for many young children and their parents. The transition from elementary school to middle or junior high school is a transition that features many elements that require attention.

We have selected three transitions and discuss these transitions in depth later in the chapter. Two of the transitions are horizontal ones and one of the transitions is a vertical one. The three transitions of interest are (1) the transition from special education to

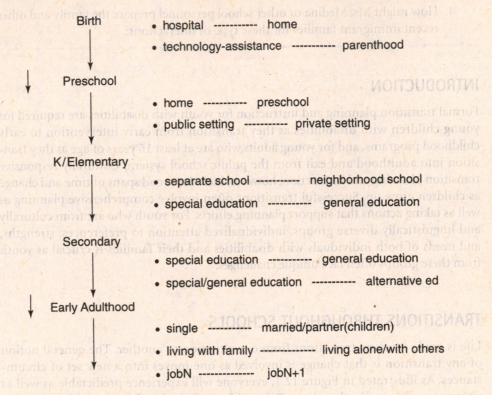

FIGURE 12.1 Vertical and Horizontal Transitions

Source: From *Transition from School to Young Adulthood,* by J. R. Patton and C. Dunn, 1998, Austin, TX: Pro-Ed. Reprinted by permission of the authors.

inclusive settings, (2) moving from bilingual to English-only instruction, and (3) the transition from high school to postsecondary education settings.

Key Elements of Successful Transitions

One can successfully navigate a transition without dedicating too much energy to this event. However, the likelihood that this transition will go well is uncertain. As Patton and Dunn (1998) noted:

> A few key provisions allow individuals to navigate the many transitions faced throughout life. In our opinion, all transitions can be accomplished more smoothly, with reduced hassles and complications, if the following elements are in place: comprehensive planning, implementation of a plan of action, and coordination. . . . Although other factors, such as motivation or disposition of the person making the transition should also be recognized as important, the basic elements . . . are the *sine qua non* for successful transition. (pp. 2–3)

Each of these key elements is explained below.

- **Comprehensive Planning.**   This element includes two crucial and sequential components. The first one is a comprehensive assessment of the needs of the individual as well as an assessment of the new situation into which the person is going to identify the demands of that setting. As Patton and Dunn (1998) point out, "the more the professional knows about the receiving environment . . . and the exiting competencies of the person who must deal with this subsequent setting, the better the chances for creating an effective transition to this new setting" (p. 3). The second component is the development of a plan to address the needs and the demands identified in the first phase.

- **Implementation of a Plan of Action.**   This second key element is a simple one and implies that the plan developed must be put into action. This element assumes that the plan that was developed is comprehensive and appropriate and that reasonable effort is given to its execution.

- **Coordination.**   Although Patton and Dunn (1998) choose one factor to represent this key element, it is more appropriate to think about this element as being composed of multiple factors. In addition to coordination, we feel these additional three features are important: communication, cooperation, and collaboration. Patton and Dunn (1998) indicate how these fit together: "Such coordination requires ongoing communication and collaboration, which contribute to cooperative efforts" (p. 3). The overriding theme of this element of successful transitions is that some system exists that links the sending setting with the receiving one.

Consideration for CLDE Learners

Working with youth with disabilities from linguistically and racially/ethnically diverse groups, as well as those from low socioeconomic backgrounds, requires an understanding of the critical issues facing these youth and their families, as well as special skills in developing and implementing transition plans both across the life span and across school settings. Of particular concern has been a consistent pattern of achievement gaps between youth of color and/or youth living in poverty, and their European American peers from middle and high socioeconomic backgrounds. These gaps are particularly glaring in the transition area of postsecondary outcomes, and they exist for U.S. young adults regardless of disability status. For example, while the 2003 high school dropout rate for all students, regardless of disability, was approximately 10 percent, this rate varied by race/ethnicity (National Center for Education Statistics, 2005; see Figure 12.2.).

Postsecondary degree attainment varies by demographic characteristics as well. In 2000, 26 percent of European Americans over age 25 had obtained bachelor's degrees, whereas the same is true for 14 percent of African Americans, 12 percent of American Indians and Native Alaskans, 44 percent of Asian Americans, and 10 percent of Latinos (Bauman & Graf, 2003). Postsecondary outcomes in employment and education, as

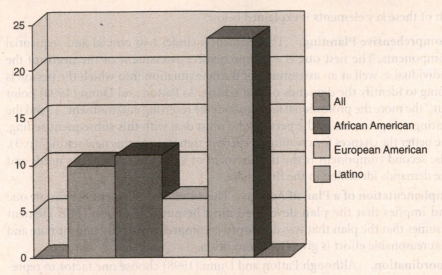

FIGURE 12.2 U.S. High School Dropout Rates
Source: National Center for Educational Statistics (2005b).

well as community participation, are interrelated. For example, for students with disabilities, obtaining a high school diploma was positively correlated with participating in postsecondary education, whereas enrollment in vocational programs and courses during high school was not (Baer et al., 2003). Additionally, according to 2003 data collected as part of the second National Longitudinal Transition Study (NLTS2), both graduation and postsecondary enrollment rates vary by disability category as well. (See Figure 12.3 for the NLTS2 rates of postsecondary enrollment in any postsecondary educational setting by disability category.)

Employment is closely linked to educational attainment. Therefore, it is not surprising that unemployment rates for Asian Americans and European Americans, who garner more advanced education credentials, are lower than other racial/ethnic groups. Similarly, young adults with disabilities who attain postsecondary degrees will be eligible for a broader range of employment opportunities. According to U.S. census data, unemployment rates for African Americans (13.3%) and American Indians and Native Alaskans (14%), are more than double unemployment rates for European Americans (6.1%) and Asian Americans (6.3%). Unemployment rates for Latinos (8.9%) fell squarely in between those of the other four groups (U.S. Census Bureau, 2004a). Wages and compensation are also closely linked to levels of education. People of color are also disproportionately more likely to live below the poverty rate. Although the national percentage of the population living below the poverty rate is 5.7 percent, that same rate for European Americans is 4.3 percent, whereas for African Americans it is 12.6 percent, for American Indians it is 11.4 percent, for Asians it is 5.6 percent, and for Latinos it is 8.6 percent (U.S. Census Bureau, 2004b).

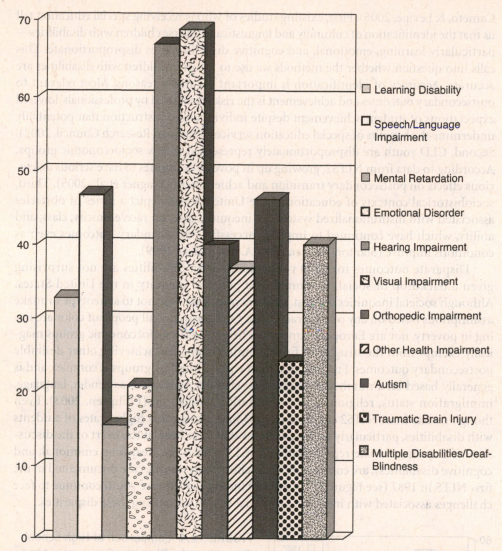

FIGURE 12.3 Rates of Enrollment in 2003 in Any Postsecondary Education Setting by Disability Category

Source: Wagner, Newman, Cameto, & Levine (2005).

Transition for young adults from diverse backgrounds is further complicated when disability status is considered. This phenomenon is sometimes referred to as "double jeopardy," because individuals with disabilities face additional obstacles as people from CLD backgrounds (Blackorby & Wagner, 1996). Although recent reports from the NLTS2 show important gains in employment and education across racial/ethnic groups of young adults with disabilities, inequity continues to be a concern (Wagner, Newman,

Cameto, & Levine, 2005). First, existing studies of who is receiving special education tell us that the identification of culturally and linguistically diverse children with disabilities—particularly learning, emotional, and cognitive disabilities—is disproportionate. This calls into question whether the methods we use to identify children with disabilities are accurate. Accuracy of identification is important for many reasons. Most relevant to postsecondary outcomes and achievement is the risk introduced by professionals' lowered expectations of student achievement despite individualized instruction that potentially undermine the benefits of special education services (National Research Council, 2002). Second, CLD youth are disproportionately represented in low socioeconomic groups. According to data from NLTS2, growing up in poverty continues to have serious deleterious effects on postsecondary transition and achievement (Wagner et al., 2005). Third, sociohistorical contexts of education in the United States depict a series of obstacles associated with institutionalized systems of inequity based on race/ethnicity, class, and ability, which have continued to impede successful postsecondary outcomes even as conditions improve (Stanton-Salazar, 2001; A. Valenzuela, 1999).

Disparate outcomes for CLD young adults with disabilities are not surprising given a backdrop of social, economic, and political inequity in the United States. Although societal inequities do exist, teachers must take care not to stereotype or make assumptions based on any one characteristic. Obviously, not all people of color are living in poverty, nor are European Americans from middle socioeconomic groups magically exempt from the struggle of finding employment and achieving other desirable postsecondary outcomes. Further, affiliation with cultural in-groups is complex and is generally based on a number of interrelated characteristics such as gender, language, immigration status, religion, sexual orientation, and so on (Philipsen, 2003). Even though results from NLTS2 collected in 2003 have shown that higher rates of students with disabilities, particularly in the categories that have been at the heart of the discussion of disproportionate representation of CLD youth (i.e., learning, emotional, and cognitive disabilities), are completing high school than was the case documented in the first NLTS in 1987 (see Figure 12.4), understanding that diverse youth continue to face challenges associated with inequity is a crucial step in addressing these disparities.

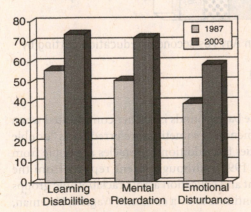

FIGURE 12.4 Comparison of High School Completion by Disability Category in 1987 and 2003
Source: Wagner et al. (2005).

TRANSITION ISSUES FOR CLDE LEARNERS

This section highlights a number of key issues related to the transition of CLDE learners. As indicated previously, many transitions exist during the school careers of students. The main issues discussed here focus on the transition from school to any number of postschool settings and include assessment, planning, self-determination, and family involvement. We are aware that other important issues related to transition could have been covered; however, we feel that these four topics are particularly important.

Teaching Implications: Teachers must be aware of their own biases and preferences for values and beliefs that are foundational to transition. For example, do teachers believe that children should live away from home after high school? Additionally, teachers must recognize the extent to which these beliefs and values are congruent with those of the families they serve. Lastly, teachers must realize that individuals with disabilities and their families must make choices that work for them.

Assessment

One of the key elements of any transition process is comprehensive planning that includes two subcomponents: assessment and individual planning. Assessment is an important and often mandated aspect of many aspects of education and historically has always been fraught with potential problems for CDLE learners and their families. Much of what occurs in transition planning avoids some of the problems associated with appropriately assessing CDLE learners, but caution remains.

To better recognize some of the assessment issues that must be considered during the transition process, it is important to understand what is meant by the term *transition assessment* and to provide an overview of the various assessment activities that should occur. Transition assessment can be defined as "a planned, continuous process of obtaining, organizing, and using information to assist individuals with disabilities of all ages and their families in making all critical transitions in students' lives both successful and satisfying" (Clark, 2007, p. 2).

Transition assessment involves activities that ideally begin in the earlier grades and continue throughout a student's secondary program. Clark (2007) stressed that assessment pervades many transitions throughout the school lives of students. Clark (2007) discussed critical phases where transition-related assessment should be conducted, as depicted in Figure 12.5, originally developed by Patton and Dunn (1998).

As noted in Figure 12.5, various facets and manifestations of assessment can be found at all points of the model. During the early stages of the transition process, students should be provided opportunities to examine how and what they think about the future. Students ought to be able to "dream" and then be provided experiences to determine whether these dreams can be accomplished. When the formal phase of the transition process begins, it is essential to assess the transition needs of students so that appropriate planning can ensue. Often, after a thorough transition needs assessment has been conducted, more detailed information is needed, as depicted in Figure 12.5.

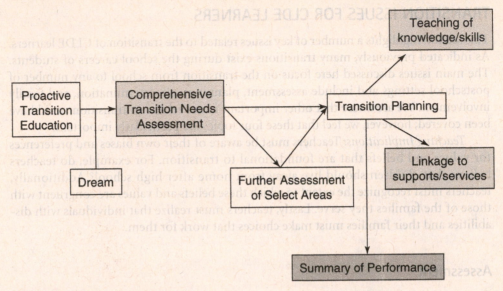

FIGURE 12.5 Transition Assessment

Source: "Transition and students with learning disabilities: Creating sound futures" by G. Blalock and J. R. Patton, 1996, *Journal of Learning Disabilities, 29*, 7–16. Copyright 1996 by PRO-ED, Inc. Reprinted with permission.

The 2004 reauthorization of IDEA added an additional phase to the transition process by requiring a "summary of performance" for all students who formally exit school.

Because the various assessments related to transition are so important, caution is warranted when obtaining data from CLDE students and their families. Anyone who collects transition assessment information on and from CLDE learners and their families must consider the following questions.

CLDE learner:

- Has the student been provided time to pursue his/her dreams?
- Has the student been asked about his/her personal preferences and interests about adult-referenced topics, as required by law?
- Has the student's response style been taken into consideration when collecting information?
- Is the student able to understand the questions/items being asked?
- Is the student able to read the questions/items presented?

Family of the CLDE learner:

- Have the parents/guardians been provided adequate opportunities to participate in the transition process?
- Have the parent's/guardian's been asked about their preferences and interests about adult-referenced topics in relation to their son/daughter?

- Are the parents/guardians able to understand the questions/items being asked?
- Are the parents/guardians able to read questions/items presented?
- Are alternative methods (e.g., translated forms in the parent's/guardian's native language) available to convey critical transition information?
- Have family values been acknowledged and considered in the planning process?
- Has a determination of the parent's/guardian's level of participation in carrying through on transition goals and activities been accomplished?

Transition assessor:

- Does the person collecting transition information harbor any biases toward CLDE students?

Instruments used:

- Are the questions/items on formal or informal instruments appropriate for the student based on his/her background?
- Are the questions/items on formal or informal instruments appropriate based on family or community values?
- Do formal and informal instruments that might be used include ways of obtaining information from students who may be learning the English language?

Interpretation of the results:

- Has transition information been collected from more than one source—ideally from the student, his/her parents/guardians, and school personnel?
- Have assurances been taken to make sure that school-based personnel reporting on transition-related assessment understand the personal context and values from which a student comes?
- Are responses considered within the context of a student's and his/her family values and expectations?

Planning

Transition planning should use a strength-based approach to address students' goals for life after high school (Leake & Black, 2005). Strength-based approaches help youth identify competencies that foster their interests while building on skills that are in the early stages of development (Laursen, 2005). Further, transition planning should address multiple aspects of adult living that extend beyond planning for future employment (Blalock & Patton, 1996; Halpern, 1985). Although IDEA 2004 requires transition services that have included consideration of employment, education, independent living, and community involvement, other key domains include interpersonal relationships, health, communication, recreation and leisure, and self-determination (Clark & Patton, 1997).

Several tenets of the Individuals with Disabilities Education Improvement Act of 2004 (IDEA, 2004) guide the process of transition for students with disabilities who receive special education services. IDEA requires transition planning to have begun by age 16, but consumers, practitioners, and scholars agree that planning in earlier developmental stages has more potential for goal attainment. In many cases, beginning to establish transition plans by age 16 has the potential to limit postsecondary opportunities. For example, a student with a learning disability who is considering attending college after high school would need to gain access to college preparatory courses well before age 16, which generally corresponds to one's junior year in high school.

Second, effective transition planning involves families (Morningstar, 2002; Morningstar, Turnbull, & Turnbull, 1995). The importance of parent participation, and the obligation teachers have to include parents in the educational planning process of their children, is stated throughout IDEA. Parents' expectations of their children's future educational and employment success can impact the decisions and actions taken by youth during transition planning and instruction (Morningstar et al., 1995). Yet, parental expectations may vary according to disability status. Parents of children with low-incidence disabilities, for example, are more likely to prefer that their child with a disability remain in the family home after high school than parents of children with high-incidence disabilities (Grigal & Neubert, 2004). Additionally, parents have important information about the preferences, strengths, and needs of their children that should guide transition planning.

Third, according to IDEA, transition plans should be based on the preferences and goals of the student. Teachers must take care to include students in decision-making processes about their futures both during planning meetings *and* during instructional activities. Students with disabilities need numerous opportunities to provide input regarding their future goals (Field, 1996; Martin et al., in press; Thoma, Nathanson, Baker, & Tamura, 2002). Involving adolescents with disabilities in the transition planning process is based on the commonsense idea that people are more likely to strive for and achieve goals that they set for themselves, rather than goals others determine for them. Nevertheless, families from diverse communities may have perspectives, influenced by the cultural identities, regarding their conceptualization of disability, adulthood, and communication between children and adults (Harry, Rueda, & Kalyanpur, 1999). Theoretically, assertive and active student participation during formal school meetings might be outside the realm of socially and culturally acceptable behavior for some groups of people (Kasahara & Turnbull, 2005; Valenzuela & Martin, 2005).

Fourth, planning must include explicit connections to community agencies that provide services for people with disabilities. Linking adolescents in secondary settings to key adult service agencies is vital as young adults with disabilities move from a system of entitlement to one of eligibility (Cozzens, Dowdy, & Smith, 1999). Teachers should be explicit about the options available to students and allow students and their families to set goals and pursue goals they deem appropriate. Lost opportunities can be avoided by the efforts of educators who make educational processes visible and help students and families establish connections to important community resources.

For students who will seek competitive employment after high school, connections to vocational experiences and training prior to graduation has proved pivotally important (Benz, Yovanoff, & Doren, 1997; Bullis, Moran, Benz, Todis, & Johnson, 2002; Taylor-Ritzler et al., 2001). Consideration for adult services must include citizenship and immigration status, however, for children of immigrants and migrants because eligibility may include documentation of citizenship or residency.

Self-Determination

Self-determination is one of the few transition practices consistently among those recommended and increasingly among those supported by empirical data (Collet-Klingenberg, 1998; Flexer, McMahan, & Baer, 2001; Powers et al., 2005). Self-determination is an important outcome of postsecondary transition for youth with disabilities (Field, Martin, Miller, Ward, & Wehmeyer, 1998). Self-determination refers to individuals' application of self-knowledge and personal goals to inform decision-making processes (Field & Hoffman, 1994; Wehmeyer & Lawrence, 1995) and to make those decisions free from undue interference or pressure from other people (Wehmeyer, 1992; Wehmeyer, Palmer, Agran, Mithaug, & Martin, 2000). Numerous self-determination curricula are available and their use is supported by preliminary research efforts (Algozzine, Browder, Karvonen, Test, & Wood, 2001; Allen, Smith, Test, Flowers, & Wood, 2001; Zhang, 2001). Still, questions remain regarding the culturally responsive nature of existing approaches to self-determination (Kasahara & Turnbull, 2005; Trainor, 2002). Self-determination approaches, for example, may require the youth with a disability to assume a position of equal power to adults during transition planning meetings. Further, from this position, youth are expected to articulate their preferences, strengths, and needs to the transition planning team. This stance might be unacceptable to people whose cultural norms include recognizing hierarchies and showing deferential attention to elders and professionals such as teachers. Recognizing children (particularly those who have disabilities) as autonomous and independent is connected to cultural models of parenting that are not universally practiced (Rueda, Monzo, Shapiro, Gomez, & Blacher, 2005). People with diverse perspectives regarding self-determination and youth with disabilities do acknowledge that self-determination and independence are important; however, teachers must consider how families define these constructs and demonstrate preferences for their application in interdependent contexts.

Family Involvement

Parental expectations of postsecondary transitions may also vary according to cultural models of parenting. Among diverse families, the importance placed on establishing a "normal" life with typical opportunities for adult pursuits may vary (Harry, 1992; Harry, Rueda, & Kalyanpur, 1999). Living outside the family home, for example, may not be a priority for all people though it has been emphasized in transition research and practice. Some Latina mothers of children with significant disabilities, for example, do not share the same concerns about and expectations for community involvement during transition that have been identified by parents using dominant cultural models of parenting (Rueda et al., 2005).

Of course family members do much more than set expectations for outcomes. As is indicated by the emphasis of parent participation stipulated in IDEA, families are important members in decision-making processes about special education services and IEPs. Families also have invaluable information about students' preferences, strengths, and needs to contribute to decision-making processes. Cross-cultural collaboration is a key aspect of successful transition. Conflicts regarding values and beliefs about transition and disability may occur when educators and families develop transition plans together, particularly if the underlying values and beliefs between school and home differ significantly. For example, the dominant preference for independence and normalcy for people with disabilities may be unfamiliar or uncomfortable for families whose cultural perspective focuses more on interdependence and do not hold "normal" as one standard by which to compare all people.

Culturally and linguistically diverse families face barriers that range from the prejudicial or stereotyping attitudes of school personnel to language barriers to logistical barriers such as transportation, child care, and limited time off from work (Thorp, 1997; Voltz, 1994). An adapted list of Al-Hassan and Gardner's (2002) strategies for communicating with parents who speak languages other than English includes the following tips:

- Assess the language used most by the family by observing parent and child interactions, initiating casual communication, and asking parents and family members about their preference for translators, assuring them that it is possible to include translators.
- Seek community-based translators if translators for the school district are limited.
- Allow families to choose translators with whom they have experience or familiarity.
- Reduce the professional and medical jargon in oral and written communication.
- Verify with parents that they understand the communication and provide opportunities for questions.
- Listen to parent perspectives with regard to disability and services that were available in their native countries to better understand their expectations and preferences.

Although the limited involvement of CLD parents in the school activities of their children with disabilities has been extensively noted and discussed in existing literature, less attention has been paid to the strengths that CLD families provide their children. Yet these strengths are important considerations. Families have entire funds of knowledge that can help transition teams incorporate active participation of family members in both planning and instruction. Funds of knowledge include the range and wealth of knowledge, skills, and values that fall outside of the academic domain imparted by families to their children in everyday life (Moll, Amanti, Neff, & Gonzalez,

1992). These resources should be emphasized in transition planning. For example, a child may visit his grandfather's farm every summer. During those visits, the grandfather may teach the child how to do farm chores. The transition plan should incorporate these skills as possible springboards to the development of related career interests, provided that these experiences align with the youth's preferences.

Further, many CLD families also exhibit strong familial ties that extend beyond immediate family members (Leake & Black, 2005). If family members have such relationships, teachers must help acknowledge them and capitalize on the connections members have to one another. For example, relationships with older siblings may be of utmost importance in planning and obtaining transition goals, particularly in the area of postsecondary education in families where an older sibling has already been through the application and entrance process, yet research has demonstrated that these connections have not been made explicitly important (Trainor, 2005).

Despite existing cultural differences, studies of parent participation also demonstrate that parents, across groups based on race/ethnicity, are concerned about the transitions their children with disabilities make as they enter adulthood. How parents define elements of this transition may vary, yet teachers should take care to engage families in important conversations so that opportunities to meet goals and objectives are not minimized in any way. For example, parents across groups seem to prioritize independence and development of their child with special needs; yet whereas European American parents tend to define independence in terms of place of residence (e.g., maintaining apartment, living with peers, or residing in a group home), parents from other backgrounds may expect their children to remain in the family while developing skills that incorporate self-care and family contributions that allow for more interdependence among family members (Geenen, Powers, & Lopez-Vasquez, 2001; Geenen, Powers, Lopez-Vasquez, & Bersani, 2003).

Teaching Implications: Because linguistically and culturally diverse families may conceptualize transition in ways that differ from school personnel, teachers may need to make information about formal transitions that are included in IDEA explicit. Helping familiarize youth and their families with transition requirements may increase their active participation in transition planning and instruction.

SELECTED TRANSITIONS ACROSS SCHOOL SETTINGS

Finding ways to help youth with disabilities surpass the barriers to successful postsecondary outcomes, particularly those associated with disability status, is precisely what the field of transition has attempted to address. Generally, scholarly and practical efforts to help students experience smooth transitions have focused on the transition from adolescence to adulthood. In fact, only two formal transition plans are included in the provisions of IDEA: the transition from early intervention programs, which must be addressed by age 2, and the transition from high school to postsecondary life, which must be addressed by age 16.

While educators, parents, and students with disabilities all acknowledge that other transitions (such as going from a self-contained classroom to a college-preparatory, inclusive classroom) are important and in need of attention, research and practice has focused on postsecondary transition. Within that, an even narrower focus has existed: planning for postsecondary transitions to employment and/or postsecondary education for mainstream young adults with disabilities. Youth with cognitive and learning disabilities have been the subject of much transition work. Less work has been done to examine precisely how specific characteristics such as disability type, race/ethnicity, gender, and socioeconomic status might impact the transition processes. Further, few examples of how to *implement* transition plans once they are developed exist in extant literature. With these limitations under consideration, examining what we do know about transitions likely encountered by CLDE learners can help guide how we approach guiding youth with disabilities during the inevitable changes they face as they grow up.

Bilingual to English–Only Instruction

The increasing diversity of the U.S. public school population has been documented throughout every chapter of this book. One element of diversity is the dominant language of children and their families. Many children are English language learners (ELLs) and/or come from homes in which a language other than English is the dominant or only language spoken among family members. For some children, this language transition begins with kindergarten as children transition from home to school. For others who immigrate in elementary, middle, or high school, the transition occurs during later years. Between 1979 and 2003, the number of English language learners served in public schools in the United States tripled, raising the percentage of ELLs to approximately 19 percent of the public school population (National Center for Education Statistics, 2005a), with Spanish as the most frequently spoken native language other than English in the United States. Children with disabilities who are also ELLs comprise 14 percent of the total population of children who receive special education services (U.S. Department of Education, 2002). English language instruction and the right of immigrant children without documentation to attend public schools continue to be hotly debated topics. Currently, the U.S. Office of Civil Rights continues to monitor the public education of ELLs to ensure that issues of discrimination are eliminated and that English language learners participate in standardized curricula and assessment as stipulated in the No Child Left Behind Education Act (U.S. Department of Education & Office of Civil Rights, 2003).

The transition of ELLs with disabilities to educational settings in which English is the language of instruction varies widely. Some states (California, Massachusetts, and Arizona, for example) have passed legislation that mandates English language instruction in public schools. Other states, however, maintain a range of services including native language instruction, bilingual instruction, English as a second language (ESL) instruction, transitional bilingual English, sheltered English, and immersion, or monolingual, English instruction (Winzer & Mazurek, 1998). Special education considerations, of course, further complicate the issue. Because many disabilities manifest in the acquisition and use of receptive and expressive language skills, learning two languages presents the need for careful consideration of instructional and transition services. While a detailed discussion of policy and curricular initiatives of bilingual education are beyond the scope of this chapter, it is important to consider this transition issue because ultimately language proficiency in *both* one's native language and English impacts many postsecondary transition domains including employment, education, and community participation.

Transition from one instructional setting to another (based on the language of instruction) should follow recommended practices for the transition between special and general education settings. Decisions to make any transition should include careful consideration of the child's present level of educational performance from multiple perspectives. Language proficiency is multidimensional (Cummins, 2003). For example, individuals demonstrate fluency in terms of academic language and interpersonal communication skills (Cummins, 1986). Therefore, understanding language proficiency in multiple settings is key. Further, understanding what aspects of a student's disability impact receptive and expressive language skills is also crucial. Beyond using multiple tools to assess language performance, the perspectives of the student and his family should be considered, just as they are in other transitions. Goals and objectives should be included on the student's IEP so that transition planning and instruction effectively address student's strengths and needs.

Secondary to Postsecondary Education Settings

Transition from high school to postsecondary educational settings, opportunities identified by immigrant parents as a major motivating factor for relocation to the United States (Stanton-Salazar, 2001; A. Valenzuela, 1999), may present complexities in transition planning for CLDE learners. Many parents from culturally or linguistically diverse backgrounds who did not experience education in the United States, or who have had limited academic opportunities, may be unfamiliar with procedures for enrolling in college preparatory courses or applying for college. Similarly, parents from low socioeconomic backgrounds may not have college experience. For children of adults with limited experience in postsecondary educational programs, providing information about postsecondary education to parents and extended family members is of utmost importance because students with disabilities often seek help from family members rather than educators (Taylor-Ritzler et al., 2001; Trainor, 2005).

For CLDE learners who attend urban high schools, transition to postsecondary education settings is potentially further complicated by academic preparation in schools that are underfunded and struggle to meet the educational needs of their students (Taylor-Ritzler et al., 2001). Baer and colleagues (2003) found that access to the general education curriculum was one predictor of postsecondary education enrollment for students with disabilities. This is an important finding because CLDE learners are disproportionately excluded from general education classes, with African

Americans and Latinos twice as likely as European Americans to be served outside of the general education classroom for more than 60 percent of the school day (U.S. Department of Education, 2002).

Issues of immigration and documentation also impact postsecondary educational opportunities as well. Residency status, citizenship, and other documentation is sometimes necessary for students seeking entrance in postsecondary institutions and financial aid, both from private lenders and federal sources of loans and grants (Szelényi & Chang, 2002). Because variation among the policies and application procedures of U.S. colleges and universities is vast, generalizations about access to postsecondary education, and services for students with disabilities, are difficult to make.

Teaching Implications: Teachers must be aware of the preferences, strengths, and needs that may be unique to families and youth with disabilities who are from culturally and linguistically diverse groups. Teachers can develop this awareness by getting to know youth, their families, and the communities in which they will live in early adulthood.

LIFE SKILLS AND CAREER DEVELOPMENT

This section addresses life skills instruction and career development, both of which are poignantly important for all students. Much like the cautions raised related to the assessment and planning during the transition process, as discussed earlier in the chapter, consideration of cultural and linguistic features must be applied to these areas as well. The first two subsections provide background on what life skills and career development are and why they are important in the educational programs of students. The last subsection discusses the cultural implications related to these areas.

Life Skills Instruction

Life skills include a variety of skills necessary to deal successfully with the demands of adulthood. Life skills are competencies performed across settings while completing daily living tasks (Cronin, Patton, & Wood, 2006). They are the skills that are required on a day-to-day basis.

For many students, life skills are learned at home, in the community, or in other incidental ways. For many students with special needs, these skills need to be taught. While different techniques have been recommended for covering life skills (see Cronin et al., 2006), they need to be addressed in some fashion for students to become successfully functioning adults. Life skills can be conceptualized as falling under seven different adult domains: employment, further education, home and family living, health, community participation, leisure/recreation, and interpersonal skills. Life skills domains relate closely to transition domains identified by various states and found in many transition assessment instruments.

Career Development

In many ways career development is a subset of the life skill domain of "employment." The National Occupational Information Coordinating Committee (1992) defined career development as "the process through which people come to understand themselves as they relate to the world of work and their role in it" (p. 3). The main focus of career development is to assist a student and his/her family in thinking about and ultimately obtaining meaningful employment.

Stages are typically associated with career development and are useful for planning long-range programs. Sitlington, Neubert, Begun, Lombard, and Leconte (1996) identified four stages, each of which is described briefly below.

- **Career Awareness.**   Stage when students first discover and think about the existence of work, jobs, and various careers; stage begins in elementary school.
- **Career Exploration.**   Stage when students dig deeper into various jobs and careers. They learn about specific aspects of jobs such as the educational requirements of jobs, typical salaries, etc. Stage is associated with middle school grades.
- **Career Preparation.**   Stage when students acquire specific career and vocational skills; it typically occurs during high school or in postsecondary settings.
- **Career Assimilation.**   Stage when the young adult enters the workforce and those events that may occur during one's employment career. This stage is defined by Brolin (1992) as "placement, follow-up, and continuing education" (p. 2) and is associated with a post-high school timeframe.

Most students can benefit greatly from a career development program that is systematic, comprehensive, and longitudinal. Although the career development movement was showcased years ago, many school systems retain elements of this programmatic option today. Its value to students with special needs is apparent and compelling.

Cultural Consideration

Most adults can remember a time during adolescence when their goals for some aspect of adulthood were completely different from those they pursued as young adults. Having goals that evolve over time is typical of many young people, regardless of disability status. Experiencing changing career goals throughout youth is common. For example, young people, particularly those with disabilities, are often attracted to high-profile careers. For youth with disabilities, this phenomenon can be exacerbated by a general lack of knowledge regarding their strengths and needs and a lack of opportunity for in-depth career exploration and vocational training. In fact, youth of color are more frequently excluded from vocational education programs. Further, research on the adult service of vocational rehabilitation indicates that program eligibility is more limited for young adults with disabilities who are also people of color. Additionally, adolescents' strengths and needs change over time. Once-appropriate transition-related goals and objectives on IEPs can quickly become outdated as adolescents face new challenges or move into subsequent developmental stages.

CULTURALLY RESPONSIVE TRANSITION PLANNING AND INSTRUCTION

Although the public school population in our nation is becoming diverse, 86 percent of America's teaching force is comprised of individuals from European American backgrounds (Westat Research Corporation, 2002). Educators must be highly competent in both *intra-* and *inter-*cultural collaboration with members of the transition planning team. This means that teachers must have competencies in communication and collaboration from people within, and those outside of, their own cultural groups. This may be more complex than it sounds. Harry, Kalyanpur, and Day (1999) outline four main steps in gaining competency in this area. The term *culturally responsive* refers to the ability of teachers to apply a sophisticated understanding of culture and to respond to the needs of families that have as their basis culturally held values and beliefs. Cultural responsiveness entails the following (Harry, Kalyanpur, & Day, 1999):

1. *Knowledge of cultural perspectives of teachers and schools that impact preferences, beliefs, and values of school personnel regarding students with disabilities and special education services.* For teachers, this amounts to knowledge of self and system. This can be particularly tricky, however, because to do so requires us to "see the forest through all the trees." It requires the ability to be reflective and to consider the underlying assumptions behind preferred practices.

2. *Knowledge and awareness of the values and beliefs held by families and students in transition planning.* Teachers must gain an understanding for the population with whom they work. This includes the sophisticated understanding that cultural identities are complex and vary both within groups and among groups. Cultural identities are integrated in the sense that they develop via memberships in multiple groups. They are dynamic in the sense that a person's cultural identity has the potential to shift and change over time.

3. *Explicit articulation of goals, values, and beliefs of the school that may differ from those of the family while respecting the cultural values of the family.* Although some teachers may be tempted to avoid conversations directly addressing conflicts in beliefs, being culturally responsive requires these conversations to be explicit. For example, parents should know that many schools prioritize standardized tests results and that exemption status could limit access to postsecondary educational opportunities.

4. *Negotiation and collaboration with family so that perspectives of the school and teachers can be adapted by the family without violating their cultural beliefs.* Teachers must try to involve families in collaborative transition planning and

be willing to provide information and options that the student with a disability and his or her family may or may not pursue.

Several studies of parent participation in the special education process, in particular during transition planning meetings, have documented the perceptions of parents from diverse backgrounds who report that they and their children have been subject to stereotyping and discrimination (Geenen et al., 2003). The special education community, including policy makers, scholars, administrators, and practitioners, must address these concerns and develop the necessary attitudes, knowledge, and skills that include, rather than alienate, families.

NEXT STEPS

Results from the NLTS2 document improvement in postsecondary achievement, outcomes, and satisfaction of youth with disabilities (Wagner et al., 2005). Still, much work remains undone. Existing research on transition planning for postsecondary life with youth with disabilities, although only one of two transitions required by IDEA 2004, reveals that transition planning is not effectively addressed with consistency (Williams & O'Leary, 2001). One obstacle to planning has been that, as students with disabilities are more regularly included in general education classes, there are fewer opportunities during the school day in which special education teachers can specifically address transition goals (Wehmeyer, 2002). Infusing life skills and other transition skills into general education and core courses (discussed earlier in this chapter), is a promising practice (Patton & Trainor, 2002). As programs are developed that address this challenge effectively, transition practices will be improved so that the number of potential paths available to adolescents as they move into adulthood will be acknowledged and individuals' choices will be realized (Greene & Kochhar-Bryant, 2003).

Creating opportunities for individualized paths to success is particularly important in addressing the transition needs of CLDE learners. Cultural perspectives are too often reduced to generalizations about the beliefs or preferences of *all* members of a group without respect for naturally occurring variability of beliefs and/or of the practical manifestations of those beliefs. Just as not all members of a group experience vulnerability or resilience when presented with risks such as poverty and/or disability, not all members of a group ascribe to a particular belief or value commonly observed or exhibited by other group members. Educators and other service providers should keep this in mind as they collaborate with diverse families and individuals.

As mentioned earlier, poverty, institutional racism, and ableism can coalesce and create formidable barriers to school achievement and postsecondary success for CLDE learners. Educators must have a sophisticated understanding of common barriers to successful transition for CLDE learners (such as those mentioned earlier), as well as strategies for circumventing these barriers. Aligning transition practices with effective instruction and planning strategies requires that educators help families and students maximize the resources they possess. Doing so requires strength-based approaches to each step of the transition planning process. Leake and Black (2005) describe this type of approach as one that engages students by embracing qualities students' demonstrate in their pursuit of hobbies and extracurricular endeavors, as well as their interpersonal relationships with family and friends. While understanding that some families have limited knowledge and access with regard to the services that promote successful postsecondary transitions is important, equally important is the understanding that CLDE learners come from families and communities of strength. In particular, strong family and community connections of support is an area of strength that should be incorporated into transition plans (Leake & Black, 2005), whether the plan is one designed for postsecondary life or participation in a new school setting.

SUMMARY

As the U.S. population becomes increasingly diverse, teachers must respond to a variety of preferences, strengths, and skills in the area of transition planning and instruction. High school outcome data indicate that facilitating positive postsecondary outcomes for all learners, including people from racially/ethically diverse backgrounds, people with low socioeconomic backgrounds, and youth who speak languages other than English, continues to challenge families, schools, and communities. The concept of transition needs to be expanded to include transitions that are unique to culturally and linguistically diverse populations, including the transition from being dominant in one language to learning English as a second language.

Elements of sound transition planning, however, hold promise for diverse populations. Individualized assessment and planning have the potential to open the doors to postsecondary opportunity. Self-determination instruction, as well as family involvement is essential to positive transition experiences for youth with disabilities. As earlier information in the chapter indicated, culturally responsive practices in these areas are essential for diverse populations.

Discussion Questions

1. Self-determination is a key issue in transition planning and instruction. Explain how self-determination preferences and needs might differ during various vertical and horizontal transitions.
2. Generate several long-term communication goals that would be appropriate for a child who is transitioning from the bilingual classroom to ESL classes.
3. Discuss possible responses to parents' questions regarding eligibility for adult services for a child who has significant disabilities but is not a U.S. citizen.
4. Discuss several key challenges to successful transitions for CLD youth. Generate several strategies for transition planning and instruction that could potentially address these challenges.

5. What communication strategies can teachers use to increase collaboration with parents who are more fluent in a language other than English?

References

Al-Hassan, S., & Gardner, R. (2002). Involving immigrant parents of students with disabilities in the educational process. *Teaching Exceptional Children, 34*(5), 52–58.

Algozzine, B., Browder, D., Karvonen, M., Test, D. W., & Wood, W. M. (2001). Effects of interventions to promote self-determination for individuals with disabilities. *Review of Educational Research, 71,* 219–277.

Allen, S. K., Smith, A. C., Test, D. W., Flowers, C., & Wood, W. M. (2001). The effects of "self-directed IEP" on student participation in IEP meetings. *Career Development for Exceptional Individuals, 24,* 105–120.

Baer, R. M., Flexer, R. W., Beck, S., Amstutz, N., Hoffman, L., Brothers, J., et al. (2003). A collaborative followup study on transition service utilization and post-school outcomes. *Career Development for Exceptional Individuals, 26,* 7–25.

Bauman, K. J., & Graf, N. L. (2003). *Educational attainment: 2000.* Washington, DC: U.S. Census Bureau.

Benz, M. R., Yovanoff, P., & Doren, B. (1997). School-to-work components that predict postschool success for students with and without disabilities. *Exceptional Children, 63,* 151–165.

Blackorby, J., & Wagner, M. (1996). Longitudinal postschool outcomes of youth with disabilities: Findings from the National Longitudinal Transition Study. *Exceptional Children, 62,* 399–413.

Blalock, G., & Patton, J. R. (1996). Transition and students with learning disabilities: Creating sound futures. *Journal of Learning Disabilities, 29,* 7–16.

Brolin, D. E. (1992) *Life centered career education: Competency assessment batteries.* Reston, VA: Council for Exceptional Children.

Bullis, M., Moran, T., Benz, M., Todis, B., & Johnson, M. D. (2002). Description and evaluation of the ARIES project: Achieving rehabilitation, individualized education, and employment success for adolescents with emotional disturbance. *Career Development for Exceptional Individuals, 25,* 41–58.

Clark, G. M. (2007). *Assessment for transition planning* (2nd ed.). Austin, TX: Pro-Ed.

Clark, G. M., & Patton, J. R. (1997). *Transition planning inventory.* Austin, TX: Pro-Ed.

Collet-Klingenberg, L. L. (1998). The reality of best practices in transition: A case study. *Exceptional Children, 65,* 67–78.

Cozzens, G., Dowdy, C. A., & Smith, T. E. C. (1999). *Adult agencies: Linkages for adolescents in transition.* Austin, TX: Pro-Ed.

Cronin, M. E., Patton, J. R., & Wood, S. (2006). *Life Skills Instruction: A Practical Guide for Integrating Real-life Content into the Curriculum at the Elementary and Secondary Levels for Students with Special Needs.* Austin, TX: Pro-Ed.

Cummins, J. (1986). Empowering minority students: A framework for intervention. *Harvard Educational Review, 56,* 18–36.

Cummins, J. (2003). Reading and the bilingual student: Fact and friction. In G. G. Garcia (Ed.), *English learners: Reaching the highest level of English literacy* (pp. 2–33). Rowland Heights, CA: International Reading Association.

Field, S. (1996). Self-determination instructional strategies for youth with learning disabilities. In J. R. Patton & G. Blalock (Eds.), *Transition and students with learning disabilities: Facilitating the movement from school to adult life* (pp. 61–84). Austin, TX: Pro-Ed.

Field, S., & Hoffman, A. (1994). Development of a model for self-determination. *Career Development for Exceptional Individuals, 17,* 159–169.

Field, S., Martin, J., Miller, R., Ward, M., & Wehmeyer, M. L. (1998). Self-determination for persons with disabilities: A position statement of the division on career development and transition. *Career Development for Exceptional Individuals, 21,* 113–128.

Flexer, R. W., McMahan, R. K., & Baer, R. M. (2001). Transition models and best practices. In R. W. Flexer, T. S. Simmons, P. Luft, & R. M. Baer (Eds.), *Transition planning for secondary students with disabilities* (pp. 38–68). Upper Saddle River, NJ: Merrill/Prentice Hall.

Geenen, S., Powers, L. E., & Lopez-Vasquez, A. (2001). Multicultural aspects of parent involvement in transition planning. *Exceptional Children, 67,* 265–282.

Geenen, S., Powers, L. E., Lopez-Vasquez, A., & Bersani, H. (2003). Understanding and promoting the transition of minority adolescents. *Career Development for Exceptional Individuals, 26,* 27–46.

Greene, G., & Kochhar-Bryant, C. A. (Eds.). (2003). *Pathways to successful transitions for youth with disabilities.* Upper Saddle River, NJ: Merrill/Prentice Hall.

Grigal, M., & Neubert, D. A. (2004). Parents' in-school values and post-school expectations for transition-aged youth with disabilities. *Career Development for Exceptional Individuals, 27,* 65–85.

Halpern, A. S. (1985). Transition: A look at the foundations. *Exceptional Children, 51,* 479–486.

Harry, B. (1992). Making sense of disability: Low-income, Puerto Rican parents' theories of the problem. *Exceptional Children, 59,* 27–40.

Harry, B., Kalyanpur, M., & Day, M. (1999). *Building cultural reciprocity with families.* Baltimore: Paul H. Brookes.

Harry, B., Rueda, R., & Kalyanpur, M. (1999). Cultural reciprocity in sociocultural perspective: Adapting the normalization principle for family collaboration. *Exceptional Children, 66,* 123–136.

IDEA. (2004). *Individuals with Disabilities Education Improvement Act of 2004.* Washington, DC.

Kasahara, M., & Turnbull, A. P. (2005). Meaning of family—Professional partnerships: Japanese mothers' perspectives. *Exceptional Children, 71,* 249–265.

Laursen, E. K. (2005). Rather than fixing kids: Build positive peer cultures. *Reclaiming Children and Youth,* 137–142.

Leake, D., & Black, R. (2005). *Cultural and linguistic diversity: Implications for transition personnel.* National Center on Secondary Education and Transition.

Martin, J. E., Van Dycke, J. L., Greene, B. A., Gardner, J. E., Christensen, W. R., Woods, L. L., et al. (in press). Direct observation of teacher-directed secondary IEP meetings: Establishing the need for self-determination and student participation instruction. *Exceptional Children.*

Moll, L. C., Amanti, C. C., Neff, D., & Gonzalez, N. (1992). Funds of knowledge for teaching: Using a qualitative approach to connect homes and classrooms. *Theory Into Practice, 31,* 132–141.

Morningstar, M. (2002). The role of families of adolescents with disabilities in standards-based educational reform and transition. In C. A. Kochhar-Bryant & D. S. Bassett (Eds.), *Aligning transition and standards-based education: Issues and strategies* (pp. 125–150). Arlington, VA: Council for Exceptional Children.

Morningstar, M., Turnbull, A. P., & Turnbull, H. R. (1995). What do students with disabilities tell us about the importance of family involvement in the transition from school to adult life? *Exceptional Children, 62,* 249–260.

National Center for Education Statistics. (2005a). *Language minority school-age children.* Washington, DC: Department of Education.

National Center for Education Statistics. (2005b). *Percent of high school dropouts among persons 16 to 24 years old, by sex and race/ethnicity: Selected years, 1960–2003.* Washington, DC: Department of Education.

National Occupational Information Coordinating Committee. (1992). *National occupational information coordinating committee (NOICC) fact sheets, numbers 1–14.* Washington, DC.

National Research Council. (2002). *Minority students in special and gifted education.* Washington DC: National Academy Press.

Patton, J. R., & Dunn, C. (1998). *Transition from school to young adulthood.* Austin, TX: Pro-Ed.

Patton, J. R., & Trainor, A. A. (2002). Using applied academics to enhance curricular reform in secondary education. In C. A. Kochhar-Bryant & D. S. Bassett (Eds.), *Aligning transition and standards-based education: Issues and strategies* (pp. 55–75). Arlington, VA: Council for Exceptional Children.

Philipsen, G. (2003). Cultural communication. In W. B. Gudykunst (Ed.), *Cross-cultural and intercultural communication.* Thousand Oaks, CA: Sage.

Powers, K. M., Gil-Kashiwabara, E., Geenen, S. J., Powers, L. E., Balandran, J., & Palmer, C. (2005). Mandates and effective transition planning practices reflected in IEPs. *Career Development for Exceptional Individuals, 28,* 47–59.

Rueda, R., Monzo, L., Shapiro, J., Gomez, J., & Blacher, J. (2005). Cultural models of transition: Latina mothers of young adults with developmental disabilities. *Exceptional Children, 71,* 401–414.

Sitlington, P. L., Neubert, D. A., Begun, D., Lombard, R. C., & Leconte, P. (1996). *Assess for success: Handbook on transition assessment.* Reston, VA: Council for Exceptional Children, Division of Career Development and Transition.

Stanton-Salazar, R. D. (2001). *Manufacturing hope and despair: The school and kin support networks of U.S.-Mexican youth.* New York: Teachers College Press.

Szelényi, K., & Chang, J. C. (2002). ERIC review: Educating immigrants: The community college role. *Community College Review, 30,* 55–74.

Taylor-Ritzler, T., Balcazar, F., Keys, C., Hayes, E., Garate-Serafini, T., & Ryerson Espino, S. (2001). Promoting attainment of transition-related goals among low-income ethnic minority students with disabilities. *Career Development for Exceptional Individuals, 24,* 147–167.

Thoma, C. A., Nathanson, R., Baker, S. R., & Tamura, R. (2002). Self-determination: What do special educators know and where do they learn it? *Remedial and Special Education, 23,* 242–247.

Thorp, E. K. (1997). Increasing opportunities for partnerships with culturally and linguistically diverse families. *Intervention in School and Clinic, 32,* 261–69.

Trainor, A. A. (2002). Self-determination for students with learning disabilities: Is it a universal value? *International Journal of Qualitative Studies in Education, 15,* 711–725.

Trainor, A. A. (2005). Self-determination perceptions and behaviors of diverse students with LD during the transition planning process. *Journal of Learning Disabilities, 38,* 233–249.

U.S. Census Bureau. (2004a). Employment status.

U.S. Census Bureau. (2004b). Selected characteristics of people at specified levels of poverty in the past 12 months.

U.S. Department of Education. (2002). *Twenty-fourth annual report to Congress on the implementation of the Individuals with Disabilities Education Act.* Washington, DC: U.S. Department of Education.

U.S. Department of Education, & Office of Civil Rights. (2003). *Annual Report to Congress: Fiscal Years 2001 and 2002.* Washington, DC: Education Publications Center.

Valenzuela, A. (1999). *Subtractive schooling: U.S.-Mexican youth and the politics of caring.* Albany: State University of New York Press.

Valenzuela, R. L., & Martin, J. E. (2005). Self-directed IEP: Bridging values of diverse cultures and secondary education. *Career Development for Exceptional Individuals, 28,* 4–14.

Voltz, D. L. (1994). Developing collaborative parent-teacher relationships with culturally diverse parents. *Intervention in School and Clinic, 29,* 288–291.

Wagner, M., Newman, L., Cameto, R., & Levine, P. (2005). *Changes over time in the early postschool outcomes of youth with disabilities.* Menlo Park, CA: SRI International.

Wehmeyer, M. L. (1992). Self-determination and the education of students with mental retardation. *Education & Training in Mental Retardation, 27,* 302–314.

Wehmeyer, M. L. (2002). Transition and access to the general education curriculum. In C. A. Kochhar-Bryant & D. S. Bassett (Eds.), *Aligning transition and standards-based education: Issues and strategies.* Arlington, VA: Council for Exceptional Children.

Wehmeyer, M. L., & Lawrence, M. (1995). Whose future is it anyway? Promoting student involvement in transition planning. *Career Development for Exceptional Individuals, 18,* 69–83.

Wehmeyer, M. L., Palmer, S. B., Agran, M., Mithaug, D. E., & Martin, J. E. (2000). Promoting causal agency: The self-determined learning model of instruction. *Exceptional Children, 66,* 439–453.

Westat Research Corporation. (2002, February). Study of personnel needs in special education. Rockville, MD. Retrieved August 15, 2006, from http://ferdig.coe.ufl.edu/spense/Results.html

Williams, J. M., & O'Leary, E. (2001). What we've learned and where we go from here. *Career Development for Exceptional Individuals, 24,* 51–69.

Winzer, M. A., & Mazurek, K. (1998). *Special education in multicultural contexts.* Upper Saddle River, NJ: Merrill/Prentice Hall.

Zhang, D. (2001). The effect of Next S.T.E.P. instruction on self-determination skills of high school students with learning disabilities. *Career Development for Exceptional Individuals, 24,* 121–132.

Name Index

Subject Index